3/24/92

$45 → $12.50

Word and Sentence Prosody in Serbocroatian

Current Studies in Linguistics Series

Samuel Jay Keyser, general editor

1. *A Reader on the Sanskrit Grammarians*
   J. F. Staal, editor
2. *Semantic Interpretation in Generative Grammar*
   Ray Jackendoff
3. *The Structure of the Japanese Language*
   Susumu Kuno
4. *Speech Sounds and Features*
   Gunnar Fant
5. *On Raising: One Rule of English Grammar and Its Theoretical Implications*
   Paul M. Postal
6. *French Syntax: The Transformational Cycle*
   Richard S. Kayne
7. *Pāṇini as a Variationist*
   Paul Kiparsky, edited by S. D. Joshi
8. *Semantics and Cognition*
   Ray Jackendoff
9. *Modularity in Syntax: A Study of Japanese and English*
   Ann Kathleen Farmer
10. *Phonology and Syntax: The Relation between Sound and Structure*
    Elisabeth O. Selkirk
11. *The Grammatical Basis of Linguistic Performance: Language Use and Acquisition*
    Robert C. Berwick and Amy S. Weinberg
12. *Introduction to the Theory of Grammar*
    Henk van Riemsdijk and Edwin Williams
13. *Word and Sentence Prosody in Serbocroatian*
    Ilse Lehiste and Pavle Ivić

Word and Sentence Prosody in Serbocroatian

Ilse Lehiste and Pavle Ivić

The MIT Press
Cambridge, Massachusetts
London, England

Publication of this book has been supported by a grant from the National Endowment for the Humanities.

This book was set in Times New Roman by Asco Trade Typesetting Ltd., Hong Kong, and printed and bound by Halliday Lithograph in the United United States of America.

Library of Congress Cataloging-in-Publication Data

Lehiste, Ilse.
Word and sentence prosody in Serbocroatian.

(Current studies in linguistics series; 13)
Bibliography: p.
Includes index.
1. Serbo-Croatian language—Accents and accentuation. 2. Serbo-Croatian language—Intonation. 3. Serbo-Croatian language—Prosodic analysis. I. Ivić, Pavle. II. Title. III. Series.
PG1244.L44 1986 491.8′216 85-15153
ISBN 0-262-12111-5

Contents

Series Foreword

We are pleased to present this book as the thirteenth volume in the series Current Studies in Linguistics.

As we have defined it, the series will offer book-length studies in linguistics and neighboring fields that further the exploration of man's ability to manipulate symbols. It will pursue the same editorial goals as its companion journal, *Linguistic Inquiry*, and will complement it by providing a format for in-depth studies beyond the scope of the professional article.

By publishing such studies, we hope the series will answer a need for intensive and detailed research that sheds new light on current theoretical issues and provides a new dimension for their resolution. Toward this end it will present books dealing with the widest range of languages and addressing the widest range of theoretical topics. From time to time and with the same ends in view, the series will include collections of significant articles covering single and selected subject areas and works primarily for use as textbooks.

Like *Linguistic Inquiry*, Current Studies in Linguistics will seek to present work of theoretical interest and excellence.

Samuel Jay Keyser

Preface

This book is the result of a collaboration that has lasted for more than twenty years. It may be perhaps appropriate to trace the history of this collaboration now that we are offering its results to the scientific community. Perhaps this will also explain why it has taken us so long to produce this book.

The beginnings of our collaboration go back to the year 1960. I. L., then a Research Associate at the Communication Sciences Laboratory of the University of Michigan, was just becoming interested in the role of suprasegmentals in phonetics and phonology. It happened that a Yugoslav engineer, Mr. Dušan Kalić, came to Ann Arbor to spend a few months in the laboratory; I. L. decided to take advantage of the opportunity of having a native speaker of Serbocroatian available as informant, and Mr. Kalić kindly agreed to produce a set of utterances containing one hundred test words selected to provide examples of the four Serbocroatian accents, which I. L. then analyzed acoustically. On December 28, 1960, I. L. presented her results at the meeting of the Modern Language Association in Philadelphia, in a paper entitled "Some Acoustic Correlates of Tone in Serbian" (later published under a different title in *Phonetica*; see Lehiste 1961).

It also happened that P. I. was at that time a guest professor at Columbia University in New York. Having come to Philadelphia to participate in the MLA meeting, he was in the audience when I. L. presented her paper. After the session, P. I. commented on the paper and suggested collaboration—a suggestion that I. L. was happy to accept. Neither one of us would have predicted then that this collaboration would lead to a current total of sixteen joint publications, and finally to this book.

During the past twenty-plus years we have had a chance to work closely together for only approximately two months in the summer of 1962, when a grant from the National Science Foundation made it possible for P. I. to spend the summer at the Communication Sciences Laboratory of the University of Michigan at Ann Arbor. Since then our work has proceeded mainly by correspondence. We have used available opportunities to have extensive discussions—during brief visits by P. I. to the United States and by I. L. to Yugoslavia, and on the occasion of international conferences in which both of us have participated. Opportunities for personal interaction have been few, however; this is one reason for the slow pace of publication of our research results. Another is that both of us have also been engaged in full-time teaching (I. L. at the Ohio State University from 1963 onward; P. I. at the University of Novi Sad until 1972, and at the University of Belgrade until his early retirement in 1975). And both of us have pursued other scholarly interests while continuing our work on Serbocroatian accentology, I. L. working primarily in the general field of the experimental study of prosody, and P. I. in Serbocroatian linguistics, especially dialectology.

The division of labor in our work has been determined by our training and background. I. L. has contributed the experimental methodology and most of the actual analysis and synthesis work. P. I. has selected the test materials, judged the genuineness of the productions, run most of the listening tests, and made all of the field recordings. P. I. has also contributed the information about the history of the study of Serbocroatian accentuation and the survey of the various attempts at phonological interpretation. In the writing of this book, I. L. is primarily responsible for most of chapters 2 and 3, and P. I. is primarily responsible for chapters 1 and 4. However, in all our publications we have followed the principle that everything printed must be accepted and approved by both; this holds also for the present book.

Readers familiar with our previous work may wonder to what an extent this book adds to the already published corpus. To be sure, we have summarized here the main results of our previous studies—but we are now returning to our earlier work with the perspective we have acquired in the past twenty years, and we have reevaluated many of our earlier results in the light of our present knowledge. We have also replicated some of our earlier experiments, and we are reporting here for the first time the results of two listening tests concerning the perception of short accents. Also new is the survey of earlier work by other scholars, which we have tried to make as comprehensive as possible, and the reevaluation of pre-experimental descriptive statements from the point of view of presently available knowledge. We hope that the bibliography will likewise be found comprehensive, even though we do not claim that it is exhaustive.

In the review of work done by other scholars we have tried to be scrupulously fair. If we have expressed an evaluation, and if this evaluation is somewhat critical, we hope that the criticism will be accepted in the spirit in which it is being offered: with the hope and in the belief that scholarship will be advanced through dialogue. This belief has also prompted us to publish the results of our research as they have become available, rather than postponing it until a hoped-for time when all questions will have been answered. We are reinterpreting some of our earlier results here, and we recognize imperfection in our own work; we hope that the publication of this book will advance the dialogue and that the result will be a gradual convergence of views toward recognition of the true essence of Serbocroatian accentuation.

Our work reflects another general principle that we share—namely, faith in the experimental method. Frequently we refer to phonetic reality when we evaluate conflicting claims concerning the nature of Serbocroatian accents. Indeed, without this faith a project such as ours would not be justified—and we doubt whether our collaboration would have lasted as long if we had not shared the same attitude toward the scientific method.

During the years of study and experimental investigation that have led to this book, we have received support and assistance from a number of sources and many individuals. It is with sincere appreciation and gratitude that we acknowledge the grants made to us by the National Science Foundation of the United States of America, the fellowships awarded to I. L. by the Guggenheim Foundation, and the support given by the Ohio State University. The following individuals have been helpful in various ways too numerous and diverse to list separately: Gunnar Fant, Jovan Jerković, Diane Kewley-Port, Lloyd Nakatani, Mihalj Olajoš, Charles Peck, Dragoljub Petrović, David Pisoni, Slobodan Remetić, and Svetozar Stijović. We are likewise grateful to all our subjects—speakers as well as listeners—and regret that we cannot acknowledge them all individually.

Finally, as a sign of our admiration and respect, we would like to dedicate this book to the memory of Gotthilf Leonhard Masing, Professor at the University of Tartu 1902–1925.

Word and Sentence Prosody in Serbocroatian

Chapter 1
History of Serbocroatian Accentology

This book deals mainly with the so-called Neoštokavian accentuation, that is, with the prosodic system of the Serbocroatian standard language and of somewhat more than half of the Serbocroatian dialects.

The Neoštokavian accentuation, as it is traditionally described, comprises four types of "accents," which in the scholarly literature of the twentieth century are most frequently called *short falling* (conventionally symbolized as ̏), *short rising* (̀), *long falling* (̑), and *long rising* (́). As a rule, falling accents may occur only on the first syllable of a word, and rising accents may occur on any syllable except the last. It follows, then, that monosyllabic words can have only falling accents and that the final syllable of polysyllabic words is always unaccented.

This pattern emerged as a result of the so-called Neoštokavian accent shift, which is assumed to have started in the fifteenth century. The Neoštokavian accent shift began in the southwest of the central Štokavian area and spread radially outward. The previous pattern, usually called "stariji štokavski" (older Štokavian), is still preserved, although in most cases in a partly modified form, in a number of peripheral Štokavian areas. Older Štokavian possessed only two "accents," one of them long and the other short.[1] Their distribution was completely free. The Neoštokavian shift transferred all noninitial accents to the preceding syllable. The secondary accents created in this way are rising, whereas the original initial accents, unaffected by the shift, are falling. Thus, the shift explains both the inventory and the distribution of Neoštokavian accents.

However, the analysis of the Neoštokavian pattern given above does not correspond to reality in an exact manner. It implies that the distinction between "falling" and "rising" accents is based on the (falling or rising) tonal movement within the accented syllable. But another element usually also contributes to the distinction between the two kinds of accents. This is the tonal relation between the accented syllable and the immediately following one. In words with rising accents this syllable (the syllable that carried the accent before the shift) is much higher than the syllable that follows a falling accent. Usually these intrasyllabic and intersyllabic tonal relations cooccur; instances in which only one of them is present are less frequent. The relative prominence of the two factors depends on the region, on the sentence intonation, on the quantity of the accented (and sometimes also the postaccentual) syllable, and so on. All this creates a complex situation, which makes alternative views possible. Of course, in the pre-experimental era (and even up to the 1960s) the facts enumerated here were not clearly established; lack of factual information opened the door to a multitude of interpretations. The controversy about the primacy of tone or intensity also contributed to the number of conflicting opinions. This is why even the oversimplified (and still dominant) view described at the beginning of this section was reached only after many decades of dispute.

The phonological analysis is also controversial because the strong constraints on the distribution of the four accents make it possible to reduce the number of distinctive features from three (accent, quantity, tone) to two—but in various ways.

We have anticipated here some of the contents of later chapters, in order to introduce the problems and to clarify the sources of both the difficulties encountered by early authors and the still persisting controversies.

It is also necessary to emphasize here that although the four-unit *system* is characteristic of all varieties of Neoštokavian, the actual distribution of the accents in lexical and paradigmatic forms may vary considerably. Thus, different native speakers (especially when they come from different regions) may use different accents in words otherwise "the same." The study of these differences is a branch of Serbocroatian accentology we do not deal with here. The study of morphophonological prosodic alternations likewise falls outside the scope of this book, which is an investigation of the phonetic (and phonological) nature of prosodic distinctions and not of their use in either morphophonemics or the lexicon, as does the problem of abstract "accent features" associated with individual morphemes, which have been suggested for example by Garde (1966a, 1966b, 1981).

Finally, we want to make it explicit that Serbocroatian, along with other "polytonic" European languages (such as Slovene, Lithuanian, and Swedish), should be distinguished from the "tonal" languages of, for example, Southeast Asia, West and Central Africa, and parts of Mexico, in terms of the phonological and morphophonological role of suprasegmentals.

1.1 The Earliest Descriptions of Serbocroatian Word Accents

The phonetic and phonological characteristics of the Neoštokavian accents have been the subject of controversy from the very beginning of their study, undoubtedly because of the complexity of the situation. Typical of one possible position is the careful statement of Đuro Daničić, the scholar who deserves the most credit for establishing the study of Neoštokavian accentuation: "In the Serbian language there are four accents: the first *a* is pronounced differently, for example, in each of the words *glava*, *pravda*, *magla*, and *slama*. Of these four accents the first two are long, and the other two are short." These are the first sentences of his first treatise about accents, and the only view he ever expressed in his whole opus concerning the nature of the Neoštokavian accents.[2] This is also, by the way, the only aspect of the problems connected with Neoštokavian accents that has never been controversial. The reserve shown by Daničić was not accidental: he realized the difficulty of the subject and avoided making unsubstantiated claims. Meanwhile, others were bolder and accepted the challenge. Many scholars expressed their frequently opposing opinions, based on auditory impressions. Since 1900 a considerable number of instrumental phonetic investigations have been devoted to the problem; more recently perceptual tests have also been carried out. Nevertheless, many questions remain to be answered.

The first works in which Serbocroatian accentuation is described were written at approximately the same time in Serbian and Croatian educated circles.[3]

The grammar of the Catholic priest Šime Starčević, from Lika in Croatia, was published in 1812. In this work Starčević states that the "Illyrian" language has four different accents. However, his description of them is very sketchy. Concerning the accent currently symbolized by ̏, he says only that it is "posve kratak" (completely short), concerning ̀ that it is "uzdignut pak brzo spuštan" (raised but quickly lowered), concerning ̑ that it is "malo rastegnut" (lengthened a little), and concerning ́ that it is "posve rastegnut" (completely lengthened). In marking accents on individual words Starčević made numerous mistakes, which probably contributed to the outcome that his teachings about accents were soon forgotten. For a century no one referred back to him; only in 1912 was he "discovered" by Branko Drechsler.[4] Thus, Starčević's work remained outside the mainstream of the scientific study of Serbocroatian accentuation.

The work of the Serbian author Luka Milovanov also experienced an unhappy fate. On August 10, 1810, Austrian censors approved the publication of Milovanov's book, which he had written in the reformed orthography, but for financial reasons he was unable to have it printed at that time. When the necessary money was found in the spring of 1811, the censor blocked publication, since in the meantime Sava Mrkalj's polemical booklet *Salo debeloga jera libo azbukoprotres*, printed in 1810 with the same orthography, had caused protests by the Orthodox ecclesiastical authorities, as a result of which the new orthography was banned. Milovanov did not want to retreat from his position, and so his work remained unpublished during his lifetime. It was finally published posthumously in 1833 through the efforts of Vuk Karadžić, who also provided an introduction. The usual manner of indicating accents (more precisely, the shape of three of the traditional four symbols) goes back to Milovanov: ˋ (according to Milovanov's terminology "accentus elevans"), ˆ ("accentus superelevans"), and ˊ ("accentus prolongans").[5] Milovanov used the symbol ˋ and the label *accentus elevans* to refer to both short accents; he made no distinction between them.[6] On the other hand, he introduced a superfluous category, "accentus superprolongans," symbolized ˆ, which designated the sequence of ˊ and postaccentual length. His terminology does not testify to any deeper insight into the essence of the differences between accents. In spite of that, his work constitutes the beginning of the continuous history of the study and comprehension of Neoštokavian accentuation.

1.2 The Treatment of Accents by Vuk Karadžić

Vuk Karadžić, the founder of the modern Serbian literary language and the reformer of the alphabet and the orthography, published his first grammar in 1814. On pages 11–14 he presents information about accentuation, not only basing himself on Milovanov's teachings, but also using his terminology and his manner of indicating accents. He quotes Milovanov correctly, and as though Milovanov's book, which he knew in manuscript form, had already been printed. Karadžić's own contribution is his explanation of the characteristics of each accent: on a vowel with ˋ, "glas se podiže i brzo izgovara" (the voice is raised and pronounced quickly), on a vowel with ˆ "glas se malo više podiže i razvlači, i od razvlačenja malo sledujućemu vokalu predaje" (the voice is raised a little higher and stretched, and some of the stretching is transferred to the following vowel), and on a vowel with ˊ "glas se proteže" (the voice is extended). Karadžić 1814 contains some errors in the accentuation of examples; Karadžić's later works do not.

In his publication of 1818 Karadžić continues to operate with the same accent symbols found in Milovanov 1833 and Karadžić 1814, but he abandons the previously adopted terminology.[7] Moreover, he describes accents in a new way: ˋ is pronounced "oštro" (sharply), with ˆ "glas (se) kao okrugao razlazi" (the voice goes out roundly), but with ˊ "se glas upravo proteže" (the voice stretches in a straight line). Karadžić retains the unfortunate "accent" ˆ, but introduces ˵, stating that it is pronounced "oštrije" (more sharply) than ˋ. Thus, we find here for the first time the complete inventory of four symbols that are still used to designate the four Neoštokavian accents. Meanwhile, Karadžić continues to use the symbol ˋ to indicate both short accents, with the exception of minimal pairs like *bȁcati* 'to stick' vs. *bàcati* 'to throw' or *ȍra* 'the right moment' vs. *òra* 'nut'.

The section on accentuation in Karadžić-Grimm 1824 constitutes a simple translation of Karadžić 1818; Karadžić 1833 likewise offers nothing new. This is generally also true of Karadžić 1836, where, to be sure, Karadžić describes the accent ˵ more precisely as "vrlo oštar" (very sharp) and ˋ as "nije *vrlo* oštar" (not *very* sharp, Karadžić's italics), and where he states that ˵ (e.g., in voc.pl. *žȅne* 'women') is pronounced "brže" (faster) than ˋ in nom.pl. *žène* 'women'.

1.3 Descriptions of Serbocroatian Accents Published before 1876

Kolarović (1827) expresses much more mature ideas, notably providing the first clear statement about two short and two long accents. Regarding ˵ (according to Karadžić's notation; Kolarović uses different symbols), Kolarović emphasizes that this accent is shorter and sharper than Regarding ˆ, he notes that "(se) jošt duže proteže nego ˊ" (it lasts longer than ˊ) and that "(se) u protezanju penje i spušta" (it rises and falls while extending itself). He still describes ˊ, as did Karadžić (1818), as "(se) upravo proteže" (stretching itself in a straight line). Except for that, he claims that one short and one long accent each possess common features: he states that ˵ and ˆ are "svršeni" (complete), whereas ˋ and ˊ are "zapeti" (tightened), and that after them "reč još traje" (the word goes on). The latter formulation is not completely clear, but it is difficult to avoid the impression that it resembles the conception presented by Masing (1876), according to which ˵ and ˆ are monosyllabic accents, while ˋ and ˊ are disyllabic—that is, that the high tone continues beyond the syllable that bears the accent mark.[8] In any event, Kolarović was the first to introduce into the description of Neoštokavian accents two intersecting criteria (quantity and tonal movement), so that according to one criterion ˵ and ˋ contrast with ˆ and ˊ, but according to the other criterion ̏ and ̂ contrast with ̀ and ́. However, his proposals, too, remained unnoticed and had little influence on the development of the growing body of knowledge about Neoštokavian accents.[9] Obviously, the conditions were not ripe for a more serious examination of problems connected with accentuation, either at home or in international scientific circles.

Relative to Karadžić 1818 and Kolarović 1827, Milaković 1838 constitutes a step backward. Milaković does not distinguish between the two short accents. He calls the accent ̀ (= ̀, ̏) short ("pronounced sharply"), the accent ́ "protegnut" ("pronounced in a stretched manner"), and the accent ̂ "okrugao akcenat" (round accent), "pronounced stretched in such a manner that during the stretching the voice rises and falls." His dependence upon Karadžić 1818 is obvious, as is his dependence upon Kolarović 1827 in the case of ̂.

In the new version of Karadžić's dictionary (Karadžić 1852) the two accents ̏ and ̀ are consistently distinguished,[10] and the superfluous "accentus superprolongans" is definitively eliminated: in place of ̂ one finds the sequence of the accent ́ followed by postaccentual length (thus, gen.pl. *ljúdî* 'people', *ovácâ* 'sheep'[11] in place of the earlier *ljûdi*, *ovâca*). The greatest amount of credit for this systematization of accentuation belongs to Karadžić's collaborator Daničić, who also assisted him in other ways in the preparation of the dictionary of 1852.[12] Otherwise, we find nothing in this work about the nature of the accents, which is in accordance with the cautious attitude of Daničić mentioned earlier.

The first nonnative scholar to occupy himself with Neoštokavian accentuation was Fran Miklošič (1852), a Slovene born in a region without tonal distinctions in the dialect. In Miklošič's view the contrasts among the four accents are based on differences in duration: ̏ lasts for one temporal unit, ̀ for two temporal units, ́ for three, and ̂ for four. In addition, ̀ is "scharf" (sharp), ̏ "schärfer" (sharper), ́ "lang" (long), and ̂ "den Vokal vornehmlich verdoppelnd" (doubling the length of the vowel). Surely under the influence of Miklošič's authority the aging Karadžić, returning for the last time to accentual problems (1858), characterizes the accent ̂ as "dugački" (long), ́ as "najduži" (the longest), ̏ as "najoštriji" (the sharpest), and ̀ as "onaj kratki koji se naznačuje znakom ̀" (that short one that is designated with the symbol ̀). Here Karadžić, in contrast to Miklošič, treats ́ as longer than ̂. In their school grammars Bošković (1869, 1878) and Živanović (1874) proceed from such ideas of Karadžić. According to these authors, ̏ is a very short accent, ̀ is short, ̂ is long, and is very long; thus, they create a symmetrical terminological system, in which, however, distinctions that are different in kind are placed on the same level.

The scholarly Franciscan from Bosnia M. Šunjić (1853) explicitly classifies accents according to two intersecting distinctive characteristics: ` is pronounced "breviter cum accentu acuto" (shortly, with the acute accent), ̏ is pronounced "breviter cum accentu gravi" (shortly, with the grave accent), ´ "sonat longa cum accentu acuto" (sounds long, with the acute accent), and ˆ "sonat longa cum accentu gravi" (sounds long, with the grave accent). It becomes obvious from Šunjić's explanations that for him *acutus* means the rising accent and *gravis* means the falling accent. Since his book is very rare, and since we are dealing here with the first appearance of ideas that have become dominant in the twentieth century, we quote the relevant passages more extensively:

Hae vocalium in sermone *affectiones*, si de elevanda, aut deprimenda voce agitur, *accentus*; si de corripiendo vel producendo enuntiationis tempore, *quantitas* audit. (p. 10) (The impression made by these vowels in speech, when one is dealing with raising or lowering of the voice, is that of accent; when one is dealing with the shortening or stretching of the voice, the impression is that of duration.)

Ex accentu acuto syllaba brevis, vel longa, velut per scalas, ad altiorem tonum sublevatur, ex quo deinde delabitur vox ad sequentes syllabas, modo *plano* proferendas. Accentus vero gravis ipsam syllabam non attollit, sed nec deprimit infra caeteras syllabas; verum efficit, ut per eum vox, in altiori toni incaepta descendat ad syllabam, seu longam seu brevem, pari tono caeteris proferendam. (p. 42) (With an acute accent, a short or long syllable is raised to a higher tone as if on a staircase, from which then the voice falls to the following syllables, which are produced in a level mode. The grave accent does not raise the syllable itself; neither does it push it down below other syllables, but it makes the voice, which starts on a higher tone, descend to the syllable, whether short or long, which is produced with the same tone as the others.)

Šunjić was thus the originator of the currently most widely accepted point of view, which operates with notions such as "short falling" and "long rising."[13] Accordingly, he developed a system of iconic symbols, designating Karadžić's ̏ by `, ` by ´, ˆ by >, and ´ by <. Moreover, he was the first to describe accents using musical notation (p. 41). This forced him to be much more explicit than the majority of the authors of the nineteenth century. Musical notation demands, for example, that one specify whether one is dealing with pitch or with intensity and that one indicate both the musical intervals involved in the tonal movement on the accented syllable and the relationship between the accented and the postaccentual syllable. According to Šunjić, the tone on the accented syllable either rises by a musical second (*pròbūdī* 'awakens', *spávati* 'to sleep', dat./loc.sg. *trávi* 'grass'—we transcribe his examples with traditional accent symbols) or falls by a second (*nȅka* 'let (him)', *spâva* 'sleeps'). The second syllable is on the pitch level of the lowest point within the first syllable, thus at the level of the onset with rising accents and at the level of the termination with falling accents. The distinction rests on a small difference in the tonal movement within the accented syllable, regardless of the quantity of that syllable; the behavior of the following syllable has no influence on the distinction. The picture is so symmetrical that it is difficult to escape the impression that the details of Šunjić's theory are based more on speculation than on precise musical recordings.

According to A. T. Brlić (1854), the accent symbolized by ̏ is "kurz und tief" (short and low), ̀ is "kurz, höher als ̏" (short, higher than ̏), ́ is "lang" (long), "im ersten Zeittheil tief (̏), im zweiten höher (̀)" (low (̏) in the first part of its duration, higher (̀) in the second) (thus, *grána* 'branch' = *grȁàna*), and ̂ is "lang, im ersten Zeittheil erhaben, im zweiten fällt sie herab" (long, raised in the first part of its duration, falling in the second) (thus, *prâvda* 'justice' = *pràȁvda*). Judging from the description, "tief" (low) is in this context an unsuccessful translation of Šunjić's term *gravis*, which Šunjić had used with a different meaning. Brlić, too, uses musical notation, restricted to the two long accents. His transcription corresponds in general to that of Šunjić, whom he quotes, with the sole difference that the second vowel of *prâvda* is higher by a musical second than the beginning (and simultaneously the peak) of the first syllable nucleus. In his text Brlić does not discuss the behavior of the postaccentual syllable. Brlić's concept of the accents was adopted by Macun in his revision of Fröhlich's grammar published in 1865.[14] Here, too, we find musical transcription of long accents, with a reference to Šunjić. In accordance with Šunjić (and differing from Brlić), the vowel of the syllable following ̂ is stated to be at the level of the termination of the syllable bearing ̂.

Vuić (1856) operates with three accents; that is, he does not distinguish between the two short accents and denotes both with the symbol ̀. According to Vuić, the accent ̀ is sharp and quick; with ̂ "protežući se glas diže i spušta i kao okrugao razilazi" (the voice, stretching itself, rises and falls and goes out roundly); and ́ is pronounced long, while "(se) glas nepromenjeno proteže" (the voice stretches itself without change). Here, Vuić obviously follows Karadžić's early concepts. With full justification, Daničić criticized him in the same year for his failure to distinguish between ̏ and ̀ (see Daničić 1925: 161).

The period from approximately 1860 to 1880 witnessed a rapid maturation of ideas concerning Neoštokavian accents. At that time practically everything was achieved that could be achieved without recourse to instrumental methods.

Mažuranić (1859, 1860) innovated with respect to terminology. For him, the accent ̏ is "jaki težki" (strong and heavy) or "dvostruki težki" (double heavy), ̀ "slabi težki" (weak and heavy), ̑ (for which he uses the symbol ́) "oštri" (sharp), and ́ (for which he uses ̂) "zavinuti" (twisted). He himself points out that these definitions constitute translations of the Latin terms *gravis*, *acutus*, and *circumflexus*; these translations are to be taken as labels for certain graphic symbols, not as expressions of assumptions concerning the nature of the corresponding accents. However, the qualifying terms "strong" for ̏ and "weak" for ̀ continued to be employed for a long time in the literature. Mažuranić also was the first to express the equivalences between short and long accents with the formulas *á* (read *ȃ*) = ȁa and *â* (read *á*) = aà. To be sure, Babukić (1839) had used a similar method for describing the non-Neoštokavian accentual system of his native Slavonian dialect. He represented the Slavonian long falling accent as *òo* and the long rising accent as *oò*. The parallelism is nevertheless incomplete, since in that dialect there is no opposition between two short accents, which simplifies the situation considerably. Finally, Mažuranić was the first to mention vocal intensity as a factor that is relevant for Serbocroatian accents; earlier authors had usually not been explicit about whether they had intensity or pitch in mind, but frequently it can be deduced from their formulation that they meant pitch. Concerning the nature of Serbocroatian accents, Mažuranić states that ̏ is pronounced "sasvim kratko i zbijeno" (completely shortly and compactly), that ̀ is pronounced "slabije i otegnuto poput zavinutoga" (more weakly and stretched like the twisted accent [i.e., like ́]), and that in the case of ̑ the stress beat occurs on the first half of the syllable nucleus, whereas in the case of ́ the beat occurs on the second half. Divković (1879) follows Mažuranić with regard to terminology; according to Divković, ̏ is a doubly heavy accent, ̀ is heavy, ̑ is twisted, and ́ is sharp (in fact, Divković switches the labels of the long accents, since he adopts Karadžić's usage of the symbols ̑ and ́). The characteristics of the accents are the same as those given by Bošković: ̏ is very short, ̀ is short, ̑ is long, and ́ is very long.

Ilijć (1860) distinguishes two short accents, ̏ and ̀, and two long accents, ̑ and ́. He explains that ̏ is pronounced sharply, that ̀ raises the voice slightly, but so that this raising is barely audible in speech, that stretches, but does not raise the voice, which rather bends around and falls, and that ´ stretches the voice and raises it rather high.

Less important is the contribution of Pacel (1860). He accepts Miklošič's mechanistic doctrine of the quantitative nature of the differences between accents. According to Pacel, ̏ lasts for one quarter of a temporal unit, ` for one half, ´ for three quarters, and ̑ for one whole temporal unit. He also introduces new terminology: ̏ is "oštri naglas" (sharp accent), ` is "kratki" (short), ´ is "dugi" (long), and ̑ is "obli" (round). Pacel continues to hold the same opinions in his 1864 publication, which is criticized by Jagić (1864b), who, to be sure, discusses neither the labels given to the accents nor the nature of the distinctions between them. Jagić's heaviest criticism is directed at the numerous errors made by Pacel in assigning accents.

In the 1863 edition of his grammar Vujić abandons his earlier teachings and adopts the system of four accents, referring to them by the terms introduced by Pacel: ̏ is sharp, ` is short, ´ is long, and ̑ is round. However, his description of the accents differs radically from that of Pacel: ̏ is pronounced sharply with a slightly raised voice, ` is pronounced quickly and with a slightly lowered voice, with ´ "(se) penje glasom povisoko i nepromenjeno" (the voice rises rather high without changing), and with ̑ "otežući glasom oblo se povija, te kao okruglo izgovara" (the voice, stretching itself, bends itself so the accent is pronounced as if it were round). In this respect Vujić remains essentially faithful to the early views of Karadžić; with regard to ̏ he even turns from Karadžić 1818 back to Karadžić 1814. In the 1879 edition of the grammar Vujić retains the same description of the accents, but the labels that he uses have generally been adapted to the usage of other, more influential authors. Now he calls the accent ̏ "vrlo kratak" (very short), ` "kratak (oštar)" (short (sharp)), ̑ "dug (obao)" (long (round)), and ´ "vrlo dug" (very long). Thus, he has adopted Bošković's and Živanović's terminology, but in two instances he has retained the labels from the 1863 edition in parentheses.

Jagić (1864a) speaks about two short and two long accents, both of which can be "acutus" (sharp) and "gravis" (heavy); for the second type he introduces the alternative label "utažen" (soothed), which logically contrasts better with "oštar" (sharp). Strictly separating "naglas" (accent) and quantity, he represents ̑ as ̏̄ and ´ as ̀̄. We also find in his work formulas like *ô* = ȍo and *ú* = uù.

Like Šunjić (1853), Budmani (1867) uses doubly binary terminology, but his terms for the quality of the accents are different: ̏ is "forte breve" (strong short), ` "debole breve" (weak short), ˆ "forte lungo" (strong long), and ´ "debole lungo" (weak long) (in another place he says "forte o determinato" (strong or determinate), "debole o indeterminato" (weak or indeterminate)). Here Mažuranić's contrast between strong and weak has been extended to long accents. Budmani, too, represents ˆ as ̏ ˘ and ´ as ˘ `, but he explicitly defines ̏ and ˆ as falling accents ("la voce que va quindi diminuendo gradatamente di tuono"—the voice gradually diminishes with respect to tone) and ` and ´ as rising accents ("la voce, bassa al principio della vocale, va gradatamente crescendo di tuono, finchè resta in certo modo sospesa"—the voice, low at the beginning of the vowel, gradually increases in tone, remaining finally suspended in a certain way). It must be emphasized that here *tuono* is considered as the relevant feature, probably meaning pitch.

Jagić (1870) identifies ˆ with the Greek perispomenon and ´ with the acute on a long vowel. To his earlier equations concerning the relationship between accents he adds as an argument the development of long *ě* in ijekavian dialects: under ˆ this vowel developed into *ȉ(j)e*, but under ´ into *i(j)è*: ekavian *sêno* 'hay', *déte* 'child', ijekavian *sȉjeno*, *dijète*. Jagić offers the following proportional formulas: ̏ : ` = ˆ : ´ and ̏ : ˆ = ` : ´. Obviously, the doubly binary analysis of the Neoštokavian accentual system was already solidly established. Meanwhile, on this occasion Jagić refrains from employing his earlier rather unsuccessful terminology and most frequently refers to the accents simply by their symbols—for example, ̏, `. (Nevertheless, he occasionally calls ˆ "round," and in one instance he calls ´ "acute.") Otherwise he emphasizes that ` "(se) puno blaže izgovara negoli ̏" (` is pronounced much more mildly than ̏). Finally, Jagić declares himself decisively opposed to Mažuranić's view that vocal intensity is relevant for Serbocroatian accents, and he assigns primacy to pitch.

Remarkably enough, neither Jagić nor Mažuranić, who also contributed to the recognition of the relations among the four accents, was a native speaker of Štokavian. Mažuranić was a born Čakavian, and Jagić a Kajkavian, both from areas with a three-accent system: two long accents and only one short accent.

Stanislav Škrabec (1870) joined the circle of authors who represent Neoštokavian accents with the formula of double binarity. This Slovenian scholar deals with Serbocroatian accents in passing, introducing the analytical symbols ` and ˗̀ for the short and long falling accents and ´ and ˗́ for the corresponding rising accents (such symbols are found again in foreign scholarly works in the middle of the twentieth century). Škrabec calls the falling accent "potisnjeni" (pushed) and the rising accent "potegnjeni" (pulled); nevertheless, it becomes clear from the context what he has in mind.

According to Veber-Tkalčević (1873), ̏ is a heavy accent, ̀ fairly heavy, ̂ (written ́, as by Mažuranić) sharp, and ́ (written ~) twisted. These terms refer to the labels applied to the graphic symbols—that is, to the translation of their Latin names. The term "potežki" (fairly heavy), a variant of "težki" (heavy) "gravis," constitutes an innovation. Veber states that the "fairly heavy" accent is pronounced somewhat longer and lower than ̏; he interprets the long accents according to the already established usage as combinations of short accents and unaccented short vowels ("sharp" = ȁa, "twisted" = aà).

Novaković (1873) primarily offers information gathered from earlier literature and carefully avoids expressing any opinion of his own concerning the nature of the accents. His views cannot even be deduced from terminology: like Daničić, Novaković refers to accents only by their graphic symbols. The presentation of accent and quantity ends with a sensibly compiled list of problems that should be solved by "musical measurements."

1.4 The Contribution of Leonhard Masing

Competent "musical measurements" were to appear very soon. The most important work from the pre-instrumental phase of research was accomplished by a foreigner who had been practically unacquainted with the Serbocroatian language until he started studying its accents. Leonhard Masing, a Slavist of Estonian background and later professor at the University of Tartu, was the first to carry through systematic observations; earlier authors had mostly offered generalizations drawn from auditory impressions and occasionally from speculation.[15] Masing obviously possessed exceptionally acute musical perception. Working on his doctoral dissertation (Masing 1876) under the direction of the well-known German Slavist August Leskien, he listened systematically to the pronunciation of four Leipzig students, three Serbs (of whom one, from Žarkovo near Belgrade, was the main informant) and one Croat (from Mrkopalj in Gorski Kotar). Conscious of possible complications introduced by sentence intonation, he restricted his investigation to words produced in isolation. Masing presented his results in musical transcription. He distinguished two kinds of accents: ̏ and ̂ are monosyllabic, and ̀ and ́ are disyllabic, which means that in (for example) pass. part. sg. neut. *nȍšeno* 'carried, worn' the first syllable is prominent with regard to pitch and intensity, whereas in (for example) *kràljica* 'queen' this applies both to the first and to the second syllable (we transcribe the examples with traditional notation; Masing used his own complex and sophisticated system). Furthermore, the vowel under ´ is rising, and the vowel under ˆ is falling. The long vowel immediately following ` or ´ is also falling (e.g., in *jùnāk* 'hero' or *trésēmo* 'we shake'). In essence, the distinguishing characteristic of disyllabic accents is high tone on two consecutive morae separated by a syllable boundary. As for ", this is simple prominence of the first syllable, which only in monosyllables becomes falling toward the end. The peaks of tone and intensity reach somewhat higher levels in monosyllabic accents than in disyllabic accents, where prominence is distributed over two syllables, so that the accents sound "sanfter und schwächer" (softer and weaker). Pretonic syllables have low tone; this applies also to syllables following (monosyllabic or disyllabic) accents, where each following syllable falls somewhat lower than the preceding syllable.

Masing also noticed certain differences between his Serbian and Croatian informants. The most important difference concerns the syllable usually designated by the symbol `: in examples like *kràljica* he observed simple high tone on both the first and the second syllable in the pronunciation of the Serbs, whereas in words produced by the informant from Croatia he heard a rising tonal movement within the first syllable itself, that is, a short rising accent. There were other differences as well. For example, under certain conditions, in the short second syllable of disyllabic accents (in other words, in the short syllable immediately following ` or ´), the Croat was more likely than a Serb to produce a falling tonal movement; this syllable, in the pronunciation of the Croat, was sometimes a little higher than the preceding one (i.e., the syllable bearing ` or ´), but on the other hand the preceding syllable surpassed the following one with respect to intensity. In addition, the rising and falling intervals were much greater in the pronunciation of the Croat; typically they amounted to a musical fifth, whereas those produced by the Serbs equaled a musical third. Finally, according to Masing, in Serbian pronunciation long vowels bearing either rising or falling tone are internally in balance, whereas in Croatian pronunciation the first part is shorter and the second part is longer (thus, for example, in the first syllable of the form gen.sg.fem. *tánkē* 'thin' the high part is long, but in imperfective *čûvāmo* 'we guard' or perfective *sàčūvāmo* 'we guard' the low part of the vowel *u* is long).

Masing was aware that his findings differed radically from the views of all previous authors, who heard accents only on the first syllable in words in which Masing perceived a disyllabic accent. He nevertheless did not try to discover the reasons for their error ("Irrthum"). In his conclusions he introduces an analysis that nowadays would be called structural. He notes that in Serbocroatian words one finds both a rising tone (on the syllable traditionally designated by ` or ´) and a falling tone (on the syllables bearing ̏ and ˆ as well as on the syllable immediately following a rising tone). The falling tone occurs obligatorily on every word; the rising tone occurs only in words that contain a falling tone beyond the first syllable, and its occurrence is concomitant with the occurrence of the falling tone—the rising tone occurs on the syllable immediately preceding the syllable with falling tone.

Der fallende Ton ist also, principiell betrachtet, der *bestimmende*, der steigende aber der *abhängige*, sekundare Bestandtheil des serb.-chorw. Accents. (1876:92) (The falling tone is thus, in principle, the *determining* constituent, the rising one, however, is the *dependent*, secondary constituent of the Serbocroatian accent.) (Double-spacing provided by L. M. in both instances where we use italics in the translation.)

This conclusion is based on sound logic, but Masing has distanced himself here from facts that he himself had established. Namely, according to his findings, the syllable bearing ̏ is usually not falling; this applies also to most occurrences of a short syllable immediately after ` or ´. Moreover, in the so-called "Serbian" pronunciation, the syllable bearing ` is not rising.

1.5 Reaction to Masing's Views

Masing's study made a scholarly sensation and called forth many reactions. Stojan Novaković announced his views in his letter to Vatroslav Jagić of July 24, 1877 (an excerpt from which appears in Jagić 1930:364). According to Novaković, in words with the ` accent like *vlàdika* 'bishop' the first syllable is more prominent than the second (which is in turn more prominent than the third), but since he has no talent for music, he cannot judge whether the prominence is due to intensity or pitch. In addition, he hears a falling tone on the vowel under ̏. In his letter to Jagić dated May 11, 1879, Novaković expresses himself in positive terms concerning the review of Masing's work prepared by Kovačević (Jagić 1930:365).

Kovačević (1878–79) criticizes Masing's selection of Serbian informants. Two of them were from Belgrade, where the population is of mixed origin, for which reason the pronunciation of Belgrade residents is least authoritative. The main informant was from Žarkovo, where there are likewise many settlers from different regions. This is why that informant has unusual accents of the type *nȍga* 'foot, leg' instead of *nòga* or dat.pl. *slàvāma* 'family feasts' instead of *slȁvama*, as well as shortening in examples like gen.pl. *zȅtōva* 'brothers-in-law' < *zȅtōvā*, *sàčūvam* 'I guard' < *sàčūvām*.[16] Kovačević himself, testing Masing's statements, consulted two persons with musical training, who independently of each other confirmed that in words with ˋ or ˊ the syllable immediately following the accented syllable has noticeably lower pitch and intensity than the accented one, from which it follows that those syllables are unaccented. Nevertheless, the syllable immediately following ˋ or ˊ is more prominent with respect to pitch and intensity than other unaccented syllables, which gives this syllable the characteristics of "Mittelton" (mid tone). In addition, the syllable under ˋ has rising pitch and the syllable with ̏ has falling pitch. It is indeed difficult to observe tonal movement with short accents, but with the long accents ˊ and ̑ it is very easy.

The views of two famous scholars, Miklošič and Novaković, remained uninfluenced by Masing's conceptualizations and the controversy surrounding them.

Miklošič (1879) writes:

> In diesem systeme bezeichnen ̏ und ˋ kurze, ˊ und ̑ hingegen lange accentuirte vocale; ̏ und ˋ unterscheiden sich voneinander dadurch, dass ̏ den kürzesten, ˋ einen weniger rasch ausgesprochenen vocal bezeichnet. ˊ dient der steigenden, ̑ der sinkenden länge. (p. 406) (In this system ̏ and ˋ indicate short, ˊ and ̑ however long accented vowels; ̏ and ˋ are distinguished from each other through the fact that ̏ indicates the shortest vowel, ˋ a vowel that is pronounced less quickly. ˊ serves to show rising length, ̑ to show falling length.)

At least with respect to long accents, this description constitutes a step forward compared to the position of the same author in 1852.

In his grammar textbooks (1879, 1884, 1890, 1894) Novaković speaks of sharp (̏), short (ˋ), high long (̑), and long (ˊ) accents. He states that ˋ is pronounced "glasom običnim" (with ordinary voice) and that ̏ is pronounced "glasom jačim i višim" (with a stronger and higher voice). For long accents the picture is more complicated: ˊ is pronounced with an ordinary voice that grows higher, and ̑ is pronounced with a stronger and higher voice that is strongest in the beginning, but later becomes lower. Živojin Simić (1883) uses almost exactly the same words to describe the accents; however, he does not mention Novaković's terminology.

The common features of Miklošič's and Novaković's presentations are also found in Brandt 1880. Brandt asserts that ̏ is pronounced "kratko i rezko" (shortly and sharply), whereas ˋ is "udarenie slaboe" (weak stress). He calls ̑ a falling accent and ˊ a rising accent. Brandt rejects Masing's teachings about the disyllabicity of ` and ´. Brandt's most important innovation is his denial of the assertion that ̏ is identical with ̑, except that it falls on a short vowel.

Pavić (1881), in a study concerned with accentuation in nominal paradigms, employs a terminology derived from the graphic symbols for the accents: ` and ´ are "gravis" (grave) and "akut" (acute), whereas ̏ and ̑ are "dvostruki" (double) and "obli" (round).

Maretić (1883) agrees with Kovačević's view that syllables immediately following ` and ´ are "slabiji i dublji" (weaker and lower) than the syllables bearing these accents, but he points out that Masing nevertheless has made an important discovery, since the syllables immediately following ` and ´ are in fact much more prominent than ordinary unaccented syllables.[17] Maretić remarks that this difference constitutes the only possible explanation for the fact that in the pronunciation of educated people (the "intelligentsia") postaccentual length is shortened in words like *prâznik* 'holiday' < *prâznīk*, *nȅćak* 'nephew' < *nȅćâk*, but retained in syllables immediately following ` and ´ (*jùnâk* 'hero', gen.pl. *ovácâ* 'sheep').[18] He considers the relative prominence of postaccentual syllables after ` and ´ to be a historical survival; that is, he considers that it has remained behind from the time before the Neoštokavian accent shift, when those syllables carried the accent: the form *vòda* 'water' derives from *vodȁ*, *rúka* 'hand, arm' from *rūkȁ*, etc. In other respects Maretić adopts Budmani's terminology: ̏ is the short and strong accent, ` is short and weak, ̑ long and strong, and ´ long and weak.

Even though among the native scholars Maretić reacted the most favorably to Masing's views, the fact remains that he did not accept Masing's basic thesis, namely that in the "disyllabic accents" ` and ´ the second syllable in principle does not fall behind the first syllable with respect to pitch, and to a certain degree also with regard to intensity. In other words, both Serbian and Croatian scholarship rejected that thesis. It was apparently contrary to the native speaker's intuition.

For Kušar (1884) ̏ and ̑ are "padajući" (falling) accents, and ` and ´ "rastući" (growing). The syllable immediately following growing accents is higher than other unaccented syllables, but lower than accented syllables. The same position is held by Šrepel (1886) and Šaxmatov (1888). Šrepel adds that the "Mittelton" (mid tone) on the syllable following ` or ´ exists precisely for the reason that these are growing accents, and that therefore they require a transition to the lower level.

In a practical manual for foreigners Muža (no date, 1888?) employs labels like "kurz mit abfallendem Tone" (short with falling tone), etc.

Jakšić (1891) gives a generally well-informed survey of research on Serbocroatian accentology up to his time. He describes accents in the manner of Novaković: "` (kratki), koji se izgovara kratko, običnim glasom" (short, pronounced shortly, with ordinary voice), "̏ (oštri), koji se izgovara takođe kratko, ali jačim i višim glasom" (sharp, pronounced likewise shortly, but with a stronger and higher voice), "´ (dugi) se izgovara običnim dugim glasom, koji raste naviše" (long, pronounced with ordinary long voice that grows higher), "̑ (visokodugi) izgovara se glasom, koji je u početku najviši, a posle pada na niže" (high long, pronounced with a voice that is highest at the beginning but later falls lower).[19] Using musical terms, Jakšić states further that with ` and ´ the volume of the voice increases (crescendo), whereas with ̏ and ̑ it decreases (decrescendo). He accepts Masing's theory with the modifications of Kovačević.

1.6 Further Developments in Serbocroatian Accentology up to the Beginning of the Twentieth Century

Storm (1892:210–212) uses musical notation to describe the results of his observations of the pronunciation of several educated Serbs and Croats whom he had met in Paris. According to Storm, there is no definite tonal movement on syllables bearing the short accents ̏ and `. In Croatian pronunciation these accents are distinguished by means of the pitch of the postaccentual syllable, which is much lower than the syllable bearing the ̏ accent, but after a syllable with ` is either at the same level or lower by only a musical second. (In Serbian pronunciation Storm, like Masing, found no prosodic differences between examples of the types *ȍko* 'eye' and *pèro* 'pen', which—as is now known—is characteristic of the dialect of Belgrade and part of its environs, where in a penultimate syllable before a short final syllable ` has been replaced by ̏.) Of the long accents ̑ is distinctly falling and ´ distinctly rising. The syllable following a long accent is much lower than the accented one (in the case of ´ by a musical fifth in the pronunciation of the Serbs, and even by a musical seventh in the pronunciation of the Croats!). In other words, Storm generally confirms Masing's notion of the disyllabicity of `, but rejects the disyllabicity of ´—which constitutes a kind of contradiction. Storm expresses himself negatively with regard to Masing's work; nor does he accept the "short falling" type of terminology, most probably because he finds no distinctive tonal movements associated with the short accents. He himself refers to ` as "accent 1," to ´ as "accent 2," to ̑ as "accent 3," and to ̏ as "accent 4"; the order of the short and long accents with ̑ and ̏ is the opposite of their order with ` and ´. The introduction of such terms, which have found no echo in Serbocroatian linguistics, undoubtedly reflects the Norwegian phonetician's dissatisfaction with the labels used by Masing and Muža, which his own observations did not confirm;[20] it is also possible that he was somewhat influenced by his background in Scandinavian accentology.

Stojanović (1892) (and 1898, 1901) is concise in his school grammar, limiting himself to calling ̏ sharp, ̀ gentle, ̂ strong, and ́ high.

Divković's school grammar of 1895, differing from his grammar of 1879, employs Budmani's terminology (strong short, etc.), taking over the description of the accents from Novaković's textbook (̏ and ̂ are pronounced with a stronger and higher voice, and ̀ and ́ with an ordinary voice; ̂ is a falling accent, and ́ a rising accent).

Brandt (1895) tacitly drops most of the views he had expressed in 1880. Now he simultaneously accepts labels like "nishodjaščee kratkostnoe" (short falling) and Masing's theory of the disyllabicity of rising accents, with the added explication that their second syllable bears a "vtorostepennoe udarenie" (secondary stress), generally of a falling nature. One is also reminded that ̏ is a "rezkoe udarenie" (sharp accent), while the presence of secondary stress on the following syllable makes rising accents "menee zametnym" (less noticeable), so that they give the impression of being weak accents. This may be considered a good synthesis of the various views that had been gaining ground during the preceding decades.

Florinskij (1895) adopts a position similar to that of Brandt (1895). He, too, accepts Masing's teachings with the "corrections" of Kovačević, and considers descriptive labels like "kratkoe nishodjaščee" (short falling) to be most appropriate. He opines further that "otnositel'no sily ili naprjažennosti golosa voshodjaščija udarenija možno nazvat' slabymi, nishodjaščija—sil'nymi" (with respect to the force and tension of the voice, rising accents may be called weak, and falling accents strong).

Florschütz (1895–96) likewise uses musical notation. He, too, finds that there is no distinctive tonal movement in accented syllables with ̏ and ̀, and that vowels with ̂ are clearly falling (by a musical sixth!), whereas vowels with ́ are rising (by a musical third). The syllable following ̏ and ̂ is low, and the one following ̀ and ́ is high; in the case of ̀ it is higher by a musical third than the accented syllable, and in the case of ́ it has the level of the termination (the peak) of the accented syllable. This is the first instance of complete agreement with Masing's views; with respect to the intersyllabic pitch relations in words with ̀, Florschütz goes even further. In conformity with his findings, he proposes to replace terms like "jaki kratki" (strong short), with which he had started, with "visoki kratki" (high short) for ̏, "duboki kratki" (low short) for ̀, "padajući dugi" (falling long) for ̑, and "rastući dugi" (growing long) for ́.

Rešetar (1897) energetically rejects Masing's theory as well as all assertions made by Šaxmatov, Storm, and Florschütz that either coincide with or resemble Masing's views. Rešetar agrees with Kovačević on everything except preaccentual syllables, in which he hears "eine gelinde Steigerung der Tonhöhe" (a mild raising of pitch). Rešetar also regularly uses terms of the type "short falling." He continues this usage in his later works, for example in Rešetar 1900 and 1922.

Šaxmatov (1898) expresses the opinion that the dispute between authors such as Masing and Florschütz and their opponents such as Kovačević and Rešetar is fruitless, since the differences in their results are obviously due to differences in the dialects they have investigated.

Milas (1898) proposes the completely erroneous idea that Neoštokavian accentuation distinguishes eight accents. He splits each of the four traditionally acknowledged accents into two: in each case, "težište intenziteta" (intensity focus) may be either in the first or in the second half of the duration of the accented vowel. Rešetar (1899) demonstrates that this claim is unfounded. In his review of prevailing opinions, Milas employs side by side labels of the type "jaki kratki" (strong short) and Pavić's labels that describe the graphic symbols: he calls ̏ "dvostruki" (double), ̀ "gravis" (grave), ̑ "obli" (round), and ́ "akut" (acute). His description of the characteristics of the accents corresponds to that of Novaković.

Maretić's grammar, published in 1899, one of the most serious investigations devoted to the modern Serbocroatian language, gives a summary of results achieved in the second half of the nineteenth century. Maretić retains Budmani's terminology ("jaki kratki" (strong short), etc.), but in explaining the difference between strong (̏ and ̑) and weak (̀ and ́) accents he introduces Masing's point of view (as modified by Kovačević): in words like *rȉba* 'fish' or *mȇso* 'meat' "akcenat je jak, jer se ne raspada u dva sloga, već ostaje u jednome, a u *nòga–rúka* slab je akcenat, jer ga je dio u jednome, a dio u drugome slogu" (p. 126) (the accent is strong, since it is not spread over two syllables, but remains on one syllable, but in *nòga* ['foot, leg']–*rúka* ['hand, arm'] the accent is weak, since part of it is on the first syllable and part on the second). In another place Maretić states that the accents ̀ and ́ "obuhvaća dva sloga, i to prvi slog malo jače, drugi malo slabije" (pp. 125–126) (encompass two syllables, the first syllable a little more strongly, the second more weakly). It is significant that Maretić speaks of the strength of the accents and not of their height. In principle, he considers strong expiration to be the relevant characteristic of accents as opposed to unaccentedness. In his opinion, too, ˆ is a falling accent and ˊ is rising; it becomes clear from his wording that in this case he is thinking of *pitch* movement. Conspicuously, he says nothing about the corresponding tonal movements on short vowels. Maretić also defines durational relationships on the basis of his auditory impressions. Taking the duration of a vowel under ̏ as the basic unit, he claims that the vowel under ˆ lasts for $1\frac{3}{4}$ units and that the vowel under ˊ lasts for 2 units (unaccented long vowels in various positions last for either $1\frac{1}{2}$ or $1\frac{3}{4}$ units). Presenting these estimations, he introduces a note of caution: "možda bi bio blizu istini" (p. 119) (this might be close to the truth). Nevertheless, he resists the temptation to say that the duration of the vowel under ˋ corresponds to $1\frac{1}{4}$ units, and states carefully: "Na pr. *e* u *sèlo* i *htjȅlo* kratko je, ali je u prvoj reči nešto, ako i vrlo malo, dulje, nego li u drugoj" (p. 119) (e.g., the *e* in *sèlo* ['village'] and [past part.sg.neut.] *htjȅlo* ['wanted'] is short, but in the first word it is somewhat, even though very little, longer than in the second).

Leskien (1899) operates with terms of the type "fallender Ton bei kurzer Silbe" (falling tone in a short syllable).

Boyer (1900) uses the terms "fort" (strong) for ̏, "faible" (weak) for ˋ, "descendant" (falling) for ˆ, and "montant" (rising) for ˊ; it can be seen from the description of the accents that he also finds rising pitch with ˋ and falling pitch with ̏. According to Boyer, the distinguishing characteristic of falling accents is "effort d'intensité" "au commencement de l'émission" (intensity effort in the beginning of production) and for rising accents "à la fin de l'émission" (toward the end of production).

When we look back again at the ideas expressed in the nineteenth century, we receive the impression of great disagreement, manifested in the diversity of terms and qualifications applied to accents. Thus, the accent ̏ is characterized by various authors as entirely short, (raising),[21] sharper, still shorter, very sharp, very short, short grave, round, short and low, (sharp and fast), strong /heavy/, sharpest, /doubly heavy/, sharp, strong short, short pushed, /heavy/, monosyllabic short, shortest, /double/, short falling, accent 4, high short, and strong. The accent ˋ is said to be a little raised and quickly lowered, raising, sharp, short and tense, not very sharp, short, short acute, short higher, sharp and fast, weak /heavy/, weak short, short pulled, /somewhat heavy/, disyllabic short, weak, /grave/, short rising, accent 1, mild, low short. The accent ˆ is qualified as a little stretched, "superelevans," the one where the voice goes out roundly, doubling the vowel, long, long grave, long falling, /sharp/, round, strong long, long pushed, monosyllabic long, high long, falling, accent 3, strong. The accent ˊ is said to be completely stretched, lengthening, stretched, one that stretches in a straight line, long, longest, very long, long acute, long rising, /twisted/, weak long, /acute/, long pulled, disyllabic long, rising, accent 2, high. It is noticeable that some of the terms are being used for more than one accent: "long" can apply either to ˊ or to ˆ, and "sharp" to ̏, ˋ, and ˆ.

There are instances in which the relationship between two accents is described in opposite ways by different authors. For Brlić (1854) ̏ is low and ˋ is high; for Florschütz (1895–96) ˋ is low and ̏ is high. Miklošič (1852) asserts that the difference between ˆ and ˊ is that ˆ is longer than ˊ; Karadžić (1858) asserts that the difference is that ˊ is longer than ˆ. This must have caused many misunderstandings. At first glance it is difficult to avoid the impression of arbitrariness and general chaos. Two facts are clear: the objective state of affairs is such that it cannot be easily discovered by means of simple listening, and some authors approached the problem in a superficial manner. Nevertheless, progress was made during the second half of the nineteenth century. Two competing approaches become more and more clearly outlined. One involves twofold binarism, that is, the intersection of a two-way quantity contrast with another two-way opposition (falling vs. rising, strong vs. weak, or monosyllabic vs. disyllabic); the other involves two qualitatively different oppositions, one for the long accents and one for the short accents (for the long accents, most frequently falling vs. rising; for the short accents, sharp vs. mild, strong vs. weak, etc.). Combinations of the two approaches are likewise not rare. Thus, Masing at first holds the position of twofold binarism (short vs. long and monosyllabic vs. disyllabic), but in describing the realizations of the accents he states that ˆ is falling and ˊ is rising, whereas their short counterparts generally do not exhibit this contrast. Similarly, Maretić (1899), operating with the contrast strong vs. weak in the case of both long and short accents, finds falling pitch to be associated only with ˆ and rising pitch only with ˊ. On the other hand, Boyer (1900), who on the level of terminology notes the contrast falling vs. rising only with long accents, nevertheless mentions falling pitch in the description of the realization of ̏, and rising pitch in the description of the realization of ˋ. Kovačević (1878–79) assumes a kind of middle position as well, although otherwise he belongs among those who deserve the most credit for spreading the concept of two falling and two rising accents. He points out that falling and rising pitch movements can be perceived easily in the case of long accents, but only with difficulty in the case of short accents. Thus, toward the end of the nineteenth century a scholarly consensus was being approached with regard to the contrasts in pitch movement associated with length, while the presence of such a contrast in combination with shortness remained controversial. In addition, many authors recognized that the pitch level on syllables immediately following ` or ´ is higher than that on syllables following ̏ or ̑, but there was no agreement concerning the pitch relation between postaccentual and accented syllables. The majority considered the accented syllable to be higher in any case; only Florschütz joined Masing in accepting full disyllabicity for ` and ´.

Close to the beginning of the twentieth century, the first instrumental measurements of accents made their appearance (Gauthiot 1900, Popovici 1902, Ivković 1912, Ekblom 1917; these works will be reviewed in chapter 2). It would have been logical for accentology to accept their findings as authoritative. This nevertheless did not happen, possibly not so much because the methodology had not yet been perfected as because these works were mostly produced by foreigners and were published abroad, in journals that are rarely read by scholars engaged in the study of Serbocroatian.

1.7 Serbocroatian Accentology in the First Decades of the Twentieth Century

The situation remained much the same in the first three decades of this century. The inherited disagreement continued. Moreover, the first year of the new century brought two works that heightened the disagreement: the dissertation of Ivan Šajković, and a grammar by Tomislav Maretić that proposed a change in terminology.

Šajković (1901) described his own pronunciation using musical notation (his family home was in northwestern Serbia, in the vicinity of Šabac, but he insisted that his pronunciation was representative of the educated layer of the population). His results, which differ noticeably from the positions of other authors, are reflected in the terms he introduces: "der jähe sinkende Accent (̏)" (steep falling accent), "der sanfte sinkende Accent (` )" (gentle falling accent), "der sanfte steigende Accent ( ´ )" (gentle rising accent), "der zweitönige Accent ( ̑ )" (two-toned accent). Both short accents have a falling pitch movement, which with ̏ amounts to a minor third and with ` to a minor second. The intensity peak is at the end of the accented syllable with ̏ and in the middle with `. Under the ̑ accent the pitch of the vowel first falls from E to C sharp (a minor third), and then rises to D sharp (major second). Intensity in the syllable under ̑ likewise has two peaks—the first in the middle, the second at the end. The musical notation shows that the pitch of the immediately postaccentual syllable is always somewhat lower than the termination of the accented syllable. Rešetar (1901, 1902) very sharply rejects Šajković's views.

Maretić (1901) abandons designations like "jaki kratki" (strong short), stating that they indicate the nature of the accents very well, but are quite unsuitable for use in schools, because each label consists of two words. He replaces these terms with labels consisting of single words: "brzi (̏)" (fast), "spori (̀)" (slow), "silazni (̑)" (falling), and "uzlazni (́)" (rising). He adds that the fast accent is indeed pronounced faster than any other, that ̀ is pronounced more slowly than ̏ , and that intensity seems to decrease with ̑ but to increase with ́ .

Other authors of grammars retain their previous usage. Thus, Novaković 1902 repeats Novaković 1879, 1884, 1890, 1894; Stojanović 1901 and 1920 repeat Stojanović 1892, 1898; Divković 1903 repeats Divković 1895; Rešetar 1916 repeats Rešetar 1897; and so on. Perhaps by accident, authors from the western part of the Serbocroatian linguistic area—Divković and Rešetar—hold fast to twofold binarism (which, to be sure, had been renounced by their colleague Maretić, a professor at the University of Zagreb), while the Belgrade grammarians Novaković and Stojanović operate with terms consisting of one word. The depth of the disagreement is demonstrated by the fact that each of the five most highly regarded authors uses a different terminology.

In his school grammar of 1905, Florschütz modifies to a certain degree his findings of a decade ago. For ̏ he states that the accented syllable is higher and stronger than the following one, and for ̀ that the accented syllable is stronger than the postaccentual syllable, but somewhat lower; for ̑ he asserts that the tone is falling, and for ́ that it rises from a lower level to a higher one (he does not mention syllables following long accents). Florschütz's new labels are simplifications of his earlier terms: ̏ is a high accent, ̀ is low, ̑ is falling, and ́ is rising. For purposes of comparison with Lithuanian accents, Florschütz (1910) provides a musical transcription of the word *bádem* 'almond', in which the tone under the Neoštokavian ́ accent is shown to rise by a musical fifth, and the second syllable (*-dem*) is at the level of the termination of the accented syllable.

From among other local authors of the first two decades of the twentieth century, Gopić (1907) and Grubor (1909) use the terminology of Maretić ("brzi" (fast), etc.), Ivković (1911) the terminology of Stojanović ("oštri" (sharp), etc.), Moskovljević (1913) the terminology of Rešetar ("kratki silazni" (short falling), etc.), and Katić (1915) and Živanović (1919) the terminology of Budmani ("jaki kratki" (strong short), etc.), which Maretić had abandoned. Grubor surveys and analyzes existing terminology, giving preference to that of Maretić, but at the same time pointing out—with a reference to Kovačević—that ̏ and ̑ are falling accents and ̀ and ́ are rising accents. In addition, he expresses the opinion that the definitions of Stojanović, based on tonal prominence, represent the nature of Serbocroatian accents better than those of Novaković, Maretić, and Florschütz, who claim that what is essential for the accents is prominence due to intensity. Katić provides his work with musical transcriptions of Čakavian and Štokavian accents. For the Štokavian accents, in the syllable with ̏ he finds neither a rise nor a fall in pitch; in syllables with ̑ the tone falls by a musical fourth. The following syllable is lower by a fourth in the case of ̏ and at the level of the termination of the accented syllable in the case of ̑. In vowels under ̀ and ́ the pitch rises by a semitone; here, too, the postaccentual syllable falls by a fourth.

The discussions of the musicologist Kuhač (1908) lack linguistic sophistication. He judges Masing to be incompetent, but he himself takes seriously Milas's theory of eight accents. Condemning attempts to represent speech melody by musical notation, he nevertheless introduces a large number of words transcribed in musical notation, taken from transcriptions of orally performed folk songs from different areas. The pitch relationships in these songs represent for him the tonal relationships occurring in the normally spoken pronunciation of these words. Focusing attention on words with ̀ accents, he considers that when the postaccentual syllable is lower than the accented syllable, the word belongs to the Neoštokavian accentual system; when the following syllable is at the level of the accented syllable, or even higher, he interprets this as an element of a more archaic accentual system (Old Štokavian, Čakavian, or Kajkavian). However, many examples from the first category come from areas in which the older accentuation has been preserved, and many examples from the second category come from the Neoštokavian area. Furthermore, among his examples with the ̀ accent (like *djèvōjka* 'girl') are also words that in actuality bear ̏ (e.g., voc.sg. *djȅvōjko*)—which in the folk songs behave in the same manner as the words with ̀.

Ivšić (1911) deals both with the nature of Štokavian accents and with Masing's theory, expressing the view that the "total impression of the syllable under the accents ́ and ̀ is stronger than the impression of the syllable following ́ and ̀, i.e. both the expiratory force is stronger and the pitch is higher."

Describing rising accents, Moskovljević (1913) states that the "expiratory strength of stress" falls on the accented syllable, but that from the point of view of pitch the following syllable does not lag behind, but may even be somewhat higher than the accented syllable (according to the author's observations, made in Srem). Moskovljević explains the difference between the moderately low second syllable of *mȅsto* 'place' and the very low second syllable of *prûće* 'rods' by observing that the falling interval under ˆ is much greater than under ̏ and that the pitch of the following syllable depends on the level at which the accented syllable terminates.

Unlike native authors, foreign Slavists of this period usually employ labels of the type "short falling." They do not explicitly claim primacy for these terms, but it is obvious that such designations are much more suitable for their purposes. Above all, they classify accents not by single-word terms, but by reference to their distinctive characteristics, quantity and quality (to be sure, the nature of the latter distinction is not completely uncontroversial, especially with regard to short accents). This position is attractive because of its symmetry and its structural regularity. Moreover, combining ̏ and ˆ in one set and ` and ´ in another leads to essential simplification in three respects. From a historical point of view, ̏ and ˆ are primary accents, which have basically remained in the same position they occupied in Proto-Slavic; ` and ´ are secondary accents, which have arisen as a result of a shift of noninitial primary accents to the preceding syllable. For the distribution of accents it is basic that ̏ and ˆ may occur only on the first syllable, whereas ` and ´ may occur on any syllable except the last. In morphophonology, too, the behavior of ̏ parallels that of ˆ, and the behavior of ` parallels that of ´. Typical in this regard are relationships like nom.sg. *bȍb* : gen.sg. *bòba* 'broad bean' and nom.sg. *kljûč* : gen.sg. *ključa* 'key', nom.sg. *nòga* : acc.sg. *nȍgu*, nom.-acc.pl. *nȍge* 'leg', and nom.sg. *rúka* : acc.sg. *rûku*, nom.-acc.pl. *rûke* 'hand', *nȍsīm* 'I carry' : *nòsiti* 'to carry' and *brânīm* 'I defend' : *brániti* 'to defind', *ȉgrām* 'I play' : *ìgrajū* 'they play', and *čûvām* 'I guard': *čúvajū* 'they guard'. Obviously, it is very economical to employ common descriptors for ̏ and ˆ as well as for ` and ´. Finally, members of both pairs do indeed share essential pitch and intensity characteristics. For all these reasons it is not surprising to find labels of the type "short falling" being used by Bogorodickij (1912) as well as by Leskien (1914), Kul'bakin (1915), Meillet and Vaillant (1924), and Liewehr (1927). Actually, this list should also include Rešetar, who, to be sure, was a native of Dubrovnik, but who was a professor at the University of Vienna until 1919.[22] Finally, Vondrák (1906) and Schmitt (1924) belong in this group. Primarily they report results of other authors, placing the greatest amount of trust in the views of Kovačević. They refer to accents by graphic symbols (̏, etc.), stating, however, that ̏ and ˆ are falling and ` and ´ rising.

Among the foreign scholars, the Norwegian Slavist and phonetician Olaf Broch (1910, 1911), who devoted himself seriously to the study of the nature of Neoštokavian accents, occupies a special place. According to Broch, it is true—as had been stated long ago—that the pronunciation distinguishes between long accented syllables with rising and falling intonation, short (or half-long) syllables with rising intonation, and short syllables with more energetic ("sharper") pressure and with relatively high pitch, whereby any pitch movement within that short syllable nucleus is only weakly noticeable, if at all. He adds, agreeing with Masing, that the higher pitch level that is reached at the end of the syllable bearing a rising accent (´ and `) extends (in the dialects known to him) from the "accented" syllable to the following one—to the whole syllable or at least to its first part. As for intensity movements, he finds that they generally parallel tonal movements; he does not accept the view that ˆ is characterized by two-peakedness, as Gauthiot had claimed. Unlike other foreign Slavists of his time, Broch does not use any labels for the accents, not even those of the type "short falling," contenting himself with identifying the accents by means of graphic symbols (˵, etc.). It is interesting that other phoneticians generally did the same (Gauthiot 1900, Ivković 1912, Ekblom 1917).

Divković (1917) combines elements from several approaches. His terminology is still that of Budmani (strong short, etc.), with Novaković's description of the pronunciation of accents and with the added emphasis that ˵ is pronounced "vrlo oštro" (very sharply), but he notes also that ˵ and ˆ are falling accents and ` and ´ are rising. Somewhat different combinations appear in Lukić 1923. Lukić uses in parallel terms like "jaki kratki" (strong short) and "silazni kratki" (falling short), "slabi dugi" (weak long) and "uzlazni dugi" (rising long), etc. He also states that govorna jačina *jakih* naglasaka *ostaje samo na naglašenom slogu*, a govorna jačina slabih deli se tako, da jedan i veći deo te jačine ostaje na naglašenom slogu, a drugi deo i to manji ostaje na drugom, nenaglašenom slogu. (italics J. L.) (The speech power of *strong* accents is associated only with *the accented syllable*, but the speech power of weak accents is distributed in such a way that one part—the larger one—remains on the accented syllable, but another, smaller part stays on the second, unaccented syllable.) This is Masing's position modified by Kovačević, but with intensity as the relevant feature.

Simić (1922) distances himself somewhat from his publication of 1883. Now he applies Stojanović's labels to short accents ("oštar" (sharp) and "blag" (mild)), but introduces his own terms for the long accents: ˆ is "dvoton" (double-toned) and ´ "jednoton" (single-toned). The double-tone accent is falling and in that sense contains two tones, a higher beginning tone and a lower terminal tone; ´ is considered to be level rather than rising.

Miletić (1926) calls ˵ and ˆ primary and ˋ and ´ secondary (from a historical point of view). Concerning Miletić's findings, see section 2.10.5 of this book.

Reviewing Miletić 1926, Belić (1926–27) says that even though the tonal movement in the accented syllable under ˋ and ˵ may vary, these two accents are never confused "jer je odnos drugoga sloga prema naglašenom i po visini tona i po intervalu *tako tipičan* da je udaljenost između ˵ i ˋ u govorima u kojima se ti akcenti čuvaju još *uvek* vrlo velika" (italics A.B.) (since the relationship of the second syllable to the accented syllable with regard to pitch level as well as the musical interval between them is *so typical* that the distance between ˵ and ˋ in those dialects that preserve these accents is *still* very great). Belić also presents his observations about regional variants of short accents. The vowel under ˵ is pronounced with expressly falling tone in Dubrovnik, Bosnia, and northwestern Serbia; in more eastern areas the tonal movement on that vowel is "netipično" (atypical). With ˋ there are more discrepancies. In Belgrade the rise on the accented syllable is weak, and the following syllable is either at the level of the accented syllable or lower. In northwestern Serbia and in (unspecified) other areas the rising character of the vowel under ˋ is "vrlo tipičan" (very typical) and the following syllable is "*uvek* niži" (*always* lower).[23] A third type is found in Vojvodina, where "uzlazni karakter ˋ (je) dobro razvijen, ali ... *katkada* početak potonjeg sloga može biti viši od kraja sloga pod akcentom ˋ" (italics A. B.) (the rising character of ˋ is well developed, but ... *sometimes* the beginning of the next syllable can be higher than the end of the syllable under ˋ). In the ijekavian dialects of Lika and Krbava "je mnogo češće potonji slog viši od naglašenog" (the following syllable is much more often higher than the accented syllable), and the rising interval between them is much greater than in the dialects of Vojvodina. As for intensity, Belić states that it increases during the first half of the vowel under ˋ or ´ and then decreases.

In addition to his earlier terms ("oštri, blagi, snažni, visoki" (sharp, mild, strong, high)), Stojanović (1926) introduces the terms of Budmani ("jaki kratki" (strong short), etc.), explaining that in the case of strong accents "glas pada na akcentovanom slogu i ne produžuje se dalje" (the voice falls on the accented syllable and does not extend any further), whereas with weak accents "glas se na akcentovanom slogu diže i spušta se tek na drugom do njega" (the voice rises on the accented syllable and drops only on the second, following syllable), which means that Stojanović has accepted Masing's position. Stefanović (1927) does the same, adding that the pitch rise on the accented syllable is "jedva primetno" (hardly noticeable) with ` but "vrlo primetno" (very noticeable) with ´.

In the tenth edition of his school grammar (1928) and the second edition of his scientific grammar (1931) Maretić retains his terminology from 1901. In other respects, in the 1928 publication he simply repeats the statements made in 1901, but in the 1931 publication he combines them with explanations from 1899 that ̏ and ̑ are strong accents, pronounced with greater strength than the weak accents ` and ´; in the latter case two syllables are included in the accent, "prvi malo jače, drugi malo slabije" (the first slightly more strongly, the second somewhat more weakly). This time Maretić refrains from representing the duration of vowels under the various accents with arithmetic proportions, but estimates that the vowel under ` is somewhat longer than the one under ̏ and that the vowel under ´ is longer than the vowel under ̑.

Musulin (1929) employs Maretić's new terminology, but also presents a diagram in which ̏ and ̑ are designated as strong accents and ` and ´ as weak.

1.8 Establishment of Standardized Terminology

A complete change in views concerning Serbocroatian accents took place in 1932, when the Ministry of Education of the Kingdom of Yugoslavia issued the booklet *Gramatička terminologija* (*Grammatical Terminology*) for the purpose of unifying and codifying terms used in textbooks by Serbs and Croats. In this booklet, terms of the type "kratki silazni" (short falling) are given as the only correct ones; of the others, only "brzi" (fast) and "spori" (slow) are mentioned, with reference to the more correct terms "kratki silazni" and "kratki uzlazni" (short falling and short rising). The booklet was produced by a committee chaired by Belić; at the end of the foreword it is mentioned that the whole task was accomplished by two members of the committee, A. Belić and St. Ivšić. It is interesting that up to that time these two authors had used no terms at all for Neoštokavian accents, referring to them in their works only by graphic symbols.[24] Very likely they were not enthusiastic about any of the existing terminological systems, and especially not about the chaotic disagreements that existed among them. Naturally, some kind of terminology had to be adopted for use in secondary schools; the two prominent linguists, who up to that time had not written school grammars, decided in favor of the terminology that was most appropriate for scholarly purposes. We know incidentally that Belić, for one, considered falling pitch on the accented syllable to be the characteristic feature of ̏, and rising pitch to be typical of ̀ (Belić 1926–27).

Recommendations made in the booklet *Gramatička terminologija* became obligatory for all schools and all textbooks in the Kingdom of Yugoslavia. Unification of terminology was a boon for the schools, even more so as the chosen solution was not bad. Nevertheless, the fact remains that a decree from above influenced the development of views concerning a scholarly problem. Succeeding generations learned already in secondary school to "hear" falling and rising pitch wherever these were officially expected to occur.

Terms of the type "kratki silazni" (short falling) are used in the school grammars of Belić (1934), Musulin (1935), Stefanović (1936), Stojanović (1936), and Lalević (1938). It is characteristic of the situation that among these authors are two who had earlier published textbooks using different systems, but who now submitted to the new regulation. Nevertheless, Stojanović also introduces his old labels ("oštar, blag, snažan, visok" (sharp, mild, strong, high)) and, in describing their pronunciation, designates falling accents as strong and rising accents as weak. Lalević, too, uses some of Stojanović's earlier views in a similar way: he states that ̏ is pronounced very shortly and sharply, ̀ shortly and more mildly, ̂ strongly, and ́ "kao da se glas diže i ne spušta" (as if the voice rises and does not fall).

1.9 Recent Nonexperimental Treatments of Serbocroatian Accents

Scholarly discussion continued its course independently of school grammars. In the 1930s it generally proceeded from points of view similar to those of Masing. Already in 1931 Jakobson, quoting Masing 1876, Miletić 1926, and Belić 1926–27, developed the idea that the relevant characteristic of rising accents is "Übersilbigkeit" (domain extending beyond one syllable) of high tone in some dialects and "Vollsilbigkeit" (domain extending over one whole syllable) in others, whereas the so-called falling accents are "unvollsilbig" (domain covering less than one whole syllable). Trubetzkoy (1939) states that in the case of ̀ the beginning of the first postaccentual syllable is at the tonal level of the end of the accented syllable, whereas ̏ frequently has level tone in a relatively low register. Intensity plays no role at all with so-called rising accents, but the prominence of the syllable under ̏ is based on intensity. Isačenko (1939) speaks of rising and falling accents, but emphasizes that with rising accents the first postaccentual syllable is higher than the accented syllable, and that ictus is divided between the two syllables. Nevertheless, he also considers it relevant that according to the linguistic intuition of native speakers, accent is located only on the first of these two syllables. However, van Wijk (1940) explicitly reduces the contrast between ` and ̏ to "intonation."

Like the phonologists of the Prague school, native scholars also emphasized the role of the following syllable in the case of the so-called rising accents. Belić (1935b) mentions the rising character of the syllables under ` and ´ and the falling nature of the syllables under ̏ and ̑, but adds that in words with ` and ´ the tone overflows into the following syllable, whereas with ̏ and ̑ "accent seems to detach the stressed syllable from other syllables, as if there were a pause after it" (p. 165). Belić states that falling accents are pronounced "forte," and rising accents "piano." The falling accents are characterized by "decrescendo" (decreasing intensity); the rising accents are characterized by increasing intensity in the beginning, but decreasing intensity starting from the middle of the accented syllable. Ivšić (1936:67) expresses the opinion that with the Štokavian accent ` "force is divided between the syllable with this sign and the following syllable," whereas with ̏ "the force is concentrated on the syllable bearing this sign." Regarding tone, Ivšić states that the accent ` begins with a low rising tone, but the accent ̏ starts with a high tone that may be falling.

Kostić (1937) presents his views of the Neoštokavian accents, based on the theories of Daniel Jones and on the results of measurements he himself carried out at University College, London, under instructions by Professor L. Armstrong. Apparently on the basis of his own (Vojvodinian) pronunciation, Kostić considers the syllable immediately following ` or ´ to be higher and stronger than the syllables bearing these accents. In syllables with short accents he does not find tonal movements worth mentioning, except for observing a rise in a few examples with ̏. On the other hand, in the syllable bearing ´ he notices regular rising movements, but in syllables with ̑ he observes a slight initial rise, followed by a strong fall proceeding in a convex line. He opines further that in various words with ̏ tonal falls occur between the accented and the postaccentual syllable amounting to different musical intervals, sometimes accompanied by tonal movements within the accented syllable itself. Thus, according to Kostić, in *kȕka* 'hook' the interval between the two syllables is larger than in 3.sg.pres. *kȕka* 'laments'. Likewise, in 3.sg.pres. *srȕši* 'destructs' the falling interval between the two syllables is small, whereas in the imperative of the same verb, *srȕši*, that interval is large, the first syllable being rising rather than level. In the aorist *srȕši* the interval is again smaller, but this time it is combined with a rising movement in the first syllable and the general tonal level is much higher than in the present tense. Kostić explicitly attributes distinctiveness ("fonematske funkcije") to these differences. He has not returned to these distinctions in his later works; neither have other researchers observed anything of the kind. It appears that Kostić was misled by chance occurrences of various details in his own realization of the same accent on different occasions, and possibly also by a kind of emphatic intonation in the production of the aorist and imperative forms.

Kostić (1938–39) characterizes the accent ̏ as simple stress, using this English term. Otherwise he proposes that the accent ̏ be designated in IPA transcription with the symbol ˈ before the accented syllable and that the accent ̀ be designated with the symbol for secondary stress, ˌ , before the accented syllable ("which is on a lower level than the following syllable"). Kostić solves the problem of designating the accent ̂ by combining the symbol ˌ with the symbol for length, : (thus, ˌve:z = *vêz* 'embroidery'), but he writes ́ with a single period after the syllable (du · žan = *dúžan* 'indebted'). The logic behind these two decisions remains unclear. The same transcription is employed in Fry and Kostić 1939.

The practice of employing terms of the type "short falling" in textbooks continued after World War II. This is true not only of books by native authors, such as Aleksić and Stevanović 1946, Belić 1948, 1960, Živanović 1951, Miletić 1952, Nahtigal 1952, Nedović 1960, Stevanović 1964, 1966, Ajanović and Minović 1971, Peco 1971c, Težak and Babić 1973, Silić and Rosandić 1974, Kašić and Jerković 1976, Ružić 1978, Simić and Simić 1981, but also of books by foreign authors, such as Lord 1958, Arbuzova, Dmitriev, and Sokal' 1965, Gudkov 1969, Dmitriev and Safronov 1975. Only among the Croats, where the unificatory moves of the 1930s had frequently been viewed as threats to Croatian individuality, was the practice maintained of introducing other terms, most frequently those of Maretić, alongside the generally accepted ones. Thus, for short accents Frančić (1963b) offers the alternative labels "brzi" (fast, ̏) and "spori" (slow, ̀). Brabec, Hraste, and Živković (1965) and Barić et al. (1979) use the complete set of Maretić's terms (fast, slow, falling, rising). Barić et al. also mention as "older labels" the collection of terms like "jaki kratki" (strong short). Hamm (1967) offers an alternative label only for ̏ ("oštri" (sharp)). This behavior testifies both to respect for the native tradition and to a possible realization that terms like "short falling" may not always correspond fully to physical reality. Meanwhile, in other grammars written by authors from Croatia, such as Težak and Babić 1973 and Silić and Rosandić 1974, labels of the type "short falling" are used exclusively.[25] This applies also to the 1970 reference manual of Matešić, who makes it explicit that he uses these terms for identification rather than for precise description (p. 16). Incidentally, concerning the same terminology the Serbian linguist Miletić (1952) also remarks that the main characteristics of the accents can be deduced from their names, but that the real state of affairs is much more complicated.

Of the authors listed above, Belić (1948, 1960), Živanović (1951), Miletić (1952), Gudkov (1969), Matešić (1970), Peco (1971c), Silić and Rosandić (1974), Kašić and Jerković (1976), Ružić (1978), and Barić et al. (1979) mention the tonal level of the following syllable as being characteristic of rising accents; the others do not deal with this question. To be sure, these authors, too, differ among themselves in the treatment of this problem. Thus, Belić and Peco emphasize that the phenomenon is dialect-dependent, and Barić et al. and Kašić and Jerković assign intersyllabic tonal relations an important role in connection with the distinction between short accents, but do not mention it in connection with long accents. On the other hand, Barić et al. state without reservations that in both rising accents the beginning of the following syllable is on the same tonal level as or even higher than the accented syllable. Such assertions found in grammars are certainly a reflection of the results of instrumental studies carried out in recent decades.

Peco (1971c) offers a musical transcription of three words with rising accents prepared by his student J. Jokanović. In each case the tone on the accented syllable rises by a minor third; in the second syllable of the words *govòriti* 'to speak' and *národi* 'peoples' the tone is at the level of the peak of the accented syllable, but in the word *víno* 'wine' it is lower by a semitone. The intensity peak is in each case at the end of the accented syllable.

Belić (1948, 1960) and Miletić (1952) state that with rising accents intensity rises only up to the middle of the accented syllable, and then falls. Both authors also remark that in certain areas (Belgrade, eastern parts of Serbia) the syllable under ̏ is pronounced without falling pitch. Miletić adds that in some areas the syllable under ̀ may be rising only in its first part, but level in the second part; that the falling intervals in falling accents are greater than the rising intervals in rising accents; and finally that sentence intonation exerts an influence on the tonal movements of the word accents: a rising factor comes into play at the beginning of the sentence, and a falling factor toward the end of the sentence. Ivšić (1970), according to whom in words with rising accents the syllable following the accent is likewise accented at the same pitch level, the accented syllable having higher intensity, asserts that it is difficult to perceive the raising of the voice in the syllable *že-* in nom.sg. *žèna* 'wife', but even more difficult to perceive the lowering of the voice in the syllable *žȅ-* in voc.sg. *žȅno* 'wife'. It is to be noted that the books of Belić, Miletić, Ivšić, and Peco are university textbooks of phonetics, Serbocroatian accentology, or comparative Slavic linguistics, which is not the case with other works mentioned in this context.

Among scientific treatises, those of Trager (1940), Hodge (1946), Kuznecov (1948), Belić (1951–52), Hraste (1957), Stankiewicz (1958, 1959), De Bray (1961), Jonke (1964), Shevelov (1964), Peco (1965a), Lehfeldt and Finka (1969a, 1969b), and Lehfeldt (1970) conform to the standard terminology (short falling, etc.) and do not mention the problem of high pitch on the syllable immediately following a syllable bearing a rising accent. Nevertheless, it should be added that Trager speaks about Serbocroatian accent as stress and states that the syllable following a rising accent bears secondary stress.

The following scholars consider the pitch level of the first postaccentual syllable to be characteristic of rising accents: Vinaver (1952), Hodge (1958), Ivić (1958 and several later works), Lüdtke (1959), Bidwell (1963, 1968), Hodge and Janković (1965), Browne and McCawley (1965), Kostić (1966, 1967), Junković (1968), Halle (1971), I. Miletić (1974), Bulatova (1975), and Simić (1977) (who considers this phenomenon to be a characteristic of northern Štokavian dialects). Hodge, Bidwell, Ivić (1965a), and Browne and McCawley introduce new ways of transcribing accents, based on phonological analyses whose point of departure is the high pitch found on the syllables immediately following syllables bearing rising accents (see sections 4.1.2 through 4.1.5).

Tomić (1963) occupies an isolated position. He remains faithful to Maretić's terminology (fast, slow, etc.). On the basis of five kymographic recordings, he tries to prove that the two long accents ˆ and ˊ are pronounced differently in the genitive plural of nouns than in other instances.

This survey of opinions held up to now about the physical nature of Neoštokavian accents demonstrates, we believe, that the disagreements can be eliminated only by experimental investigation, to which we devote chapters 2 and 3 of this book.

Chapter 2
Word Prosody

This chapter deals with accentual phenomena at the word level. We will first present a condensed summary of the results of our descriptive study of accentual patterns in standard Serbocroatian and in three representative dialects from areas in which the Neoštokavian accent shift has not been completed. We will then discuss listening tests that we have conducted in order to establish the perceptual significance of the patterns discovered in the descriptive phase of the investigation. Finally, we will review and comment upon relevant work performed by other investigators.

2.1 Accentual Patterns in Standard Serbocroatian

Our description of the accentual patterns in Standard Serbocroatian will proceed as follows. We will first describe fundamental frequency and intensity patterns. We will then discuss vowel duration and vowel quality, as well as possible interactions between word accent and vowel quality. More details concerning the phonetic data, test materials, and informants are to be found in our earlier publications, to which we will occasionally direct attention.

2.1.1 Method

The method adopted throughout the investigation consists of acoustic-phonetic analyses of specially prepared materials, spoken by native speakers and tape-recorded under laboratory conditions. The patterns were established through detailed study of a considerable number of utterances by one speaker; the generality of the observations was checked by analyzing the patterns appearing in a smaller subset of materials recorded by twelve additional informants.

2.1.2 Informants

The main informant for the study was P.I., one of the authors. P.I. was born in 1924 in Belgrade. His parents are from Vojvodina (father from Srem, mother from Kikinda). From 1924 to 1941 he lived in Subotica, from 1941 to 1955 in Belgrade, from 1955 to 1975 in Novi Sad, from 1975 to the present in Belgrade. He is a university professor specializing in the Serbocroatian language. His pronunciation is based on standard Serbocroatian as spoken by educated Vojvodinians, with certain regional characteristics. These concern mainly the distribution of vowel length in unaccented syllables. In the speech of P.I., long unaccented vowels never occur immediately after a long falling accent or after another unaccented long vowel. After the long rising accent, long vowels may occur in medial position; after a short falling accent or after an unstressed short syllable, long vowels may occur in medial position or in a closed final syllable. There are no restrictions in the occurrence of long vowels after a short rising accent.

The twelve additional informants speak the same dialect of modern standard literary Serbocroatian as the main informant, with only minor exceptions. At the time of the recording six of the informants were announcers of Radio Novi Sad and six were students at the Department of Serbocroatian Language and Literature at the University of Novi Sad. Half of the informants were men, the other half women, evenly distributed among the announcers and the students. All of them were living in Novi Sad at the time of the recording; three had also been born in Novi Sad or its environs. Three others had been born elsewhere within the province of Vojvodina in northeastern Yugoslavia. Of the remaining six, three had a western Štokavian background (from the jekavian dialect area), and three were from northern Serbia (one from Belgrade, two from places near the border of the jekavian dialect area). All informants had lived in Novi Sad for at least several years. At the time of the recording the informants were between 20 and 40 years old.

2.1.3 Test Materials

The test materials consisted of 146 words with the short falling accent, 144 words with the short rising accent, 83 words with the long falling accent, and 91 words with the long rising accent. (We will continue to employ these traditional labels; our use of the labels or of the symbols ̏, ̀, ̑, and ́ is for the purpose of identification only and is not meant to refer to the phonetic realization of the accents.) The words were distributed among the various accentual types as described in appendix A (see Ivić and Lehiste 1963:63–67).

To approach the problem of the interrelationship between sentence intonation and word accent, we decided to investigate first the nature of word accents in neutral position—that is, in a position where the influence of sentence intonation on the test word would be minimal and could be kept constant. The test words selected for the study were therefore placed in short frame utterances constructed in such a manner that the test words appeared in central position (that is, neither at the beginning nor at the end of the utterance) at the peak of the intonation contour, bearing primary, but not emphatic, sentence stress. Once the phonetic nature of word accents in this position has been established, it becomes possible to describe the modifications of the patterns introduced either by changing the position of the words within the same intonation contour or by changing the intonation contour.

The basic frame sentence used in the recording was *Forma ... data je kao primer* 'The form ... is given as an example'. P.I. recorded all test words in this frame. Nine additional frames were employed, constructed in such a way that the words were placed in an environment in which the grammatical form of the word would occur naturally. P.I. also recorded almost all test words in these frames. In all, P.I. recorded 877 productions of the 464 words. A summary of the number of times each accent type occurred with each syllable nucleus is given in table 2.1.

The twelve additional informants read a subset of these words and some additional words in the basic frame. The informants produced two partially overlapping lists of test utterances, one containing 51 test words, the other 65 test words. The two lists are given in appendix B. In addition, the speakers recorded several frame sentences in which certain test words appeared in initial, medial, and final position, and two sentences selected for the study of intonation. These materials will be described in Chapter 3.

2.1.4 Recording and Analysis Techniques

The 877 utterances by P.I. were recorded early in 1961 at the Communication Sciences Laboratory of the University of Michigan in Ann Arbor. The recordings were made in an anechoic chamber, using high quality equipment. The twelve additional speakers were recorded early in 1962 at the recording studio of Radio Novi Sad.

All tapes were analyzed acoustically at the Communication Sciences Laboratory of the University of Michigan. Broad-band and narrow-band spectrograms were produced using the two Model D spectrographs then

Table 2.1
Number of times each accent type occurred with each syllable nucleus in the test words produced by P. I. (After Ivić and Lehiste 1963:33.)

	/˵/		/ˋ/		/ˆ/		/ˊ/		Total	
Vowel	Words	Tokens	Words	Tokens	Words	Tokens	Words	Tokens	Words	Tokens
i	9	17	11	19	6	13	14	26	40	75
e	29	54	22	45	7	14	7	15	65	128
a	33	60	38	71	41	74	37	67	149	272
o	47	92	44	82	6	13	6	13	103	200
u	15	30	17	32	15	30	14	29	61	121
r	9	18	10	20	8	16	13	27	40	81
Total	142	271	142	269	83	160	91	177	458	877

available at the laboratory.[1] Formant frequencies were measured from broad-band spectrograms; fundamental frequency patterns were studied by means of measurements made from narrow-band spectrograms. The fundamental frequency of a periodic sound was derived by measuring the center frequency of selected higher harmonics on a narrow-band spectrogram and dividing by the order number of the harmonic. Usually the tenth harmonic was measured. In low-pitched voices, the twentieth harmonic was also measured. Repeated tests and checks indicated that the accuracy of measurement was within a 25 Hz range for formant frequencies and within a 20 Hz range for the center frequency of the twentieth harmonic, which would represent an accuracy of ± 1 Hz for the fundamental frequency (cf. Lehiste and Ivić 1963 : 5–9). These values are close to the just noticeable differences for the perception of spoken language (cf. Lehiste 1970).

Measurements of segment durations were also made from broad-band spectrograms. The determination of segment boundaries was performed according to techniques developed during an earlier study (Peterson and Lehiste 1960 : 693–703).

All tapes were further processed through a special circuit designed for the continuous portrayal of acoustic intensity (Peterson and McKinney 1961 : 65–84). The signals were displayed on a multichannel Model 1108 Visicorder Oscillograph of the Minneapolis Honeywell Company. An oscillogram of the waveform was included on the representation of each utterance; this made it possible to perform fairly accurate segmentation of the test words and to determine the acoustic intensity of the signal at various points within the syllable nuclei.

Several problems are connected with the interpretation of intensity data. It has been known for some time that differences in the phonetic quality of vowels affect their amplitudes (Lehiste and Peterson 1959 : 426–435). When articulatory effort is kept constant, high vowels may be expected to have a smaller amount of acoustic intensity than low vowels. Liprounding has a further reducing effect on output intensity. Thus, the phonetic quality of the vowels must be taken into consideration when their relative intensities are being compared in attempting to establish differences in the degree of stress.

Since changes in the positions of the formants are often reflected in the intensity patterns, some fluctuations in the continuous graph displaying the intensity of a syllable nucleus as a function of time are due to the formant transitions between the target of a syllable nucleus and the preceding and following consonants. Such fluctuations are obviously segmentally conditioned and thus cannot be significant on a suprasegmental level.

A further problem is introduced by the interaction between the fundamental frequency and the frequency of the formants. If the fundamental frequency changes over a wide range, while the formant positions remain constant, it is likely that for a certain part of the duration of the syllable nucleus the frequency of one of the harmonics coincides with the frequency of one of the lower formants, which ordinarily contain the greatest amount of acoustic intensity. At this "optimal vocal frequency" the overall level of the signal may be higher by several decibels than during other time segments of the same syllable nucleus (House 1959:55–60). Variations in intensity due to this factor obviously cannot have any linguistic significance.

The degree of precision to be sought in the measurement of intensity depends further on the discriminatory capacity of the ear. It has been established that the minimal noticeable difference (the difference limen) for overall amplitude is approximately ± 1 dB or approximately 12% of the overall amplitude (Flanagan 1957:533–534). In measurements made for the present study, a precision of ± 1 dB was attempted; however, since the variations that may be caused by the external factors mentioned above may be considerably greater, the results are judged to be significant only when the observed differences are consistently greater than approximately 3 dB.

2.2 Fundamental Frequency Patterns

The basic accentual patterns occurring in the speech of the main informant are described below with reference to table 2.2 and figure 2.1. Table 2.2 contains average fundamental frequency (F_0) values derived from 633 individual occurrences of test words with twelve accentual patterns. Figure 2.1 presents curves drawn to represent F_0 movements during the syllable nuclei of these test words. The measurements were made at the beginning of each syllable nucleus, at the peak of the F_0 movement, and at the end of each syllable nucleus. In most cases the syllable nucleus consists of a vowel; however, since syllabic /r/ can likewise carry an accent, the term "syllable nucleus" is more precise. For stylistic reasons, we sometimes talk about syllables without specifying the syllable nucleus; in cases where a distinction is relevant between syllables, syllable nuclei, and vowels, we use unambiguous terminology. The frequency scale used in figure 2.1 is logarithmic. The logarithmic scale was adopted for the presentation in order to make it easier to compare the patterns of speaker P.I. with the patterns produced by the twelve additional speakers, whose voices covered a very wide range

Table 2.2
Fundamental frequency, intensity and duration patterns in test words produced by P. I. Fundamental frequencies in hertz, intensities in decibels, durations in milliseconds. (After Lehiste and Ivić 1963 : 19.)

Accentual pattern	No. of occurrences	Syllable	Fundamental frequency			Intensity			Dur. of SN	F_0 peak at	Intensity peak at
			Beg.	Peak	End	Beg.	Peak	End			
˵ ˘	102	˵	227	245	226	42.9	42.2	41.5	143	68	46
		˘	185	185	149	40.7	41.5	39.9	95	10	34
˵ ¯	28	˵	230	253	232	41.6	41.8	40.8	141	77	52
		¯	207	207	151	41.6	38.5	37.3	150	10	11
˵ ˘ ˘	41	˵	225	246	225	42.7	42.3	41.1	139	62	45
		˘	196	196	161	41.4	42.0	39.7	87	10	28
		˘	157	157	146	37.8	37.8	37.1	88	13	10
˵ ¯ ˘	24	˵	217	241	226	42.3	43.5	42.4	136	80	66
		¯	196	196	148	42.4	41.0	38.8	139	11	10
		˘	149	150	140	36.9	38.0	37.0	80	11	35
ˋ ˘	71	ˋ	209	233	227	40.9	41.2	40.8	157	122	57
		˘	235	237	198	41.1	40.6	39.6	101	15	12
ˋ ¯	32	ˋ	220	244	240	41.4	41.5	42.2	147	129	76
		¯	243	244	165	43.0	40.7	39.0	174	14	10
ˋ ˘ ˘	49	ˋ	207	233	227	40.6	40.1	40.0	140	101	52
		˘	237	241	214	42.2	41.1	40.1	98	20	26
		˘	191	191	156	39.5	40.3	39.7	89	11	39

` ¯ ˘	25	`	209	232	229	40.2	40.1	39.6	140	120	57
		¯	240	240	177	41.6	40.6	39.7	162	13	44
		˘	165	165	149	37.2	38.5	37.3	85	11	33
⌢ ˘	94	⌢	231	249	176	42.0	41.2	40.5	223	56	77
		˘	175	176	151	39.9	40.1	38.2	101	13	32
⌢ ˘ `	41	⌢	236	252	193	40.5	40.5	39.0	200	51	74
		˘	173	176	161	38.6	39.4	37.8	83	17	31
		˘	164	164	150	37.1	38.2	37.3	90	10	34
´ ˘	88	´	211	238	234	41.3	40.5	40.4	216	194	80
		˘	231	233	196	41.8	40.4	39.9	106	14	32
´ ˘ ˘	38	´	217	241	239	40.2	39.5	38.8	188	174	69
		˘	238	240	221	38.5	38.5	37.3	85	14	26
		˘	198	198	161	39.9	39.2	38.0	87	11	27

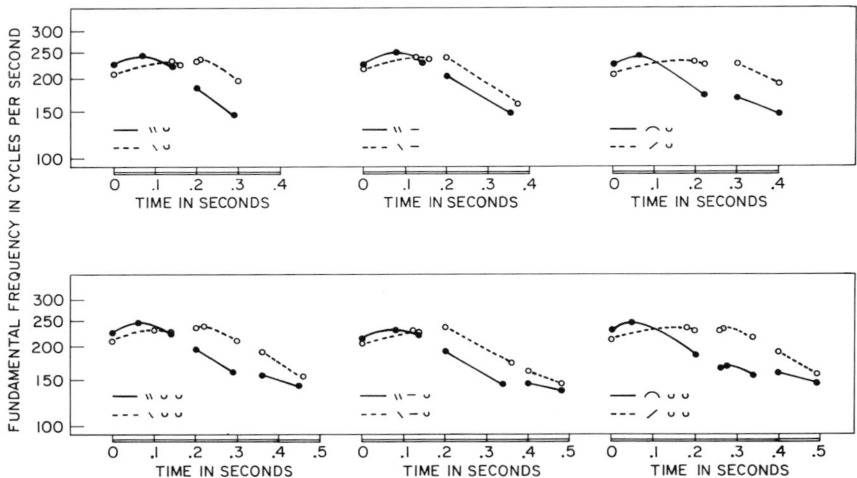

Figure 2.1
Basic accentual patterns in words produced by P. I. (After Lehiste and Ivić 1963: 18.)

of fundamental frequencies. The time scale is linear. In each case the patterns associated with falling accents are drawn with solid lines, and the corresponding minimally contrastive patterns associated with rising accents are drawn with dotted lines.

It becomes evident from a study of figure 2.1 and table 2.2 that the fundamental frequency of the accented syllable in words with the accent commonly called the short falling accent is not consistently falling. Rather, the syllable has a relatively high fundamental frequency; on the average, the peak is reached at approximately the middle of the duration of the syllable nucleus. The accented syllable in words with the accent commonly called the short rising accent is indeed predominantly rising; however, the absolute values associated with this accent in the speech of P.I. were lower than the values associated with the so-called short falling accent in comparable positions. We will continue to use the labels "short falling" and "short rising," but we wish to emphasize that these conventional labels do not necessarily reflect phonetic reality.

The values given in table 2.2 for the positions of the peak of the F_0 contour are averages. They show a distinction between words with short falling accents and words with short rising accents in terms of position of the peak. This form of presentation obscures the fact that there is actually

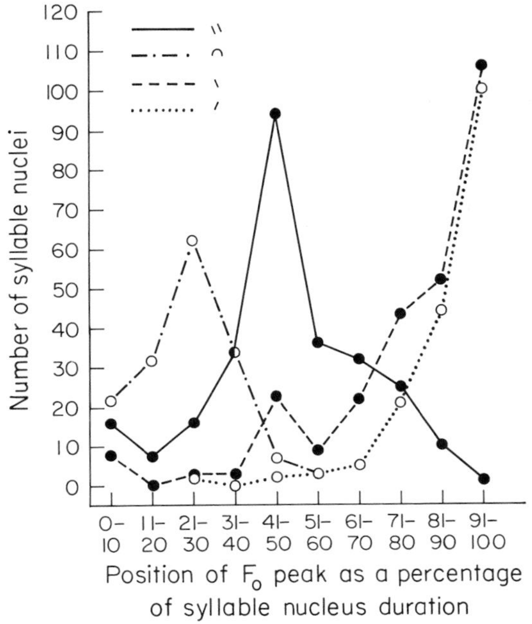

Figure 2.2
Position of F_0 peak shown as percentage of the duration of the stressed syllable nucleus in test words produced by P. I.

extensive overlap between the two distributions. A clearer picture emerges from figure 2.2 and table 2.3, which show the distribution of the positions of the F_0 peak within the syllable nucleus for all four accents. In the table the position of the F_0 peak is expressed as a percentage of the duration of the syllable nucleus. In the figure the number of times the peak was found to occur in each position is shown on the vertical axis. Peaks in words with short accents are indicated by filled circles connected by a solid line for ˵ and by a dashed line for ˋ; peaks in words with long accents are shown by circles connected by a dashed-dotted line for ˆ and by a dotted line for ˊ. Rising and falling accents are identified in the figure. Although the distributions of rising and falling accents are noticeably different, it is quite clear that particularly for the short accents, in a large number of instances the position of the peak of the F_0 contour was the same for words with both accents. The late peak in the case of rising accents is to be expected, since the following syllable has a high F_0 level and the rise during the first vowel leads directly into the high second syllable. What is more important is the

Table 2.3
Position of F_0 peak in test words produced by P. I., expressed as a percentage of the total duration of the accented syllable nucleus.

	Number of syllable nuclei			
Range	Short falling	Short rising	Long falling	Long rising
1–10%	16	8	22	
11–20%	7		32	
21–30%	16	3	62	2
31–40%	34	3	34	
41–50%	94	23	7	2
51–60%	36	9	3	3
62–70%	32	22		5
71–80%	25	43		21
81–90%	10	52		44
91–100%	1	106		100
Total	271	269	160	177

shape of the curve representing the position of the F_0 peak within syllables carrying the short falling accent. This curve is somewhat asymmetrical. The most common position for the F_0 peak is in the 41%–50% range of the duration of the syllable nucleus; 104 syllable nuclei had their peak later than in the 41%–50% range, and only 73 had their peak earlier than the middle position. It is the 198 words with a peak in the middle and in the second half of the syllable nucleus that suggest to us that the F_0 contour on the accented syllable is unlikely to constitute the only distinction between short accents.

The syllables under the two long accents may indeed be characterized as falling and rising, respectively. The long falling accent contains a high peak within the first half of the duration of the syllable nucleus. The high peak is followed by a fall to a rather low fundamental frequency. There are also numerous instances in which there is no initial rise; this is frequently the case when the initial consonant is voiceless (especially when it is a voiceless fricative). In these instances the F_0 contour has its highest value at the very beginning. Although the syllable bearing the long rising accent has a rising contour (reaching its highest value close to the end of the syllable nucleus), the F_0 rise in the syllable carrying the long rising accent is much less extensive than the fall in the syllable with the long falling accent. The F_0 contours of the two long accents are also qualitatively different. During the production of a syllable with the long falling accent, the fundamental frequency usually changes its direction from rising to falling, and the slopes are relatively steep. During the production of a syllable with a long rising accent, the F_0 contour constitutes an almost straight line, and its slope may be almost negligible.

The most prominent difference between words with rising and falling accents on the first syllable appears in the F_0 patterns of the second syllable. In all instances the fundamental frequency of the syllable following a falling accent was considerably lower than the fundamental frequency of the syllable following a rising accent. The peak F_0 value of the postaccentual syllable following a rising accent was comparable to or higher than the peak F_0 value of the syllable carrying the rising accent. In syllables following a falling accent the fundamental frequency was much lower than in the accented syllable. The highest F_0 value, which was usually lower than the lowest F_0 value of the accented syllable, occurred immediately at the beginning of the syllable, and the syllable contained no separate F_0 peak. In words with three syllables the curve representing the F_0 movement in the third syllable of a word with a rising accent on the first syllable resembles that of the syllable following a falling accent.

Table 2.4 offers data exemplifying the difference between the two kinds of accents with regard to the relationship between the fundamental frequencies of the accented and postaccentual syllables. In constructing this table, we calculated the ratio between the F_0 peaks of the accented and postaccentual syllables in test words produced by P.I. The ratio is equal to 1 when both peaks have the same value. It is smaller than 1 when the F_0 peak of the accented syllable is lower than that of the postaccentual syllable, and larger than 1 when the F_0 peak of the accented syllable is higher than that of the postaccentual syllable. A ratio of 1.25 corresponds to a major third, a ratio of 1.5 to a fifth, and a ratio of 2.0 to an octave. Since spoken language operates only rarely with pure musical intervals, the ratios constitute a continuum.

As the table indicates, the rising accents show a concentration of tokens whose F_0 peak ratios fell between .901 and 1.00: the F_0 peak of the accented syllable was either slightly lower than or equal to the F_0 peak of the postaccentual syllable. No large intervals are involved; the distribution of the ratios is very compact. The falling accents, on the other hand, are characterized by a rather steep fall (ratios higher than 1.10) from the F_0 peak of the accented syllable to the F_0 peak of the postaccentual syllable. The largest interval for the short falling accents was approximately a major sixth; for the long falling accents the largest interval was close to a seventh.

Table 2.4
Distribution of ratios of F_0 peak on accented syllable/F_0 peak on postaccentual syllable in test words produced P.I.

Ratio	Short falling	Short rising	Long falling	Long rising
.701–.750				
.751–.800				
.801–.850		3		
.851–.900		15		
.901–950		38		6
.951–1.000	2	150		59
1.001–1.050	6	56	1	89
1.051–1.100	14	7	6	22
1.101–1.150	15		8	1
1.151–1.200	37		1	
1.201–1.250	33			
1.251–1.300	27			
1.301–1.350	43		4	
1.351–1.400	32		11	
1.401–1.450	20		12	
1.451–1.500	10		23	
1.501–1.550	10		30	
1.551–1.600	5		20	
1.601–1.650	2		15	
1.651–1.700			7	
1.701–1.750			8	
1.751–1.800			3	
1.801–1.850			1	
1.851–1.900				
1.901–1.950				
1.951–2.000				
Total*	256	269	150	177

*These numbers are smaller than the totals given in table 2.1, since monosyllabic words are not included in this table.

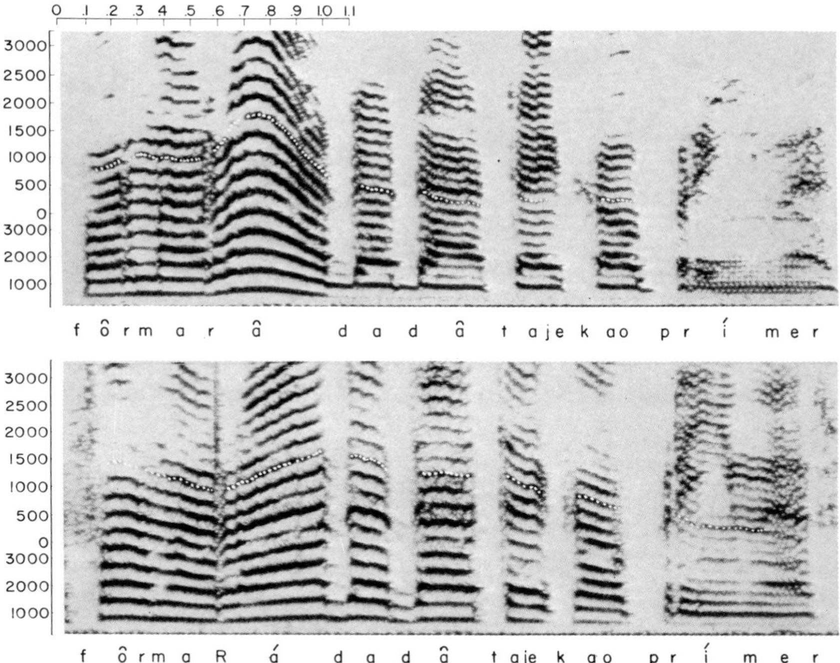

Figure 2.3
Narrow-band spectrograms of the test words *râda* and *Ráda*, produced by P. I. in the frame *Forma . . . data je kao primer*. (After Ivić and Lehiste 1963: fig. 3b.)

The ratios associated with long falling accents are somewhat greater than those associated with short falling accents; this is probably because the falling movement takes some time to be completed—in the case of a long syllable nucleus the movement is fully realized on the accented syllable itself, whereas in the case of short falling syllable nuclei the falling movement continues into the second syllable. The F_0 peak occurs at the beginning of the second syllable, and the intervals are correspondingly smaller.

Examples of test words with long falling and long rising accents produced by P.I. are given in figure 2.3, which contains narrow-band spectrograms of the utterances *Forma râda data je kao primer* 'The form *râda* (gen.sg.masc. 'work') is given as an example' and *Forma Ráda data je kao primer* 'The form *Ráda* (fem. proper name) is given as an example'. The tenth harmonic has been dotted with white paint and provides a visual representation of the F_0 movement expanded by a factor of ten. Figure 2.4

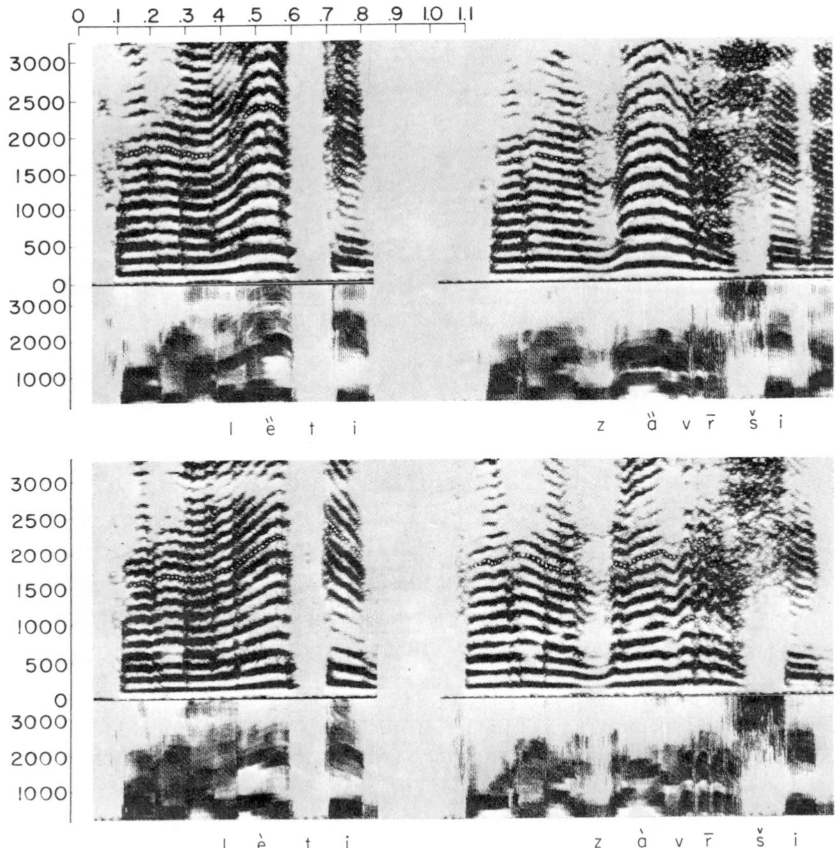

Figure 2.4
Broad-band and narrow-band spectrograms of the test words *lȅti*, *lèti*, *zȁvr̄ši*, and *zàvr̄ši*, produced by P. I. in the frame *Forma . . . data je kao primer*

offers broad-band and narrow-band spectrograms of productions of the test words *lèti* 'in summer', 3.sg.pres. *lèti* 'flies', 3.sg.aor. *zȁvr̄ši* 'finished', and 3.sg.pres. (perf. asp.) *zàvr̄ši* 'finishes' spoken by P.I. in the same frame. The tenth harmonic (and in the *zavr̄ši* pair, the fifth) has again been dotted with white paint.

The F_0 movement associated with long postaccentual syllables after rising accents is in many respects similar to the falling movement associated with the syllable under a long falling accent. The postaccentual long syllable is, however, shorter than the stressed falling syllable and does not contain the initial rise characteristic of the long falling accent when it follows a voiced initial consonant. The slope of the curve representing the F_0 movement in a long syllable after a short rising accent differs from that of a long syllable after a short falling accent: after the rising accent the curve is convex, whereas after a falling accent it is concave. Words containing long postaccentual syllables are illustrated in figure 2.5, which presents broad-band and narrow-band spectrograms of the test words *kȕvār* 'cook', *čùvār* 'guard', 3.sg.aor. *ȍdlūči* 'decided', and 3.sg.pres. *òdlūči* 'decides'. Again, the tenth harmonic has been dotted with white paint to make the F_0 movement easier to follow. Since the vowel /u/ contains very little energy in the region of the tenth harmonic, the fifth harmonic has been traced in addition to the tenth in the words *kȕvār* and *čùvār*.

Since the voices of the twelve additional speakers covered a very wide range, the informants were divided into three groups according to their average peak fundamental frequencies, and measured values were averaged within the three groups. Table 2.5 contains data for six low-pitched speakers, table 2.6 data for three medium-pitched speakers, and table 2.7 data for three high-pitched speakers. The intensity data also contained in the tables will be discussed later.

Figure 2.6 presents graphically the F_0 movements during words of six accentual types. The top set of curves shows the patterns for the group of high-pitched speakers; the middle set represents the average patterns found in the same test words produced by the group of low-pitched speakers. A logarithmic scale was used for the presentation of frequency. The time scale is linear. Solid lines represent falling accents, dotted lines rising accents. This figure is directly comparable to figure 2.1, which presents information for the same test words produced by the main informant. (The lower set of curves in figure 2.6 represents the intensity patterns observed in the speech of the six low-pitched informants. This material will be discussed in a later section.)

Comparison of figures 2.1 and 2.6 clearly shows that the F_0 patterns used

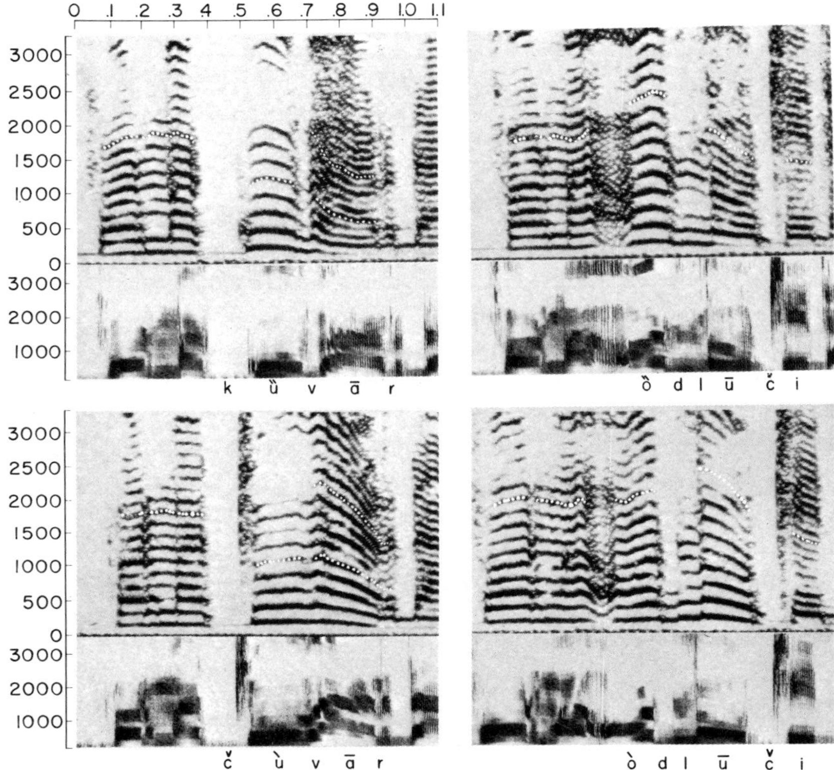

Figure 2.5
Broad-band and narrow-band spectrograms of the test words *kȕvār*, *čùvār*, *ȍdlūči*, and *òdlūči*, produced by P. I. in the frame *Forma . . . data je kao primer*. (After Lehiste and Ivić 1963 : 23.)

by all speakers are essentially identical. In most instances the F_0 movements observed in the speech of the main informant were corroborated by the results obtained from the twelve additional informants. As before, the syllable carrying the falling accent was found to have a somewhat higher fundamental frequency than the syllable carrying the rising accent. The chief difference between words with falling accents and minimally contrastive words with rising accents on the first syllable again appeared in the fundamental frequency of the second syllable: in words with rising accents the fundamental frequency of the second syllable was either the same as or higher than that of the accented syllable, whereas in words with falling

Table 2.5
Fundamental frequency, intensity, and duration patterns in test words produced by six low-pitched speakers. Fundamental frequencies in hertz, intensities in decibels, durations in milliseconds. (After Lehiste and Ivić 1963 : 40.)

Accentual pattern	No. of occurrences	Syllable	Fundamental frequency			Intensity			Dur. of SN	F_0 peak at	Intensity peak at
			Beg.	Peak	End	Beg.	Peak	End			
˵ ˘	58	˵	120	128	115	42.1	43.8	40.0	106	43	43
		˘	101	101	88	36.6	36.8	33.4	85	20	28
			(8 laryng., 1 voiceless)								
˵ ˘ ˘	20	˵	119	131	121	42.6	43.5	40.6	103	58	41
		˘	108	109	99	39.1	38.6	37.5	70	19	31
		˘	98	98	93	37.1	37.1	34.1	77	28	21
			(2 laryng.)								
ˋ ˘	33	ˋ	117	126	121	42.3	43.4	41.5	108	62	42
		˘	125	130	113	40.9	41.1	37.1	83	31	27
ˋ ˘ ˘	34	ˋ	109	116	113	41.4	42.7	40.5	107	62	42
		˘	124	127	112	41.4	42.7	40.6	80	25	29
		˘	103	103	90	38.2	36.5	33.3	86	23	14
			(4 laryng.)								
ˆ ˘	40	ˆ	124	131	98	38.3	42.3	36.6	179	45	42
		˘	95	97	90	35.9	36.0	34.0	88	23	33
			(11 laryng.)								
ˊ ˘	42	ˊ	106	120	117	40.2	41.7	40.8	195	144	94
		˘	120	122	104	39.0	39.2	36.5	82	17	26

Table 2.6
Fundamental frequency, intensity, and duration patterns in test words produced by three medium-pitched speakers. Fundamental frequencies in hertz, intensities in decibels, durations in milliseconds. (After Lehiste and Ivić 1963:41.)

Accentual pattern	No. of occurrences	Syllable	Fundamental frequency			Intensity			Dur. of SN	F_0 peak at	Intensity peak at
			Beg.	Peak	End	Beg.	Peak	End			
˵ ˘	23	˵	219	229	210	44.2	44.0	40.4	123	48	38
		˘	170	172	155	36.0	35.4	30.9	77	28	28
			(3 laryng.)								
˵ ˘ ˘	7	˵	217	241	220	44.3	43.8	40.8	114	63	23
		˘	181	181	169	36.8	36.5	36.3	79	29	38
		˘	166	173	170	35.5	34.7	32.8	75	39	20
ˋ ˘	15	ˋ	196	198	182	42.2	43.0	39.8	123	40	45
		˘	211	230	219	40.9	41.0	36.8	67	57	40
ˋ ˘ ˘	15	ˋ	186	188	182	43.6	43.1	41.4	129	47	41
		˘	198	214	205	42.2	42.8	39.7	87	57	37
		˘	200	204	192	39.1	37.8	34.5	93	30	21
ˆ ˘	16	ˆ	229	240	156	43.5	43.7	35.1	205	37	48
		˘	162	164	149	34.4	35.4	31.4	88	34	28
			(2 laryng.)								
ˊ ˘	21	ˊ	188	195	192	43.5	43.4	41.1	215	126	84
		˘	214	224	206	41.1	39.7	35.1	92	38	19

Table 2.7
Fundamental frequency, intensity, and duration patterns in test words produced by three high-pitched speakers. Fundamental frequencies in hertz, intensities in decibels, durations in milliseconds. (After Lehiste and Ivić 1963:42.)

Accentual pattern	No. of occurrences	Syllable	Fundamental frequency Beg.	Fundamental frequency Peak	Fundamental frequency End	Intensity Beg.	Intensity Peak	Intensity End	Dur. of SN	F_0 peak at	Intensity peak at
˵ ˘	37	˵	289	320	298	40.4	41.1	37.0	129	86	52
		˘	210	211	189	34.2	34.1	32.4	84	14	28
			(1 voiceless)								
˵ ˘ ˘	13	˵	272	314	303	40.4	42.4	37.5	128	107	59
		˘	210	210	188	35.2	35.8	33.7	80	12	34
		˘	186	189	187	33.1	33.8	32.2	72	43	39
			(1 laryng.)								
` ˘	25	`	258	273	257	40.6	41.1	38.4	136	78	59
		˘	297	314	294	40.3	39.1	37.6	92	37	26
` ˘ ˘	21	`	256	277	268	41.5	42.1	39.5	135	78	53
		˘	309	326	277	37.6	38.9	38.1	92	39	47
		˘	231	231	193	36.8	35.3	33.1	74	10	15
ˆ ˘	20	ˆ	296	325	213	39.5	40.2	35.8	205	46	74
		˘	196	197	188	33.8	34.2	33.9	81	22	41
´ ˘	22	´	259	284	277	40.9	41.2	39.4	202	147	69
		˘	305	316	291	39.1	39.7	39.0	88	32	53

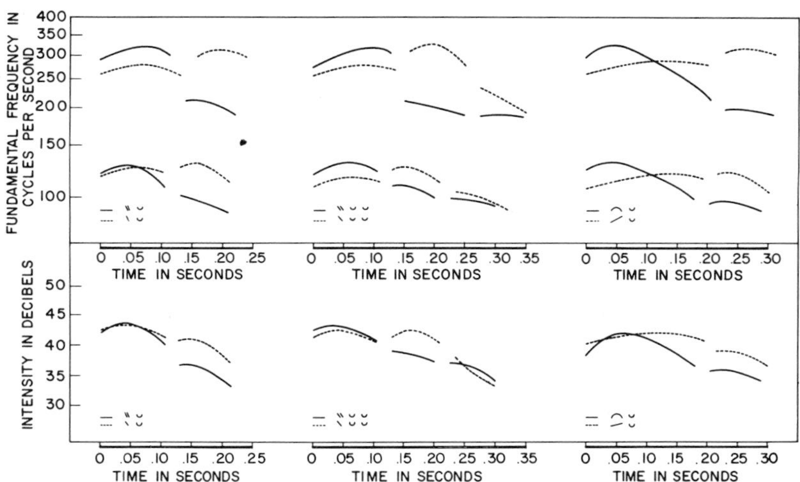

Figure 2.6
F_0 and intensity patterns in six test words produced by nine speakers. (After Lehiste and Ivić 1963: 55.)

accents the fundamental frequency of the second syllable was considerably lower. In the speech of most of these informants the syllable following the rising accent was relatively even higher than in the pronunciation of the main informant. In numerous instances the fundamental frequency in syllables following falling accents became so low that the speakers shifted into a mode of phonation called laryngealization, characterized by slow and irregular vibration of the vocal folds.

The movement of the fundamental frequency within the accented syllable was generally rising-falling within vowels with a long falling accent, with a peak in the first half of the syllable nucleus. In words with a long rising accent the F_0 curve was generally rising, with a peak close to the end of the syllable nucleus. In the case of short accents the difference in F_0 movement within the accented syllable was nonsystematic. The averages presented in tables 2.5, 2.6, and 2.7 show that for Group 1 (table 2.5, six low-pitched speakers) the peak occurred earlier for ̏ than for ̀ (an average of 50 vs. 62 msec from the beginning of the syllable nucleus); for Group 2 (table 2.6, three medium-pitched speakers) the peak occurred later for ̏ than for ̀ (an average of 56 vs. 44 msec from the beginning of the syllable nucleus); and for Group 3 (table 2.7, three high-pitched speakers) the peak occurred considerably later for ̏ than for ̀ (an average of 97 vs. 78 msec from the beginning of the syllable nucleus).

With respect to direction of the F_0 movement, nine out of twelve subjects had the same pattern in vowels bearing either short accent. For five of these subjects the direction was generally falling (the end of the syllable nucleus had a lower fundamental frequency than the beginning) for both accents; for three subjects the direction was generally rising; and for one subject the direction was falling in disyllabic words and rising in trisyllabic words. For the rest of the subjects (three out of twelve) the direction varied for different word types. The most curious case is that of speaker E13. In her pronunciation the vowel under ̏ had a rising F_0 contour, and the vowel under ̀ a falling contour (Ivić and Lehiste 1965:86). In no case did the direction of F_0 movement show a consistent association with accent type (Ivić and Lehiste 1965:91).

Productions of test words by a high-pitched speaker are illustrated in figure 2.7, which presents broad-band and narrow-band spectrograms of the test words past part.sg.neut. *sȅlo* 'sat down', nom.sg.neut. *sèlo* 'village', gen.sg.masc. *kȏsa* 'blackbird', and fem. *Kósa* (proper name) produced by speaker E11. Because of the relatively high fundamental frequency, the seventh harmonic has been traced in white on these spectrograms instead of the tenth. The words were produced in the basic frame; however, part of the utterance following the test word has been removed in each case.

The study of F_0 movements thus has shown that the main difference between words with falling and rising accents is in the fundamental frequency of the postaccentual syllable, which in the case of words with rising accents is as high as or possibly even higher than that of the accented syllable. (Postaccentual vowels have the same predominantly falling contour after both kinds of accents, but the F_0 level of the postaccentual syllable is considerably higher after rising accents than after falling accents.) In light of these findings, it is interesting to consider further the problem of what constitutes accentedness in Serbocroatian. The question appears relatively simple in the case of words with falling accents, in which the postaccentual syllables were always considerably lower than the stressed syllables. The higher fundamental frequency of syllables with falling accents lends them so much relative prominence that little doubt is likely to arise regarding their accentual status. However, in words with rising accents the postaccentual syllable cannot be differentiated from the accented syllable on the basis of fundamental frequency alone. Other factors that may contribute to the identification of accented syllables

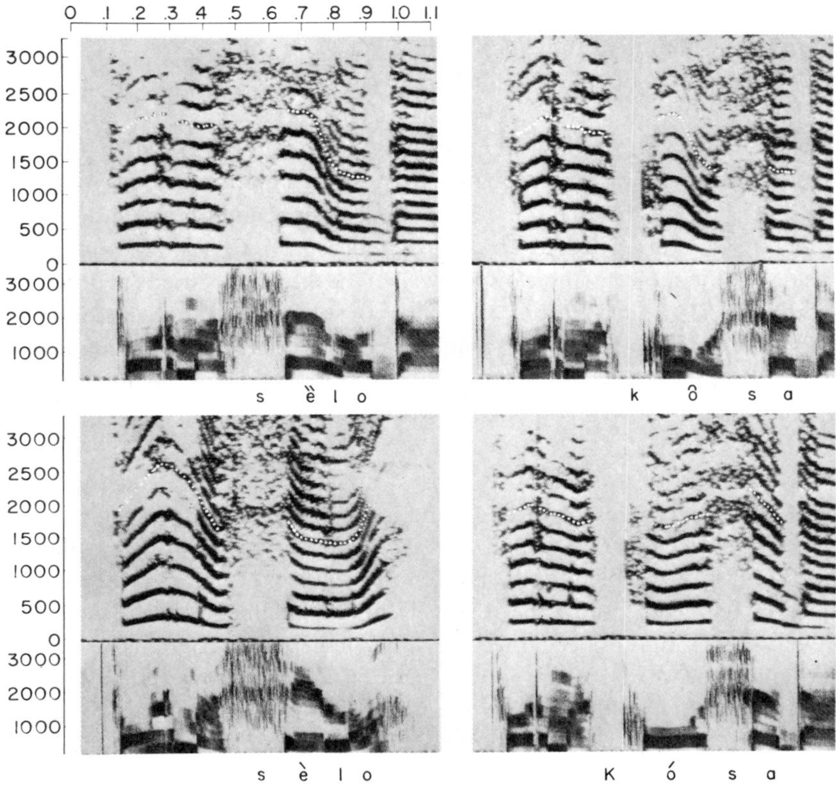

Figure 2.7
Broad-band and narrow-band spectrograms of the test words *sȅlo*, *sèlo*, *kôsa*, and *Kósa*, produced by speaker E11 in the frame *Forma . . . data je kao primer*. (After Lehiste and Ivić 1963 : 59.)

include intensity, duration, and phonetic quality. We will consider these factors in turn.

2.3 Intensity Patterns

Table 2.2 contains information about the intensity patterns observed in the speech of the main informant. Measurements were made at the beginning and end of syllable nuclei as well as at the intensity peak observed on each syllable nucleus. The moment at which the intensity peak occurred is likewise indicated, measured in milliseconds from the beginning of the syllable nucleus. Since the influence of preceding and following consonants is particularly great during transitions, only the peak values deserve consideration.

A study of the intensity information contained in the table indicates that in the speech of P.I. intensity plays no systematic role in distinguishing between the various accents. There was no clear-cut difference in intensity either between accented and postaccentual syllables or between the two types of accent.

The intensity patterns observed in the speech of the twelve additional informants were ambiguous in many respects. In utterances by some of the speakers, regular intensity differences appeared to be associated with the different F_0 patterns. In the case of other speakers, as in the case of the main informant, no clear correlation between intensity and fundamental frequency could be established. Tables 2.5, 2.6, and 2.7 offer intensity information averaged for the groups that had been established on the basis of fundamental frequency. These groups, however, were not homogeneous with regard to the character of the intensity patterns. Table 2.8 was therefore constructed from tables originally prepared for each informant. In this table only the average difference in intensity between the peak of the stressed syllable and the immediately following syllable is presented in test words produced by each of the twelve speakers. A negative value (for example the value −9.9 for speaker D1 under word type ̏ ˘) indicates that the intensity of the second syllable was 9.9 dB lower than the intensity of the first syllable. A positive value (such as +0.3 in the same row under word type ` ˘) shows that the second syllable was 0.3 dB higher in intensity than the first syllable. The differences averaged for all rising patterns and for all falling patterns are presented in the second and third columns from the end. The last column contains a general evaluation of the extent and regularity of intensity differences between accents. Differences of 5 dB or more are indicated by +, differences between 3 and 5 dB by ?, and differences of less than 3 dB by −.

As table 2.8 shows, differences between the intensity patterns of words with rising and falling accents are larger than 5 dB in the speech of seven informants, between 3 and 5 dB in the speech of two informants, and less than 3 dB in the speech of three informants. It is possible that this reflects regional variation between the speakers. No systematic conclusions can be drawn on the basis of our data, but we would not want to exclude the possibility that a special study of this question might yield significant results. The presence of this variability in our materials nevertheless sug-

Table 2.8
Average intensity differences (in decibels) between the accented and the postaccentual syllable in test words produced by twelve speakers. (After Ivić and Lehiste 1965:96.)

Speaker	˵ ˘	ˋ ˘	˵ ˘ ˘	ˋ ˘ ˘	ˆ ˘	ˊ ˘	All falling patterns	All rising patterns	Probable Significance
D1	−9.9	+0.3	−8.0	+1.2	−7.4	−2.3	−8.4	−0.3	+
D2	−9.0	−5.0	−10.7	−2.8	−10.8	−4.1	−10.2	−4.0	+
D3	−5.2	−2.7	−1.0	+2.2	−6.5	−1.8	−4.2	−0.8	?
D5	−8.0	−1.3	−2.6	−0.4	−5.0	−2.5	−5.2	−1.4	?
D6	−8.2			−1.2	−6.3	−2.1	−7.3	−1.1	+
D7	−4.7	−1.3	−4.5	−1.5	−7.7	−6.7	−5.6	−3.2	−
D8	−7.6	−2.5	−10.8	−5.2	−7.2	−2.2	−8.5	−3.3	+
E10	−8.7	−0.8	−4.0	+3.0	−7.8	−5.0	−6.8	−0.9	+
E11	−5.0	−1.0	−4.2	−3.1	−3.8	−1.7	−4.3	−1.9	−
E12	−9.2	−3.9	−7.3	−0.2	−7.6	+0.4	−8.0	−1.2	+
E13	−8.3	−2.4	−4.7	−1.4	−6.9	−0.8	−6.6	−1.5	+
E14	−5.2	−2.9	−5.7	−1.6	−3.4	−2.2	−4.8	−2.2	−
Average	−7.4	−2.0	−5.8	−0.9	−6.7	−2.6	−6.7	−1.8	?

gests that intensity has but little relevance in distinguishing between the rising and falling accents.

The general movement of intensity within a word is falling, even more so than is the case with the F_0 movement. Table 2.8 contains almost exclusively falling intensity relations between successive syllables; even the relations between a syllable under a rising accent and the following syllable are in most cases falling. Moreover, the intensity of preaccentual vowels in words such as 3.sg.pres. *zelèni* 'becomes green' or nom.sg.masc. *barjàktār* 'ensign' is usually higher than that of the accented (and postaccentual) vowels in the same words (Ivić and Lehiste 1967: table 14), whereas the fundamental frequency of preaccentual vowels in the same material always remains below the level of the accented and postaccentual vowels (Ivić and Lehiste 1967: 10–12). Finally, intrasyllabic intensity movements are predominantly falling in more than 90% of the cases, in contradistinction to the F_0 movements in the same material, which are frequently rising (Ivić and Lehiste 1967: tables 2–14).

We would like to emphasize again that for the purpose of establishing contrastive accent types we consider the difference in the overall intensities between the syllables (as reflected in the height of the intensity peak) to be potentially significant, and not the shape of the curve representing the intensity of a syllable nucleus as a function of time. Figure 2.8 may serve as illustration. This figure contains intensity curves and oscillograms of four test words produced by informant D1, in whose speech intensity differences between postaccentual syllables after rising and falling accents are regularly present. All test words were produced in the basic frame, the first part of which is included in the figure. In the word pair gen.sg.masc. *sȍli* 'salt' and 2.sg.imper. *sòli* 'salt', the intensity curve does seem to follow the F_0 curve, but this is not the case for the word pair gen.sg.masc. *rûža* 'lipstick' and nom.sg.fem. *rúža* 'rose'. The intensities of the second syllable have the same relationship as in *sȍli* and *sòli*. The shape of the curve on long /u/, however, reflects the F_0 movement only in the case of *rûža*. In *rúža* a rising F_0 movement is associated with a falling intensity during the syllable nucleus. Examples of this kind are abundant, and they prevent us from attributing contrastive value to the direction of intensity movement or to the position of the intensity peak.

2.4 Duration

Next we consider the contribution of duration to the identification of an accented syllable. Table 2.9 presents the duration of syllable nuclei in words

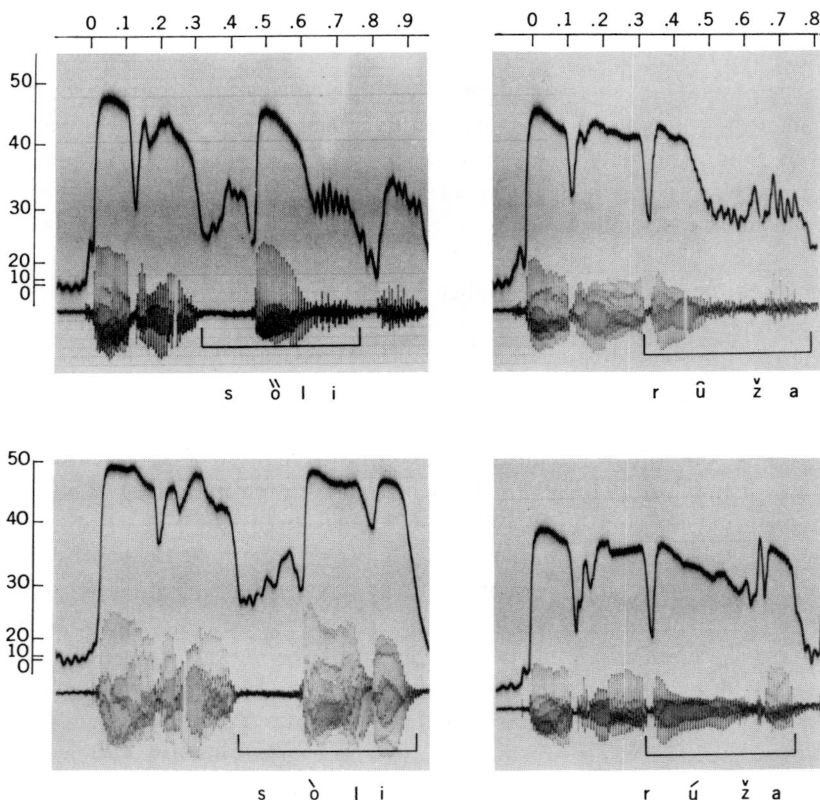

Figure 2.8
Intensity curves and oscillograms of the test words *sȍli*, *sòli*, *rûža*, and *rúža*, produced by speaker D1 in the frame *Forma . . . data je kao primer*. (After Ivić and Lehiste 1965: fig. 4.)

with ten accentual patterns produced by P.I. and in words with six accentual patterns produced by the twelve additional informants. We discuss first the duration of vowels in words produced by P.I.

A study of the durations given in table 2.9 shows a systematic dependence of the duration of the vowel of the first syllable on the total length of the word. For all accent types, this duration is greatest in disyllabic words with a short postaccentual syllable, somewhat shorter in words with a long postaccentual syllable, and shortest in words with two postaccentual syllables. (Longer words will be discussed in section 2.6.) Note also that for the short accents, the vowel bearing the short rising accent is somewhat

Table 2.9
Duration of syllable nuclei in words with ten accentual patterns produced by P. I. and six accentual patterns produced by twelve speakers. N = number of tokens. Average durations in milliseconds.

Accentual pattern	P. I.				12 Speakers			
	N	1.syll.	2.syll.	3.syll.	N	1.syll.	2.syll.	3.syll.
˵ ˘	102	143	95		118	116	83	
˵ ¯	28	141	150					
˵ ˘ ˘	41	139	87	88	40	111	74	75
ˋ ˘	71	157	101		73	119	82	
ˋ ¯	32	147	174					
ˋ ˘ ˘	49	140	98	89	70	119	85	85
ˆ ˘	94	223	101		76	192	86	
ˆ ˘ ˘	41	200	83	90				
ˊ ˘	88	216	106		85	202	86	
ˊ ˘ ˘	38	188	85	87				

longer than the vowel bearing the short falling accent in all positions; the opposite is true for long accents.

These observations are partly corroborated by the data derived from the speech of the twelve additional informants. This material is relatively limited; still, for the short falling accents it holds true that vowels in the initial syllables of disyllabic words are longer than vowels in the initial syllables of trisyllabic words. It is likewise true that vowels bearing the short rising accent are longer than comparable vowels bearing the short falling accent. However, here the duration of the vowel with a short rising accent is the same in disyllabic and trisyllabic words, and the relationships in the duration of long accents are the reverse of those found in the speech of P.I. Of course, this applies to the averages; there is a considerable amount of individual variation (Ivić and Lehiste 1965: tables 2–14).

A comparison of accented short syllables with their long counterparts in the speech of P.I. shows a ratio of 1.6 for ˵ ˘ vs. ˆ ˘ and 1.4 for ˋ ˘ vs. ˊ ˘. The comparable ratios for the twelve additional speakers are 1.7 and 1.7. Half of the speakers of this group were radio announcers who were striving to avoid regionalisms in their pronunciation; the tendency toward lengthening in the production of short accents, especially the short rising accent, is one such regionalism. We assume this to be the primary cause of the observed difference between the productions of P.I. and the larger group (Ivić and Lehiste 1965: 88–90).

A general feature is the difference in the duration of accented and unaccented vowels of the same phonemic length. In the speech of P.I. the ratio between vowel durations in words with ˵ ˘ was 1.5; in words with ˋ ˘ it was 1.6. In comparable words produced by the group of twelve informants the ratios were 1.4 for both accents. In the speech of P.I. the ratio between the long accented vowel in ˆ ˘ and the long unaccented (postaccentual) vowel in ˋ ¯ was 1.3. Comparable material was not available for the twelve additional speakers.

Thus, in every case the accented vowel is considerably longer than its unaccented counterpart. The difference is greatest for P.I. in words with short rising accents and short postaccentual vowels. There is also a tendency for postaccentual vowels to be longer after rising accents than after falling accents. This tendency is clearly present in the speech of P.I. The twelve additional speakers provided partial support for this observation: one comparison out of three displayed a substantially longer postaccentual vowel after a rising accent. In the second case there was no difference, and in the third case there was a minimal (1 msec) difference in the opposite direction.

It should be emphasized here that we are talking about tendencies and not about statistical significance. Clearly, differences on the order of a few milliseconds may be the result of measurement error, and are also below the threshold of perception. Moreover, the numbers given in table 2.9 represent averages; there is extensive overlap between the ranges (Lehiste and Ivić 1963: fig. 3).

We are likewise not claiming that an accented syllable can be immediately identified on the basis of its duration, out of the context provided by other syllables within the same word. On the other hand, we do consider it probable that differences in the ratios of successive syllables contribute to the perception of a particular accentual pattern. These matters will be discussed in more detail in a later section.

2.5 Vowel Quality in Relation to the Prosodic System

We turn now to the possible influence of suprasegmental features upon the allophonic nature of syllable nuclei. In order to study the relationships between the segmental and the suprasegmental systems, the formant positions of all syllable nuclei in the corpus were measured and tabulated. Table 2.10 presents the average values of the frequencies of the first three

Table 2.10
Formant positions of accented and postaccentual syllable nuclei occurring in test words produced by P. I. (After Lehiste and Ivić 1963:82.)

Accent type	/i/			/e/			/a/			/o/			/u/			/r/		
	F_1	F_2	F_3	F_1	F_2	F_3	F_1	F_2	F_3	F_1	F_2	F_3	F_1	F_2	F_3	F_1	F_2	F_3
̏	385	2010	2570	550	1745	2415	765	1440	2095	545	1045	1925	450	825	1885	490	1470	1815
̀	435	2075	2615	550	1775	2425	790	1450	2040	570	1025	1910	455	810	1950	485	1425	1855
Accented short	410	2045	2595	550	1760	2420	780	1445	2070	560	1035	1920	455	820	1920	490	1450	1835
̑	395	2140	2685	490	2005	2475	910	1545	2120	490	990	1915	450	785	1930	515	1445	1955
́	375	2165	2770	470	1960	2465	885	1500	2075	495	925	1875	455	765	1995	475	1405	1850
Accented long	385	2155	2730	480	1985	2470	900	1525	2100	495	960	1895	455	775	1965	495	1425	1905
Short after ̏, ̑	365	1950	2485	555	1690	2405	620	1415	2060	575	1190	1955	400	1130	2020			
Short after ̀, ́	445	1945	2500	500	1685	2340	660	1480	2115	560	1175	1960	425	1215	1985			
Long after ̏				490	1910	2525	735	1405	2010	475	1125	2100	380	860	1850	555	1315	1850
Long after ̀, ́	430	2175	2670	470	1955	2530	825	1525	2095	525	960	1950	440	990	1920	495	1370	1865
Short postaccentual	405	1950	2495	530	1690	2375	640	1450	2090	570	1185	1960	415	1175	2005			
Long postaccentual	430	2175	2670	480	1935	2530	780	1465	2055	500	1045	2025	410	925	1885	525	1345	1860

Table 2.11
Number of occurrences of various syllable nuclei in test words produced by P. I. (After Lehiste and Ivić 1963:83.)

Syllable nucleus	Under falling accents	Under rising accents	After short falling	After long falling	After short rising	After long rising	Total accented	Total postaccentual
i	17	19	57	44	57	68	36	226
ī	13	26			10	2	39	12
e	54	45	44	8	36	10	99	98
ē	14	15	16		6		29	22
a	60	71	33	62	45	63	131	203
ā	74	67	29		52	2	141	83
o	92	82	35	24	33	18	174	110
ō	13	13	2		7	2	26	11
u	30	32	22	12	8	12	62	54
ū	30	29	10		6		59	16
r	18	20					38	
r̄	16	27	5		7		43	12
Total short	271	269	191	150	179	171	540	691
Total long	160	177	62		88	6	337	156
Total	431	446	253	150	267	177	877	847

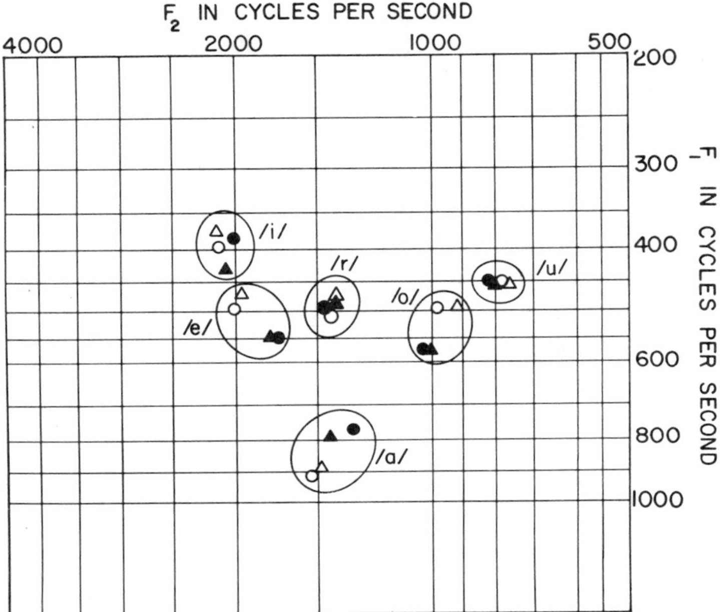

Figure 2.9
Acoustical vowel diagram of accented syllable nuclei occurring in test words produced by P. I. (After Lehiste and Ivić 1963:84.)

formants in syllable nuclei produced by the main informant. The formant frequencies are averaged according to syllable nucleus and accent type. The number of times each syllable nucleus occurred in a given position may be derived from table 2.11.

The information contained in table 2.10 appears in a more easily surveyable manner in the acoustical vowel diagrams of figures 2.9, 2.10, and 2.11. The symbols represent average positions of the first two formants, displayed on a two-dimensional acoustical vowel diagram whose vertical axis represents the position of the first formant and whose horizontal axis represents the position of the second formant. A logarithmic scale is employed in order to achieve better correlation with perception. On these and subsequent vowel diagrams, filled dots represent occurrences of syllable nuclei either bearing the short falling accent or immediately following a syllable with the short falling accent. Filled triangles are associated in the same way with the short rising accent, circles with the long falling accent,

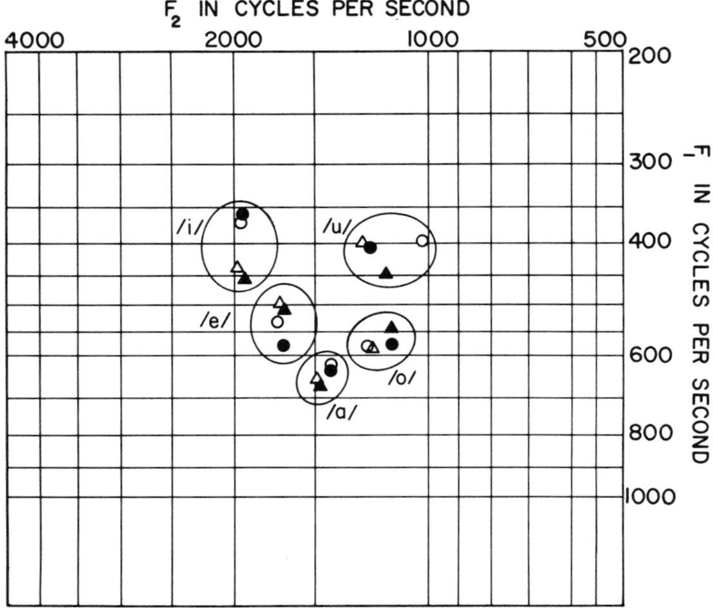

Figure 2.10
Acoustical vowel diagram of short postaccentual syllable nuclei occurring in test words produced by P. I. (After Lehiste and Ivić 1963: 85.)

and triangles with the long rising accent. The approximate area into which the individual realizations fall is circled for each phoneme.

Figure 2.9 contains an acoustical vowel diagram of the accented syllable nuclei occurring in the test words spoken by P.I. Figure 2.10 contains an acoustical vowel diagram of short postaccentual syllable nuclei, and figure 2.11 a diagram of long postaccentual syllable nuclei. Since the corpus did not contain any occurrences of long postaccentual vowels after long falling accents, figure 2.11 does not contain circles, which in this case would indicate occurrence of length after long falling accents. Not every syllable nucleus was represented in every position among the words on which figure 2.11 is based. In particular, there were very few instances of length after a long rising accent, and only two examples of long /o/ after a short falling accent. Table 2.11 may be consulted for details.

A study of the acoustical vowel diagrams leads to the following general observations. In accented syllables the formant structure of the syllable nuclei appeared to be independent of accent type, but in the case of /e/, /o/,

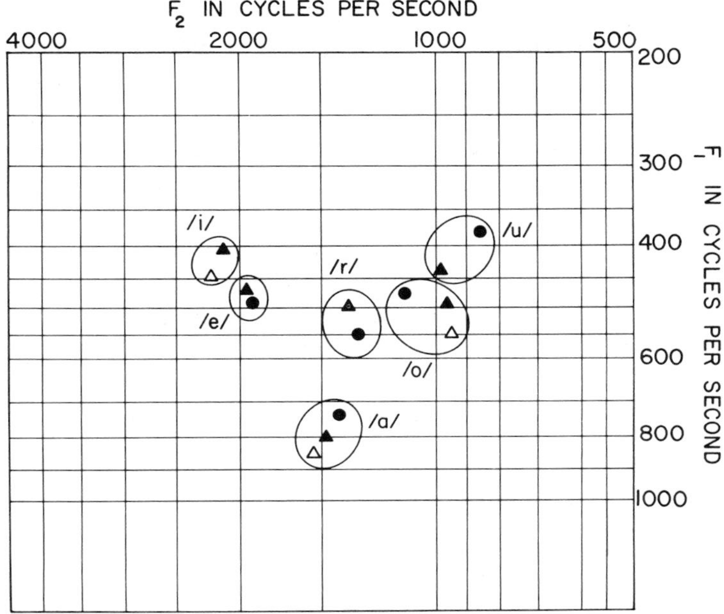

Figure 2.11
Acoustical vowel diagram of long postaccentual syllable nuclei occurring in test words produced by P. I. (After Lehiste and Ivić 1963:86.)

and /a/ it was dependent on length. Figure 2.9 reflects the well-known fact that in the eastern Serbocroatian pronunciation the short allophones of /e/ and /o/ are considerably more open than the long allophones (that is, the shorter allophones have greater first formant values). The long allophones of /e/, /o/, and /a/ were also less centralized; that is, they were farther removed from the center of the acoustical vowel diagram. In the case of /e/ and /o/ this took the form of a fronting for /e/ (higher values for the second formant) and farther backing for /o/ (lower values for the second formant) than was the case for the short allophones. In the case of /a/ the more extreme position was realized by higher values for both the first and the second formant for the long allophones than were associated with short allophones.

In postaccentual syllables the short vowels /a/, /o/, and /u/ were considerably centralized (figure 2.10). (The corpus contained no examples of postaccentual short /r/.) The whole vowel diagram appears to have been pulled together toward the center, and extreme values did not occur.

Postaccentual long vowels, on the other hand, had values very similar to those of the accented allophones of long vowels (figure 2.11). The formant structure of postaccentual vowels was therefore also conditioned by length, as was the formant structure of three of the accented syllable nuclei. This dependence applied to all vowels, however, not only to those that had separate length-conditioned allophones in accented position.

In many respects the relationships between the segmental and the suprasegmental systems observed in the utterances produced by the group of twelve informants resembled those observed in the speech of the main informant. There was some regional variation, but the most frequent pattern was the same: two phonetically different allophones for /e/ and /o/, conditioned by length; allophonic differentiation between long and short /a/; and strong centralization of postaccentual short /a/ and /u/.[2]

2.6 Prosodic Characteristics of Words

In order to make conclusions regarding the prosodic characteristics of the word as a whole, we examined data about fundamental frequency and duration patterns in a number of comparatively long word types. These data, presented in table 2.12, were not included in table 2.2. The number of examples for each of the word types is four or more; various other long word types, represented by fewer examples, are to be found in Ivić and Lehiste 1963 (tables 5, 10, 14, 19). Table 2.12 is arranged in such a way that syllables with falling accents appear in double column 4; syllables with rising accents in double column 3; preaccentual syllables in double columns 2 and 1; postaccentual syllables following falling accents in double columns 5, 6, and 7; and postaccentual syllables following rising accents in double columns 4, 5, and 6.

A set of regularities valid also for shorter words (cf. table 2.2) can be observed. Most numerical values in the corpus appear to be basically results of the interaction of various factors, some of them pertaining to the inherent characteristics of the given accents, and others connected with the length of the word or the position of a syllable within the word.

Words with different syllabic and accentual patterns exhibit two common regularities. It is generally true that the beginning of the F_0 contour on a word is higher than the F_0 value at the end of the word. Thus, the general F_0 movement within the word is predominantly falling. Furthermore, the level of the F_0 peak reached within the word depends on the distance of the peak from the beginning of the word. The so-called falling accents occur

Table 2.12
F_0 and duration patterns in polysyllabic words produced by P. I. Average F_0 values (in hertz) at the beginning, peak, and end of a vowel are presented in the first part of a double column; average durations (in milliseconds) and position of the F_0 peak are shown in the second part.

Accentual	1		2		3		4		5		6		7	
pattern	F_0	Dur.	F_0	Dur.	F_0	Dur.	F_0	Dur.	F_0	Dur.	F_0	Dur.	F_0	Dur.
˵ ˘ -							225	125	203	98	158	131		
							249	68	204	13	158	10		
							231		165		140			
ˋ - ˘ ˘					212	131	245	153	187	78	156	81		
					232	113	247	15	187	10	156	13		
					227		189		155		146			
˘ ˋ ˘			202	101	216	130	238	125						
			210	54	243	113	238	14						
			203		241		179							
˘ ˋ -			204	105	224	115	245	148						
			211	83	243	82	246	13						
			209		231		165							
˘ ˋ ˘ ˘			199	84	214	112	234	81	194	82				
			202	33	234	88	237	19	194	12				
			202		232		215		157					
˘ ˋ ˘ -			203	85	218	128	238	80	179	130				
			204	35	241	120	242	25	179	10				
			202		237		223		138					
˘ ˋ - ˘			203	88	229	94	247	154	165	90				
			208	48	241	76	250	14	165	10				
			202		228		186		140					

Table 2.12 (continued)

Accentual pattern	1		2		3		4		5		6		7	
	F_0	Dur.	F_0	Dur.	F_0	Dur.	F_0	Dur.	F_0	Dur.	F_0	Dur.	F_0	Dur.
ˆ ˘ ˘ ˘							232	213	171	78	153	60	147	85
							246	50	173	18	153	15	147	10
							178		155		148		142	
˘ ´ ˘ ˘			204	89	205	175	236	83	196	80				
			209	47	236	160	236	12	196	10				
			200		233		216		162					
˘ ˘ ´ ˘	208	77	209	73	223	188	233	83						
	212	42	213	32	241	170	233	10						
	208		203		233		191							

closest to the beginning of the word, and they are associated with the highest F_0 peaks. Rising accents on the first syllable usually have later peaks and lower F_0 values than falling accents. When rising accents are preceded by unstressed syllables (and thus are located farther from the beginning of the word), their peaks have progressively lower values.

The last high fundamental frequency appears on the accented syllable in words with falling accents, and on the first postaccentual syllable in words with rising accents. Thus, in both cases the last high fundamental frequency is on the syllable that was accented before the Neoštokavian accent shift. Anticipating here the discussion in section 4.2.5, we will call this syllable the "tonal center" of the word. In words with falling accents this syllable always contains the F_0 peak of the word, and in words with rising accents this is the case in the majority of instances. However, in a considerable number of instances the fundamental frequency of the syllable presently bearing a rising accent slightly exceeds that of the tonal center, especially in polysyllabic words with an accent on the penultima, where the overall falling F_0 contour characterizing all words tends to lower the postaccentual syllable, which in this case is word-final.

Table 2.12 is arranged in such a manner that the tonal centers of all types of words are in the same column. This makes it possible to observe the characteristics of the tonal center as well as for the syllables that precede and follow.

The tonal center that follows a rising accent has considerably shorter duration than the tonal center under a falling accent, provided that the phonemic quantity of the two vowels is the same. It also exhibits a basically simple F_0 fall, whereas the fundamental frequency under a falling accent is usually rising-falling, and in words with a short falling accent often even prevailingly rising (that is, the terminal frequency of the F_0 contour on the accented syllable is higher than its frequency at the beginning of the syllable).

The syllable that immediately precedes the tonal center in words with rising accents (the syllable carrying the rising accent) usually has a predominantly rising fundamental frequency. With respect to the level of the F_0 peak, this syllable is the only one comparable to the tonal center, which means that in words with rising accents there are two syllables that bear high fundamental frequency. With respect to duration, the syllable immediately preceding the tonal center has the characteristics of an accented syllable.

The F_0 level of preaccentual syllables is considerably lower than that of the tonal center and of the syllable under the rising accent, but much higher than the level of the syllables following the tonal center. In sequences of preaccentual syllables the F_0 level remains basically constant; only in longer sequences is the last preaccentual syllable somewhat higher. These observations are based on a relatively small number of examples and are therefore tentative. For example, in the word type ˘ ˘ ˘ ˘ ` ¯ (not included in table 2.12 because the number of examples was only two) the average F_0 peaks of successive syllables were 215, 218, 217, 227, 239, and 240 Hz. Sequences of postaccentual syllables are characterized by a gradual fall; for example, 246 Hz on the accented syllable and 173, 153, and 147 Hz on successive postaccentual syllables in word type ̑ ˘ ˘ ˘ given in table 2.12. In general, there is virtually no fall before the tonal center and no rise after it.

The duration of a long vowel is shorter than the sum of the durations of two short vowels. Correspondingly, the F_0 fall in long tonal centers does not reach the falling interval between the peak of the short tonal center and the end of the following syllable. Also, the rising interval within a syllable under the long rising accent is smaller than the interval in the sequence ˘ ` (constituting part of a longer word), and the fall within a long syllable occurring after the tonal center is smaller than the fall in a sequence ˘ ˘ in a comparable position.

All accented words may be viewed as segments of an idealized long word-level F_0 contour having a tonal center, preceded by another syllable with high fundamental frequency and additional syllables with a lower F_0 level, and followed by a sequence of syllables with gradually declining fundamental frequency. An important feature of this contour is that a rise cannot occur after a fall. Words with falling accents may be viewed as segments of the idealized contour that begin with the tonal center; words with rising accents may be viewed as segments starting at least one syllable before the tonal center. The tonal center is the only part of the ideal contour that is necessarily present in every accented word.

Once the segmental structure of the word and the position of its tonal center have been determined, the behavior of tone and duration can be predicted on the basis of the regularities outlined in this section, taking into account a number of other factors such as the durational differences between high and low vowels, the tendency of voiced consonants to lower the beginning fundamental frequency of the following syllable nucleus carrying a falling accent, the continuity of the F_0 contour through an intervocalic sonorant, and the position of the word within the sentence.

2.7 The Relationship between Accentuation and Juncture

In this section we consider realizations of sequences of unstressed proclitic elements plus word, and compare these with lexically similar (or identical) sequences in which the accent has been shifted to the proclitic element. The material discussed here consists of the following items: *u ràt* 'to the war (acc.sg.masc.)', *ù rat* 'to the war' (alternative accentuation), *da mȍli* 'that he requests (3.sg.pres.)', and *zàmoli* 'requests (3.sg.pres., perf.asp.)'. These sequences were produced by the group of twelve speakers as part of their regular recording session in the same basic frame as the other test materials.[3]

Table 2.13 contains phonetic data concerning productions of these items by the twelve speakers. Durations are averaged over all twelve subjects, as are the values reported for the location of the F_0 peak (in milliseconds from the beginning of the syllable nucleus). Average intensity peak values in decibels (relative to a constant reference level) are given for the seven speakers with regular intensity patterns. F_0 values are presented separately for three groups of speakers established on the basis of their average speaking range.

As table 2.13 indicates, shifting the accent from *ràt* to the proclitic resulted in shortening the formerly accented word and changing the durational ratio between the two syllables. Even clearer is the change in duration in the pair *da mȍli–zàmoli*, with the additional difference that all syllables are shorter in a trisyllabic word.

For the seven speakers with regular intensity patterns, shifting the accent to the proclitic in *ù rat* was accompanied by an increase in the intensity of the accented syllable without a reduction in the intensity of the (now) postaccentual syllable. In the case of *da mȍli* and *zàmoli* the accent shift was not accompanied by any significant change in intensity pattern.

Shifting the accent to the preceding syllable causes the F_0 peak of the formerly preaccentual syllable to move toward the end of the syllable nucleus, and the F_0 peak of the formerly accented syllable to move toward the beginning of the syllable nucleus.

The F_0 contours show the same general pattern for all three groups: shifting the accent to the formerly preaccentual syllable raises the fundamental frequency on that syllable without lowering it on the formerly accented syllable. This may be seen by comparing *u ràt* with *ù rat* and *da mȍli* with *zàmoli* for all three groups of speakers.

This material suggests that the contribution of the three main prosodic

Table 2.13
Average durations (in milliseconds), positions of F_0 peak, intensity peaks (in decibels), and F_0 values (in hertz) at the beginning, peak, and end of the syllable nucleus, occurring in four test items produced by twelve speakers

	u r̀ät		ù rat		da m̀öli			zàmoli		
	1.syll.	2.syll.	1.syll.	2.syll.	1.syll.	2.syll.	3.syll.	1.syll.	2.syll.	3.syll.
Average duration	108	138	108	103	80	129	70	116	79	79
Position of F_0 peak	37	102	96	48	22	74	31	63	38	26
Average intensity peak (7 subjects)	34.9	43.1	41.7	43.1	42.6	42.4	35.7	43.0	42.0	36.4
F_0 values for 4 low-pitched subjects	89	94	100	115	86	93	74	94	99	75
	89	102	111	115	86	102	75	95	99	75
	86	95	111	91	84	86	71	93	78	65 (1 lar.)
F_0 values for 4 medium-pitched subjects	138	145	157	167	141	153	146	148	159	147
	147	166	165	173	144	165	150	153	164	149
	138	157	162	165	140	145	144 (1 lar.)	148	157	141
F_0 values for 4 high-pitched subjects	293	244	285	309	271	305	204	249	294	245
	293	318	315	336	272	331	205	259	319	252
	285	315	312	319	269	286	200	257	285	228

parameters to the difference between the accentual types ˘ ̏ and ` ˘ is as follows: duration is relatively most important, followed by fundamental frequency. Intensity is of relatively little importance in distinguishing between these two accent types.

2.8 Word Accents in Three Dialects outside the Neoštokavian Linguistic Area

In parallel with our studies of accentual patterns in the standard language, we carried out smaller-scale investigations of three dialects in which the Neoštokavian accent shift has not been completed. The dialects are representative of Čakavian, Kajkavian, and Slavonian dialect areas. The recording and analysis techniques used in these studies were the same as those used in the main part of the investigation. This section summarizes the results of these studies.

2.8.1 Čakavian

Čakavian (Lehiste and Ivić 1973a) represents the most archaic accentual system found in Serbocroatian, assumed to be almost identical to the system that evolved into the contemporary Štokavian accentual system through the merger of the earlier two long accents and the Neoštokavian accent shift. Our investigation is based on recordings made of the dialect spoken in the village of Jelenje, located north of Rijeka. In the dialect of this village there are two long accents: a long falling accent and a long rising accent (the so-called neoacute). Short syllables may also be accented, but there is no distinction between rising and falling in the case of short accents. Long and short vowels may also occur in unstressed syllables without dependence on the position of the accent.

The recordings were made by one of the authors (P.I.) in 1963, in the radio station at Rijeka. Three subjects, representing three generations, participated in the recording session: one male speaker (identified as Č1), 70 years old at the time of the recording, and two female speakers, Č2 (39 years old) and Č3 (26 years old). All three subjects had lived most of their lives in Jelenje.

The material recorded by each subject consisted of 240 sentences. Two-thirds of the sentences were frame utterances. Eighty nouns occurred in one frame in medial position and in another frame in final position. Eighty sentences contained verbs. There were 40 declarative sentences; of these, 20 contained two verbs, one in medial position and the other in final position, and 20 contained a verb in final position. Of 40 interrogative sentences, 20

Table 2.14
Average F_0 values (in hertz) and durations (in milliseconds) in six accentual types occurring in test words produced by three Čakavian speakers. N = number of tokens. (After Lehiste and Ivić 1973: 165.)

	Č1						Č2						Č3					
Accent type		F_0						F_0						F_0				
and position	N	Beg.	Peak	End	Dur.	F_0 peak	N	Beg.	Peak	End	Dur.	F_0 peak	N	Beg.	Peak	End	Dur.	F_0 peak
Medial																		
ˆ	8	207	228	213	151	70	13	222	235	226	145	46	11	235	244	241	132	68
˜	10	203	232	222	150	106	5	208	223	215	150	103	8	239	247	246	134	73
ˆ ¯	1	225	253	235	120	70							1	230	250	235	160	90
		192	192	185	100	10								205	205	200	100	10
˜ ˘	3	182	202	199	160	133	3	197	233	233	180	147	4	241	260	256	120	70
		192	199	194	87	37		228	228	202	133	10		238	238	238	100	10
˘ ˆ	2	180	181	170	95	15	2	200	225	225	100	25	1	210	210	210	100	50
		179	183	169	135	30		235	235	220	130	10		220	245	245	140	120
˘ ˜	3	180	183	167	90	20	3	210	210	207	77	10	2	223	223	215	80	10
		194	223	217	163	130		230	247	240	127	77		228	240	240	110	110
Final																		
ˆ	27	206	235	212	227	114	11	213	237	230	207	128	18	234	236	192	252	23
˜							7	214	250	249	193	156	1	200	200	180	300	10
ˆ ¯	2	195	243	227	175	110	1	190	220	200	160	100	2	220	230	200	160	25
		240	240	215	220	10		225	230	220	200	40		190	190	180	200	10
˜ ˘	3	207	253	250	190	180	3	193	213	212	160	103	5	232	234	230	164	48
		231	231	185	217	10		217	220	210	170	40		196	196	178	168	10
˘ ˆ	6	185	186	166	100	11	1	215	215	200	120	10	2	220	220	200	125	10
		202	234	229	242	148		200	200	200	200	10		220	225	195	225	25
˘ ˜							4	200	200	184	88	18	1	240	240	235	100	10
								208	233	233	195	105		200	200	180	200	10

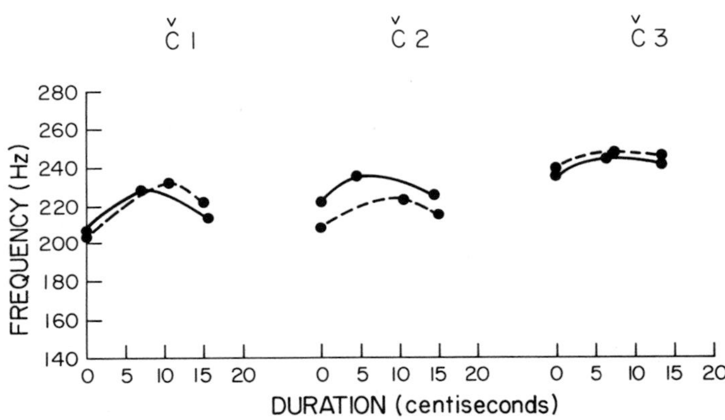

Figure 2.12
Average F_0 contours in monosyllabic words with the long falling accent (solid line) and the neoacute accent (dashed line) produced by three Čakavian speakers in medial position in two frames. (After Lehiste and Ivić 1973:167.)

had the verb in initial position and 20 had the verb in final position. The test words were selected for the purpose of illustrating the occurrence of all three accents in various word types and positions. The recordings were analyzed acoustically in the same manner as the recordings of the standard language. The results of measurements made from spectrograms are summarized in table 2.14 and illustrated in figures 2.12 and 2.13.[4]

Figure 2.12 presents average F_0 contours in monosyllabic words produced in the frame *Tvõj . . . nĩ dȍbār* 'Your . . . is no good' for masculine nouns and *Tvojȁ . . . nĩ dobrȁ* 'Your . . . is no good' for feminine nouns. The solid line represents F_0 contours associated with the long falling accent, and the dotted line the contours associated with the long rising accent (neoacute). Curves for the three subjects are presented side by side, the oldest speaker on the left, the youngest speaker on the right. It can be seen that for the representatives of the two older generations, the two curves differ with regard to the position of the F_0 peak: the peak occurs earlier in the long falling accent, and closer to the end of the syllable nucleus

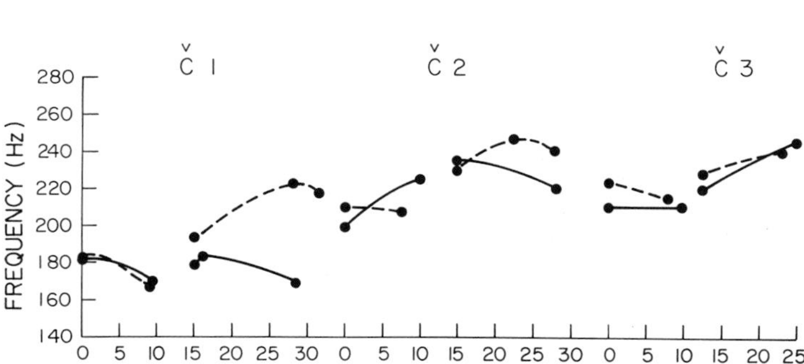

Figure 2.13
Average F_0 contours in disyllabic words with either the long falling accent (solid line) or the neoacute accent (dashed line) on the second syllable, produced by three Čakavian speakers in medial position in two frames. (After Lehiste and Ivić 1973 : 167.)

in the long rising accent. There is practically no difference in the position of the F_0 peak in test words produced by the representative of the youngest generation.

There seems to be no reason to associate relative F_0 level with accent type: the two curves cross each other in the case of speaker Č1, whereas in the case of Č2 and Č3 the average levels associated with the two accents have the opposite relationship—the F_0 level of the falling accent is higher than that of the rising accent in the speech of Č2, but lower than that of the rising accent in the speech of Č3.

Figure 2.13 presents average F_0 contours for disyllabic words with either the long falling accent or the neoacute on the second syllable. The test words occurred in medial position of frame utterances. Both older speakers, Č1 and Č2, show the same kind of distinction on the accented second syllable as they showed on accented monosyllables: the F_0 peak is close to the beginning of the syllable nucleus in the case of the long falling accent, and considerably closer to the end of the syllable nucleus in the case

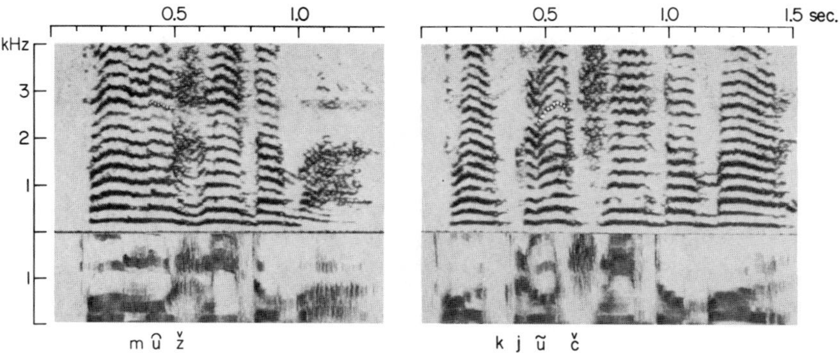

Figure 2.14
Broad-band and narrow-band spectrograms of the test words *mûž* and *kjũč*, produced by speaker Č1 in the frame *Tvoj . . . ni dobar*. (After Lehiste and Ivić 1973 : 168.)

of the neoacute. No distinction between the two accents is observable in comparable test words produced by speaker Č3.

Figures 2.14 and 2.15 show broad-band and narrow-band spectrograms illustrating the F_0 patterns occurring in the speech of subject Č1. The words were produced in the frame *Tvõj . . . nĩ dȍbār/Tvojȁ . . . nĩ dobrȁ*. Figure 2.14 shows the words *mûž* 'man', with the long falling accent, and *kjũč* 'key', with the neoacute. Figure 2.15 shows the test words *butîga* 'shop' and *Terẽza* (proper name). The tenth harmonic has been dotted with white paint to make it easier to follow the F_0 movements visually.

More details are presented in table 2.14, which is based on productions of nouns by the three subjects. The number of tokens is not uniform because of variation between speakers; for example, one or the other subject may have produced a word with a long falling accent instead of the expected long rising accent. There were also instances of repetition and of hesitation by the subjects, providing additional tokens or making a particular token unusable for comparative purposes.

The table confirms the general observation: those subjects who retain the distinction between long falling and neoacute have a difference in the position of the F_0 peak, which occurs earlier in the case of the long falling accent. The youngest subject, Č3, has no systematic distinction. We would like to emphasize that we could not detect any indication of the presence of the "broken tone" mentioned by some earlier authors, either in Čakavian, Kajkavian, or Slavonian.

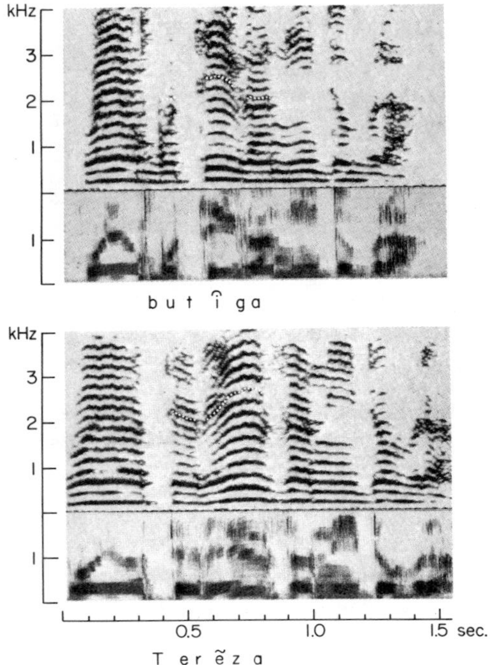

Figure 2.15
Broad-band and narrow-band spectrograms of the test words *butîga* and *Terẽza*, produced by speaker Č1 in the frame *Tvoja . . . ni dobra*. (After Lehiste and Ivić 1973 : 170.)

2.8.2 Kajkavian

The Kajkavian dialect that we studied (Ivić and Lehiste 1979) was that of Donja Pušća, one of the most conservative of Kajkavian dialects, reported to have retained the old Kajkavian accentual system almost without change. The recordings were made in 1963 by P.I. in the Zagreb radio station. The informants consisted of one male speaker, K1, 61 years old at the time of the recording, and two female speakers, K2 (58 years old) and K3 (67 years old). Speaker K2 made a large number of mistakes (mispronunciations and stuttering) during the recording; the description summarized below is based on materials produced by the other two speakers.[5]

The test materials consisted of 238 sentences. Included were 80 nouns, produced in two frames in which the test words occurred both in medial and in final position. Seventy-eight sentences contained a total of 116 verb forms. There were 38 declarative sentences in which verb forms occurred in both medial and final position, 20 declarative sentences with the verb in final position, and 20 questions with the verb in final position.

The results of measurements from broad-band and narrow-band spectrograms are presented in table 2. 15 and figure 2.16. The basic difference between the two long accents appears in the F_0 pattern on the accented syllable. In the case of the neoacute the fundamental frequency shows a rising movement within the syllable nucleus, with a peak very close to the end of the accented vowel; in the case of the long falling accent the high peak is located closer to the beginning of the syllable nucleus. This is essentially the same pattern that we found in Čakavian; the differences between the accents are even more clearly manifested.

The fundamental frequency of the postaccentual syllable starts at a higher frequency in medial position after the neoacute than after the long falling accent. However, this is evidently conditioned by the terminal F_0 level of the accented syllable nucleus. There is no difference in the postaccentual syllables in final position: as the table indicates, the second syllable reaches equally low F_0 levels, and there is a comparable number of words in both categories in which the whole postaccentual syllable is laryngealized. The data of speaker K3 should be considered rather carefully. Although in her data the average postaccentual F_0 levels (in final position) are higher after the neoacute than after the long falling accent, only after the neoacute was there extensive laryngealization (rare for a medium-high pitched female voice). In 6 out of 16 cases the last syllable was laryngealized in her productions in words with the ˜ ˘ accentual pattern. Of course, only the nonlaryngealized productions were averaged, with the result that the fundamental frequency given in the table for postaccentual syllables in ˜ ˘ appears higher than that of postaccentual syllables in ˆ ˘, productions of which contained no laryngealization.

Final position has a further effect on the realization of the F_0 contour on the accented syllables: the peak of the F_0 contour on the neoacute occurs in the middle of the accented syllable, rather than close to the end of the syllable nucleus, as is the case for medial position. Nevertheless, the contours on the two long accented syllables remain distinctively different. There was no difference in postaccentual syllables.

The short accent had both rising and falling realizations. Since there are no contrasts in short accents, data concerning the short accent were not included in the table.

Figure 2.17 illustrates the pronunciation of four disyllabic words by speaker K3. Narrow-band spectrograms of the test words *škôla* 'school', *strãža* 'watch, sentry', *hȉža* 'house', and *rĩža* 'rice' are presented, produced

Table 2.15
Average F_0 values (in hertz) and durations (in milliseconds) in four accentual types occurring in test words produced by two Kajkavian speakers, K1 and K3. N = number of tokens. (After Ivić and Lehiste 1979: 189.)

Speaker	Accent type and position	N	F_0 Beg.	F_0 Peak	F_0 End	Dur.	F_0 peak at
K1	Medial						
	⌢ ˘	9	119	127	113	166	88
			117	118	112	90	24
	~ ˘	8	120	125	122	198	161
			122	122	112	95	18
	⌢	8	130	136	124	231	58
	~	2	121	129	121	150	115
K1	Final						
	⌢ ˘	12	127	134	111	183	59
			106	106	96	111	13
			(3 lar.)	(3 lar.)	(4 lar.)		
	~ ˘	13	118	124	115	234	123
			102	102	88	117	13
			(2 lar.)	(2 lar.)	(3 lar.)		
	⌢	7	133	136	100	197	29
	~	1	115	122	100	250	120
K3	Medial						
	⌢ ˘	7	225	240	213	117	41
			199	199	183	72	10
	~ ˘	7	204	234	228	144	129
			223	223	196	86	10
	⌢	7	216	230	204	126	60
	~	2	199	210	206	130	120
K3	Final						
	⌢ ˘	8	219	233	165	150	38
			133	135	120	90	13
	~ ˘	16	200	220	203	167	75
			161	161	127	90	10
			(5 lar.)	(6 lar.)	(6 lar.)		
	⌢	4	214	236	145	170	53
	~	4	188	249	240	158	135

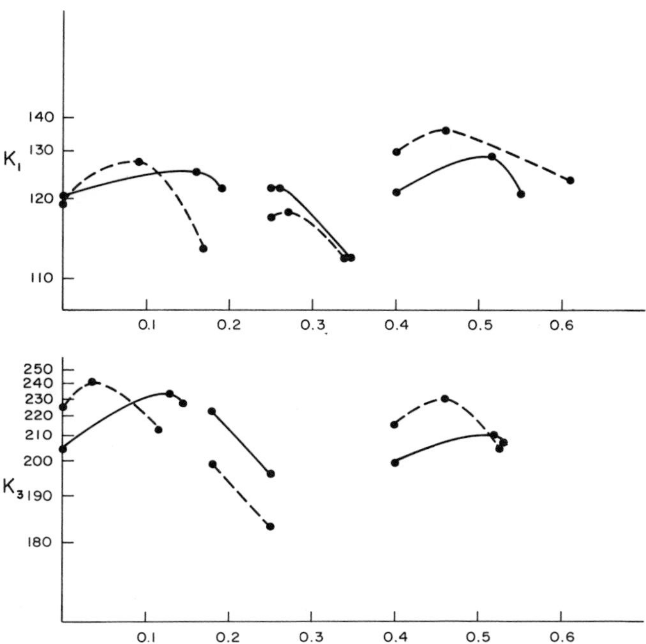

Figure 2.16
Curves representing F_0 positions in disyllabic and monosyllabic words with the neoacute (solid line) and long falling (dashed line) accents produced by two Kajkavian speakers in medial position. (After Ivić and Lehiste 1979: 190.)

in the frame *Tvojȁ . . . nĩ dobrȁ* 'Your . . . is no good'. Figure 2.18 illustrates the production of four monosyllabic words—*bîk* 'bull', *strĩc* 'father's brother', *mêd* 'honey', and *hlẽv* 'stable'—produced in the frame *Tvõj . . . nĩ dȍber* by the same speaker.

2.8.3 Slavonian

The Slavonian dialect possesses one of the most interesting accentual systems in the Slavic linguistic area, for it constitutes a transitional form between the archaic three-accent system and the Neoštokavian four-accent system. Slavonian has three long accents, opposed to two short accents, and thus constitutes a five-accent dialect.

Our study (Lehiste and Ivić 1977) was based on recordings made of the speech of four informants from Strizivojna in 1962 by P.I. at the radio station in Osijek. The informants were about half a generation apart in age,

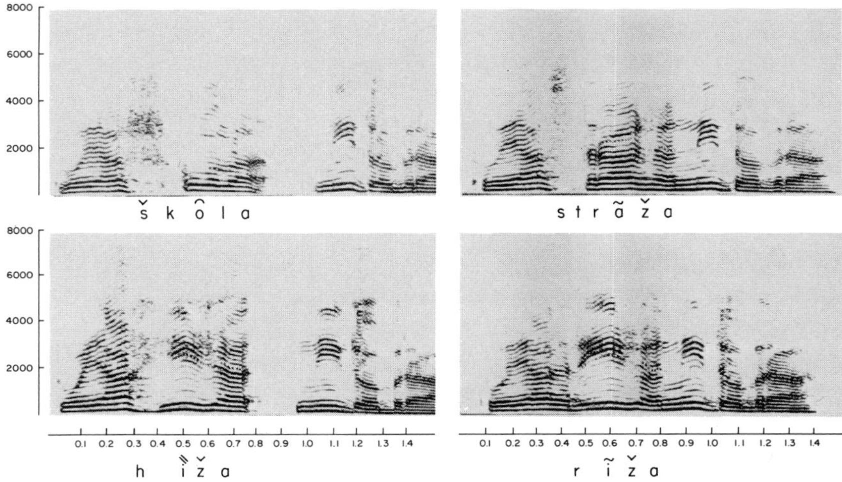

Figure 2.17
Narrow-band spectrograms of the test words *škôla*, *strãža*, *hȉža*, and *rĩža*, produced by speaker K3 in the frame *Tvoja . . . ni dobra*. (After Ivić and Lehiste 1979: 191.)

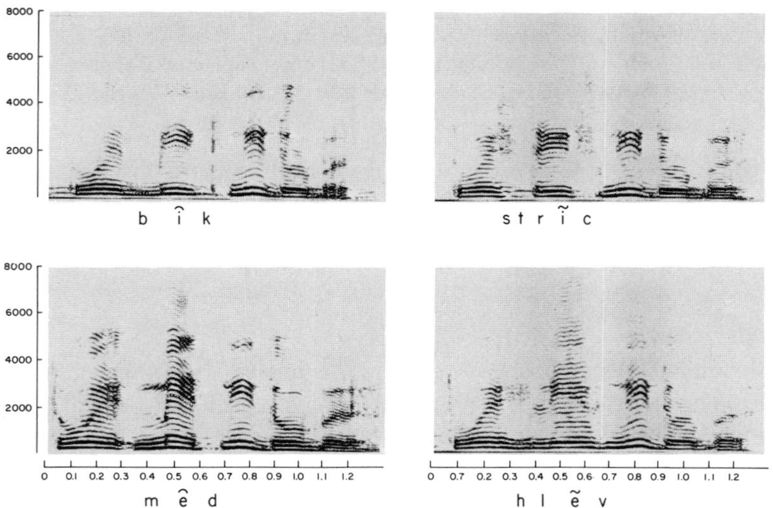

Figure 2.18
Narrow-band spectrograms of the test words *bîk*, *strĩc*, *mêd*, and *hlẽv*, produced by speaker K3 in the frame *Tvoj . . . ni dober*. (After Ivić and Lehiste 1979: 191.)

ranging from 76 to 34 at the time of the recording. One of the two male informants (J1) was 76 years old; the other (K2) was 60 years old. Of the two female informants, K3/L3 was 42 years old, and L4 was 34 years old. All were considered typical representatives of the dialect under study.

The materials recorded by the informants consisted of a total of 216 sentences. However, some informants recorded only subsets of the material, and one (K3/L3) produced almost all sentences twice. Details are presented in Lehiste and Ivić 1977; the summary offered here is based mainly on the speech of informant K3/L3, who produced the largest number of utterances.

The set of sentences included 80 nouns, produced in two frames, so that the nouns occurred both in medial position and in final position. There were also 56 sentences involving verbs. Of these, 40 were statements, 24 having verbs in both medial and final position, and 16 having verbs in final position, and 16 were questions with verbs in initial position.

The results of the measurements are presented in tables 2.16 and 2.17 and in figure 2.19. Table 2.16 presents average F_0, duration, and intensity patterns for informant K3/L3, derived from nouns occurring in medial position. Table 2.17 presents comparable data for the same set of nouns occurring in final position. Figure 2.19 shows some of the patterns in graphic form. Figure 2.20 contains narrow-band spectrograms of the test words *šâtra* 'tent', *strãža* 'watch, sentry', and *gréda* 'beam', produced in medial and final position by speaker K3/L3.

The most important phenomenon is the opposition between the three long accents. All three are phonologically contrastive, and one would thus expect them to be phonetically different. The traditional description—associating tonal differences with the stressed syllable—would predict three contrastive F_0 movements within the accented syllable nucleus. However, tables 2.16 and 2.17 do not confirm such a view. The F_0 movements in the vowels under ˜ and ´ are practically identical in the word types ˘ ˜ ˘ vs. ˘ ´ ˘ in medial position and in the word types ˜ ˘ vs. ´ ˘ and ˘ ˜ ˘ vs. ˘ ´ ˘ in final position (the disyllabic words in final position are also represented in the lower half of figure 2.19). All these categories display moderately falling F_0 movements, contrasting with the strongly falling fundamental frequency in the vowel under ˆ. The only category where a noteworthy difference can be observed is the category of disyllabic words in medial position (see also the upper half of figure 2.19). Here the vowels under both accents have a rising F_0 movement, with the peak at practically the same place, but the intervals of the rise and the slight final fall are different in the two cases. Nevertheless, the actual spectrograms

Table 2.16
Average F_0 values (in hertz), durations (in milliseconds) and intensity peaks (in decibels) in thirteen accentual types occurring in test words produced by a Slavonian speaker (K3/L3). Nouns in medial position. N = number of tokens. (After Lehiste and Ivić 1977: 74.)

Accent type	N	F_0 Beg.	F_0 Peak	F_0 End	Dur. of SN	F_0 peak at	Intensity peak in dB
⌢	3	228	253	213	187	57	44.3–42.3
~	3	191	226	199	317	17	39.7–35.7
⌢ ˘	3	237	241	170	210	27	44.7
		170	170	169	103	10	35.0
~ ˘	12	219	252	242	223	154	42.8
		202	202	172	112	10	37.4
				(2 lar.)			
´ ˘	10	204	214	211	239	161	40.1
		225	230	212	86	35	40.4
˵ ˘	5	211	257	252	136	116	43.2
		200	200	182	78	10	38.8
˘ ˵	10	195	201	194	108	43	38.3
		220	230	210	134	42	41.6
˘ ~	3	187	189	180	80	27	37.7
		191	246	244	223	207	41.3
˘ ⌢ ˘	2	204	206	196	105	15	39.5
		245	261	203	220	30	43.0
		194	194	179	125	10	38.5
˘ ~ ˘	6	212	217	204	95	32	40.2
		216	219	199	178	17	41.5
		182	182	162	128	10	36.2
		(1 lar.)	(1 lar.)	(1 lar.)			
˘ ´ ˘	1	230	230	220	110	10	40.0
		220	220	205	290	10	41.0
		215	220	220	110	110	40.0
˘ ˵ ˘	4	210	217	210	88	56	37.3
		240	249	236	125	60	37.0
		188	188	153	125	10	32.5
˘ ˋ ˘	1	190	210	205	110	80	37.0
		210	217	217	110	110	39.0
		220	220	190	150	10	41.0

Table 2.17
Average F_0 values (in hertz), durations (in milliseconds) and intensity peaks (in decibels) in twelve accentual types occurring in test words produced by a Slavonian speaker (K3/L3). Nouns in final position. N = number of tokens. (After Lehiste and Ivić 1977:74–75.)

Accent type	N	F_0 Beg.	F_0 Peak	F_0 End	Dur. of SN	F_0 peak at	Intensity peak in dB
⌢	3	180	195	135	243	40	37.0–29.0
				(1 lar.)			
~	3	206	208	180	317	30	41.0–37.3
⌢ ˘	4	212	220	160	225	30	44.8
		160	160	150	110	10	38.5
		(1 lar.)	(1 lar.)	(2 lar.)			
~ ˘	11	203	205	191	225	39	41.4
		169	169	155	103	10	35.4
		(1 lar.)	(1 lar.)	(1 lar.)			
´ ˘	9	197	198	183	262	17	40.1
		189	193	181	101	29	39.1
˵ ˘	5	192	196	188	142	58	43.6
		169	169	155	100	10	35.6
		(1 lar.)	(1 lar.)	(2 lar.)			
˘ ˵	9	187	188	178	109	12	37.2
		192	200	189	123	33	39.8
˘ ~	3	199	201	187	87	20	40.3
		187	187	166	243	10	39.7
˘ ⌢ ˘	2	204	217	210	80	35	42.0
		229	239	175	170	35	44.5
		180	180	167	130	10	35.5
		(1 lar.)	(1 lar.)	(1 lar.)			
˘ ~ ˘	6	193	195	185	92	18	38.7
		198	204	191	187	47	39.8
		174	174	162	107	10	35.8
				(1 lar.)			
˘ ´ ˘	1	200	200	195	110	10	38.0
		201	201	185	330	10	40.0
		185	189	180	100	50	42.0
˘ ˵ ˘	3	196	197	189	78	20	38.5
		221	234	205	140	33	40.3
		202	202	183	115	10	37.5
		(1 lar.)	(1 lar.)	(2 lar.)			

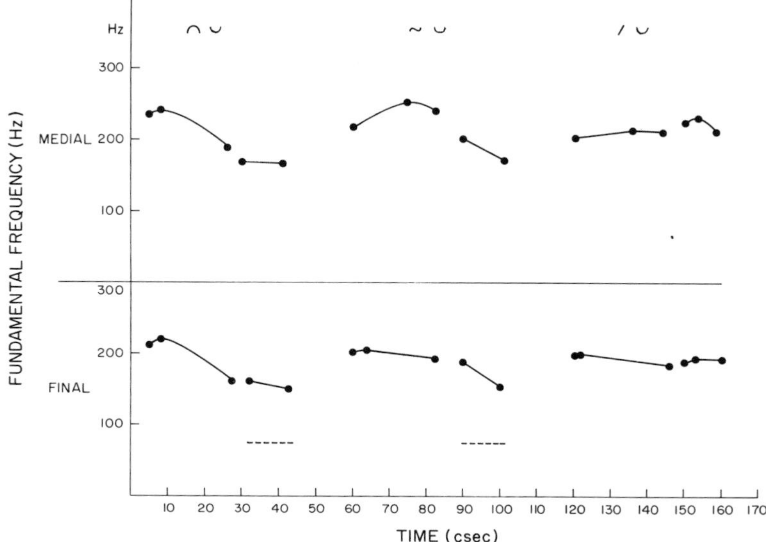

Figure 2.19
Curves representing F_0 positions in three types of disyllabic words occurring in medial and final position in frame utterances produced by speaker K3/L3. (After Lehiste and Ivić 1977:79.)

reproduced in figure 2.20 show that the differences are more apparent than real.

Let us consider the F_0 curves associated with the postaccentual syllable. In medial position the long falling accent is followed by a second syllable with low fundamental frequency. The old rising accent (neoacute) is followed by a second syllable that starts somewhat higher than the second syllable after a long falling accent, but drops to the same low frequency. The new, Neoštokavian rising accent has a second syllable that has a higher fundamental frequency than the stressed syllable itself. (This is the well-known characteristic of the Neoštokavian long rising accent, amply documented in our earlier publications and reviewed in section 2.2.)

In final position the long falling accent and the neoacute both have second syllables that start at the termination frequency of the first syllable and drop to a low frequency; both cases also show laryngealization. The Neoštokavian rising accent is followed by a syllable with a fundamental frequency that is on the average as high as the fundamental frequency on the stressed syllable. There is never any laryngealization, at least in the materials we analyzed for this part of the study.

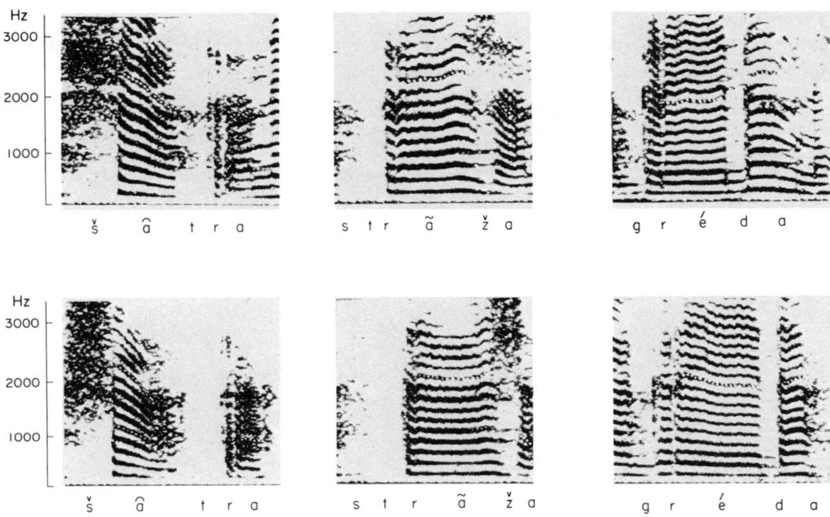

Figure 2.20
Narrow-band spectrograms of the test words *šâtra*, *strãža*, and *gréda*, produced in medial (top) and final (bottom) position by speaker K3/L3. (After Lehiste and Ivić 1977:82–83.)

We can conclude that the characteristic difference between the two old accents rests within the stressed syllable itself, whereas the new long rising accent differs from the two old accents by being primarily characterized by the relationship between the fundamental frequencies of the accented and postaccentual syllables. It should be emphasized that the two old accents can, and do, contrast in monosyllabic words, while the new long rising accent is only found in words in which at least one syllable follows the stressed syllable.

The long falling accent and the neoacute differ in that the long falling accent is really falling: it has a slightly rising and then sharply falling F_0 curve, the initial rise depending on the phonetic nature of the initial consonant. The neoacute has its peak much later in the accented syllable and thus differs from the long falling accent by being basically rising. Both old accents are followed by a syllable with low fundamental frequency; however, this cannot be considered an essential part of the accent, because the two accents can contrast in monosyllabic words. The fact that the second syllable starts at a higher frequency after the neoacute is automatically conditioned by the higher termination frequency of the stressed syllable, as compared to the termination frequency of a stressed syllable

Table 2.18
Intensity patterns in words of three accentual types produced by two Slavonian speakers in medial and final position. Intensities in decibels. N = number of tokens. (After Lehiste and Ivić 1977: 75, 77.)

Speaker	Accent type	Medial position			Final position		
		N	1.syll.	2.syll.	N	1.syll.	2.syll.
K3/L3	ˆ ˘	2	46.0	34.0	2	45.5	38.0
	˜ ˘	3	45.0	38.0	3	40.3	33.7
	´ ˘	2	44.0	41.5	2	42.0	40.5
L4	ˆ ˘	2	47.0	42.5	2	45.0	40.0
	˜ ˘	4	41.3	37.8	5	41.5	32.2
	´ ˘	2	43.0	42.0	2	42.5	39.5

with long falling accent. In final position both second syllables can be laryngealized, and of course in such instances there is no difference between the beginning and ending frequency of the second syllable.

The Neoštokavian long rising accent differs from the neoacute basically through its high second syllable. Here the second syllable is an essential part of the accent: since the new rising accent does not occur on monosyllabic words, its presence is obligatory. For both long rising accents the peak of the F_0 curve is at the same point in the accented syllable. Thus, the two long rising accents are distinguished only on the basis of the postaccentual syllable. We published this result in Ivić and Lehiste 1965: 75. Junković (1968: 54) has expressed the same opinion, whereas Mahnken and Matešić (1970) believe that a break in the F_0 movement is crucial for the neoacute.

The F_0 patterns on trisyllabic words confirm the findings in disyllabic words. Tables 2.16 and 2.17 contain comparable data for trisyllabic words produced by the same informant.

The two short accents had basically the same manifestations as the short rising and short falling accents found in the standard language.

The distinction between the two old long accents, on the one hand, and the new (Neoštokavian) long rising accent, on the other hand, can also be observed in the intensity patterns found in the material produced by the Slavonian informants. Table 2.18 shows the average intensity peaks in words with identical vowels in both syllables, produced by speakers K3/L3 and L4 in medial and final position. For each speaker and position the intensity difference between the two syllables in the two old accents is larger than the intensity difference between the two syllables of words carrying the Neoštokavian long rising accent.

2.8.4 Slavonian Accents and the Neoštokavian Accent Shift

The four speakers who produced our test material also produced many words whose accentual patterns were not clearly identifiable with any of the five standard patterns just described. We did not include the unstable productions in the analysis presented in Lehiste and Ivić 1977 and summarized on the preceding pages. However, these productions were transcribed and analyzed in the same manner as the other test materials, and they provide crucial evidence for the accent shift in progress (see Lehiste and Ivić 1982).

To change from the old unshifted system (as found in the Čakavian and Kajkavian dialects) to the Neoštokavian system, several steps are necessary. The opposition between the old falling accent and the neoacute must be eliminated. Both old long accents must acquire the phonetic shape of the long falling accent. Accents occurring on noninitial syllables must be moved toward the beginning of the word by one syllable; disyllabic sequences must be created with high pitch and intensity on both the formerly pretonic syllable and the formerly accented syllable. Our four informants produced instances of all these steps, several of them having preferred patterns. Speaker K2, for example, produced long falling accents on the first syllable in 6 out of 21 words in which speakers K3/L3 and L4 produced the neoacute on the first syllable. All speakers produced instances of incomplete shifts, in which the preaccentual syllable has already acquired relatively high pitch and intensity, but the postaccentual syllable still carries its original pattern, including duration appropriate to a stressed syllable. Often a different stage of the accent shift was found in productions of the same word by different speakers. For example, speaker L4 produced the word *voda* 'water' with its original pattern, that is, with a short falling accent on the second syllable (/vodȁ/); speakers K2 and K3/L3 produced versions with an incomplete shift (/vòdȁ/); and speaker J1 had the Neoštokavian shifted form, with a short rising accent on the first syllable (/vòda/). Exactly the same distribution of stages was found for *koza* 'goat'; other words showed variations of this pattern. The word *igla* 'needle', for example, was produced with the original unshifted pattern (/iglȁ/) by speakers K2 and L4, with an incomplete shift (/ìglȁ/) by speaker K3/L3, and with a complete shift by speaker J1 (/ìgla/).

The phonetic analysis of incomplete shifts suggests that the first step in the accent shift involves anticipation of high fundamental frequency and intensity on the pretonic syllable. Completed shift involves an additional durational change, relatively greater length being shifted from the originally accented syllable to the originally pretonic syllable. There is no direct way to establish whether the change in the domain of accentual pattern from the accented syllable to the disyllabic sequence has already taken place in the systems of any of the speakers; indirectly, one might conclude that as soon as minimal pairs arise in the language involving disyllabic words with the neoacute (or falling) accent on the first syllable, on the one hand, and the Neoštokavian long rising accent on the first syllable, on the other hand, the relationship between the accented and postaccentual syllables must have become the crucial distinguishing factor. We did not include minimal pairs in our test materials, but they contain a fair number of instances in which the accentual patterns are minimally contrastive: *svíla* 'silk' vs. *strĩna* 'wife of father's brother', *tráva* 'grass' vs. *šâtra* 'tent', and so on. Nor did we carry out listening tests; clearly, the problem can only be solved through systematic investigation of perception.

2.9 Listening Tests

Two informal listening tests were carried out at the beginning of the investigation. In the first, a randomized tape containing all minimal pairs from the corpus recorded by the main informant P.I. was presented to him for identification. He achieved 100% success. In the second, a randomized tape was again presented to the main informant for identification; the tape contained only the first syllables of minimally contrastive disyllabic words with short rising and short falling accents. When the intervocalic consonant was eliminated together with the nucleus of the second syllable, identifications were completely random. When a voiced intervocalic consonant was included in the truncated test words, identifications became much better than chance. Inclusion of the complete second syllable resulted in complete identification. This suggested to us that the relationship between the accented and the postaccentual syllable is important for perceiving the distinction.

Systematic listening tests were carried out with synthetic speech. The purpose of the experiments was to test the perceptual significance of the various acoustic patterns observed in the speech of the informants in the course of the investigation. The same methodology was employed in all experiments: test stimuli were generated on an electronic, computer-controlled synthesizer, and tapes containing randomized stimuli were presented to panels of listeners for identification of the stimuli. The results of the listening tests were submitted to statistical analysis.

A basic issue had to be decided before the synthetic F_0 patterns were generated to test the significance of F_0 movements in the perception of

Serbocroatian accents. The issue concerns the shape of the falling contour. In most instances a long falling accent is realized as a rising-falling movement, with a peak in the first third of the syllable nucleus. The initial rise is usually present, if the initial consonant is voiced; after a voiceless obstruent the F_0 contour usually starts at the peak. On the other hand, a rising-falling contour may occasionally end at a frequency that is higher than the beginning frequency of the rising part of the contour. It was decided to investigate whether there was any perceptual distinction between those falling contours whose terminal fundamental frequency was higher than their beginning fundamental frequency and those whose fundamental frequency, after an initial rise, dropped below the beginning frequency. In both cases, of course, we are dealing with a rising-falling pitch contour; the question is whether the listener attaches any significance to—or is even able to hear—the difference between the initial and terminal frequencies.

2.9.1 Experiment 1

This experiment started with the production of a set of stimuli consisting of the vowel /a/ with different F_0 contours. The synthesis was performed at the Royal Institute of Technology in Stockholm, using a Control Data 1700 computer to control OVE III, a serial formant synthesizer.[6] Figure 2.21 shows the kinds of stimuli used in the experiment. All F_0 movements were superimposed on the synthetic vowel /a/. There were eighteen stimuli in all, in two sets. The first set consisted of eleven stimuli starting at 100 Hz and having a peak at 118 Hz. The duration of the stimuli was 275 msec; the peak occurred 50 msec from the beginning of the stimulus. There were five instances in which the terminal frequency was higher than the initial frequency, one instance in which they were equal, and five instances in which the terminal frequency was lower than the initial frequency. A second set consisted of seven stimuli starting at 178 Hz, peaking at 200 Hz, and ending at three frequencies above 178 Hz, one at 178 Hz, and three frequencies below 178 Hz. A listening tape was prepared in which each of the eighteen stimuli appeared twice in random order. The stimuli followed each other at five-second intervals.

The tape was presented to two groups of listeners, one consisting of native speakers of Serbocroatian in Novi Sad, Yugoslavia, the other consisting of native speakers of American English in Columbus, Ohio, who had no acquaintance with tone languages. There were 19 Yugoslav listeners and 10 American listeners. Each stimulus was judged 38 times by Yugoslavs and 20 times by Americans. The Yugoslav listeners were asked to make an essentially linguistic judgment. If a changing F_0 contour is per-

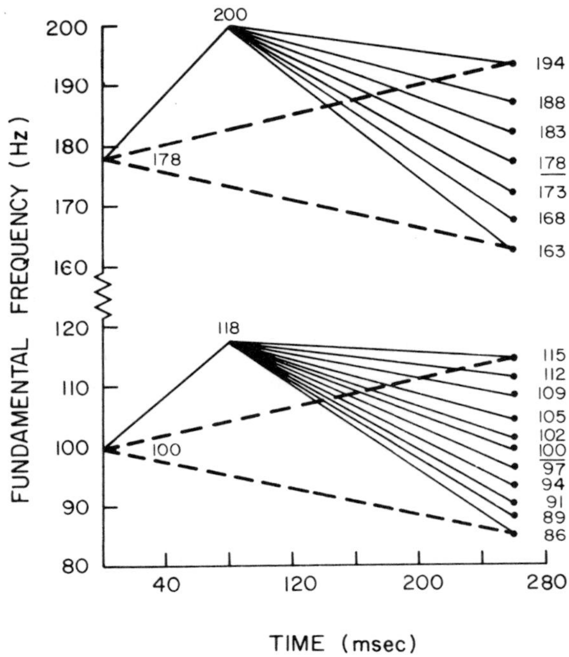

Figure 2.21
F_0 patterns occurring on synthetic stimuli used in Experiment 1. (After Lehiste and Ivić 1972:3.)

ceived as rising when its end has a higher frequency than its beginning, the listeners for whom a rising contour carries a special lexical meaning should be able to associate this meaning with the F_0 contour. In the same way, a changing contour whose terminal pitch is lower than its beginning should be assigned to the falling tonal category. The Serbocroatian speakers were asked to make an identification in terms of two different accents; they were instructed to indicate whether the long synthetic vowel seemed to them to fit better into a word with a long falling accent or into a word with a long rising accent. The English-speaking listeners were asked to make a phonetic judgment: they were instructed to listen carefully to the difference between the beginning and terminal frequencies of the rising-falling F_0 curve and to check whether the stimulus was "predominantly rising" or "predominantly falling."

The results of the test were inconclusive in many respects.[7] It seemed that neither group of listeners could hear the difference between initial and

Table 2.19
Judgment of stimuli as "falling" or "rising" by thirteen Yugoslav subjects

Stimulus	F_0 contour	"Falling"	"Rising"
1	100–118–86	25	1
2	100–118–89	22	4
3	100–118–91	21	5
4	100–118–94	19	7
5	100–118–97	23	3
6	100–118–100	20	6
7	100–118–102	16	10
8	100–118–105	14	12
9	100–118–109	12	14
10	100–118–112	4	22
11	100–118–115	1	25
Total		177	109

terminal frequencies of a rising-falling F_0 contour. Both groups substituted a strategy of labeling the high-pitched stimuli as "rising" and the low-pitched stimuli as "falling." Because the test yielded no clear-cut answer to the question concerning the perception of a rising-falling F_0 contour, we decided to circumvent the problem by synthesizing the F_0 contours with a straight line in the next experiment. It should be remembered that the realization of the long rising accent generally approximates a straight line, and that an initial peak followed by a fall (without an initial rise) is one of the possible realizations of the long falling accent.

At a later date we decided to replicate the experiment with Yugoslav listeners. It appeared in retrospect that the inclusion of stimuli in two pitch ranges may have confused the subjects to the extent that they adopted an alternative strategy. In the replication experiment we used only the eleven low-pitched stimuli, which were included twice in a randomized listening test. The test was administered to 13 subjects (native speakers of Serbo-croatian) in Belgrade on March 23, 1981. There were 26 judgments per stimulus, for a total of 286 judgments. The results of the listening test are presented in table 2.19.

The results of the replication test indicate that the stimuli were perceived by the subjects as belonging to three categories. Stimuli 1–6 were assigned to the "falling" category. Stimuli 7–9 were indeterminate; the listeners gave random responses. Stimuli 10–11 were reliably assigned to the "rising" category.

We interpret these results to mean that the listeners attended to the whole F_0 curve and based their judgments on the relative magnitudes of the rising movement in the first half of the stimulus and the falling movement in the second half. In general, the falling second part appears to have exerted a stronger influence than the rising first half: stimulus 6, in which both F_0 movements were of equal magnitude, was reliably assigned to the "falling" category. However, when the interval of the fall was minimal compared to the rise (stimuli 10 and 11), the rising first part appears to have dominated the listeners' perception to the extent that the stimuli were reliably assigned to the "rising" category.

2.9.2 Experiment 2

These results were, of course, unavailable to us when we designed our first experiment using synthesized Serbocroatian words as stimuli. The purpose of this experiment was to establish the perceptual value of F_0 patterns associated with long rising and long falling accents. The test word selected for the experiment was *radi*, a form of the verb *raditi* 'to work, to do', which may occur with a long falling accent (in the 3.sg.pres.) and with a long rising accent (in the 2.sg.imper.). The synthetic stimuli were produced at the Royal Institute of Technology in Stockholm under the same conditions as the test materials used in the first experiment.

The synthesized patterns are shown in figure 2.22. The first set of eleven stimuli had a steeply falling first syllable (183–122 Hz), combined with six level and five falling second syllable contours. The second set of eleven stimuli had a similar pattern generated with a narrower range: 163–141 Hz on the first syllable, followed by six level and five falling second syllables. The third and fourth sets of eleven had a level first syllable (at 149 Hz) and a rising first syllable (141–163 Hz), respectively, both combined with the same second syllables as the second set. The duration of all first vowels was 260 msec, and that of the vowels of the second syllable was 120 msec. There was a total of 44 stimuli.

A randomized listening tape was prepared, on which the stimuli appeared at five-second intervals. The listening tests were given to 25 listeners in Novi Sad. The listeners were asked to identify each word as a lexical item by checking one of two columns, the heading of which gave a paraphrase of the meaning of the word; they were specifically not asked to assign a "tone" to each word. The scores were, however, tabulated in terms of "falling" responses. The results are presented in table 2.20 and in figures 2.23, 2.24, 2.25, and 2.26. For 25 listeners, the scores are significantly different from chance (at the 0.05 level) if they are either above 17.5 or below 7.5.

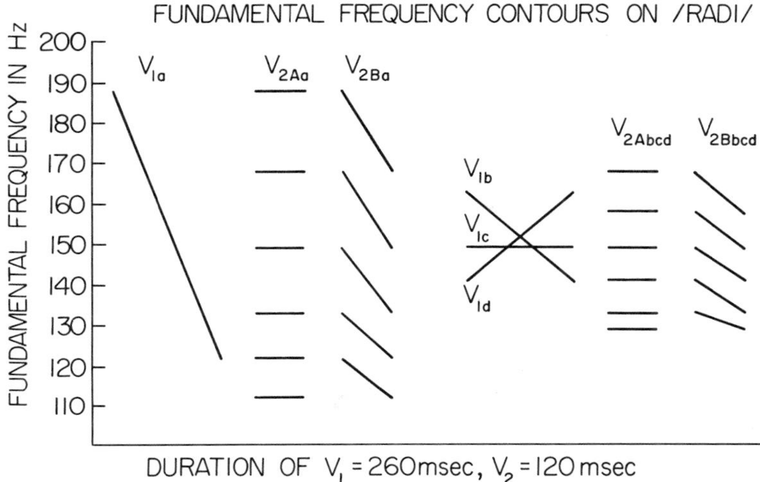

Figure 2.22
F_0 patterns occurring on the first and second syllable vowels of the synthesized test word *radi* used in Experiment 2. (After Lehiste and Ivić 1972: 8.)

Figure 2.23 shows the results of listener judgments of stimuli with a steep fall (a musical fifth) on the first syllable, followed by either a level or a falling second syllable. In the case of the level second syllable, judgments were random until the second syllable assumed the value of 133 Hz. Then they were significant (at the 0.05 level) for "falling." When the second syllable had a falling fundamental frequency, the highest second syllable gave borderline judgments for "falling"; all lower values (from 168–149 Hz to 122–112 Hz) gave significant "falling" responses.

Figure 2.24 presents the results of listener judgments of stimuli of the same type, but with a narrower range. The results are interestingly different. With a steep fall in the first syllable, even the highest second syllable value could not shift listener judgments to "rising"; with a small interval on the first syllable, the highest level second syllable gave significant "rising" responses. The shift to significant "falling" responses took place at the same level frequency as before (133 Hz); with a falling second syllable, there was an abrupt change (at 141–133 Hz) from random to significant "falling" responses.

Figure 2.25 presents listener responses to stimuli with a level first syllable. Here a level second syllable produced significant "rising" responses until the second syllable acquired a lower frequency than the first; at that

Table 2.20
Number of "falling" judgments obtained with synthetic productions of the word *radi* with different F_0 contours. The group of 25 listeners includes all those who participated in the test; the group of 14 includes those listeners who made fewer than 2 mistakes in judging 8 extreme contours. (After Lehiste and Ivić 1972:10.)

		Number of subjects			Number of subjects	
V_1	V_2	25	14	V_2	25	14
183–122	188–168	17	10	188	16	12
	168–149	18	10	168	14	10
	149–133	19	13	149	16	11
	133–122	19	14	133	22	14
	122–112	25	14	122	19	13
				112	21	14
163–141	168–158	8	3	168	6	3
	158–149	9	3	158	9	4
	149–141	10	6	149	13	7
	141–133	19	12	141	15	6
	133–129	19	12	133	22	12
				129	21	12
149–149	168–158	8	3	168	0	0
	158–149	4	0	158	3	1
	149–141	11	2	149	5	1
	141–133	11	5	141	11	5
	133–129	12	7	133	8	4
				129	12	6
141–163	168–158	5	0	168	6	1
	158–149	5	0	158	4	2
	149–141	9	1	149	3	2
	141–133	8	4	141	3	1
	133–129	12	6	133	12	7
				129	11	5

point (141 Hz) the judgments became random. With a falling second syllable, the results appear ambiguous: the single stimulus for which responses were significant for "rising" has an intermediate value, flanked by random responses.

Figure 2.26 presents responses to stimuli with a rising first syllable. Here the judgments shifted from significantly "rising" to random, when the level second syllable acquired a level below the frequency of the first syllable (133 Hz), or when a falling second syllable reached a terminal value that was equal to the initial value of the first syllable (149–141 Hz).

Table 2.20 presents the information numerically. The table includes the scores for the total group of 25 and the scores for a selected subgroup of 14.

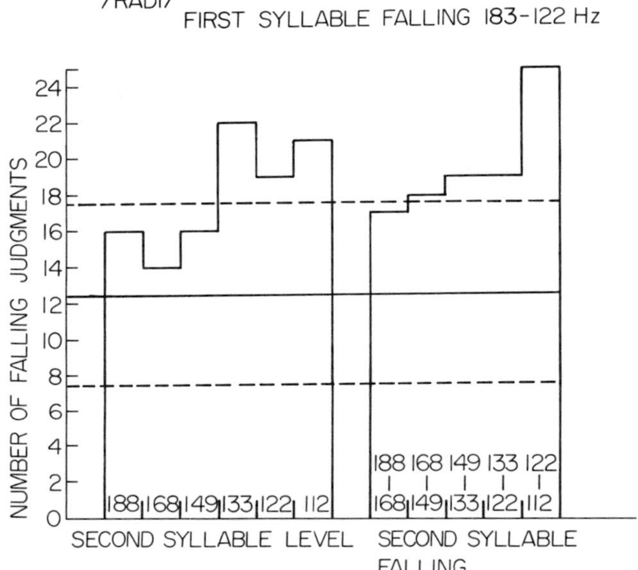

Figure 2.23
Listener judgments of the F_0 contour on *radi* as "falling," when a steeply falling F_0 contour on the first syllable was combined with eleven different second syllable contours. (After Lehiste and Ivić 1972:8.)

This group of 14 was obtained by eliminating all subjects who made two or more mistakes in judging the eight extreme stimuli, namely those in which the F_0 patterns corresponded to contours expected on the basis of measurements made from actual speech. The eight extreme stimuli included those with an F_0 fall on the first vowel of 183–122 Hz and second syllables with 133–122, 122–112, 133, 122, and 112 Hz, as well as those with a rise in the first vowel of 141–163 Hz and second syllables of 168–158, 168, and 158 Hz. Eleven subjects who made two or more mistakes—that is, judged stimuli from the first set as rising and stimuli from the second set as falling—were excluded from the subgroup of 14. The smaller number of subjects makes the statistics less reliable; however, the elimination of listeners who were either less careful or less able to judge F_0 movements makes the picture somewhat sharper. The judgments are significant (at the 0.05 level) for 25 subjects when they are either below 7.5 (significant for *rádi*) or above 17.5 (significant for *râdi*). For the subgroup of 14 subjects the corresponding values are 3 or fewer (*rádi*) or 11 or more (*râdi*).

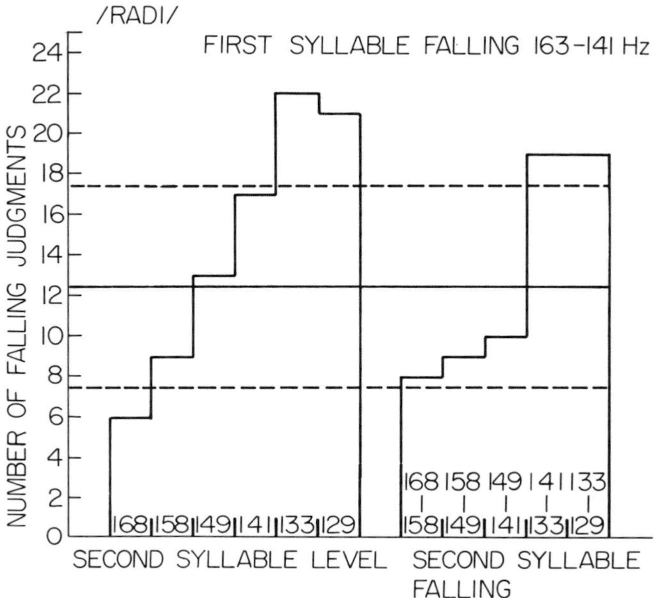

Figure 2.24
Listener judgments of the F_0 contour on *radi* as "falling," when a moderately falling F_0 contour on the first syllable was combined with eleven different second syllable contours. (After Lehiste and Ivić 1972:9.)

The *radi* set was synthesized to represent a continuum of tonal patterns spaced equally between values characteristic of natural productions of words with long falling and rising accents occurring at the peak of the intonation contour in a nonemphatic declarative sentence. It was expected that the listeners would identify the extreme values with "rising" and "falling" accents and that the intermediate values would evoke intermediate responses. In the whole set there was only one case in which perception shifted from "rising" to "falling" (fig. 2.24); in all other cases the shift was between either "rising" or "falling" and random. The case in which the shift was from "rising" to "falling" is, however, singularly unimpressive: it happens to be the clearest case in the whole set of a gradual shifting of judgments rather than a categorical one.

It is interesting to note the frequencies at which the shifts from "falling" or "rising" to random (and vice versa) take place. The results of the listening test make it clear that for this group of listeners the F_0 pattern on the first syllable is not sufficient for identifying the accent. Otherwise, we

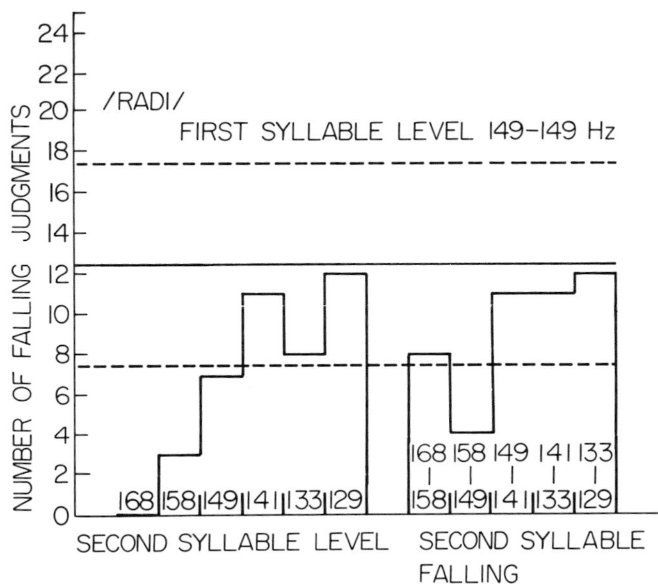

Figure 2.25
Listener judgments of the F_0 contour on *radi* as "falling," when a level F_0 contour on the first syllable was combined with eleven different second syllable contours. (After Lehiste and Ivić 1972:11.)

should have obtained "falling" judgments in all cases in which the first syllable had a falling fundamental frequency. Evidently something additional had to be present before the listeners agreed in their "falling" responses. This additional factor was the fundamental frequency of the second syllable. For a falling first syllable, the second syllable had to reach a fairly low value before the judgments shifted from random to "falling"; in other words, a high fundamental frequency on the second syllable counteracted the fall on the first syllable, with the result that the listeners could not classify the word with any degree of certainty. For significant "rising" judgments with a rising first syllable, the second syllable had to have a frequency that was at least as high as the frequency of the first. It is noteworthy that "rising" judgments were also obtained with a level first syllable when the fundamental frequency on the second syllable was as high as or higher than the level of the first. A rising contour on the accented syllable is thus not a necessary characteristic for the stimulus to be perceived as bearing a rising accent; the necessary characteristic is the F_0

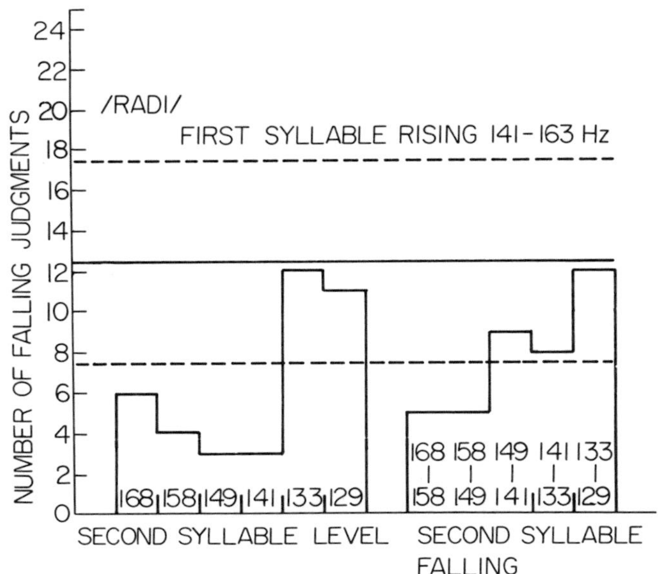

Figure 2.26
Listener judgments of the F_0 contour on *radi* as "falling," when a rising F_0 contour on the first syllable was combined with eleven different second syllable contours. (After Lehiste and Ivić 1972: 12.)

relationship between the accented syllable and the postaccentual syllable. Recall that a high second syllable evoked significant "rising" responses even then the first syllable carried a moderately falling F_0 contour (fig. 2.24).

What emerged from this experiment is a set of identifying features, characteristics that must be present in order to evoke significant agreement among listeners in assigning a stimulus to an accentual category. For the long falling accent these characteristics include a falling fundamental frequency on the first syllable and a second syllable with a fundamental frequency as low as or lower than the terminal frequency of the first syllable. For the long rising accent successful identification presupposes absence of a prominent F_0 fall on the first syllable and a second syllable with a fundamental frequency at least as high as that on the first syllable.

It is thus clear that the patterns extend over two syllables. Within this set of synthesized words, these features seem to distinguish not between two accents (or two words), but rather between the presence and absence of an identifiable accent (between a word and a nonword).

2.9.3 Replication of Experiment 2

The listeners who had participated in the *radi* test were mainly from Vojvodina. In the course of further listening tests (to be described later in this chapter) we found that dialect background played a part in the responses given by listeners to various stimuli. This prompted us to replicate the original *radi* test, using a larger number of subjects and controlling for dialect background.

The same tape that had been used in the original test was employed in the replication tests, which were carried out at the universities and in the Linguistic Institutes of Novi Sad and Belgrade in February and March 1980. Again those subjects were eliminated who made two or more mistakes in identifying the eight extreme stimuli. The subjects whose results were used for the analysis constitute three regional groups: 29 subjects from Vojvodina, 22 subjects from Serbia, and 20 subjects from western (jekavian) dialect areas. The results of the listening tests are presented in table 2.21. Data for listeners from Vojvodina are presented in columns labeled 1, data for listeners from Serbia in columns labeled 2, and data for listeners from western areas in columns labeled 3. The table presents the numbers of "falling" judgmants given by the three groups of listeners to each stimulus.

Let us consider first the subjects from Vojvodina. With 29 subjects the judgments are significant (at the 0.05 level) for "rising" if they number 8 or fewer; they are significant for "falling" if they number 21 or more. In the set of stimuli with a steep fall on the first syllable, subjects made "falling" judgments on the basis of the F_0 pattern on the first vowel when the second syllable had level fundamental frequency, regardless of the frequency value. With a falling second syllable, the three stimuli with relatively high second syllable frequencies received random identifications, but the two lowest second syllable frequencies combined with a steep fall on the first syllable produced significant agreement for "falling."

With a moderate fall on the first syllable, listeners from Vojvodina identified the stimuli as rising as long as the frequency of the second syllable was as high as or higher than the frequency of the first syllable. Intermediate second syllable frequencies produced random identifications; only the lowest level second syllable value produced reliable "falling" responses.

Level and rising first syllables produced significant "rising" responses as long as the second syllable was as high as or higher than the first syllable; with lower second syllables, the judgments became random.

This group of listeners thus behaved basically in the same fashion as the listeners who served in the original experiment. We conclude that for

Table 2.21
Replication of *radi* experiment. Group 1—29 subjects from Vojvodina; group 2—22 subjects from Serbia; group 3—20 subjects from western (jekavian) dialect areas.

		Number of "falling" judgments				Number of "falling" judgments		
V_1	V_2	1	2	3	V_2	1	2	3
183–122	188–168	19	18	20	188	21	19	18
	168–149	21	21	20	168	21	18	19
	149–133	18	19	20	149	27	20	20
	133–122	28	21	19	133	24	20	19
	122–112	29	22	20	122	29	22	20
					112	28	22	19
163–141	168–158	5	13	19	168	6	12	18
	158–149	4	10	17	158	6	13	20
	149–141	7	10	20	149	10	19	19
	141–133	23	20	19	141	17	17	20
	133–129	14	16	16	133	15	17	18
					129	24	19	20
149–149	168–158	2	3	0	168	1	0	3
	158–149	1	2	1	158	5	2	7
	149–141	11	3	3	149	5	4	4
	141–133	9	2	2	141	13	6	0
	133–129	15	6	1	133	14	7	0
					129	11	4	0
141–163	168–158	0	3	1	168	0	3	0
	158–149	9	0	0	158	4	3	0
	149–141	12	5	1	149	8	1	0
	141–133	12	8	0	141	8	0	0
	133–129	11	8	0	133	9	7	1
					129	13	5	1

listeners from Vojvodina the relationship between the F_0 levels of the accented and postaccentual syllables plays a very important role. We note that with this larger set of subjects, a steep fall on the first syllable was not completely sufficient for producing "falling" responses: when the second syllable had a high falling F_0 pattern, listener responses were random. Other contradictory cues, such as a rise on the first syllable combined with a low second syllable, likewise produced random judgments.

Listeners from western dialect areas (columns labeled 3) show a clear-cut pattern. Here, with 20 subjects, the judgments are significant for "rising" when they number 5 or fewer and for "falling" when they number 15 or more. Listeners belonging to this group evidently base their judgments entirely on the F_0 movement within the accented syllable: falling F_0 movements are heard as "falling," and level and rising F_0 movements on the first syllable are assigned to the "rising" category, regardless of the F_0 level on the second syllable.

Listeners from Serbia (columns labeled 2) occupy a middle position between those from Vojvodina and those from western dialect areas. The judgments of the 22 listeners from Serbia are significant for "rising" when they number 5 or fewer and for "falling" when they number 17 or more. Here the judgments were significant for "falling" for all stimuli with a steep fall on the first syllable. With a moderate fall, the judgments were significant for "falling" when the second syllable had a lower frequency than the first; when the second syllable had a higher frequency, the judgments were random. In this respect the subjects from Serbia behaved like those from Vojvodina. Random judgments were also obtained when the first syllable was rising, but the second syllable had a low fundamental frequency. However, with both level and rising first syllables, the judgments tended to go in the "rising" direction, fluctuating between significant for "rising" and random. With respect to this tendency toward "rising" judgments, responses by listeners from Serbia resembled those of listeners from western dialect areas.

2.9.4 Experiment 3

This experiment was designed to test the perceptual relevance of the F_0 patterns that had been observed in productions of disyllabic words with short accents. In the experiment, fundamental frequency was changed gradually from one observed pattern to that of its minimally contrastive counterpart.[8] The technique that was employed in the preparation of the stimuli involves analysis and resynthesis of the speech signal, whereby at the resynthesis stage, any parameter can be changed as desired.[9] For the

Table 2.22
Base forms of stimuli synthesized for testing the perception of short accents. Durations in milliseconds, fundamental frequencies in hertz.

Test words	Dur. of V_1	F_0 on V_1	Position of F_0 peak	Dur. of V_2	F_0 on V_2
mȍstu	160	232–243–208	50	100	158–142
mòstu		198–222–215	140		226–190
sȅdi	160	256–263–243	70	100	196–149
sèdi		190–245–245	160		250–218
sȅlo	180	233–238–204	70	100	156–138
sèlo		199–220–220	160		220–180
nòsi	180	180–222–212	130	90	238–208
nȍsi		190–230–205	90		180–135

purposes of this test, the fundamental frequency was manipulated; all other parameters remained unchanged. The test words were taken from productions by P.I. at an earlier stage of the study. Six minimal pairs were chosen, produced in the frame *Forma . . . data je kao primer*. For three of the test words—dat.sg.masc. *mȍstu* 'bridge'/loc.sg.masc. *mòstu* 'bridge', 2.sg.imper. *sȅdi* 'sit down'/3.sg.pres. *sèdi* 'sits', and past part.nom.sg.neut. *sȅlo* 'sat down'/nom.sg.neut. *sèlo* 'village'—the falling member of the pair constituted the base from which the F_0 modifications started; for the other three test words—3.sg.pres. *nȍsi* 'carries'/2.sg.imper. *nòsi* 'carry', 3 sg.pres. *vȍde* 'leads'/gen.sg.fem. *vòde* 'water', and 3.sg.pres. *mȍli* 'requests'/2.sg.imper. *mòli* 'request'—the base was the production bearing the short rising accent.[10] The starting and terminal values of relevant parameters are given in table 2.22.

In each pair the member that served as basis for the manipulation of fundamental frequency is listed first. All other parameters were kept constant at the values of the original production. Thus, for *mostu* the duration of the first vowel remained constant at 160 msec and that of the second vowel at 100 msec. The base stimulus had an F_0 contour on the first vowel starting at 232 Hz, having a peak value of 243 Hz at a point 50 msec from the beginning of the vowel, and terminating at 208 Hz. The second vowel had an F_0 contour that fell smoothly from 158 to 142 Hz. The values of all these parameters were changed in ten equal steps until the target value for the same word with short rising accent was achieved. This target value was taken from the corresponding production by P.I. at the time the whole set of words had been recorded. (Recall that the words had not been produced one after another as minimal pairs; rather, a large number of test words were recorded in random order, each word being embedded in the basic test frame. The majority of the words were not members of minimal pairs.)

To change the production of *mȍstu* into a production with short rising accent, the beginning F_0 value was changed from 232 Hz to 198 Hz, the peak value was changed from 243 Hz to 222 Hz, and the position of the peak was changed from 50 msec to 140 msec from the beginning of the vowel; the terminal value was changed from 208 Hz to 215 Hz, and the F_0 contour on the second syllable was changed from 158–142 Hz to 226–190 Hz. All changes were made in equal steps. Similar procedures were used in the preparation of test materials involving the other test words. The frames were kept constant from stimulus to stimulus.

A test tape was prepared, in which the test sentences occurred in two blocks with a different permutation in each. There was a seven-second interval between test sentences. Three practice sentences were presented before the start of the test. The listening test was administered to 76 subjects at the Universities of Belgrade and Novi Sad. Of these subjects, 42 were from Vojvodina and thus spoke the same version of standard literary Serbocroatian as P.I., the speaker whose productions formed the basis of the test; 34 had various other backgrounds. The test was administered to small groups of listeners in a quiet environment.

The results of the listening test are presented in table 2.23 and figures 2.27 and 2.28. In the table, listener responses are presented according to stimulus number. In every case stimulus 1 is the contour that is given for the falling accents in table 2.22. It should be remembered that for the first three pairs (*mostu*, *sedi*, *selo*) the synthesis was based on the production with short falling accent. The fundamental frequency was changed in ten steps from the original falling pattern to the rising pattern that occurred in the production of its minimally contrasting partner with short rising accent in the same recording session. For the pair *nosi* the production with the short rising accent constituted the base; the fundamental frequency was changed in ten steps from the original rising pattern to the falling pattern that occurred in the production of its minimally contrasting partner with the short falling accent in the same recording session. In every case all other parameters remained unchanged; for *mostu*, *sedi*, and *selo* these parameters reflect the short falling accent, and for *nosi* they reflect the short rising accent.

A difference between the two groups of listeners emerges from an analysis of the data (table 2.23). Group 1 (listeners from Vojvodina) identified

Table 2.23
Identification of stimuli as bearing the short falling accent by 76 Serbocroatian listeners. Group 1—listeners from Vojvodina (N = 42); Group 2—listeners with other backgrounds (N = 34).

Test word	Group	Stimulus number									
		1	2	3	4	5	6	7	8	9	10
mostu	1	37	40	40	34	37	28	14	5	5	0
	2	34	34	34	28	24	9	2	0	0	0
	Total	71	74	74	62	61	37	16	5	5	0
sedi	1	40	41	36	26	15	12	9	5	7	3
	2	33	30	28	18	10	15	5	2	3	6
	Total	73	71	64	45	25	27	14	7	10	9
selo	1	37	39	40	36	41	34	32	19	10	8
	2	33	32	34	28	27	14	8	5	3	1
	Total	70	71	74	64	68	48	40	24	13	9
nosi	1	26	27	19	12	3	1	0	0	0	2
	2	7	11	1	3	1	0	1	1	1	1
	Total	33	38	20	15	4	1	1	1	1	3

more stimuli as 'falling" than listeners from other regions: of a total of 42 × 40 = 1680 judgments, these listeners chose "falling" in 813 instances, or 48.33%, while Group 2 (listeners from other regions) made 527 "falling" judgments out of 34 × 40 = 1360 instances, or 38.75%. This difference is reflected in the graphs depicting the "falling" judgments of the two groups (figures 2.27 and 2.28). For the three words that started out as falling accents, the graph crosses the 50% line between stimuli 4 and 6 for Group 2, but between stimuli 4 and 8 for Group 1. For the test word that started out as a rising accent, Group 2 listeners heard rising accents throughout; Group 1 listeners heard considerably more falling accents, and the conversion of the F_0 pattern from that of a rising accent to that of a falling accent resulted in shifting the perception from "rising" to random.

The change in fundamental frequency was thus sufficient to turn a short falling accent into a short rising one. The attempt to turn a short rising accent into a short falling one by manipulation of the F_0 pattern was much less successful. We believe that this result may be due to the nature of the synthesized F_0 contours. As table 2.22 indicates, the rising-falling F_0 pattern on the accented syllable nucleus involved a smaller rise and larger fall in the cases of *mȍstu*, *sȅdi*, and *sȅlo*, so that the terminal fall was always unambiguously greater than the initial rise. The production of *nȍsi* by P.I. that had been selected as the target value for the synthesis happened to have a relatively larger rise and smaller fall—a relationship similar to that found

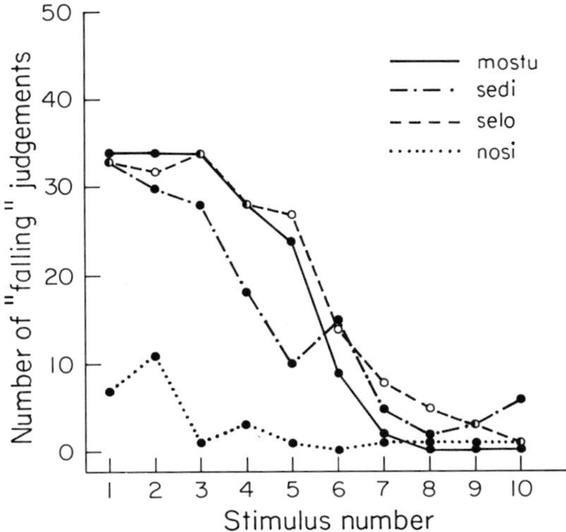

Figure 2.27
"Falling" judgments of 40 synthetic tokens made by 42 listeners from Vojvodina

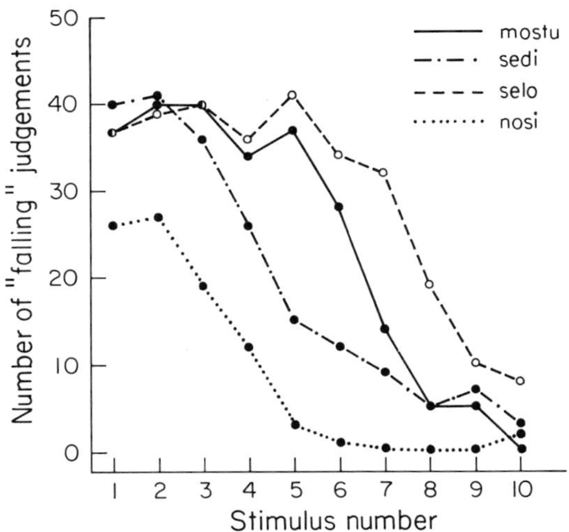

Figure 2.28
"Falling" judgments of 40 synthetic tokens made by 34 listeners from Serbia and western areas of Yugoslavia

in his production of *nòsi*. In addition, the falling interval between the peaks of the two syllables of this production of *nȍsi* was smaller than in other examples, and, on the other hand, both the intrasyllabic and the intersyllabic F_0 relationships in *nòsi* were strongly rising, more so than in the examples *mòstu*, *sèdi*, and *sèlo* used in the same test. The internal structure of the synthesized F_0 contours thus remained to a large extent characteristic of *nòsi* for all stimuli. At the time this experiment was designed, the results of the replication of Experiment 1 were not available to us, and we were therefore not alerted to the possible ambiguity in the stimulus. (Individual productions may, of course, vary within a certain range, and this production by P.I. had been identified by him in a previous listening test as an acceptable production of the word with a short falling accent.)

The difference between listeners from Vojvodina and listeners from other regions was particularly noticeable in their reactions to the stimuli bearing successive approximations to the short falling accent: the number of "falling" responses by the Vojvodinians was much greater than that of the other group at the "falling" end of the continuum, even though it did not reach significance. We believe that they were influenced by the relatively long (180 msec) duration of the first vowel of the stimulus. One of the characteristics of the northeastern dialect is the greater duration of the vowel under ` in comparison with ̏, which causes the perceptual boundary between short and long vowels to lie at a considerably larger value for rising accents than for falling accents (see section 2.9.6, Experiment 5). The length of the vowel of the first syllable provided a clue for `, whereas the low F_0 value of the second syllable provided a clue for ̏; this, in our opinion, caused the responses to the stimuli at the ̏ end to remain within the random range.

As for the subjects from the other areas, their judgments appear to have been more strongly determined by the prominent initial F_0 rise and the relatively smaller fall within the accented syllable nucleus than by the low frequency of the second syllable: they made prevailingly "rising" judgments for the whole set of stimuli. We offer the above suggestions with caution, bearing in mind the considerable variability in the production of short accented syllable nuclei by our group of twelve speakers reported in section 2.2.

A second possible reason for the failure of F_0 change alone to turn a rising accent into a falling one is the possibility that words originally produced with falling accents have some additional phonetic characteristics that do not occur in words with rising accents. We hypothesized that this might be intensity. Although intensity differences did not play a systematic role in distinguishing between rising and falling accents in the speech of this informant (P.I.), we had found that approximately half of our subjects whose speech we had analyzed earlier (Lehiste and Ivić 1963:71) always had a lower intensity on posttonic syllables after falling accents than they did after rising accents. This particular production of *nòsi* by P.I. had a peak value of 42 dB on the first syllable and 39 dB on the second syllable. Because of the different intrinsic intensities of /o/ and /i/, the difference is negligible. Conceivably, the absence of a larger intensity drop may have prevented some of the listeners from positive identification of the stimuli as falling accents. The intensity pattern present on this word certainly did not influence the subjects in the direction of "falling" identification.

A third possible reason is regional differences in the perception of accents. Most of our studies had involved subjects with Vojvodinian background. It may well be that the same phonetic parameters receive different interpretations depending on the dialectal background of the listeners.

2.9.5 Experiment 4

To investigate these new hypotheses, we prepared another listening test, using shorter syllable nuclei that would be appropriate for both short rising and short falling accents, averaged F_0 curves, and manipulation of intensity as well as fundamental frequency. We also decided to specify more precisely the dialectal background of the listeners.

The stimuli synthesized for Experiment 4 consisted of various manipulations of the test word *vode*. The synthesis was performed at the Experimental Psychology Laboratory of the University of Indiana in Bloomington.[11]

The segmental structure of the test word was based on a production by P.I. The suprasegmental structure was set to vary between two prototypical patterns provided by the average values found in disyllabic words with short falling and short rising accents on the first syllable, produced by P.I. The duration of the first vowel was kept constant at 140 msec; that of the second vowel was constant at 120 msec. This duration is longer by approximately 20 msec than the average value, but the averages had been calculated on the basis of words occurring in the middle of a frame sentence, whereas the test words of the present experiment were to be presented in isolation, without a frame. The small amount of preboundary lengthening (20 msec) that was added to the second vowel improved the naturalness of the stimuli.

The manipulations of fundamental frequency and intensity are summarized in table 2.24. The dimensions that were manipulated include F_0

Table 2.24
Manipulations of F_0 contours and intensity patterns of the test word *vode*. Fundamental frequencies in hertz, intensity differences in decibels. Position of F_0 peak in milliseconds from the beginning of the syllable nucleus.

		First vowel				Second vowel		Intensity difference between
Block	Item	Beg.	F_0 peak at	Peak	End	Beg.	End	V_1 and V_2
1	1	227	70	245	226	185	149	
	2	222	90	242	226	185	149	
	3	217	110	239	226	185	149	
	4	213	120	236	227	185	149	
	5	209	130	233	227	185	149	
2	6	227	70	245	226	237	198	
	7	222	90	242	226	237	198	
	8	217	110	239	226	237	198	
	9	213	120	236	227	237	198	
	10	209	130	233	227	237	198	
3	11	227	70	245	226	185	149	
	12	227	70	245	226	198	161	
	13	227	70	245	226	211	173	
	14	227	70	245	226	224	185	
	15	227	70	245	226	237	198	
4	16	209	130	233	227	185	149	
	17	209	130	233	227	198	161	
	18	209	130	233	227	211	173	
	19	209	130	233	227	224	185	
	20	209	130	233	227	237	198	
5	21	227	70	245	226	185	149	−10
	22	227	70	245	226	198	161	−7
	23	227	70	245	226	211	173	−4
	24	227	70	245	226	224	185	−1
	25	227	70	245	226	237	198	+2
6	26	209	130	233	227	185	149	−10
	27	209	130	233	227	198	161	−7
	28	209	130	233	227	211	173	−4
	29	209	130	233	227	224	185	−1
	30	209	130	233	227	237	198	+2

contour on the first vowel, F_0 contour on the second vowel, position of the peak of the F_0 contour on the first vowel, and the intensity ratio between the first and second vowels. The stimuli consisted of six blocks of five items each. The basic short falling pattern appeared on stimulus 1. The stimulus had an F_0 contour of 227–245–226 Hz on the first vowel and an F_0 contour of 185–149 Hz on the second vowel. The peak of the F_0 contour of the first vowel appeared at 70 msec, that is, in the middle of the 140 msec long vowel. This is the position in which the average peak was found in natural productions of the disyllabic ˵ ˘ pattern. The intensities of the two vowels were adjusted to be equal; the reference points were the middle of V_1 and the first third of V_2. The test word *vode* had been selected partly because the intrinsic intensities of the two vowels are approximately equal, and intensity could therefore be controlled without introducing additional distortion.

The basic short rising pattern had an F_0 contour of 209–233–227 Hz on the first vowel, with the F_0 peak at 130 msec (close to the end of the 140 msec long vowel), and an F_0 contour of 237–198 Hz on the second vowel. These values, too, represent the averages found for this word type (` ˘) in productions by P.I. Stimulus 10 represents this basic pattern. The intensities of the two vowels were again adjusted to be equal. This applies in general to the twenty stimuli contained in the first four blocks.

In blocks 1 and 2 the F_0 contour on the first vowel was changed from the contour appropriate for the falling pattern to the contour appropriate for the rising pattern. Both the actual F_0 values and the position of the peak were changed in five steps. In block 1 (stimuli 1–5) the second syllable was kept constant at the value appropriate for the falling pattern; in block 2 (stimuli 6–10) the fundamental frequency on the second vowel was kept constant at the value appropriate for the rising pattern.

In block 3 (stimuli 11–15) the fundamental frequency on the first vowel was kept constant at the value appropriate for the falling pattern, while the fundamental frequency of the second vowel was changed, in five steps, from that appropriate for the falling pattern to that appropriate for the rising pattern. In block 4 (stimuli 16–20) the fundamental frequency of the first vowel was kept constant at the value appropriate for the rising pattern, while the fundamental frequency of the second vowel was changed in the same manner as in block 3.

Blocks 5 and 6 are identical with blocks 3 and 4 except for intensity, which changes in 3 dB steps from −10 to +2, in parallel with the change of the F_0 contour on V_2 from the contour appropriate for ˵ ˘ to the contour appropriate for ` ˘. We hypothesized that the intensity drop of −10 dB should enhance the falling accent cues already present in the F_0 pattern, and that the intensity rise of +2 dB might constitute an additional cue for positive identification of a rising pattern.

Five different randomizations were prepared of the 30 stimuli. The onset of each randomized set of 30 stimuli was signaled by 500 msec tone bursts; the number of tone bursts indicated the order number of the set. The listeners were thus able to catch up with the test in case they made an error in any of the sets. A pause of five seconds separated the stimuli within each randomized set. The task of the listeners was a linguistic one: to identify the stimulus word *vode* either as gen.sg.fem. or as nom.pl.fem., corresponding to the short rising accent and the short falling accent, respectively.

The listening test was administered in Belgrade on two occasions (March 19 and March 23, 1981) to eleven subjects on the first occasion and five subjects on the second occasion. Four of the subjects took the test twice. One of the subjects produced only 3, and another only 2, usable sets of responses. Since four subjects produced 10 responses per stimulus, five produced 5 responses per stimulus, one produced 3, and one 2, there were 70 responses per stimulus, for a total of 2100 responses.

Table 2.25 presents the results in terms of "falling" judgments. The listeners have been divided into three groups on the basis of the patterns that became apparent in their responses. The dialectal background of the subjects seems to have had a decisive influence in almost all instances. Figure 2.29 indicates the birthplace and original family residences of the subjects. We will refer to this information during the discussion.

Group 1 shows a sharp contrast between blocks 1 and 2. Recall that block 1 had a varying F_0 contour on the first syllable and low F_0 on the second syllable. The judgments of subjects in Group 1 appear to have been consistently based on the F_0 relationships between the two syllables: the stimuli of block 1 are all assigned to the short falling category, regardless of the change introduced in the F_0 contour and in the position of the F_0 peak.

Likewise systematically assign Group 1 listeners the stimuli of block 2 to the short rising category regardless of the F_0 pattern on the first syllable. The only difference between blocks 1 and 2 is the fundamental frequency on the second syllable, which is appropriate for the rising pattern in block 2. For this group of subjects, the F_0 movement and position of the peak in the accented syllable plays no role; the relationship between the F_0 patterns on the two syllables is decisive.

This observation is reinforced by the responses of the subjects to stimuli in blocks 3 and 4. In block 3 the first vowel carries an optimal falling pattern, and this is what the subjects perceive as long as the changing fundamental frequency in the second syllable is appropriate for the falling

Table 2.25
Listener responses to *vode* stimuli, expressed as number of "falling" judgments. Eleven subjects combined into three groups. NR = number of responses per subject.

Stimulus block	Stimulus number	Group 1				Group 2				Group 3					
		M.S.	P.I.	E.F.	Total	Lj.L.	V.B.	V.P.	Total	S.R.	D.C.	P.S.	S.S.	M.N.	Total
NR		10	10	5	25	5	5	10	20	10	5	5	3	2	25
1	1	10	10	5	25	5	5	10	20	10	5	5	3	2	25
	2	10	10	5	25	5	5	10	20	8	5	5	3	2	23
	3	10	10	4	24	5	5	8	18	1	3	1	1	1	7
	4	10	10	3	23	5	2	2	9	1	1	0	1	2	5
	5	9	10	4	23	2	5	4	11	0	0	0	1	0	1
					120				**78**						**61**
2	6	0	0	0	0	3	5	6	14	10	5	0	3	2	20
	7	2	0	0	2	0	4	1	5	5	2	0	3	2	12
	8	0	0	0	0	0	1	0	1	0	1	0	0	0	1
	9	0	0	0	0	0	0	0	0	0	0	0	0	0	0
	10	0	0	0	0	0	0	0	0	0	0	0	0	0	0
					2				**20**						**33**
3	11	10	10	5	25	5	5	9	19	10	5	5	3	2	25
	12	10	10	4	24	4	5	8	17	10	5	5	3	2	25
	13	10	10	2	22	5	5	9	19	10	5	5	3	2	25
	14	8	2	1	11	5	5	7	17	10	5	1	3	2	21
	15	2	0	0	2	3	5	9	17	9	5	1	3	2	20
					84				**89**						**116**

Table 2.25 (continued)

Stimulus block	Stimulus number	Group 1				Group 2				Group 3					
		M.S.	P.I.	E.F.	Total	Lj.L.	V.B.	V.P.	Total	S.R.	D.C.	P.S.	S.S.	M.N.	Total
4	16	10	10	5	25	4	3	5	12	2	1	0	1	0	4
	17	9	10	4	23	2	2	1	5	0	1	0	1	0	2
	18	1	2	3	6	2	2	0	4	0	0	0	0	0	0
	19	0	0	0	0	0	0	0	0	0	0	0	0	0	0
	20	0	0	0	0	0	1	0	1	0	0	0	0	0	0
					54				**22**						**6**
5	21	10	10	5	25	5	5	10	20	10	5	5	3	2	25
	22	10	10	2	22	5	5	10	20	10	5	5	3	2	25
	23	10	10	2	22	4	5	9	18	10	5	5	3	2	25
	24	9	5	0	14	4	4	9	17	10	5	3	3	2	23
	25	1	0	0	1	3	4	7	14	10	5	0	3	2	20
					84				**89**						**118**
6	26	10	10	3	23	5	4	1	10	1	0	0	0	1	2
	27	9	9	2	20	3	4	0	7	0	3	0	1	0	4
	28	3	4	2	9	1	0	0	1	0	2	0	1	0	3
	29	0	0	0	0	0	0	0	0	0	0	0	0	0	0
	30	0	0	0	0	0	1	0	1	0	0	0	0	0	0
					52				**19**						**9**

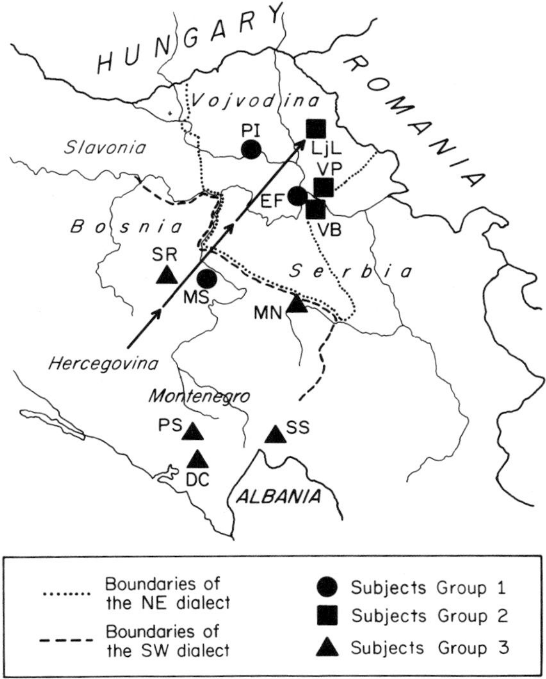

Figure 2.29
Birthplace and original family residence of subjects participating in Experiment 4

pattern (stimuli 11–13). They switch to perceiving the rising pattern when the second vowel acquires the F_0 level appropriate for the rising pattern (stimuli 14–15). The crossover point differs for the three subjects, but the pattern of responses is the same. Likewise, in block 4 these listeners hear the falling accent as long as the F_0 level of the second vowel is appropriate for the falling pattern (stimuli 16–17), even though the first vowel carries an optimal "rising" contour, and they switch to perceiving the rising pattern when the F_0 level of the second syllable reaches the appropriate value for "rising" (stimuli 18–20). A comparison of blocks 3 and 4 with blocks 5 and 6 shows that intensity had no influence on their decision: the falling pattern was positively identified both when the vowels had the same intensity (stimulus 11) and when the second vowel was lower by 10 dB (stimulus 21). Optimal perception of the rising pattern was likewise achieved both with and without the 2 dB intensity rise provided in stimulus 30 (as compared to stimulus 20). Blocks 3 and 5, on the one hand, and 4 and 6, on the other hand, will be treated together from now on.

Group 3 listeners exhibit behavior that is in many respects the opposite of that of Group 1 listeners, and Group 2 listeners occupy an intermediate position. Group 3 will be discussed next.

The members of this group based their judgments primarily on the F_0 contour of the first vowel. Thus, in block 1 they showed an almost categorical shift between perceiving ˵ ˘ and perceiving ` ˘ when the $F_0$ peak shifted into the last quarter of the first vowel and the $F_0$ contour thus became rising (stimuli 3–5). In block 2 four of the five subjects displayed a similar categorical shift from perceiving ˵ ˘ to perceiving ` ˘ (stimuli 8–10). It should be noted that the F_0 level of the second vowel did not affect their judgments in these instances: they assigned stimuli 3–5 to the short rising pattern regardless of the low frequency of the second vowel, and they assigned stimuli 6–7 to the short falling pattern in spite of the contradictory cue provided by the high fundamental frequency of the second vowel (although the crossover from ˵ ˘ to ` ˘ occurred earlier in block 2). One of the subjects (P.S.) differed from this pattern in a systematic way: he assigned all stimuli without exception to the rising pattern either when the second syllable carried high fundamental frequency (block 2) or when the first syllable carried a rising F_0 contour (blocks 4 and 6). He assigned stimuli with changing fundamental frequency on the first syllable to the falling category when two conditions were present: fundamental frequency on the accented syllable was appropriate for ˵˘, and fundamental frequency on the second syllable was relatively low (stimuli 1–2, 11–13, 21–23).

Blocks 3 and 4 have fixed F_0 patterns on the first vowel and changing F_0 patterns on the second vowel. With the exception of subject P.S., the listeners in Group 3 again based their judgments on the first vowel, assigning the stimuli of block 3 to ˵ ˘ and the stimuli of block 4 to ` ˘. Blocks 5 and 6 replicate the response patterns observed in blocks 3 and 4. This indicates that for these subjects, too, identification was achieved without any necessary contribution from intensity.

The listeners we have assigned to Group 2 appear less certain in evaluating the relative importance of the cues. Their responses to block 1 stimuli (changing fundamental frequency on the first vowel, low fundamental frequency on the second vowel) show positive identification of ˵ ˘ when both syllables carry F_0 contours appropriate for ˵ ˘ (stimuli 1–3). These subjects evidently require the presence of both cues (some individual differences will be discussed below); their responses to stimuli 4–5, in which the two cues contradict each other, suggest that they are simply guessing.

Compare this with the subjects in Group 1, who perceived these stimuli unambiguously as ̏ ˘, and with the subjects in Group 3, who perceived them just as unambiguously as ̀ ˘.

The responses of subjects in Group 2 to block 2 stimuli (changing fundamental frequency on the first vowel, high fundamental frequency on the second vowel) reinforce the finding that both cues are required for firm identification of the accentual pattern: stimuli 8–10 are positively identified as ̀ ˘, whereas the responses to stimuli 6–7 include a fair (but nonsignificant) number of "falling" judgments.

In blocks 3 and 5 (first vowel carrying an F_0 contour appropriate for ̏ ˘, second vowel carrying a changing F_0 contour) these listeners perceive ̏ ˘, but the certainty of their identification of ̏ ˘ decreases as the fundamental frequency of the second vowel acquires higher values and the cues thus gradually become contradictory. Stimuli 11 and 21 are identified as ̏ ˘ in 98% of the instances, but stimuli 15 and 25 receive only 78% ̏ ˘ identifications. Recall that subjects in Group 1 showed a categorical shift from ̏ ˘ to ̀ ˘ depending on the change in the second vowel from an F_0 level appropriate for ̏ ˘ to one appropriate for ̀ ˘; they identified stimuli 11 and 21 in 100% of the cases as ̏ ˘, and stimuli 15 and 25 in 94% of the cases as ̀ ˘. On the other hand, the subjects in Group 3 responded very much like the subjects in Group 2: stimuli 11 and 21 evoked 100% identification of ̏ ˘, and stimuli 15 and 25 evoked 80% identification of ̏ ˘.

In blocks 4 and 6 (first vowel carrying an F_0 pattern appropriate for ̀ ˘, second vowel carrying a changing F_0 contour) listeners in Group 2 changed from positive identification of ̀ ˘ (95% for items 20 and 30) to considerably less certain identification of ̀ ˘ when the second syllable carried a contradictory F_0 cue (45% for items 16 and 26). Recall that listeners in Group 1 had a categorical shift from perceiving ̏ ˘ (98% identifications for items 16 and 26) to perceiving ̀ ˘ (100% identifications for items 20 and 30). The subjects in Group 3, on the other hand, based their judgments entirely on the F_0 contour of the first syllable (appropriate for ̀ ˘): their perception of ̀ ˘ for items 16 and 26 was 88%, and for items 20 and 30, 100%.

Certain individual differences between subjects are worth observing. Subject P.S. of Group 3 has already been discussed. Subject V.B. (Group 2) appears to base his identifications of ̏ ˘ more on the F_0 contour of the first syllable than his identifications of ̀ ˘: in blocks 3 and 5, with fundamental frequency appropriate for ̏ ˘, he gives 48 (out of 50) ̏ ˘ responses, or 96%, whereas in blocks 4 and 6, with fundamental frequency on the first syllable appropriate for ̀ ˘, he gives only 33 ̀ ˘ responses, or 66%. He also identifies items 6 and 7 (block 2) positively as ̏ ˘. This pattern of responses resembles that of Group 3. On the other hand, he also identifies items 26 and 27 positively as ̏ ˘; in this his responses resemble those of Group 1. It is certainly justifiable to consider V.B.'s pattern of responses to be transitional between the patterns of Groups 1 and 3. Consideration of the geographical origin of the speakers belonging to the different groups sheds some light on the patterning of their responses.

The geographical distribution of the subjects is shown in figure 2.29. In general, the grouping based on response patterns appears to correlate fairly well with this distribution. The subjects in Group 1 come from the northeast (mainly from Vojvodina), those in Group 3 from the southwest, and those in the transitional Group 2 from the central region. Subject M.S. might have been expected to belong to Group 3, and he is indeed the least typical member of Group 1. Subject Lj.L. might have been expected to belong to Group 1; her family, however, had moved to their present residence from a territory in which western Štokavian dialects are spoken (territory of subjects in Group 3), and her responses may reflect some dialect mixture.

The results of this test thus show that the relative importance of prosodic characteristics in the perception of short accents depends on regional factors. In the territory in which the subjects in Group 1 are at home, the F_0 relationship between the first and second vowels is crucial for the distinction between short falling and short rising accents. In the home territory of subjects in Group 3, F_0 movement on the accented syllable is the decisive factor. Transitional between the two is the territory of subjects in Group 2: here both cues must be present before positive identification of ̏ ˘ and ̀ ˘ is made. Intensity plays no role in achieving this positive identification.

2.9.6 Experiment 5

A separate set of experiments was conducted to explore the perception of quantity and the interaction between tone and quantity. Traditionally, tone and quantity have been considered independent, and, looking only at overall averages, the data we had accumulated seemed to support this view. However, upon a closer analysis of word pairs with minimally different accentual patterns, it emerged that vowels bearing the short rising accent were longer than vowels bearing the short falling accent, all other factors being kept constant. There also appeared to be a difference in the durations of the two long accents, as well as a greater amount of overlap in the durations of short and long rising syllable nuclei than in the durations of short and long falling syllable nuclei. These observations suggested that the

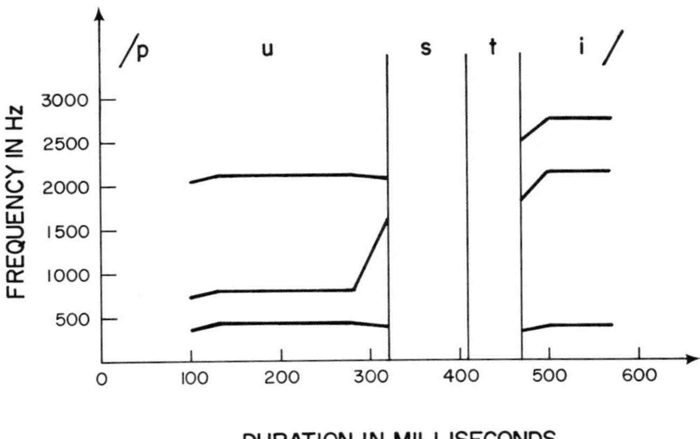

Figure 2.30
Schematic representation of the formant frequencies and temporal structure of the synthesized test word *pusti*. (After Lehiste and Ivić 1973b: 183.)

maintenance of the length opposition could be different for the two accent types. A perceptual test was designed to investigate this hypothesis.[12]

The test materials consisted of synthesized versions of the test word *pusti*. This sequence of phonemes may have four meanings, depending on the type of accent. *Pȕsti*, with a short falling accent, is the 3.sg.pres.ind. form of the verb *pùstiti* 'to leave, quit, relinquish'; *pùsti*, with a short rising accent, is the 2.sg.imper. of the same verb; *pûsti*, with a long falling accent, is the nom.sg.masc. of the definite form of the adjective *pûst* 'waste, deserted'; and *pústi*, with a long rising accent, is the nom.sg.masc. of the indefinite form of the same adjective. The synthesis was performed on the JAWORD synthesizer at the phonetics laboratory at the Department of Linguistics of the Ohio State University. The JAWORD synthesizer, a parallel resonance synthesizer, was controlled by a PDP-10 computer. A schematic representation of the formant frequencies and temporal structure of the test word is given in figure 2.30 (Lehiste and Ivić 1973b: 183, figure 1).

The figure shows a version of *pusti* with a first vowel duration of 220 msec; the duration of /s/ was 80 msec, that of /t/ 60 msec, and that of the second vowel 100 msec. In producing the test stimuli, the duration of the steady state of the first vowel was changed in 10 msec steps; all other parameters were kept constant. The overall duration of the vowel /u/ ranged from 120 msec to 240 msec, for a total of 13 different durations.

Three different F_0 patterns were used in the synthesis. The first set of 13

Table 2.26
Fundamental frequencies and durations used in synthesizing *pusti* stimuli. Durations in milliseconds, fundamental frequencies in hertz. (After Lehiste and Ivić 1973: 184.)

Duration of /u/	F_0 on first vowel			F_0 on second vowel		
	Beg.	Peak	End	Beg.	Peak	End
120	210	240	220	190		157
130	210	240	210	190		157
140	210	240	200	190		157
150	210	240	195	190		157
160	210	240	190	185		157
170	210	240	185	180		157
180	210	240	180	175		157
190	210	240	175	170		157
200	210	240	170	167		157
210	210	240	167	163		157
220	210	240	163	160		157
230	210	240	160	157		157
240	210	240	157	157		157

stimuli was synthesized on a monotone: fundamental frequency was kept constant at 100 Hz on both syllables. The second set of 13 stimuli was synthesized with rising tone: fundamental frequency rose smoothly from 210 Hz to 240 Hz on the first syllable, and fell from 240 Hz to 200 Hz on the second syllable. The third set of 13 stimuli was synthesized with a falling tone: the fundamental frequency of each stimulus started at 210 Hz, rose to a peak of 240 Hz at a distance of 50 msec from the beginning of the first vowel, and then dropped to a value that decreased with increasing length of the syllable nucleus. The beginning frequency of the second syllable was always one step lower than the ending frequency of the first syllable. All final syllables ended at a frequency of 157 Hz. The precise values are given in table 2.26 (Lehiste and Ivić 1973b: 184, table 1).

A listening test was prepared in which the 39 stimuli appeared twice in random order. The listening test was presented to eighteen listeners in Novi Sad. The task of the listeners was to identify each stimulus as either a form of the verb *pustiti* (which would entail judging the duration of the first vowel to be short) or form of the adjective *pust* (which would entail judging the duration of this vowel to be long).

Two of the listeners had to be eliminated because they failed to provide

Table 2.27
Number of "short" judgments made by twelve subjects listening twice to *pusti* stimuli. Durations in milliseconds. N = 24. (After Lehiste and Ivić 1973: 186.)

Duration of /u/	Number of "short" responses			
	Monotone	Falling	Rising	Total
120	21	23	23	67
130	20	20	23	63
140	20	15	20	55
150	4	9	17	30
160	4	10	12	26
170	4	8	10	22
180	5	5	12	22
190	1	2	3	6
200	1	4	4	9
210	1	3	2	6
220	0	1	3	4
230	0	1	1	2
240	0	1	2	3
Total	81	102	132	315

responses to some of the stimuli. The responses of the remaining sixteen listeners were checked for reliability by the following procedure. All responses to the shortest and longest stimuli (vowel durations of 120, 230, and 240 msec) were noted. Eighteen responses for each listener fell into this group of extreme values (3 durations × 3 tonal patterns, each occurring twice in the listening test). Listeners who made more than 4 errors out of 18 in identifying these stimuli were eliminated. This screening resulted in the exclusion of four additional listeners. The remaining group of twelve listeners consisted of three linguists who are (or were at the time) faculty members of the Department of Serbocroatian Language and Literature at the University of Novi Sad, and nine students from the same department.

The results of the listening test are presented in tables 2.27 and 2.28 and in figure 2.31 (Lehiste and Ivić 1973b: 186, table 2; 187, table 3; 185, figure 2). Table 2.27 shows the number of "short" responses, presented separately for each F_0 pattern. ("Short" responses mean that the listeners identified the stimulus as a form of the verb *pustiti.*) Each stimulus occurred twice in the listening test taken by these twelve subjects; thus, the maximum number of possible "short" responses is 24. The number of "long" responses is equal to the difference between the given number and 24.

Table 2.28
Number of "short" judgments made by twelve subjects listening twice to *pusti* stimuli, presented separately for each subject. F = falling F_0 contour, L = level F_0 contour, R = rising F_0 contour. Durations in milliseconds. (After Lehiste and Ivić 1973: 187.)

Speaker	F_0 contour	Duration of /u/													Total in each category	Overall total
		120	130	140	150	160	170	180	190	200	210	220	230	240		
AM	F	2	1	1											4	
	L	2	2	2											6	
	R	1	1												2	12
DP	F	2	2	1	1										6	
	L	2	2	2			1	1							8	
	R	2	2	2	1		1	1					1		10	24
PI	F	2	2												4	
	L	2	2	2											6	
	R	2	2	1	2	1									8	18
1	F	2	2	2											6	
	L	2	1	2		1									6	
	R	2	2	2						1					7	19
2	F	2	2	1		1									6	
	L	1	1	1											3	
	R	2	2	2	2			1						1	10	19
3	F	2	2	2	2	1		1	1						11	
	L	2	1	1							1				5	
	R	2	2	1	1			1							7	23
5	F	1	1	1		1	2	2	1	1					10	
	L	2	2	1		1	1	1	1						9	
	R	2	2	2	2	1	2	2	1	1	1	2		1	19	38

6	F	2	2	2	1	2	2			1	1	1	1	1	16	
	L	1	1	2											4	
	R	2	2	2	2	2	2	2	1		1	1			17	37
8	F	2		1	1	1									5	
	L	1	2	2		1		1							7	
	R	2	2	2	2	2		1							11	23
9	F	2	2								1				5	
	L	2	2	2											6	
	R	2	2	2	2	2	1	1							12	23
10	F	2	2	2	2	2	2	2		1	1				16	
	L	2	2	2	2	1	1	1		1					12	
	R	2	2	2	2	2	2	1	1	1					15	43
11	F	2	2	2	2	2	2			1					13	
	L	2	2	1	2		1	1							9	
	R	2	2	2	1	2	2	2		1					14	36
Total in each category	F	23	20	15	9	10	8	5	2	4	3	1	1	1	102	
	L	21	20	20	4	4	4	5	1	1	1	0	0	0	81	
	R	23	23	20	17	12	10	12	3	4	2	3	1	2	132	
Overall total		67	63	55	30	26	22	22	6	9	6	4	2	3	315	

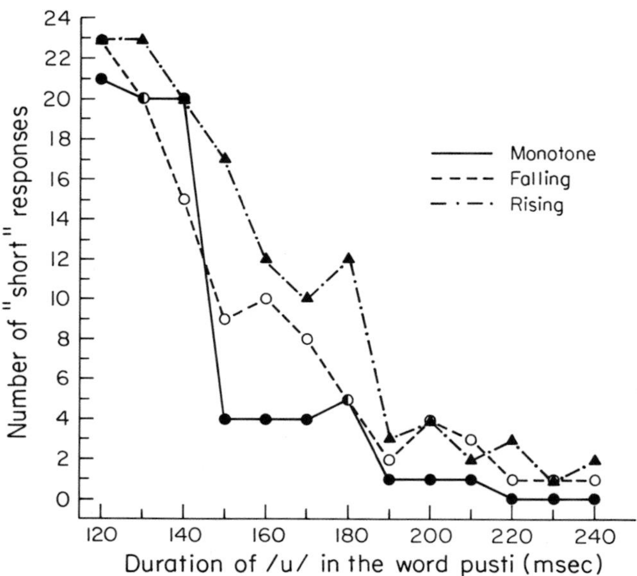

Figure 2.31
Listener responses to the test word *pusti* synthesized with different accentual patterns. (After Lehiste and Ivić 1973b: 185.)

The same material is presented graphically in figure 2.31. The graph shows the number of "short" responses, displayed as a function of the duration of /u/. Points that fall above 16.9 or below 7.1 are significantly different from chance (at the 0.05 confidence level).

A study of table 2.27 and figure 2.31 reveals that monotone intonation was accompanied by the clearest perception of quantity differences; the perception is obviously categorical, since a change in duration from 140 msec to 150 msec produced an abrupt shift from the "short" to the "long" category. The boundary between the two categories appears to fall at 145 msec.

With both rising and falling accents, there is a region of uncertainty during which the points representing listener responses fall in the random region. With falling fundamental frequency durations of 120 and 130 msec were perceived as short, durations between 140 and 170 msec produced random judgments, and durations above 180 msec were perceived as long. The crossover point between the two categories is identical with the crossover point for monotone intonation (145 msec), but the extended region of random judgments makes this value less reliable. With rising fundamental frequency, values of 120, 130, and 140 msec were reliably judged as short, and 150 msec fell just on the borderline of statistical significance. Durations between 160 and 180 msec produced random responses; durations longer than 180 msec were reliably judged as long. The crossover point between the two categories appears to fall at 170 msec.

The overall results of the listening test indicated that to a certain extent, the assignment of "long" and "short" responses depends on the tonal pattern. In the crucial region (between 140 and 180 msec) the same durations are more likely to be assigned to the "short" category when the word has a rising accent than when the word has either a monotone fundamental frequency or a falling accent. Conversely, durations that are already judged as long with monotone or falling fundamental frequency may still be perceived as short when they have a rising accent. It is interesting that stimuli with a monotone F_0 pattern do not behave in the same way as stimuli with a rising F_0 movement. In earlier literature, monotone has been treated as a possible way of realizing the rising accent, and in our experiments with *radi*, stimuli produced on a monotone were identified as carrying a long rising accent when the postaccentual syllable had a higher fundamental frequency than the first syllable.

The extensive area of random responses prompted us to study the responses of each listener separately, to establish whether the random patterns recurred in the test materials of all listeners or whether the results were due to grouping together different responses from individuals who might nevertheless have clearly distinguished between the two categories, but placed the boundaries at different durations. Table 2.28 presents the responses of all listeners separately.

A study of the table reveals a considerable amount of individual difference. Subjects 5 and 6 seem to have made largely random judgments, even though they had passed our screening. Subjects A.M., D.P., P.I., and 1 have fairly consistent boundaries between short and long categories, as do several of the other subjects. For example, subject 2 has a higher perceptual boundary between short and long categories with rising accent than with either monotone or falling accent. With subject 3, the picture is reversed. Subject 8 has a higher boundary between short and long rising accents than is the case with either a falling or a monotone F_0 pattern. Subject 9 is particularly interesting: with a low crossover value for falling fundamental frequency and an only slightly higher crossover value for monotone stimuli, this subject has a relatively large crossover value for rising stimuli. Subjects 10 and 11 are characterized by little difference between accent types, but the highest overall crossover values between "long" and "short" responses.

These patterns become more meaningful when the dialect background of the listeners is taken into account. The dialect of Vojvodina is characterized by a relatively longer duration of short rising accents (Ivić 1949–50: 143). Nine of the twelve listeners are natives of Vojvodina; three come from other regions (A.M., D.P., and 1). The average numbers of "short" responses for the two groups show a considerable difference: with falling fundamental frequency non-Vojvodina listeners gave 5.3 "short" responses, with monotone stimuli 6.7 "short" responses, and with rising stimuli 6.3 "short" responses. The corresponding average scores for Vojvodina listeners were 9.6, 6.8, and 12.6, respectively. This indicates that the Vojvodina listeners were much more inclined to judge the stimuli as short, especially in the rising category. (The importance of the F_0 pattern in producing these results becomes obvious from the fact that with monotone fundamental frequency there was no difference between the two groups.) Translated into crossover points, the boundary between short and long falling accents occurred at 142 msec and the boundary between short and long rising accents at 147 msec for non-Vojvodina listeners; for listeners from Vojvodina the corresponding boundaries were at 163 and 178 msec.

The listeners from Vojvodina thus placed the perceptual boundary between short and long accents at a considerably higher value. They also showed a difference between falling and rising accents: rising accents had a higher boundary value. Thus, the differences that had been observed in production were also confirmed for perception. The results reinforce the earlier conclusion that regional differences must be taken into account in describing the phonetic realization of prosodic structure.

2.10 Experimental Research Concerning Word Tone by Other Scholars

In this section we will review experimental phonetic investigations of the production and perception of Serbocroatian accents by other scholars during the time span covered by our research, as well as some earlier work. In a number of cases these investigations have used our research as a point of reference. Advances in scholarship are often achieved in the course of a dialogue; a scientific discovery can best be understood in the context of this dialogue. This is the primary reason why we sometimes draw parallels between the reviewed studies and the stage our own investigations had reached at the time those studies were published. In our own research we have gone through a number of stages in the evaluation of our experimental data and in setting up and testing new hypotheses. Some of our earlier interpretations now appear to us less convincing; in this book we are offering the interpretation that appears to us most satisfactory in light of the experience we have accumulated in the past twenty years. In this review we sometimes criticize others' results from the point of view of our present knowledge; we are fully aware of the fact that some of this knowledge was not available at the time this earlier work was performed, and we recognize and appreciate the contributions made by other scholars to the developing field of instrumental research concerning Serbocroatian accentology.

The scholars whose work will be reviewed include R. Gauthiot (1900), I. Popovici (1902), M. Ivcovitch (1912), R. Ekblom (1917, 1924–25), B. Miletić (1926), W. Appel (1950), D. Kostić (1949–50), P. Jacobsen (1967, 1969b, 1973a), P. Rehder (1968a), T. Magner and L. Matejka (1971), A. Peco and P. Pravica (1972), E. Purcell (1973, 1976, 1981), and J. Gvozdanović (1980). The order is determined by the publication date of the first study; further contributions by the same author are treated together, even though this disrupts the precise chronology. The treatment is not exhaustive—relatively minor papers are subsumed under major ones, especially where a later major publication reviews several earlier ones (e.g., in the case of Gvozdanović 1980).

2.10.1 Robert Gauthiot (1900), "Étude sur les intonations serbes"

Gauthiot's study represents the first experimental investigation of the phonetic realization of Serbocroatian accents. The study was carried out in Rousselot's laboratory at the Collège de France in Paris, using methodology and instrumentation available at that time. Gauthiot had one speaker from Belgrade, who produced an unspecified small number of isolated words. Measurements were made of fundamental frequency, intensity, and duration. Gauthiot offers no numerical data, but presents four graphs on which he has traced the pitch and intensity curves of the accented syllables of *ȅto* 'this', *sûh* 'dry', *íći* 'to go', and *òtac* 'father' (Gauthiot's informant was from Belgrade, but three of his examples do not reflect Belgrade pronunciation: the word for 'dry' is normally *sûv*, 'to go' is pronounced *ȉći*, and 'father' is pronounced *ȍtac*). Gauthiot does not specify the units of pitch and intensity and he presents both curves on the same scale; he provides a time scale (in centiseconds) for each graph and claims to have preserved temporal information (which is improbable in view of the fact that all four stressed syllables turn out to have approximately the same duration). The data for the four accented syllables, as far as they can be extracted from the graphs, are summarized below.

The pitch pattern for *ȅto* consists of a straight line level at 130 (this value may represent Hz). The intensity pattern is level at 105 (if this means dB, the reference level has not been specified). The duration is 125 msec.

The pitch pattern for *sȗh* starts at 250, and falls steeply in the beginning and then gradually toward the end, the final value being 75. (If the numbers represent Hz, the drop was close to two octaves!) The intensity curve starts at 210 and drops in parallel with pitch until reaching a valley at approximately 70 in the third quarter of /ȗ/; then the curve rises again fairly steeply to 200. The second peak thus is slightly lower than the first peak. The duration is 120 msec.

This report by Gauthiot haunts later descriptions of ̑: scholars continue to claim that Gauthiot found two intensity peaks associated with ̑, and the schematic curves drawn to represent Gauthiot's finding usually look more like /\/\ than like Gauthiot's actual curve (e.g., Nikolaeva 1973: 159). In a footnote on p. 338, Gauthiot notes, correctly, that the difference between the height of the two peaks is *not* a characteristic of the ̑ accent; he assumes that the first peak is due to the explosion of the initial consonant. In the text he notes that the second peak is absent when the word ends in a vowel. Spectrographic analysis had not been invented at Gauthiot's time; thus, he had no way of discovering the fact that both peaks in his graph are due to transitions between the initial and final consonants and the vowel /u/. This vowel has relatively low intrinsic intensity; in fact, the intensity valley observed by Gauthiot appears to coincide with the period during which the /u/ in *sȗh* maintains its target value between two transitions. (One must assume here that /h/ stands for a velar fricative.) (It is interesting to consider the influence on future research of the accidental choice of a test item by a pioneer in the field. It is quite probable that two-peaked ̑ accents would never have become part of the canon if Gauthiot had chosen to use a word like *sȃt* as an example.)

The syllable under ` in *òtac* has a pitch curve that rises slowly but uniformly from 210 to 295. The intensity curve shows a steep rise from 45 to 300. The duration is 100 msec.

The accented vowel in *íći* has a pitch curve that rises, in a straight line, from approximately 180 to 210 (on this graph, no numerical values are attached to the endpoints of the line, and the scales are imprecisely marked). The intensity curve starts at approximately 5 and remains at that value for the first quarter of the duration of the syllable nucleus; then it rises steeply to approximately 250. The duration of the vowel is 112.5 msec.

In his general description of the accents Gauthiot states that a syllable under ̏ never shows any internal variation, either in pitch or in intensity, regardless of whether it constitutes a monosyllable or part of a disyllabic or trisyllabic word. The only characteristic of such syllables is that they are clearly marked off ("nettement coupées") from following syllables by their intensity and height.

Syllables marked by ˆ have two intensity peaks, one initial, the other final, and a single initial pitch peak followed by a fall. Gauthiot notes that this characteristic is probably better perceivable than the first.

In both rising accents intensity increases from the beginning to the end of the accented syllable. Pitch is likewise rising, and its rise is not strictly connected with the rise in intensity. Gauthiot concludes that pitch and intensity are independent of each other and may enter into complex relationships in the manifestation of accentual patterns.

2.10.2 I. Popovici (1902), "Sur l'accent ˵ en serbocroate"

We were unable to consult this work in the original and must content ourselves with the information offered by Miletić (1926:15). Popovici made measurements of five words—presumably by means of a kymograph—and found that two of them (nom.sg.neut. *ȍko* 'eye', nom.sg.neut. *ȕho* 'ear') had a falling tone on the first syllable, and three of them (gen.sg.masc. *brȁta* 'brother', *ȅto* 'this', nom.sg.fem. *žȁba* 'frog') a moderately rising tone. On the basis of Popovici's numerical data Miletić prepared diagrams, which he published among the illustrations for his book. It appears that in the first syllable of *ȍko* the "melody" is level and that in *ȅto* the first syllable has a level beginning followed by a fall; the other three examples Popovici appears to have described correctly.

2.10.3 Miloche Ivcovitch (1912), "Contribution à l'étude des intonations serbes"

Ivcovitch reports the results of a kymographic study of words with the accent ˵, carried out in the laboratory of the Collège de France in Paris. The test words were nom.sg.masc. *gȁd* 'vile person' and nom.sg.masc. *gȁdan* 'vile, disgusting'. Seven subjects from different Serbocroatian dialect areas produced a total of 11 examples of *gȁd* and 8 examples of *gȁdan*. Ivcovitch presents numerical values for each pitch period for both fundamental frequency and intensity; an original registration of the word *gȁd* is reproduced, as well as a graph drawn on the basis of measurements made of this registration. The graph is calibrated for frequency (on a musical scale), but not for intensity.

Ivcovitch draws the following conclusions:

1. Fundamental frequency rises a little at the beginning of the vowel, remains constant in the middle, and drops toward the end.
2. In the majority of instances (11 out of 18) intensity follows fundamental frequency—increasing in the beginning, remaining constant in the middle, and becoming gradually weaker toward the end.
3. In disyllabic words the unaccented syllable is both lower in pitch and weaker in intensity than the accented syllable.

2.10.4 R. Ekblom (1917), "Beiträge zur Phonetik der serbischen Sprache"
Ekblom carried out a kymographic analysis of the speech of one informant from Belgrade. The instrumental work was done in the physiological department of the Karolinska Institute in Stockholm in 1916. Measurements were made of duration, intraoral pressure, and fundamental frequency.

Ekblom reports that long vowels are a little more than twice as long as short vowels, with some fluctuation in the averages depending on environment; in monosyllabic words, for example, the duration of vowels under ̏ is 11 csec and that of vowels under ̑ is 23 csec.

The intonational aspects of the study are based on approximately 160 productions of around 100 words, some of which were pronounced more than once. Ekblom used a short frame, *To je* . . . 'This is . . .', so that the words appeared, in effect, in sentence-final position. Examples of all four accents are offered on 49 reproductions of F_0 curves and 4 reproductions of intraoral pressure curves.

The short falling accent is characterized by a slightly falling F_0 movement. Among the 36 instances are also some with rising fundamental frequency and some with level pitch.

The long falling accent falls steeply after an initial rise. The rising part is generally shorter than the falling part. When the initial consonant is voiceless, the initial rise is heightened and shortened, until sometimes the falling second part extends for the whole duration of the vowel. There is one word (*bȃr* 'bar, nightclub') in which the rising first part of the curve is longer than the second, and the two endpoints have the same fundamental frequency; two out of three productions of this word have such a realization. There are 59 examples of words with ̑.

The short rising accent is characterized by rising fundamental frequency. Only very few deviations from the typical rise are found among the 24 examples of this intonation; in those cases F_0 movement is level or slightly falling. Ekblom observes that the realization of ̀ as a rising movement is much more constant than the realization of ̏ as a falling movement.

The long rising accent is generally slightly rising. Of 41 examples none are either level or falling; there are some cases of a steeper rise.

Regarding postaccentual vowels Ekblom makes the following observations.

1. The last syllable of a word drops to the same low F_0 range regardless of accent.

2. When more than one unstressed syllable follows the accented syllable, there is a continuous fall on the postaccentual syllables after ̂ and ̏. After ́ and ̀, however, all unstressed syllables (except the last) remain at the level at which the accented syllable terminates.

Ekblom states that these results agree with Masing's views, as far as disyllabic and trisyllabic words are concerned. Masing had said that only the syllable immediately following a rising accent has high pitch; Ekblom differs from Masing in claiming that all postaccentual syllables except the last have high pitch after a rising accent.

Ekblom also measured intraoral pressure during the production of [p] in test words consisting of the sequence *papa*, produced four times with each accent. On the basis of pressure during adjacent consonants, Ekblom concludes that expiratory pressure increases during ̏, decreases during ̂, remains unchanged during ̀, and rises strongly during ́.

Ekblom's informant also produced three readings of a short anecdote consisting of two sentences. Ekblom deduces from these data that there are no basic differences between tones on isolated words and in continuous speech. Sentence intonation nevertheless has some influence on word tone. Sentences have a rise in the beginning, remain more or less level during the middle, and show a fall at the end. Initial position within a sentence increases the rises of rising tones and decreases the falls; final position has the opposite effect. This could also be expressed, Ekblom says, in terms of angles between the ideal sentence intonation curve and the curve that is actually observed: the nature of the word-level accent determines the angle.

R. Ekblom (1924), "Zur čechischen und serbischen Akzentuation"

Ekblom 1924–25 is devoted to a comparison of word-level intonation in Czech with the F_0 movements occurring in Serbian words bearing the falling accents ̂ and ̏. The Czech material is new; the Serbian data derive mainly from Ekblom's earlier publications. New for Serbocroatian are average curves calculated from 30 occurrences of words with ̏ and 59 occurrences of words with ̂. The curves are presented graphically; the axes of the diagrams are not calibrated, and no numerical values are given. The curve for the syllable with ̏ is basically level or even slightly rising; the curve for ̂ has an overall convex shape with a minimal rise in the beginning, followed by a steep fall.

Ekblom also reproduces six original curves (derived by means of a kymograph and calibrated on a musical scale) of the utterances *dȏba i bȇdan* 'age and poor' and *bȁba i dȅda* 'grandmother and grandfather', produced by one speaker in three versions: with equal emphasis on both conjuncts, with emphatic stress on the first conjunct, and with emphatic stress on the second conjunct. As Ekblom notes, the curves show that the F_0 contour is generally rising in initial position, probably due to the influence of sentence intonation. Emphatic stress is accompanied by sharply rising F_0 movements in syllables with ̏.

2.10.5 Branko Miletić (1926), *O srbo-chrvatských intonacích v nářečí štokavském*. (Reviewed in Belić 1926–27.)

For this study, which was carried out between 1923 and 1925 in the Laboratory of Experimental Phonetics of the Charles University in Prague, Miletić used four speakers from various regions who pronounced test words in isolation and in short phrases. The utterances were recorded kymographically; Miletić used a microscope to measure the duration of each period within voiced sounds, which he then converted to frequency. Intensity was similarly calculated from amplitude. For the study of intensity, Miletić chose words with identical vowels. The number of test words analyzed in the course of the study was 988; of these, 415 carried the short falling accent, 230 the long falling accent, 206 the short rising accent, and 137 the long rising accent. The bulk of the material consisted of isolated words, but a number of words incorporated into sentences, usually in final or initial position, were also analyzed. The book does not contain numerical results of measurements, but offers basically a survey of pitch movements observed on kymograms (rising, falling, level, level-falling, etc.) in accented vowels with information about the frequency of these types with various accents.

According to Miletić's findings, the short falling accent in isolated words had two basic manifestations: either level melody ending in a fall, or falling throughout. The level melody occurred normally when the speaker was in good physical condition, and the falling melody when he did not feel well. Miletić states that in a minority of cases a greater part of the accented vowel or even the whole accented vowel is rising. Isolated words that have a level F_0 contour carry a falling contour at the end of a sentence; isolated words with an initial rise replace that by a level contour terminating in a fall. In initial position the pronunciation is as in isolated words if the word does not carry the sentence accent; under this accent the melody is rising.

Long falling accents are similar to short falling accents except for greater duration. They, too, either have a level melody ending in a fall or are falling throughout. An initial rise is frequent, and the influence of sentence intonation is parallel to that on ̏ .

The regular form of the short rising accent is rising throughout or at least predominantly rising. There are two other possibilities: either the syllable bearing ̀ can be level like some productions of ̏ , or the F_0 contour can be level, ending in a fall, which is the regular pattern associated with ̏ . In those cases, however, Miletić observes that the high tone in the next syllables preserves the distinction between ̀ and ̏ . Phrasal intonation changes the F_0 pattern of the word by increasing the rise in initial position and decreasing the rise in final position. In exceptional cases even the last traces of a rising melody disappear, the intersyllabic interval increases, and ̀ becomes ̏ .

The long rising accent is likewise ordinarily rising either for the whole duration of the vowel or for the greater part of its duration. In exceptional cases the F_0 contour can be either level or level with a slight final fall. Again the small interval between the accented and the postaccentual syllables preserves the character of the rising accent. In connected discourse the rising melody is generally retained. All words are rising in sentence-initial position; in final position the rise is less prominent, and the melody can approach that of ̂ except for the fact that the next syllable is at about the level of the accented one.

The chapter on intersyllabic intervals was prepared with the help of a musicologist. With falling accents, the interval between the accented and the postaccentual syllable usually fluctuates between a major second and an augmented fifth; with rising accents, either the two syllables are on the same level or the interval between them is relatively small in either direction.

Intensity curves generally parallel F_0 curves. The intersyllabic intensity difference is greater for falling accents, especially ̏ , than for rising accents; for ̀ and ́ , both syllables can have the same force. Miletić finds no two-peaked intensity curves in words with long falling accents, which Gauthiot (1900) had considered typical.

Miletić gives no information about the duration of syllable nuclei.

2.10.6 Wilhelm Appel (1950), *Gestaltstudien. A. Untersuchungen über den Akzent in der serbokroatischen Sprache*

Appel analyzed ten isolated words, five short sentences, and two lines from a poem, spoken by M. Rešetar in 1927 during a visit to Vienna. The registration was made by means of a kymograph; fundamental frequency, intensity, and duration were calculated on the basis of measurements made of individual periods of the sound waves. The results may be summarized as follows.

Long vowels are almost twice as long as short vowels. The F_0 patterns in words with ̏ can be rising, level, or falling. In words with ̀, fundamental frequency rises during the first (accented) vowel; the second vowel may be either higher or (somewhat) lower than the accented vowel.

In long vowels it is unnecessary to compare the fundamental frequency of the accented vowel with the following vowel, since the long duration of the vowel makes it possible to observe contrasts within the accented syllable itself. Nevertheless, the participation of the postaccentual vowel in the realization of the rising accent can also be observed when the accented vowel is long. The F_0 curve is moderately rising in the three words with ́. Words with ̑ have generally falling F_0 contours. Intensity runs generally parallel to the F_0 movement.

Appel concludes from his (very limited) data that the falling accents are expiratory rather than tonal. The F_0 movement is irrelevant and depends on sentence intonation: in the rising part of the sentence intonation curve (at the beginning of a speech unit) it is rising or level, in the falling part (at the end of a speech unit) it is always falling. Long vowels with expiratory accent (i.e., with ̑) can have rising, rising-falling, or falling F_0 contours. The rising accents are, on the contrary, musical accents. The rising F_0 contour is not subject to change through sentence intonation; it is retained as rising, or at least it has an inhibiting effect on falling sentence intonation. Essential in the case of rising accents is the participation of the postaccentual syllable; therefore, the musical accent has a restricted distribution and does not occur on final syllables. Pitch and intensity go hand in hand in expiratory accents, but are relatively independent in musical accents.

2.10.7 Đorđe Kostić (1949–50), "O jačini naglaska dvosložnih reči pod (̏) i (̀) akcentom"

Kostić investigated the intensity of vowels in seven disyllabic minimal pairs: 3.sg.pres. *ȉgra* 'plays, dances'-nom.sg.fem. *ìgra* 'play, game, dance', nom.sg.fem. *zȅlen* 'greens, vegetables'-nom.sg.masc. (adj.) *zèlen* 'green', nom.sg.fem. *rȁčva* 'fork, bifurcation'-3.sg.pres. *ràčva* 'forks, divides', 3.sg.pres. *snȍsi* 'stands, bears, endures'-2.sg.imper. *snòsi* 'stand, bear, endure', 3.sg.pres. *prȍsi* 'begs'-2.sg.imper. *pròsi* 'beg', nom.sg.fem. (adj.) *kȍsa* 'oblique'-nom.sg.fem. *kòsa* 'hair', nom.pl.fem. *ȕši* 'ears'-gen.pl.fem. *ùši* 'ears'. The fourteen words were pronounced by the author (presumably in the given sequence). The analysis was carried out in the laboratory of Radio Belgrade. In a second reading the author pronounced again seven minimal pairs of words with short accents, and one other speaker pronounced four such pairs. Thirty-six words appear to have been analyzed in all. Intensity was measured in decibels.

In disyllabic words in Kostić's recordings the first syllable with ̏ has higher intensity than that with ̀; the syllable following ̏ has lower intensity than that following ̀. The difference between the intensities of the two successive syllables is considerably greater with ̏ ̆ than with ̀ ̆. The second set of words gives similar results.

Kostić notices considerable variability in the intensities associated with a given position. In his discussion he does not take the different intrinsic intensities of the vowels into account. Two of his minimal pairs have the same vowels in both syllables. We recalculated the intensity relationships in *zȅlen-zèlen* and *rȁčva-ràčva*. The intensity drop between the two syllables of *zȅlen* and between the two syllables of *rȁčva* was 8.525 dB and 7.225 dB, respectively, for an average of 7.875 dB. In *zèlen* the two syllables had equal intensity; in *ràčva* the second *a* was higher by .750 dB (not 1.750 dB, as given by Kostić), for an average rise of .375 dB. The average difference between the intensity drops in words with ̏ ̆ and ̀ ̆ was 8.250 dB.

The second production by Kostić does not include the pair zȅlen-zèlen, and the stressed and postaccentual syllables for *rȁčva-ràčva* have the following intensities: *rȁčva* 15.50 and 16.25 dB, *ràčva* 14.75 and 21.50 dB. These values look suspicious—both relationships are rising. Instead of a drop in intensity in *rȁčva*, the data show a .75 dB rise; instead of an approximately level relationship in *ràčva*, the data show a 6.75 dB rise.

Kostić concludes that the relationship between the intensities of the two syllables is one of the characteristics of Serbocroatian accents.

2.10.8 Karl-Heinz Pollok (1964), *Der neuštokavische Akzent und die Struktur der Melodiegestalt der Rede*. (Reviewed in Peukert 1969.)

Pollok's research was conducted between 1952 and 1954; publication of the results was delayed until 1964. Thus, Pollok's research essentially antedates ours, although the study was published in the time period presently under consideration.

Pollok used four speakers who produced a large number of separate sentences as well as free conversation. Two of the speakers were born in western Serbia, one in Bosnia, and one in Slavonia. None of the sentences were designed to compare test words in identical sentence environments; thus, Pollok's results are not directly comparable to those of most other experimental studies. The recordings were analyzed at the Physikalisch-Technische Bundesanstalt in Braunschweig, where F_0 and peak speech power curves were produced using the Grützmacher-Lottermoser method. Pollok considered primarily fundamental frequency and intensity; duration was treated in passing. The results are presented in descriptive rather than quantitative form. For example, a table may indicate that in x productions of a word with a particular accent, fundamental frequency was rising in y% of them.

Concerning intensity, Pollok concludes that there exists a tendency for expiratory strengthening of the falling accents; in free conversation this tendency is fully developed only in the case of ˆ, whereas the two short accents may become similar to each other under certain circumstances. With rising accents, peak speech power coincides with the accented syllable in approximately 60% of 185 measured instances of words with ´ and 515 measured instances of `; with the long falling accent, peak speech power and accented syllable coincide in 79.6% of 108 cases, and with the short falling accent, they coincide in 70.2% of 516 cases.

The F_0 contours can be described as follows. In 130 instances of ´ the F_0 movement is rising in 85.4% of the instances and nonrising in 14.6% (111 and 19 tokens, respectively). All 19 nonrising F_0 curves occur in final position. In 217 instances of ` the F_0 movement is rising in 92.7% of the instances and nonrising in 7.3% (201 and 16 tokens, respectively). Most of the nonrising curves occur in final position. Of 140 words with ˆ, 80% (112 tokens) have a falling F_0 curve; 20% (28 tokens) do not. A considerable number of these occur at the beginning of either a sentence or a new unit of speech ("Redeabschnitt") within a sentence; nonfalling realizations also occur at the end of nonfinal clauses.

Words with ̏ constitute a special case. Only a relatively small number have really falling F_0 curves. The characteristic F_0 pattern is what Pollok calls "Stoßton mit einem Umbruch in der Tonbewegung"—perhaps to be translated as a "sharp tone with a rapid frequency change," although "sharp tone" is quite inadequate for "Stoßton." The Stoßton is rising-falling in every case; either the first or the second half can be longer, yielding a "rising Stoßton" and "falling Stoßton," respectively, symbolized by Pollok as ╱ˎ and ˏ╲. Out of 276 cases, 196 (71%) have the rising Stoßton; 69 (25%) have the falling Stoßton. Together these two types account for 265 cases, or 96%. Only 11 words with ̏ have no Stoßton, constituting 4% of the cases.

Pollok recognizes that description of the accented syllable alone is not sufficient; in a footnote (p. 51) he mentions that the relatively low F_0 value of the postaccentual syllable is often considered an essential criterion in differentiating ̏ from ̀. However, he does not limit his attention to postaccentual syllables, but proceeds to build an extensive theory of complex hierarchical patterns in which syllables, words, and higher-level units are embraced in a network of parabolic melody curves. Since our work has proceeded from different premises, we will not review Pollok's theories further here; we note simply that Pollok's theory provides no way to account for realizations of accents that proceed in a straight line, as is the case with many realizations of the long rising accent.

2.10.9 Per Jacobsen (1967), "The Word Tones of Serbo-Croatian: An Instrumental Study"

Jacobsen (1967) carried out an instrumental investigation of word tones in Serbocroatian in the spring of 1967. Four informants from various regions recorded a total of 982 test utterances consisting of selected monosyllabic and disyllabic words placed in the frame sentence *Piše . . . na karti* '. . . is written on the card'. The utterances were subjected to acoustic analysis by means of an intensity meter and a pitch meter and were recorded on a Mingograph. Measurements were made of duration, F_0 values in three positions within the vocalic portions of the recordings, and intensity. The average duration of short accented vowels and long vowels in Jacobsen's materials was 113 msec and 198 msec, respectively, for a ratio of .57. There was no significant difference between rising and falling accents in terms of duration. With regard to fundamental frequency, Jacobsen's observations confirm practically every aspect of our earlier findings. Jacobsen notes that the opposition between short accents cannot be regarded as an opposition between falling and rising tone in the stressed syllable; rather, the distinction is based on the relation between the tone of the stressed syllable and that of the following syllable. The tone of the postaccentual syllable in words with the short rising accent starts as high as or higher than the end of the preceding stressed syllable; in words with the short falling accent the tone of the postaccentual syllable is considerably lower. In words with long accents the tonal movement on the stressed syllable itself is sufficient to establish the opposition. The role of intensity could not be established on the basis of the study.

A special feature of this work is that the author takes into account the consonantal environment, giving separate F_0 values for words beginning with voiced and voiceless consonants. His results confirm the observation that a voiceless consonant tends to raise the F_0 level of the following vowel (Lehiste and Peterson 1961). Jacobsen also finds that intensity level in the first postaccentual syllable is higher after rising accents than after falling accents. However, he states cautiously that "it is difficult to tell . . . whether intensity plays any role for the identification [of accents] . . . ; experiments with synthetic speech . . . might throw light on this question."

Per Jacobsen (1969b, 1973a), "Falling Word Tones in Serbo-Croatian"
In these studies Jacobsen examined words with short and long falling accents to establish whether the primary distinction between them is duration or tone. In the earlier study one speaker produced the four words *kȉm* 'caraway', instr.sg. *kîm* 'who', nom.sg.fem. *dȕga* 'long', and gen.sg.masc. *dûga* 'debt'. The words were produced normally and with different kinds of articulatory modifications: words with the short falling accent were lengthened, while the tone was kept as constantly level as possible; words with the long falling accent were spoken with a shorter duration, while preserving the characteristic rising-falling tonal contour. From this set of words Jacobsen selected productions in which the words of each contrasting pair had equal duration but different tonal contours. A randomized listening test was administered to an unspecified number of subjects, who performed perfectly in identifying the normally produced words and randomly in identifying the distorted words. Jacobsen concluded that the listeners distinguished among the words on the basis of length rather than tonal contour.

In the second study the test materials consisted of 24 synthetic words with the segmental structure *grad.* For 18 of the stimuli, the vowel had three durations: 100, 150, and 200 msec. The fundamental frequency on the vowel was either rising-falling (100–130–75 Hz) or falling (110–100 Hz). Each duration and F_0 contour was combined with three intensity patterns: level, rising by 3 dB, or falling by 3 dB. Six stimuli had a duration of 260 msec, two F_0 contours, and three intensity conditions. A randomized listening test was presented to an unspecified number of native speakers. The listeners identified words with 100 msec vowel duration as *grȁd* 'hail', identified words with 200 and 260 msec vowel durations as *grâd* 'city', and made random guesses for words with 150 msec vowel duration. Jacobsen concludes that the distinctive feature of the falling word tones in Serbo-croatian is duration; neither tonal movement nor intensity plays a part.

2.10.10 Peter Rehder (1968a), *Beiträge zur Erforschung der serbokroatischen Prosodie. Die linguistische Struktur der Tonverlaufs-Minimalpaare.* (Reviewed in Lehiste 1969, Peukert 1969.)

This is a revised version of the author's University of Munich dissertation. The methodology and some of the results are also described in Rehder 1968b.

Rehder carried out an acoustic analysis of minimal pairs established through the use of listening tests. Twelve informants from Belgrade recorded members of 6 to 18 minimal pairs embedded in meaningful sentences as well as in isolation. The informants also participated in listening tests in which they identified words produced by themselves and by the other speakers. The results of these listening tests separated the informants into two groups. The majority of the informants—nine out of twelve—were unable to produce disyllabic words with contrastive short accents, nor were they able to recognize the distinction. The smaller group of three informants who distinguished between disyllabic words with short rising and falling accents consisted of a professor of Serbocroatian who was fully conscious of the expected realization of the accents in the literary language, and two informants whose families came from dialect areas in which the distinction is preserved (Novi Sad in one case, Titovo Užice in the other). Both groups had the distinction in trisyllabic words with short accents and in disyllabic words with long accents; however, individuals differed in whether a particular minimal pair was distinctive in their idiolect. In this way, a considerable number of minimal pairs were eliminated that had originally been excerpted from dictionaries and grammars. Although time-consuming, this procedure is necessary from a methodological point of view when the investigator is not a native speaker in order to avoid operating with ghost minimal pairs.

The test words recorded by the three informants who distinguished between short accents in disyllabic words were analyzed spectrographically. The same material was also processed by means of a mingograph, which was used to produce continuous curves of fundamental frequency and intensity. The results achieved in this part of Rehder's study are, for all practical purposes, identical with our results (Ivić and Lehiste 1963, 1965); as Rehder remarks, the results of the two studies confirm each other. Rehder, too, finds that F_0 differences play a more consistent part than intensity differences. In words with short falling accents the F_0 peak of the stressed syllable is much higher than that of the postaccentual syllable; in words with short rising accents the postaccentual syllable has a higher F_0 peak. In words with long falling accents the F_0 curve is rising-falling during the accented syllable itself, and the postaccentual syllable is low. In words with long rising accents F_0 is rising during the accented syllable. The relationship between the fundamental frequencies of the accented and postaccentual syllables in minimal pairs with long accents is the same as in minimal pairs with short accents. However, this applies without reservation only to Rehder's speakers I2 and I3. The speaker I1 (personally known to P.I.), a language specialist who has worked for many years in a theater teaching orthoepy, apparently pronounced Rehder's test minimal pairs as he was accustomed to pronounce them to actors in order to make them aware of prosodic distinctions. This exaggerated pronunciation is manifested in a drastic F_0 rise in the vowel under ´ (the averages were 110.8–181.8 Hz in one set of examples and 123.6–206.6 Hz in the other set) and even more in exceptionally great falling intervals in the vowel under ˆ (in one set of examples even 265.0–99.2 Hz, thus much more than an octave). In such examples with ´ the postaccentual vowel remained considerably below the level of the accented one (peaks 181.8 vs. 169.5 Hz and 206.6 vs. 152.5 Hz, respectively). In his conclusions (p. 161) Rehder proceeds from the pronunciation of I1, stating that for a falling accent a falling F_0 relation is characteristic, and for a rising accent a rising relation, in such a way that in words with short accents these relations transcend the syllable boundary, whereas in words with long accents they fail to cross this boundary. However, the fall in the vowel under ˆ continues in the next syllable in the pronunciation of all three speakers, and the rise in words with ´ embraces the next syllable in the pronunciation of I2 and I3. About the importance of this finding, Rehder says, "Dieses Schema ist das entscheidende Interpretationsergebnis der Substanzanordnung im Messbereich der Signalfrequenz" (This scheme is the decisive interpretational result of the distribution of substance in the measurement range of the frequency of the signal) (p. 161). With regard to duration, Rehder states that the ratio between vowels carrying short accents and those carrying long accents is approximately 1 : 2 (p. 110). In fact, the averages for ˵ are 12.3 and 12.4 csec, for ` 12.6 and 12.8 csec, for ˆ 20.2 csec, and for ´ 21.1 csec. This means that actual ratios vary between 1 : 1.6 and 1 : 1.7, which is much closer to our findings (the data presented here concern the pronunciation of I1, since for I2 and I3 Rehder gives no measurement results regarding the short accents; it turned out that these informants distinguished confidently only one or two minimal pairs with short accents).

Rehder also attempted to establish the relative importance of fundamental frequency and intensity as distinctive components of the accents by using what he called "purposeful destruction" and "purposeful construction" ("gezielte Destruktion" and "gezielte Konstruktion") of the signals. Two devices were used for this investigation: a vocoder for manipulating the fundamental frequency, and a specially built intensity compressor for manipulating intensity. Selected minimal pairs (established during another part of the study) were processed and rerecorded under the following conditions: (a) fundamental frequency unchanged, intensity leveled by means of the intensity compressor; (b) intensity unchanged, frequency monotonized at 155 Hz by means of the vocoder; (c) both parameters leveled at the same time in the manner described above. Listening tests indicated that fundamental frequency was the decisive parameter in identification. Under condition (a) the identification score for the distinction between 3.sg.pres. *râdi* 'works' and dat.sg. *Rádi* (masc. proper name) and between gen.sg.masc. *svêta* 'world' and nom.sg. *Svéta* (masc. proper name) was 99.3%, under condition (b) it was 57.4%, and under condition (c) it was 54.6%. For nom.sg.masc. *gȍri* 'worse'/3.sg.pres. *gòri* 'burns' and past part.nom.sg.neut. *sȅlo* 'sat down'/nom.sg.neut. *sèlo* 'village', comparable scores were (a) 98.3%, (b) 44.2%, (c) 33.3%; for nom.sg.fem. *ȕpala* 'inflammation'/past part.sg.fem. *ùpala* 'fell in', they were (a) 88.5%, (b) 64.8%, (c) 63.0%; and for the whole set, they were (a) 95.4%, (b) 53.6%, (c) 47.8%.

This experiment by Rehder was an important event in the history of the investigation of Neoštokavian accents. It proved conclusively that intensity differences do not distinguish between rising and falling accents: accents were correctly perceived with leveled intensity, and randomly perceived with leveled fundamental frequency under original intensity. The identification scores were generally somewhat lower when both fundamental frequency and intensity were leveled, suggesting that intensity may make a moderate supplementary contribution for the identification of an accent.

In a second series of tests modeled on the well-known experiments of Isačenko and Schädlich (1963), Rehder attempted to show that the contrastive accents of Serbocroatian can be produced by the use of two and only two F_0 levels, and that the principle of binarity can thus be applied to phenomena of word-level prosody. For this purpose, ten members of minimal pairs produced by one informant were processed through the intensity compressor and monotonized at 155 Hz and 161 Hz. Tape-splicing techniques were used to produce stimuli for perceptual testing. Disyllabic words with short accents were spliced at the syllable boundary. Words with long accents were spliced both at the syllable boundary and in the middle of the accented syllable. The following F_0 patterns were thus produced (where: indicates syllable boundary): for short and long accents,

155:161 and 161:155; for long accents only, 155–161:161, 155–161:155, 161–155:161, and 161–155:155. Listening tests showed approximately 80% agreement among listeners in assigning the stimuli to either the falling or the rising category. The decisive factor was the first stepwise change: if the first change was from 155 to 161, the word was heard as having a rising accent, and if the first change was from 161 to 155, the word was assigned to the falling category.

The author draws the following conclusions (pp. 189–190). (I) The phonologically relevant factor in Serbocroatian disyllabic and trisyllabic accentual minimal pairs is a change in frequency (rise or fall) during the first syllable nucleus and the quantity (short or long) of the first syllable nucleus. (II) There is a polar opposition between members of an accentual minimal pair: each member has either a distinctive rise or a distinctive fall. (III) The distinctive rise and distinctive fall can be interpreted as theoretical constructs without a time dimension; they constitute input signals for generating the phonological shape of words. (IV) The voice of the speaker, in generating the fundamental frequency, realizes the input signal in the time dimension of speech production, so that the change in fundamental frequency is gradual rather than instantaneous.

Rehder's conclusion I must be interpreted as "what is phonologically relevant is the change in frequency within the first syllable or at its end." Interpreting the phrase "Frequenzstufenwechsel . . . des ersten Silbenträgers" to mean "F_0 change within the first syllable nucleus" would hardly be acceptable and would even contradict the results of Rehder's own test, which has shown that both with short and with long accents an F_0 change at the syllable boundary can be distinctive. Moreover, even the theory operating with the first frequency change in the word is contradicted by the facts that the syllable under ˆ often contains an initial F_0 rise and that sometimes a considerable rise also occurs in the syllable carrying ˵.

In order to verify conclusion II a listening test must be carried out that includes a pattern with no frequency change within the first syllable or at the syllable boundary. If such a test shows that the listeners' responses are random, conclusion II is right, and if these responses give a significant advantage to either kind of accent (we have reason to suppose that this might be the rising accent), the opposition would prove to be privative rather than polar. However, Rehder excluded such a pattern from his test. Likewise, he did not include a stimulus in which the first syllable would have carried a rising-falling contour. If listeners were to qualify such a stimulus as a falling accent, this would invalidate Rehder's conclusion that the direction of the first F_0 change is distinctive. It is interesting in this connection that two of the three speakers whose pronunciation was analyzed instrumentally by Rehder had predominantly rising frequency movements in the vowel under ˆ. The F_0 peak of that vowel was at 58% of its duration for one speaker and at 61% for the other, and its termination was higher than its beginning by a musical interval that was comparable to the interval with which Rehder operated in his listening tests. It is, of course, important that the *first* change in frequency under ˆ in the pronunciation of these two speakers was not only rising, but quite substantially so: 121–144 Hz and 133.3–157.2 Hz, which is much greater than the interval employed in Rehder's tests (155–161 Hz).

2.10.11 Thomas F. Magner and Ladislav Matejka (1971), *Word Accent in Modern Serbo-Croatian*. (Reviewed by Browne 1972, Butler 1972, Jacobsen 1973b, Kalogjera 1973, Kolarič 1975, Kravar 1975a, Neweklowsky 1973, Nikolaeva 1974, Peco 1973, Šivic-Dular 1973; also see Matejka 1967, Magner 1968, 1981, Kravar 1968b, 1982–83, Pešikan 1968–69.)

The aim of Magner and Matejka's investigation was to establish whether the prosodic system described by Karadžić and Daničić and codified in Serbocroatian grammars is still in current use. The test materials consisted of sentence pairs differing in the prosodic structure of one word—for example, *I danas* pàra *igra ulogu* 'Even today, *money* plays a role', *I danas* păra *igra ulogu* 'Even today, *steam* plays a role'. The sentences were recorded by two experienced accentologists born in Bosnia-Hercegovina. The tapes were played, and listening tests given, to approximately 1600 high school students (and some university students) in a number of cities (Belgrade, Zagreb, Novi Sad, Subotica, Niš, Osijek, Rijeka, Split, Sarajevo) as well as in smaller towns (Loznica, Sisak, Dubrovnik, Banja Luka, Travnik, Mostar, Gacko, Trebinje, Stolac, Titograd, Nikšić). The task of the listeners was to indicate on prepared test sheets which member of the sentence pair they heard. There were two tests, one consisting of 100 sentences, the other of 50 sentences; the shorter test was also read in each class by one of the students and judged by fellow students. Finally, the test was administered to a group of accentologists, with the result that only those linguists who had been born in Bosnia and Hercegovina were able to turn in an error-free performance.

In general, the listening tests showed that listeners from smaller towns, especially those from Bosnia and Hercegovina, were much more successful in identifying the sentences than listeners from large cities, primarily those from Zagreb and Belgrade. The location of the accent was well perceived everywhere, as well as quantity oppositions in accented syllables (with the exception of Niš and, to a certain extent, Zagreb). Posttonic quantity was better distinguished in smaller towns. Tone oppositions in short accents appeared neutralized everywhere. There was a considerable amount of variation in the identification of long accents, both geographically and with regard to individual minimal pairs. In a hierarchy of prosodic features, location of the accent thus plays the most significant role, followed by the quantity of accented syllables; quantity oppositions in unstressed syllables and tone oppositions in general seem to be relatively less relevant. Magner and Matejka regard the low scores on a number of test items as proof that "the accentual system presented in Serbocroatian grammars, dictionaries and textbooks has little or no relationship with the accentual system(s) employed in many urban areas" (p. 191). Therefore, they propose a far-reaching revision of the prosodic norm of the standard language. They are inclined to accept only the place of stress and quantity under stress as relevant prosodic features (p. 191). They also express "unavoidable scepticism" concerning earlier accentological studies of Serbocroatian dialects (p. 185) and the belief that "a generative or typological treatment of Contemporary Standard Serbo-Croatian . . . cannot be more than a mere scholastic exercise" if it is based on the classical description of the prosodic pattern (p. 181).

All of Magner and Matejka's statements regarding the preservation of particular elements of the classical pattern are certainly true. For instance, postaccentual quantity is very much alive "in rural communities in Bosnia and Hercegovina" (and in general in that republic), the accent place contrasts are present everywhere, and quantity in accented vowels is relevant in all the regions where the authors found it. Also, many of the statements pointing to the loss of a distinction correspond to reality. For example, quantity and tone contrasts do not exist in Niš, postaccentual quantity tends to be eliminated or reduced in many other areas, and the tone distinction is alien to the natives of Zagreb. In such cases Magner and Matejka's results bring welcome confirmation of facts already known to Serbocroatianists. The authors are also right in criticizing a certain rigidity of most Serbocroatian grammarians, who tend to ignore the actual pronunciation in the two most important cultural centers, Belgrade and Zagreb.

However, in a number of instances the claims of the two authors are unsubstantiated. For example, they mention the "instability of tonal differentiation" even in long vowels in places such as Dubrovnik (p. 112), and they state that "the students . . . in Vuk's Loznica" cannot readily distinguish gen.sg.masc. *ùčitelja* 'teacher' from gen.pl.masc. *ùčitēljā* (pp. 100–101). They report that "the gloomiest picture by far was observed in the testing of the distinctive power assigned to the difference between short falling and short rising accent" (p. 183). "The situation with short rising and short falling accent, as represented in Test I and II, was a thoroughgoing failure" (p. 114); the share of listeners who succeeded in distinguishing between *òrao* 'eagle' and *ȍrao* 'plowed' was nowhere greater than 24%, and in Stolac in Hercegovina and Titograd in Montenegro it was even zero. "Judging from the test and the analysis of the local voices, one would have to say that the most dubious 'distinction' appeared to be the difference between short falling and short rising accent, although *some individuals* with Bosnian and Hercegovinian background tested rather well. They were, however, in such a striking minority that it is legitimate to ask whether the language planning which promotes the classical Vukovian accentual system is not facing insurmountable obstacles" (p. 190) (italics I.L. and P.I.). However, in this case the failure is on the side of the authors. Although the contrast between the two short accents is one of the crucial points in the pattern, their test forms did not include a single minimal pair that would have been lexically adequate. In all the pairs they used (instr.sg. *vòdōm* 'water' vs. instr.sg. *vȍdom* 'squad', *sȁd kao* 'now like' vs. *sàtkao* 'wove', *pàra* 'money' vs. *pȁra* 'steam', gen.sg. *kȍsti* 'bone' vs. gen.pl. *kòstī* 'bones', *òrao* 'eagle' vs. *ȍrao* 'plowed') at least one of the two members has either a different accent or a different form in large parts of the Neo-štokavian area. The authors based their conclusions on the pair *òrao* vs. *ȍrao*; yet on pp. 152–153 they note that the local speaker in Novi Sad used the form *órao* rather than *òrao* (the form *órao* is indeed common in many regions), and Kravar (1982–83) cites the forms *òrao* and *òrāo* 'plowed' and the same forms *òrao* and *òrāo* 'eagle' from various places. Obviously, conclusions based on such a "minimal pair" are on shaky ground. Moreover, it is surprising that the authors did not themselves notice the difference between ˋ and ̏ in most places they visited. In fact, the area of this distinction encompasses a huge territory, from the Adriatic coast to the Hungarian and Romanian border, and from western Croatia to central Serbia. It is also unrealistic to propose abandoning the "Vukovian" pattern in descriptive and normative works on modern standard Serbocroatian. This is still the most widespread prosodic pattern. Its relatively archaic character corresponds to the general tendency of literary languages to favor continuity embodied in time-honored linguistic forms. It is easy to deduce (or to "generate") most other patterns represented in Magner and Matejka's book from the classical accentuation, but not vice versa. Thus, if alternative possibilities were to be admitted to the norm, the right procedure would be to add some facultative rules (e.g., concerning the loss of postaccentual quantity oppositions at least in some positions, or concerning tone neutralization in short accented vowels) to the description of the "full" pattern. And finally, only the "full" pattern is well defined; everything else observed by the two authors is in a state of flux.

The study has provoked a considerable amount of discussion and criticism, some of which appears well warranted. The procedure applied by the authors has at least three methodological weaknesses:

1. Their choice of lexical examples was often inadequate. For example, in some localities the words *râdio* 'radio' and *rádio* 'worked' have the same accent (*rádio*), and in many areas both *pȁra* 'steam' and *pàra* 'money' are pronounced *pȁra*, although the tonal distinctions are otherwise preserved. Moreover, some of the lexemes chosen are unknown or at least unfamiliar in various regions. In spite of all this, the authors failed to distinguish consistently between lexical facts and phonological mergers.

2. The questions in the test forms were not always properly formulated. For example, on p. 104 the authors mention that the test frame *Broj konduktera nije poznat* 'The number of conductors is not known' "clearly favored" one of the possible answers, and on p. 133 they report that the multiple choice in cases such as *sȁd kao* 'now like'-*sât kao* 'like an hour'-3.sg.past *sàtkao* 'wove' and inst.sg.masc. *lȕkom* 'onion'-inst.sg.masc. *lûkom* 'arch'-inst.sg. *Lûkōm* (masculine name)-inst.sg.fem. *lúkōm* 'harbor' turned out to be a confusing factor. And in general, Kravar 1968b (and 1975b) is probably right in his opinion that the high school students must sometimes have been confused by the procedure and the whole situation of testing; he reports that he himself experienced some of the examination atmosphere when he and his colleagues at Zadar University were tested by Magner and Matejka.

3. Magner and Matejka's method of scoring and statistical analysis was unsound. They carried out no tests of statistical significance. By applying an elementary statistical test of Goodness of Fit, the Chi-Square Test, to results produced by Belgrade listeners, Browne (1972) has shown that the probability is much less than 0.001 that the Belgrade listeners could have achieved their results concerning postaccentual quantity in *ȕčitēljā* vs. *ȕčitelja* by random guessing. The authors, however, interpreted these results simply as a failure to distinguish postaccentual quantity oppositions. The difference between the scores of subjects from Belgrade and (for example) from Gacko and Stolac is nevertheless a fact that should be accounted for. Browne suggests that the distinctiveness of a contrast is not

an all-or-nothing matter, and that it can be greater for some speakers and smaller for others. We might add that in large cities the audience is more likely to be mixed, so that a lesser degree of distinctiveness can be the result of the inclusion of subjects who do and subjects who do not distinguish between members of a minimal pair.

It appears that the methodological shortcomings of Magner and Matejka's study are such that their conclusions cannot be accepted at full value.

2.10.12 Asim Peco and P. Pravica (1972), "O prirodi akcenata srpskohrvatskog jezika na osnovu eksperimentalnih istraživanja"

Peco and Pravica recorded 760 sentences produced by 32 subjects. The recorded tapes were analyzed spectrographically and were also processed through a Frøkjær-Jensen Trans-Pitch Meter and displayed on a Mingograph. Measurements were made primarily from narrow-band spectrograms. The authors present illustrations of test words on which they have traced F_0 contours through voiceless consonants like /t/ and /s/. Since the vocal folds are not vibrating during voiceless consonants, there is no periodicity and consequently no fundamental frequency. However, the tables contain measurements of F_0 movements purportedly taking place during these consonants (pp. 212–214).

The article contains F_0 measurements made of the production of 46 words, 8 with an ̏ accent, 11 with ̑, 14 with ̀, and 13 with ́. Intensity and duration values are not reported. Unfortunately, in words with falling accents only F_0 values in the first syllable were measured; in words with rising accents the first postaccentual syllable was also included. The results are given for each particular word rather than in the form of averages. As a rule, references are added concerning the sentence in which the word appeared, along with the name and place of origin of the speaker. Although the words are not classified according to their position within the sentence, this information can be obtained on the basis of the sentences for which references are given. In the case of 7 words that are wrongly identified in the references (that is, the sentence to which the table refers does not contain the word) and of 6 words, all with the ̑ accent, for which no references are given, it is possible to determine their position by searching through the lists of sentences. The resulting data are shown in table 2.29. There is no information concerning the reasons for such an unequal representation of various categories.

The test contains a reference to the influence of sentence intonation on the realization of word tones, but this influence is not systematically

Table 2.29
Position of 46 words for which measurements are reported in test sentences analyzed by Peco and Pravica (1972)

	Position			
Accent	Initial	Medial	Final	Total
˵	1	4	3	8
⌢	3	6	2	11
ˋ	8	4	2	14
ˊ	11	1	1	13
Total	23	15	8	46

Table 2.30
Average F_0 values, in hertz, measured within accented and postaccentual syllable nuclei of words occurring in initial, medial, and final position in test sentences analyzed by Peco and Pravica (1972). The measurements were made at the beginning of the syllable nucleus, at the peak of the F_0 contour within the syllable nucleus, and at the end of the syllable nucleus.

	Position								
Accent	Initial			Medial			Final		
˵ first syllable	200	250	250	223	245	228	113	115	65
⌢ first syllable	230	285	253	208	259	246	210	218	159
ˋ accented syllable	221		294	238		284	225		268
ˋ postaccentual syllable	294		263	270		248	268		220
ˊ accented syllable	217		298	225		250	200		250?
ˊ postaccentual syllable	298		248	250		240	no information		

accounted for. This obliges readers to establish for themselves the averages for each accent in each position. The figures that we compiled from Peco and Pravica's data are shown in table 2.30.

Most of these data correspond basically to our own results. The most striking exception concerns the rising syllable under ⌢ not only in initial, but also in medial, position. Another difference is that Peco and Pravica have found rising F_0 contours "from the beginning to the end of the accented vowel" in all words with ˋ and ˊ, whereas our data displayed no such regularity, at least in the case of the short rising accent. Especially remarkable is the consistently rising F_0 movement in the vowels under ˋ and ˊ in final position.

Even though the F_0 data and spectrograms published by Peco and Pravica reveal that the first postaccentual syllable in words with rising accents has high initial fundamental frequency, they draw conclusions very different from ours (and from those of a number of other authors). In particular, they insist that their data prove that the Serbocroatian rising accents are not disyllabic. This conclusion appears to be based on an assumption not made explicit in the article, namely that in order for a rising accent to be disyllabic, the fundamental frequency must continue its rise from the beginning of the first syllable to the end of the second (pp. 213, 214, 215). They argue that "a partial spread [of high tone] to the next syllable [after a rising accent] is quite natural and phonetically understandable. Since with rising accents the tone lasts till the end of the accented vowel, it is clear why this rise embraces also some centiseconds of the postaccentual syllable. If this were not so, we would have the picture which characterizes the falling accents, especially the long falling one" (pp. 214–215). However, we submit that Peco and Pravica's assumptions are unwarranted, for the following reasons.

1. The correct definition of a disyllabic accent is "an accent with high F_0 peaks in two consecutive syllables." This is how we use the term, how other authors use it, and how it was used by Leonhard Masing, who introduced it into Serbocroatian accentology. In order to prove that rising accents are not disyllabic, it would be necessary to show that words in which they occur contain only one syllable with a high F_0 peak.

2. There are no reasons to assume that the initial part of a syllable following a rising accent automatically has high initial fundamental frequency. Rising accents without such a concomitant high tone are known from many languages, including the Čakavian, Kajkavian, and Slavonian dialects of Serbocroatian. In Slavonian such a rising accent even contrasts with the Štokavian ˊ precisely by not having high fundamental frequency on the next syllable (cf. section 2.8.3). Of course, this Slavonian accent is monosyllabic, and the Štokavian accent disyllabic.

3. Peco and Pravica emphasize that the high tone in the beginning of the postaccentual syllable distinguishes the rising accents from the falling ones ("if this were not so, we would have the picture which characterizes the falling accents," p. 215). In their opinion, based on their own measurements, even the two long accents would be indistinguishable without high fundamental frequency in the beginning part of the syllable following the ˊ accent. In other words, the level of the F_0 peak in the first postaccentual syllable appears to be phonologically relevant. The authors probably overlooked the implications of their own statement, for they did not present F_0 values for second syllables in words with falling accents.

4. The falling accents normally have a peak in the first half of the syllable

nucleus, followed by a fall whose duration is usually longer than that of the (initial rise and) peak. The postaccentual syllables of rising accents owe their prosodic shape to the original presence of a (falling) accent on that syllable, not to the extension of the prosodic characteristics of the syllable currently carrying the rising accent to the postaccentual syllable. Thus, there is no reason to expect the rise of the syllable currently bearing a rising accent to be extended up to the termination of the formerly accented, now postaccentual, syllable; it is natural to expect the F_0 curve on the postaccentual syllable to resemble that which it carried originally. The innovation is in the formerly preaccentual syllable, not in the currently postaccentual one.

5. It is true that the peak at the beginning of the first postaccentual syllable is sometimes lower than the F_0 level reached in the syllable carrying the rising accent (the phenomenon is infrequent in Peco and Pravica's material, and they do not use this argument). We attribute this to the position of the syllable within the overall F_0 contour characterizing the "ideal" shape of a word (cf. section 2.6). The F_0 curve within a word is generally falling; the farther a syllable is from the beginning, the lower the F_0 value of its peak, all other factors being kept constant. The postaccentual syllable is farther from the beginning of the word than the accented syllable, and thus its lower peak has a natural explanation. This also means that, when the two peaks are at the same level, the intersyllabic relation appears rising if measured against the general tonal contour of the word.

6. In the opinion of Peco and Pravica, "as far as tone is concerned, the postaccentual syllable [in words with rising accents] is as a whole considerably inferior to the accented syllable" (p. 215). This view is contradicted by their own material. True, the initial peak of the postaccentual syllable is usually followed by a fall and thus by lower fundamental frequency, but in the accented syllable too the tone is not constantly on the same high level: the parts that precede the final peak are lower. Table 2.30 shows clearly that in words with ` or ´ the initial fundamental frequency of the accented vowel is as a rule lower than the final fundamental frequency of the postaccentual one, both in initial and in medial position (221 vs. 263 Hz and 238 vs. 248 Hz, respectively, in words with `, and 217 vs. 248 Hz and 225 vs. 240 Hz, respectively, in words with ´). Since the final fundamental frequency of the accented vowel and the initial value of the postaccentual one are in most cases equal, the averages for the postaccentual syllable are higher. Thus, the "postaccentual syllable as a whole" is not at all "inferior as far as tone is concerned."

7. Finally, the relevance of the second syllable for the perception of the

distinction between rising and falling accents has been amply demonstrated by listening tests.

We agree with Peco and Pravica that the dialect background of the subjects must be considered. Some of our own data (replication of Experiments 2 and 4, sections 2.9.3 and 2.9.5) show that dialect background may influence the relative importance of the F_0 contour on the accented syllable and the F_0 pattern on the postaccentual syllable in the perceptual identification of the accents.

The spectrograms published by Peco and Pravica show realizations of all four accents that do not differ in any essential way from realizations described in our publications.

Basically the same ideas expressed in Peco and Pravica 1972 were expounded in Peco 1971c and Peco 1976. The results of Peco and Pravica's measurements were analyzed in Simić 1977.

2.10.13 Edward T. Purcell (1973), *The Realization of Serbo-Croatian Accents in Sentence Environments: An Acoustic Investigation.* (Reviewed by Lehiste 1976.)

Purcell's book is a slightly modified version of his doctoral dissertation, presented to the Graduate School of the University of Wisconsin in 1970. An excerpt from the book dealing with sentence intonation had been published earlier (Purcell 1971); this article will be referred to in the section on sentence intonation.

Five male informants from [Bosnia-]Hercegovina, residing in the Chicago area, recorded a reading text containing 50 test words in six sentence environments and in a frame sentence. The test words consisted of 5 examples each of words with 10 accentual patterns: monosyllabic, disyllabic, and trisyllabic words with short and long falling accents and disyllabic and trisyllabic words with short and long rising accents. The 1,750 productions were analyzed acoustically by means of a Frøkjær-Jensen Trans-Pitch Meter and an amplitude analyzer designed at the University of Wisconsin, and recorded graphically on a Siemens Oscillomink. The resulting four-channel oscillograms showed F_0 curves, intensity curves, duplex oscillograms, and a time calibration. Measurements of fundamental frequency, intensity, and duration were made from the oscillograms.

On the basis of these data, Purcell arrived at what he labeled the "normal pattern of accentual differentiation": "a pattern of higher/lower relationships which may distinguish a short rising from a short falling accent, or a long rising from a long falling accent within the same sentence environ-

Table 2.31
Average durations, in milliseconds, for accented vowels in test words analyzed by Purcell (1973)

Disyllabic Words				Trisyllabic words			
Short falling	Long falling	Short rising	Long rising	Short falling	Long falling	Short rising	Long rising
81	148	111	157	79	117	78	123

ment" (p. 93). The normal pattern is based on the average data for all five speakers collectively, for test words in all seven sentence environments dealt with in the study.

Systematic durational differences were found to be associated with long and short accents. The average durations, in milliseconds, for the accented vowels were as shown in table 2.31 (Purcell 1973:85).

The differences in the F_0 contours can be summarized as follows (pp. 94–95):

1. Within the accented vowel,
a. the fundamental frequency at the start of the accented vowel is higher for a falling accent than it is for a corresponding rising accent, except for trisyllabic words bearing long accents (surprisingly enough, here the F_0 value at the start of the accented syllable is lower for ˆ than for ´);
b. the fundamental frequency at the end of the accented vowel is lower for a falling accent than for a corresponding rising accent;
c. the F_0 peak within the accented vowel occurs closer to the start of the vowel for a falling accent than for a rising accent.
2. Within the first postaccentual vowel, the F_0 value is lower for a falling accent than for a corresponding rising accent at all points of comparison (start, middle, and end of the vowel).

These relationships are stated to hold for all sentence environments, even though deviations from the normal pattern might occur.

Purcell's criteria 1a–c correspond to our parameter of "intrasyllabic relation," and criterion 2 carries information that is, in connection with the F_0 peak of the accented syllable, relevant for our second parameter ("inter-syllabic relation"). The two approaches are similar; the difference is that we compare *relations* (within the accented syllable and between the two syllables), whereas Purcell, in five out of six cases, compares *absolute* F_0 values in words with falling and rising accents.

Purcell also calculated correlation coefficients for a subset of his data (test words produced in frame sentences) and a subset of ours (test words produced in frame sentences by P.I. and by the group of low-pitched subjects whose data were given in Lehiste and Ivić 1963: table 5). The correlations were uniformly high, ranging between .72 and .99, and averaging .9175. A correlation coefficient of $+1.0$ would mean that there was an exact match between the data produced by Purcell's subjects and those produced by the group with which they were being compared. The high correlation coefficients make it possible to say that the production patterns reported by Purcell are basically identical with those reported by us in 1963. This emerges especially clearly if we bear in mind that a considerable part of the differences concerns the initial fundamental frequency in trisyllabic words with long accents, where Purcell's findings contradict his results in the rest of the material. Characteristically enough, Purcell's rules correspond 100% to the data for our main informant (except for the anomaly in trisyllabic words with long accents, which did not occur in our material).

However, we were puzzled by the fact that subjects from Vojvodina and subjects from western territories responded differently to our listening tests. If the productions of the accents are identical, there would be no reason for listeners from western territories to develop different expectations. Returning to Purcell's data, we found several points of difference between the patterns produced by his subjects and those produced by our eastern subjects. The main difference appears in the relative F_0 levels of postaccentual syllables in words with rising accents (cf. Purcell's footnote 13, p. 209). We checked the tables Purcell provides for statement mid and frame sentence environments for all of his subjects and found that the peak F_0 value on the postaccentual syllable after rising accents was regularly lower than the peak F_0 value on the accented syllable (even though this value is higher than the peak F_0 value on the postaccentual syllable following falling accents). In eight possible comparisons per speaker, three speakers had lower F_0 peaks in postaccentual syllables than in syllables bearing rising accents, and two had such relationships in 6 instances out of 8, for a total of 36 out of 40, or 90% of the instances. Our subjects, on the other hand, had the opposite relationship—equal or higher F_0 peaks on postaccentual syllables after ˋ and ˊ—in 92.8% of comparable instances (tables 2.2, 2.4, 2.5, and 2.6). We found in our listening tests that the F_0 level of the postaccentual syllable was a stronger cue for eastern than western listeners; this finding becomes entirely reasonable in light of Purcell's data, which show that in realizations of accents by speakers from western areas the difference in the height of postaccentual syllables after rising and falling accents is considerably reduced.

True, it might seem possible to explain the falling intersyllabic relations in Purcell's material by two circumstances in the biographies of his informants: two of them (A.Č., N.D.) had lived during their childhood and youth on the island of Brač, where a Čakavian dialect is spoken, and two of them (A.R., L.H.) had left Yugoslavia almost a quarter of a century before Purcell recorded their speech, so that one might expect their pronunciation to have been influenced by the languages of the countries where they had lived in the meantime (Syria, Italy, and the United States in one case; Italy, Argentina, and the United States in the other). However, a serious argument can be adduced against such an attempted explanation: the same falling intersyllabic relations in words with rising accents appeared also in the speech of the fifth informant, R.G., who never lived in a Čakavian-speaking region and who left Yugoslavia shortly before his pronunciation was recorded.

Edward T. Purcell (1976), "Pitch Peak Location and the Perception of Serbo-Croatian Word Tone"

For this study, Purcell produced a set of 21 versions of the sequence [ra:di] with a JAWORD terminal analogue speech synthesizer. Except for the first and twenty-first versions, all stressed vowels started at 100 Hz, peaked at 120 Hz, and ended at 100 Hz. The stressed vowel of the first sample started at 120 Hz and ended at 100 Hz; the twenty-first sample started at 100 Hz and ended at 120 Hz. The position of the peak varied in 10 msec steps from the beginning to the end of the syllable nucleus, which was 200 msec long. The second syllable was kept constant at 100 Hz.

A randomized test tape was prepared, on which each stimulus occurred twice. Listeners had to identify the words as one of the forms of the verb *raditi* 'to work'—2.sg.imper. or 3.sg.pres.indic. Since the imperative carries a long rising accent and the 3.sg. form carries a long falling accent, selection of the imperative was interpreted as perception of the long rising accent, and selection of the 3.sg. as perception of the long falling accent. Eleven listeners participated in the experiment at the University of Sarajevo, and nine at the University of Belgrade. The results were pooled for the two groups; thus, there were 40 judgments for each stimulus.

The results showed that an F_0 peak located in the final 24% of the stressed vowel was reliably judged as "rising"; peaks located earlier were heard as "falling." There was a crossover between stimuli 15 and 16; the rapid switch from falling to rising evaluations suggested a near categoricity of perception. Purcell concluded that the crucial feature in the perceptual distinction between long rising and long falling accents is the position of the F_0 peak rather than the pitch relationship between syllables.

We accept Purcell's data, but we do not agree with his conclusions. For 20 out of 21 stimuli, Purcell's test words included a second syllable at the F_0 level of the terminal value of the F_0 contour of the preceding syllable, but Purcell ignored the presence of that syllable in the interpretation of his results. Purcell tried to explain the surprising fact that the crossover did not take place when the peak of the F_0 contour was in the middle of the syllable nucleus by proposing three different theories, none of them convincing. We believe that the explanation is very simple: the second syllable in Purcell's materials was 20 Hz below the peak of the first syllable and thus favored falling judgments.

Under the conditions of Purcell's experiment, pitch peak location was a sufficient cue for distinguishing between long rising and long falling accents. Purcell has not demonstrated that pitch peak location was a necessary cue. Our earlier experiments with the same word pair (Lehiste and Ivić 1972) show that even the presence of a pitch peak is not necessary for the identification of rising accents: significant recognition was achieved with a monotone first syllable, when the second syllable had an appropriate value. Our experiments also show that an appropriate F_0 contour is not always sufficient without an appropriate relationship between syllables: a rising F_0 curve by itself was not sufficient for the perception of a long rising accent unless the second syllable had an appropriately high value, and a falling F_0 curve by itself was not sufficient for the perception of a long falling accent unless the second syllable had an appropriately low value.

Edward T. Purcell (1981), "Two Parameters in the Perception of Serbo-Croatian Tone"

In his 1973 and 1976 publications Purcell had advanced the view that it is the position of the F_0 peak within the accented syllable that distinguishes rising accents from falling ones. We had maintained that the crucial difference lies in the relationship between the F_0 levels of the accented and the postaccentual syllables. We had also considered the possibility that the relationship between the initial and final F_0 values within the accented vowel may be important for the perception of Serbocroatian tone, but had rejected it on the basis of the results of our first experiment (1972, reviewed here as Experiment 1 (original study), section 2.9.1). In the study reported in 1981, Purcell investigated the relative importance of F_0 peak location, on the one hand, and the relationship between initial and final F_0 values within the accented syllable, on the other hand, for the perception of long rising and falling accents.

The word pair *râdi–rádi* was again chosen as the basis for the 15 synthetic stimuli prepared for the listening tests. The durations of the two vowels were 200 and 100 msec. Five F_0 patterns were applied to the first vowel; the initial and final values of the F_0 contour were as follows:

1. Steep fall: start at 110 Hz, end at 92 Hz
2. Slight fall: start at 105 Hz, end at 96 Hz
3. Level: start at 100 Hz, end at 100 Hz
4. Slight rise: start at 96 Hz, end at 105 Hz
5. Steep rise: start at 92 Hz, end at 110 Hz

The contour applied to the first syllable also had a peak occurring in three positions: at 25%, 50%, and 75% of the duration of the vowel. Though the F_0 value of the peak is not given in the article, a graph indicates that it occurred at approximately 120 Hz. The contour was therefore rising-falling in every case; for example, the "steep fall" involved a rise from 110 Hz to 120 Hz and a fall from 120 Hz to 92 Hz, and the "steep rise" involved a rise from 92 Hz to 120 Hz and a fall from 120 Hz to 110 Hz. The frequency values of second syllables are not given in Hz in the article; however, all second syllables carried a falling F_0 contour that seems (on the basis of the graph) to have started from the frequency at which the first syllable terminated. Purcell states that "in all instances the fundamental frequency of the second vowel decreased linearly and proportionally to the frequency change exhibited in the first syllable" (p. 190). Since the first syllable carried a rising-falling F_0 pattern, this statement is difficult to interpret.

The 15 items were presented twice each in random order to eleven native listeners in Sarajevo and to nine in Belgrade. Listeners were asked to identify each stimulus as one or the other member of the minimal pair. There were 40 judgments per stimulus, for a total of $15 \times 40 = 600$ judgments. A statistical analysis was performed on the data, which led Purcell to the following conclusions. Listeners appear to track both peak location and initial-final relationships, and they seem to give them equal weight in their determinations. If the two parameters agree in their indications—if both indicate falling or both indicate rising—then the two reinforce each other. The effects of the two together are greater than the effects of each alone. There is no basis for claiming that one or the other parameter is more important for the perception of Serbocroatian accents.

One factor Purcell does not consider sufficiently in the interpretation of his data is the overall prevalence of "falling" judgments. Purcell does not show the actual distribution of the responses, but the distribution is recoverable from his table I, which was prepared as follows. The 600 judgments by twenty subjects were coded 1 for falling and 2 for rising. Coded

Table 2.32
Number of "rising" responses given by 20 listeners to synthesized forms of the test word *radi*, differing in F_0 contour and in the placement of the F_0 peak (expressed in percentage of the duration of the accented vowel), reported in Purcell (1981)

Peak location	Steep fall	Slight fall	Level	Slight rise	Steep rise	Row means
25%	4	1	8	13	17	8.60
50%	8	9	11	15	31	14.80
75%	19	18	12	15	22	17.20
Column means	10.33	9.33	10.33	14.33	23.33	13.53

vectors were prepared to represent the two independent variables of the experiment: 1, 2, and 3 for early, mid, or late F_0 peak location, and 1, 2, 3, 4, or 5 for steeply falling, slightly falling, level, slightly rising, or steeply rising initial-final frequency relationships. Means and standard deviations were calculated for the 15 combinations; these values are given in Purcell's table I. Lower values (close to 1) indicate "falling" judgments, higher values (close to 2) indicate "rising" judgments.

Using the means given in table I, we have reconstructed table 2.32, showing "rising" judgments given by twenty listeners to 2 × 15 = 30 stimuli. There were 40 responses to each stimulus, for a total of 600 responses. There were thus 203 "rising" judgments out of 600, or 34%. Furthermore, not all of the "rising" judgments represent true identifications; some are simply due to guessing. In the absence of intrasubject reliability estimates, values clustering around 1.5 (on Purcell's scale from 1 to 2) might represent statistically random choices; translated into the data presented in table 2.32, the interval between approximately 14 and 26 would therefore correspond to guessing. Out of 15 stimuli, 8 received statistically significant "falling" identifications, 1 received significant "rising" responses, and 6 received potentially random responses. There were thus 254 significant "falling" identifications, 31 significant "rising" identifications, and 315 random choices (we are assuming that the minority choices to stimuli with significant majority agreement were likewise potentially random judgments).

We believe that many of the choices were in fact random, resulting from contradictory information present in the stimuli. The falling second syllable constituted a strong cue for "falling" judgments. There were no stimuli in the set in which the second syllable would have had an F_0 level comparable to the peak of the preceding accented syllable. This conflict between the cues provided by F_0 peak position and by falling second syllable becomes especially clear from a study of the judgments made with the F_0 peak at 75% of the duration of the first vowel. Here the judgments fall in the random range of 14 to 26 regardless of the relationship between the beginning and the ending frequencies of the F_0 contour on the accented syllable: steep fall, slight fall, slight rise, and steep rise all evoke apparently random responses. Only the case with level intonation—that is, with the same value for the beginning and end of the F_0 contour, and a peak at 75% of the duration of the first vowel—receives a significant identification score, and this stimulus is significantly identified as "falling," in spite of the F_0 peak at 75% of the duration of the first vowel.

We agree that Purcell's data show a trend toward more "rising" judgments both with later placement of the F_0 peak and with an increasingly rising relationship between the beginning and end of the F_0 contour on the accented syllable. It seems to us, however, that neither factor was very powerful in producing significant "rising" judgments by the listeners in the presence of the contradictory cue provided by the second syllable.

2.10.14 Jadranka Gvozdanović (1980), *Tone and Accent in Standard Serbo-Croatian*. (Reviewed by Micklesen 1981.)

This publication is Gvozdanović's doctoral dissertation; it includes the results of several earlier articles, which we will not review separately. The book constitutes a thoroughgoing and theoretically well-founded exploration of tone and accent in Serbocroatian, based on a critical survey of previous investigations as well as some independent experimental research. Here we will review some of its basic assumptions and experimental data.

Gvozdanović starts from a generalization based on data concerning the relative position of the F_0 peak, which, she states, she has derived from our published materials. She defines three types of F_0 contours: falling F_0 contour, characterized by the occurrence of the F_0 peak at some point within the first quarter of the duration of the vowel; nonfalling, nonrising F_0 contour, characterized by the occurrence of the F_0 peak in the second or third quarter of the duration of the vowel; and rising F_0 contour, characterized by the occurrence of the F_0 peak within the last quarter of the duration of the vowel. In addition, she recognizes high fundamental frequency (higher than that of the preceding syllable nucleus), low fundamental frquency (lower than that of the preceding syllable nucleus), and indifferent fundamental frequency (neither higher nor lower than that of the preceding syllable nucleus). She says nothing about determining the height of the fundamental frequency in an initial syllable, where no preceding syllable nucleus is present. Where contrastive, these F_0 contours are called "tones." Gvozdanović uses other terms that are not explicitly defined, but may be understood on the basis of earlier definitions. Thus, "nonfalling" appears to refer to tones with a peak anywhere except in the first quarter of the duration of the vowel; "nonindifferent" appears to refer to a F_0 level that is either higher or lower than that of the preceding syllable nucleus; and so on.

"Accent" is defined as a change from nonfalling to falling fundamental frequency. Accent is a feature of "prosodic words" (that is, morphological words and associated proclitics and enclitics, if any). Gvozdanović has devoted much attention to the concept of prosodic word and has made a substantial contribution to its elaboration. According to Gvozdanović, prosodic words are established with reference to initial and final boundaries specified in terms of fundamental frequency: they start with a rising or a high nonfalling fundamental frequency and end with a nonrising fundamental frequency. A boundary between prosodic words consists either of a falling fundamental frequency that is followed by a nonfalling fundamental frequency or of a nonfalling, nonrising fundamental frequency that is followed by a nonindifferent, nonfalling fundamental frequency.

Gvozdanović's definition of accent makes it possible to describe traditional rising accents as being "characterized either by a rising or by a nonfalling non-rising fundamental frequency which is followed by a high falling fundamental frequency in the next syllable nucleus" (p. 11). A falling accented syllable nucleus "is characterized by a non-falling nonrising fundamental frequency which is followed by a low falling fundamental frequency in the next following syllable nucleus" (p. 12). However, some problems arise in connection with traditional falling accents, which, in Gvozdanović's opinion, never have a peak in the first quarter of their duration: falling F_0 contours are exclusively associated with postaccentual syllables. No prosodic word starts with a falling F_0 contour (pp. 36–37). It is this claim—that no accented syllable has a peak in its first quarter—that makes it possible to define accent as a change from nonfalling to falling fundamental frequency.

Gvozdanović bases her definitions on our data, not taking into account the fact that averages constitute generalizations over a considerable range of observations. She quotes the average position of the F_0 peak in productions of test words by P.I. as being at 27% of the duration of a syllable nucleus bearing the long falling accent (Ivić and Lehiste 1963). However, the same table that contains this average value (table 12, p. 49) also gives individual peak positions for six different syllable nuclei averaged according to the syllable nucleus, and the table shows that for 74 words in which the long falling accent is realized on the vowel /a/, the position of the F_0 peak was at 21.6% of the duration of the syllable nucleus. At least some of these 74 words would have falling F_0 contours on the first syllable even according to Gvozdanović's definition. As may be seen from table 2.3, 54 out of 160 test words with the long falling accent produced by P.I. had the F_0 peak within the first 20% of the duration of the syllable nucleus, amounting to 33.75% of the instances. Moreover, 23 out of 271 test words with the ̏ accent and even 8 out of 269 words with the ̀ accent had the F_0 peak within the first 20% of the duration of the syllable nucleus, which renders Gvozdanović's statements about these accents inaccurate. There seems to be no principled reason why 25% should constitute a cutoff point.

Information about twelve additional speakers was likewise available (Lehiste and Ivić 1963). The position of the F_0 peak in syllable nuclei bearing the traditional long falling accent, produced by twelve informants and expressed as a percentage of the duration of the syllable nucleus, was as follows: 8.2%, 12.8%, 18.3%, 14.8%, 12.9%, 24.3%, 29.6%, 26.8%, 18.8%, 17,8%, 19.7%, and 67.4%. Thus, for nine out of twelve speakers, the peak occurred in the first quarter and the F_0 contour on these syllable nuclei would be falling according to Gvozdanović's definition. The data from these speakers also show that there exist individuals in whose pronunciation the *average* place of the F_0 peak in syllable nuclei under ̏ and even under ̀ is in the first quarter of the duration of the syllable nucleus (see the data from speakers D1, D2, D3, and D5 for ̏ and from speakers D1 and D2 for ̀). Finally, in the pronunciation of speakers D1, D6, E10, E11, and E13 the syllable following ̀ had a rising F_0 contour.

According to Gvozdanović's terminology, syllables with an F_0 peak in the first quarter of the syllable nucleus would have a falling F_0 contour, but would not carry falling tone. Indeed, a large number of words bearing a traditional falling accent would not have any accent at all according to Gvozdanović's definitions, since they do not contain a nonfalling syllable followed by a falling syllable. Nor should any prominence be heard in such words, for Gvozdanović claims that accent is perceived as prominence, and the perception of prominence is brought about by the change from nonfalling to falling fundamental frequency. If no such change is present, no prominence should be perceived. It appears to us that premises leading to such improbable results cannot be valid.

Gvozdanović takes issue with our attempt to characterize accentedness in Serbocroatian. In Lehiste and Ivić 1963 we had tried to identify the phonetic factors that enter into marking a syllable as the bearer of accent. Intensity seemed to play no systematic part; high fundamental frequency did not distinguish between two syllables of which the first carried a rising accent. We found that in our materials accented syllables were always longer than unaccented syllables (in comparable positions) of the same *phonological quantity* (italics added now). We admitted that "the durational cues remain ambiguous in the case of words containing a short rising accent and a posttonic length" (1963: 29); we never claimed, as Gvozdanović seems to believe (1980: 34–35), that the longest syllable nucleus in a word is accented. However, the combination of the accent ` and length of the following syllable constitutes the best kind of evidence for the importance of greater duration as a clue to accentedness. All those who have experience in teaching standard Serbocroatian accentology know that not only foreigners, but also native students, make frequent mistakes or are unsure of themselves in identifying the place of accent in words like *dèvōjka* 'girl' and *jùnāk* 'hero'. The most important evidence in this respect is provided by the works of early authors. In the first edition of Vuk Karadžić's dictionary (1818) such examples were always written as *devôjka, junâk*, etc. It would not be right to explain away this fact by supposing that the Neoštokavian accent shift had not yet been completed in these word categories in Karadžić's native dialect—in other words, by supposing that accent was in fact pronounced on the second syllable. Karadžić marked examples of length after the accent ̏ in the same manner; thus, he wrote *kamên* 'stone', *Cigânka* 'gypsy woman' instead of *kȁmēn, Cȉgānka*. To be sure, he was aware (as shown by his statement on p. XXXVI) that in such words accent is nevertheless present on the first syllable, but he considered it unnecessary to indicate this accent, since its presence would be understood. He considered postaccentual long vowels as bearers of accent as well, since he wrote (for example) *pâmćênje* (= *pâmćēnje*) 'memory'. He did add a reservation: "One could almost say that this sound, too, is twofold in those words in which two occur in one word, e.g. *pâmćênje*, *sûdîm*, *šârân*, *vêzêm* etc." (p. XXXVI; 'memory', 1.sg.pres. 'judge', 'multicolored', 1.sg.pres. 'bind'). The fact that of the two "accents" in words like *dèvōjka* or *kȁmēn* he wrote only the second suggests that for him that "accent" appeared more prominent. This conclusion is also indicated by his practice in connection with the sequence ´ ¯ in verbal nouns, where naturally the long accent is more prominent than unaccented length. In such cases Karadžić wrote only ´ (*písanje* 'writing', etc.), and he stated on the quoted page that in all such examples ˆ is pronounced on the following syllable. In other words, where he thought that he could give a general rule according to which a certain sign automatically implies another, he omitted one of the two signs—namely, the one that seemed to him less prominent. Karadžić was, by the way, not the only one to treat postaccentual length as more prominent than a preceding short accent. He took over this system of indicating accents from Milovanov (see section 1.1). Milovanov also wrote (for example) *junâk*, *orâč* 'plower', *kolâč* 'cake', *držânje* 'holding'; however, differing from Karadžić, he asserted explicitly that there is no accent on the first syllable of such words. This agrees with the practice of still earlier writers like J. Raić (1793) and J. Muškatirović (1806), who placed an accent mark only on the long syllable in words like *kakáv* (= *kàkāv* 'which') or *kováč* (= *kòvāč* 'blacksmith'). Kolarović (1827) also used a comparable way of indicating the accent in the words *levâk* 'left-handed man' (= *lèvāk*, p. 154) and imper.sg. *prepisûj* 'copy' (= *prepìsūj*, pp. 155, 156). All this testifies that among the first authors who indicated Neŏtokavian accentuation the impression prevailed that in such examples the long syllable is more prominent than the preceding syllable, which bears a short accent. Nevertheless, one can observe a development in Karadžić's views: in 1833 he was already aware of the fact that in words like *ovčar* 'shepherd' and *kamen* 'stone' (in contemporary transcription, *òvčār* and *kȁmēn*) "the first syllable is pronounced more sharply than the second, but the second is stretched more than the first." He adds, "It may be that according to Greek prosody one might say that the first syllable has an accent, while the second syllable is long" (Karadžić 1895: 379). In the second edition of Karadžić's dictionary, prepared with the help of Daničić, accentuation of the first syllable is systematically carried out in words like *òvčār* and *kȁmēn*, but postaccentual length continues to be indicated by the same symbol as the accent ˆ. Gifted with an extremely sharp logical sense, Karadžić was obviously the first to evaluate the prominence of phonologically short vowels relative to other phonologically short vowels, and the prominence of phonologically long vowels relative to other phonologically long vowels. However, his follower Daničić considered postaccentual length to be a manifestation of the ˆ accent.

During the second half of the nineteenth century the debate continued between supporters of this view and supporters of the view that unaccented long vowels must be distinguished from accented vowels. Only the victory of the second point of view brought about the present situation in which all those who have studied Serbocroatian accentuation *know* that words like *jùnāk* bear a short accent followed by unaccented length; only those who are still learning are unsure of themselves.

The experiments reported by Gvozdanović were designed to test the hypothesis that accent is manifested as a change from nonfalling to falling fundamental frequency and that durational differences are irrelevant. According to this hypothesis, a syllable nucleus with a nonfalling fundamental frequency should be perceived as accented independently of its duration, and if it has a falling fundamental frequency, it should be perceived as unaccented independently of its duration and of its F_0 height (Gvozdanović 1980:59).

The materials selected for a perception test consisted of pairs of items like *ù-kuću–u kȕću* 'into a/the house'. Gvozdanović analyzes these examples as constituting either one or two prosodic words. *Ù-kuću*, with a nonfalling fundamental frequency on the first syllable followed by a high falling fundamental frequency on the second syllable, constitutes a single prosodic word. The sequence *u kȕću* contains a prosodic word boundary, signaled by a nonrising fundamental frequency on *u* and a high nonfalling fundamental frequency on the first syllable of *kȕću*.

Six native speakers from various parts of Yugoslavia produced the test materials used in the study. There were four subsets of items. The first consisted of combinations of the type *u kuću*, in which all syllables were short. Items in the second subset differed from those in the first in having a long second syllable. The third subset consisted of disyllabic items comprising a proclitic and a monosyllabic word with a long vowel. The fourth subset consisted of minimal pairs bearing either the short rising or the short falling accent. The test words were incorporated into sentences presupposing contrastive vs. noncontrastive usage; frame sentences were not used, and the location of the test items in the sentences varied from initial to final position. The speakers were asked to perform transformations on the sentences (e.g., to put them into the past tense or to change a statement into a question) in order to divert their attention from the real purpose of the study and to cause the test items to be produced naturally. In addition, fifteen minimal pairs were produced in isolation.

A listening test was prepared, consisting of two kinds of test items: "isolated" test words, excised from normally spoken sentences, and "composed" test words, constructed from parts of prosodic words produced in isolation. The composition was performed by means of a segmentator built at the Instituut voor Fonetische Wetenschappen in Amsterdam. In the composition process, preaccentual proclitics were combined with corresponding postaccentual words spoken by the same subject. For example, the unaccented *u* of *u kȕću* was combined with the unaccented *kuću* of *ù-kuću*, which means that a syllable with a nonfalling fundamental frequency was combined with syllables characterized by falling fundamental frequency. Gvozdanović reasons as follows (p. 64):

If it does indeed hold that the fundamental frequency contour is the relevant feature determining perception of the place of the accent, the combination *u* + *kuću* described above should be perceptually identified as *ù-kuću*, i.e. as having the accent on the initial syllable nucleus, even though this syllable nucleus does not have a long duration. Similarly, when a non-falling *u* is combined with a falling *pūti*, this combination *u* + *pūti* should be perceived as one prosodic word, with the accent on the first syllable nucleus.

The items included in the test were analyzed acoustically.

The testing was performed in Loznica, a Yugoslav town situated at the border between territories in which the southwestern and northeastern varieties of the Serbocroatian standard language are spoken. The 50 listeners were chosen randomly from among the pupils and teachers of a secondary school center for chemistry and metallurgy in Loznica. They included 13 male speakers of the southwest variety of Serbocroatian, 12 male speakers of the northeast variety, 12 female speakers of the southwest variety, and 13 female speakers of the northeast variety. In fact, the roster of listeners shows that this classification is incorrect. The majority of the "speakers of the northeast variety" come either from the valley of the Drina in western Serbia, where a basically southwestern dialect is spoken, or from places even farther west. Only eight subjects can be considered more or less representative for the northeastern pronunciation; in addition, there are two or three borderline cases.

The subjects were tested individually through headphones. Their task was to indicate on an eight-page test instrument whether a particular test item had been accented on the proclitic or on the morphological word. Subjects could also choose the response "undecided," but Gvozdanović states that this was generally avoided. In the statistical treatment of the responses, percentages of "undecided" responses were divided between the two categorically opposed choices.

The statistical method used was Stepwise Linear Regression. The following acoustic parameters were used in the statistical analysis: the relative position of the F_0 peak in each of the three syllable nuclei; the duration of each of the three syllable nuclei; and the maximal F_0 value in each syllable nucleus, transformed into a logarithmic measure (neither intensity nor intersyllabic F_0 relations were taken into account). For each acoustic variable entered into the regression equation, F- and t-coefficients were computed and their level of significance was established. All of the independent variables had F-values that were significant at the .01 level. Only the relative position of the F_0 peak had t-values significant at the .01 level; the maximal F_0 value of the second and third syllable was significant at the .05 level. The position of the peak in the second syllable was significant at the .001 level, which means that there is a 99.9% probability that it is a relevant perceptual cue to accentedness.

The crucial results for Gvozdanović's hypothesis concern the "composed" trisyllabic items with short syllable nuclei. Here, too, the t-value of the F_0 peak position of the second syllable was significant at the .001 level; F_0 levels on the second and third syllables were significant at the .05 level. There is a 99.9% probability that a relatively early occurrence of the F_0 peak in the second syllable nucleus, which makes this syllable nucleus acoustically falling, coincides with the perception of the accent on the first syllable nucleus.

As for F_0 levels, a low fundamental frequency of the second syllable nucleus was correlated with the perception of the accent on the first syllable nucleus. We find this puzzling, since in a prosodic word bearing a rising accent on the first syllable, the second syllable normally has high fundamental frequency. Likewise puzzling is the finding that perception of accent on the first syllable was correlated with a high fundamental frequency on the third syllable nucleus.

Duration was found to have F-values that were significant at the .01 level, as was the case with all other independent variables; however, none of the t-values for duration turned out to be significant. The fact that all F-values had comparable significance, and that all independent variables had significant F-values, appears to require explanation.

An interesting additional finding was a difference between isolated and composed items concerning the relevance of the F_0 contour on the first syllable nucleus: in isolated items a relatively late peak contributed to the perception of the first syllable as being accented, whereas in composed items the F_0 contour on the first syllable showed no systematic variation. Instead of this clue, the F_0 levels of the second and third syllable nuclei were perceived as relevant in composed items. Gvozdanović does not comment about the curious result that perception of accent on the first syllable nucleus is correlated with a relatively low second syllable nucleus and a relatively high third syllable nucleus. She states, though, that the plurality of the relevant acoustic cues may be due, to some extent, to differences between speakers and to differences among listeners, who included individuals speaking both of the major varieties of standard Serbocroatian.

On the basis of the test results, Gvozdanović formulates two different acoustic rules that can account for accentedness in standard Serbocroatian:

1. The rising syllable in a prosodic word, or in its absence the first syllable, which is acoustically nonfalling nonrising, is accented.
2. The last acoustically nonfalling syllable in a prosodic word is accented.

Gvozdanović proposes that the first rule applies to the southwestern and western varieties of standard Serbocroatian, and that the second rule may be basic to the prosodic system of the northeastern variety.

Gvozdanović bases her distinction between the two variants of the standard language in this respect on the assumption that in the northeastern variant ̏ and ̑ can occur in noninitial syllables of a prosodic word, which is impossible in the (south)western variant. Under consideration here are examples such as *u kȕću, u grȃd* in the northeast vs. *ȕ kuću, ȕ grād* in the (south)west, and some compound words and loanwords (see note 8 of chapter 4). In our opinion Gvozdanović overestimates here a rather marginal problem. Moreover, her own exposition indicates that in syntagms with prepositions both possibilities are represented in both areas, with certain differences in distribution. The differences between the two variants, insofar as they exist, are of a statistical rather than an absolute nature. In practice, in all major cultural centers in Croatia (Zagreb, Rijeka, Osijek, Split) instances without the accent shift to the preposition are even more frequent than in typical northeastern pronunciation. Likewise, compounds and loanwords with falling accents in noninitial syllables are widespread in the west; see the works of Croatian authors cited in note 6 of chapter 4. All this makes Gvozdanović's dual solution unsatisfactory. It would be more appropriate either to describe examples such as *u kȕću* using junctures and treat the examples in loanwords and compounds as exceptions in the whole territory (which we consider more correct; see chapter 4) or to operate with ̏ and ̑ in noninitial syllables, again in the whole territory.

As noted, the problem with these acoustic rules is their dependence on the position of the F_0 peak within a syllable. The first rule would assign no accent at all to those words with falling accents whose F_0 peak falls within the first quarter of the syllable nucleus. The second rule would assign no accent to words in which there is no acoustically nonfalling syllable—that is, in which all syllables have a peak at the beginning of a syllable nucleus. Words with falling accents frequently have such realization in noninitial position within a sentence, and words with rising accents have such realizations in sentence-final position.

It must be concluded that specifying the position of the F_0 peak within a syllable is not a sufficient basis for identifying an accented syllable, at least according to the rules formulated by Gvozdanović.

2.11 Summary of Production and Perception of Word Accents

The studies reviewed in the preceding sections reveal a certain amount of agreement and some differing opinions. There is a wide area of consensus in the description of the phonetic realization of different types of accent. The phonetic characteristics of falling accents include a high F_0 peak on the accented syllable and a low fundamental frequency on the postaccentual syllable. The position of the F_0 peak relative to the duration of the syllable nucleus varies slightly depending on the length of the vowel: in long falling accents the F_0 peak is relatively close to the beginning of the syllable nucleus, whereas in short falling accents it tends to be approximately in the middle of the syllable nucleus (the average absolute distance from the beginning tends to be the same). There is a continuous decline in the fundamental frequency after the peak in the first syllable until the lowest F_0 level has been reached in the second syllable. As a result, the terminal fundamental frequency within the accented syllable is frequently lower than the initial fundamental frequency at the beginning of the accented syllable. The accented syllable also usually has somewhat higher intensity than the postaccentual syllable. There seems to be general agreement, though, that intensity plays no systematic role in differentiating between rising and falling accents.

The rising accents usually have a postaccentual syllable whose F_0 peak is as high as or even higher than the F_0 peak reached during the accented syllable. In rising accents the F_0 peak occurs in most cases relatively close to the end of the accented syllable nucleus. There is a continuous F_0 rise from the beginning of the accented syllable toward the F_0 peak, which is very often reached in the postaccentual syllable; the F_0 peak on the accented syllable, if separately manifested, is superimposed on the general rise. As a result, the terminal F_0 value in the accented syllable is, as a rule, higher than its initial value, and the F_0 level reached in the postaccentual syllable is likewise often higher than the peak or terminal F_0 value of the accented syllable. In many instances the intensity of the second syllable is approximately equal to the intensity of the accented syllable. The syllable under a rising accent is integrated into the word without a sharp contrast. In words consisting of at least three syllables the disyllabic sequence consisting of the accented syllable and the immediately following syllable is set off by higher F_0 level.

The perceptual relevance of the characteristics summarized above has been tested in a number of experiments. The aim of the experiments has generally been to identify the one crucial feature that distinguishes the falling accents from the rising accents. The main candidates for this feature have been the F_0 movement within the accented syllable and the relationship between the F_0 levels of the accented and postaccentual syllables. We have previously advanced the view that it is the relationship between the F_0 levels of the two syllables of a disyllabic sequence with accent on the first syllable that determines the identification of an accent as rising or falling. The results of our last experiment, however, have persuaded us to modify our view. It appears indeed that the same phonological judgment can be reached by different perceptual evaluations of the same phonetic material. For listeners from certain regions (the west), the F_0 movement within the accented syllable serves as the primary cue; for listeners from other regions (the northeast), the F_0 relationship between the two successive syllables of the accented disyllabic sequence is of crucial importance; and there seem to be transitional regions (parts of Serbia) in which listeners require the presence of both kinds of cues in order to correctly identify the accents. Everywhere, the role of the intersyllabic relationship is greater in words with short accents. In view of these results, it appears futile to try to identify a single crucial parameter that carries the distinction between rising and falling accents: insofar as communication between speakers of different varieties of the standard language is possible, the phonetic manifestation of the accents must be rich and redundant enough to contain all the cues that listeners may find necessary.

It is our opinion that in western (or at least southwestern) regions syllable nuclei under "falling" accents are more consistently falling and those under "rising" accents are more consistently rising than in the northeast. This would provide a material basis for the observed differences in the evaluation of test stimuli. To be sure, such a supposition has thus far not been confirmed by experimental research in a conclusive way. At any rate, Purcell's findings suggest that the difference between falling and rising accents with respect to the F_0 level of the first postaccentual syllable is smaller in the southwest than in the northeast. This could naturally contribute to the fact that listeners from the southwest attribute greater significance to the intrasyllabic cue in judging the stimuli of listening tests. It is clear that much remains to be done with regard to the investigation of regional variation in the pronunciation of Neoštokavian accents.

We nevertheless continue to believe that among the different cues, primary importance belongs to the relationship between the F_0 levels of the two syllables constituting the accented disyllabic sequence. The reason is inherent in the phonological structure of the language: contrastive accentual patterns presuppose a disyllabic sequence, since there are no contrasts on monosyllabic words. If the shape of the F_0 curve alone were capable of carrying the distinction, we would expect monosyllabic words to be potentially rising or falling. This is not true for Neoštokavian. A comparison with the other three dialects treated in section 2.8 is instructive. In the Čakavian and Kajkavian materials we found distinctive differences in the position of the F_0 peak (i.e., differences in the F_0 contour) on monosyllabic words as well as on accented syllables in polysyllabic words. In Slavonian we were able to observe the difference between the old rising accents and the new (Neoštokavian) rising accents. The old rising accents differ from falling accents on the basis of the F_0 contour on the accented syllable; the new rising accents differ from both old accents on the basis of the F_0 level of the postaccentual syllable.

The domain of the accentual pattern in Neoštokavian is therefore a disyllabic sequence. This disyllabic sequence has certain phonetic properties; for speakers from different regions in which the standard language is spoken, different aspects of these phonetic characteristics may carry greater perceptual value in identification, but what these differential identifications all presuppose is the presence of two syllables.

2.12 Accentual Words and Accentual Measures

Words in Neoštokavian, as well as in other dialects of Serbocroatian, can be accentogenic words or clitics (the latter include proclitics and enclitics). The distinction is based on different semantic properties and syntactic functions. Clitics include shorter forms of auxiliary verbs and of personal pronouns, as well as most prepositions and conjuctions. The main prosodic characteristic of accentogenic words is that they introduce an accent into the spoken chain, whereas clitics do not. Examples: *sîn* 'son', *brȁt* 'brother', and *sèstra* 'sister' are accentogenic words; *je* 'is', *ga* 'him' (shorter form), and *za* 'for' are clitics. Syntagms like *sîn je* 'the son is' or *za sèstru* 'for the sister' have one accent each. However, accentogenic words do not always carry an accent, and clitics are not always unaccented. In cases like *zȁ sīna* 'for the son' or *òd brata* 'from the brother' the initial falling accent is "transferred" to the proclitic as ̏ or as ̀ according to rules that are well described in Serbocroatian grammars. In many cases such a recession is regulated by semantic or syntactic factors. In contrastive usage (*za brȁta, a ne za sîna* 'for the brother, but not for the son') the accent remains on the accentogenic word. There are syntagms in which the transfer is very common (*ȕ vodu* 'into the water', *nè rādi* 'does not work', etc.) and syntagms in which the pronunciation of educated people keeps the accent always on the accentogenic word (*da vȉdī* 'that he sees', *i sȋn* 'and the son'; forms like *dà vidī, ȉ sīn* sound rustic). The retraction is more widespread in the western regions than in the northeast, but all over the Neoštokavian territory one finds both instances with the retraction and instances without it.

We propose to call prosodic units containing only one accent *accentual words*. These units may consist of an accentogenic word, or of such a word and one or more clitics (*sèstra* 'sister', *sèstra je* 'the sister is', *za sèstru* 'for the sister', *za sèstru je* 'it is for the sister'). The function of the accent in syntagmatic combination is connective. It signals the close syntactic link between components of an accentual word. However, in combinations such as *za brȁta* or *i sȋn* the situation is more complex. The fact that there is only one accent in such syntagms signals the syntactic link between the components of the syntagm, but the fact that the accent is not transferred to the clitic implies a weaker degree of connective function (a looser link). The description of such cases requires a special type of juncture. The details concerning the occurrence of such junctures belong to the descriptive grammar; we shall only mention that the frequency of a syntagm and regional differences also play important roles. Grammarians are inclined to favor the retraction, whereas the actual pronunciation of educated people tends to limit it to a number of set expressions and to verbal forms with the negative particle *ne*. The general public has a feeling of regularity that requires words in sandhi position to be pronounced with their "normal" characteristics (for example, the pronunciation *s njȋm* 'with him' rather than *š njȋm*, or the frequent restitution of the final consonant of the preposition in examples such as *bez zákona* 'without a law' rather than *be zákona, pod dàskōm* 'under the board' rather than *po dàskōm*). (Obviously we are dealing here with instances of analogic restoration.)

We propose to reserve the term *accentual word* for parts of the spoken chain held together by a connective accent (*zà brata, ȕ vodu, za sèstru*, as well as *brȁt je* or *sèstra je*) and to introduce the concept of *accentual measure* to cover all units having only one accent, including those in which at least one proclitic precedes a word with a non transferred falling accent (*da vȉdī, i sȋn, i za brȁta* 'and for the brother'). Needless to say, in syntagms where the accentogenic word carries a rising accent, the concepts of accentual word and accentual measure overlap.

2.13 Re-evaluation of Pre-experimental Views Concerning Word Accents

The reported results of our investigations, as well as works of other authors, make it possible to turn our attention again to the ideas described in chapter 1 and to extract from that multitude of frequently contradictory assertions those that have been confirmed by experimental studies and those that have not. We will follow the sequence of presentation of chapter 1 in both instances, starting with those assertions that have turned out to be correct. Each will ordinarily be referred to only once, on the occasion of its first appearance in the literature.

When discussing the very earliest contributions—those of the first half of the nineteenth century, a time when systematic scientific thinking about this topic had not yet been developed—it is often necessary to try to interpret the meaning of the statements in order to establish whether they are backed by acceptable observations.

If we interpret Starčević's qualification of the ̏ accent as "completely short" to mean that this accent is shorter than all the others, it appears that the statement stands. It is likewise correct that ̑ and ́ are long accents (Starčević calls them "lengthened"). As far as the relative length of the two long accents is concerned, not only did different authors give different answers on the basis of auditory impressions, but different instrumental investigations too have given different results.

The notion of Milovanov (1833) and Karadžić (1814) that ̏ is "accentus elevans" (raising accent) and ̑ "accentus superelevans" (greatly raising accent) appears realistic in view of the fact that the pitch level of syllables with ̏ and ̑ stands out from the intonational context much more than that of syllables with ̀ and ́. However, the validity of this statement is weakened by the fact that neither Milovanov nor Karadžić (1814) distinguished between ̏ and ̀.

The accents ̏ and ̀ are indeed pronounced "sharply" (Karadžić 1818), if this is understood to mean shortness of production. It is even more true that accent ̏ is sharper than ̀: its greater sharpness derives not only from the fact that it is usually somewhat shorter than ̀, but also from the abrupt pitch drop between the accented syllable and the one following. If Karadžić's description of ̑—"the voice goes out roundly"—is really based on the observation that the pitch movement changes direction ("roundly") during the pronunciation of the vowel under ̑ and that the accent is falling ("the voice goes out"), one would have to conclude that Karadžić had an exceptional ear for F_0 movements. This interpretation is supported by his observation that under ́ "the voice stretches in a straight line." It is true that in vowels bearing this accent, the direction of the pitch movement within the accented syllable usually remains unchanged. Karadžić's descriptions sound as if they had been based on spectrograms.

In harmony with Karadžić (1818) is Kolarović (1827), when he states that ̏ is shorter and sharper than ̀ and that ́ stretches itself in a straight line. However, with regard to ̑ he is more explicit than Karadžić: "it rises and falls while extending itself." It is true that ̏ and ̑ are "complete" accents in the sense that occurrence of high tone is limited to the accented syllable. If in contrast with that we interpret Kolarović's claim that after ̀ and ́ "the word goes on" as an expression of the observation that high tone is carried over into the following syllable, then this claim would be accurate. The remarks that ̀ and ́ are "tightened" might possibly constitute an imprecise reflection of the realization that high tone lasts longer and is carried over into the following syllable. In any event, Kolarović deserves a great deal of credit for having been the first to notice the doubly binary relationship between the distinctive characteristics of the four Neoštokavian accents.

Šunjić (1853) was the first to state clearly that the accents ̏ and ̑ are falling and ̀ and ́ rising, which is generally true for long accents—at least under neutral (unmarked) sentence intonation condition. The statement is also valid for ̀ in the majority of dialects, and for ̏ in a certain number of them.

Mažuranić's (1860) formulas *â* = ȁa and *á* = aà correspond quite well to physical reality, and they are also quite revealing with regard to the genetic and distributional characteristics of the accents. Mažuranić also makes the accurate judgment that ̏ is pronounced "completely shortly and compactly"; his assertion that ̀ is pronounced "more weakly and stretched like the ́ accent" is likewise not without factual basis.

Ilijć's assertion (1860) that ̀ raises the voice slightly, but so that this raising is barely audible, is certainly correct, when raising is interpreted as rising pitch; this interpretation is supported by the statements that ̑ does not raise the voice, but that ́ raises it rather high. It is also true that under ̑ the voice bends around and falls.

Vujić's teaching (1863) that ̏ is pronounced with a slightly raised voice and ̀ with a slightly lowered voice is acceptable only if the term "raising" refers not to rising pitch (in talking about the ́ accent, Vujić uses the term "rise" rather than "raising") but to prominence relative to the following syllable.

Budmani's description (1867) of ̏ and ̑ as strong and ̀ and ́ as weak was frequently, and justifiedly, interpreted to mean that strong is the accent that is concentrated on one syllable and places that syllable in contrast to others, whereas weak is the accent that is spread over two syllables and does not single out the accented syllable by means of clear-cut prominence. The meaning of Budmani's observation that the accents ̏ and ̑ are determinate and ` and ´ are indeterminate also becomes clear in light of this interpretation.

Jagić's proportional formulas (1870) ̏ : ` = ̂ : ´ and ̏ : ̂ = ` : ´ do, in principle, correspond to reality.

Masing's conception (1876) of ̏ and ̂ as monosyllabic accents and ` and ´ as disyllabic accents has been fully confirmed by instrumental measurements. In all Neoštokavian areas the syllable immediately following ` or ´ is considerably higher than the syllable following ̏ or ̂; in the greater part of the Neoštokavian territory the F_0 peak of the syllable following ` or ´ is usually at the level of the syllable bearing the ` or ´ accent or even higher. Masing is correct in making a distinction between long and short accents with regard to the falling or rising nature of the accented syllable. The syllable under ̂ is in fact falling within a sentence produced with neutral sentence intonation, and the syllable under ´ is rising, but under ̏ a falling F_0 movement is not a regular phenomenon, nor is pitch rise regular under ` in some dialects (Masing himself notices both the difference between the long and short accents in this respect and the lack of complete parallelism in the behavior of the short accents). In any event, those terminological systems (Brandt 1880, Boyer 1900, Maretić 1901, Florschütz 1905) are not necessarily wrongly conceived that designate only ̂ and ´ as falling and rising, respectively, and employ different characterizations for ̏ and ` (sharp vs. weak, strong vs. weak, fast vs. slow, high vs. deep). Even in those cases in which the syllable under ̏ is in fact falling and the syllable under ` does carry a rising F_0 contour, the physical difference between them is by far smaller and less noticeable than the difference between the two long accents, and is therefore far less significant for the distinction.

Masing's observation is correct that disyllabic accents are "milder and weaker" than monosyllabic accents: it is true that disyllabic accents lack a sharp contrast with regard to prominence between the accented and the postaccentual syllable.

The view of Kovačević (1878–79), since adopted by many other authors, that the syllable immediately following ` or ´ has noticeably lower pitch than the accented syllable, is accurate for only part of the dialects. The dialect of Purcell's informants may have belonged in this group.

In light of the preceding paragraphs, it is clear how one should understand Novaković's (1879) claim that ` and ´ are pronounced with an ordinary voice and ̏ and ̂ with a higher voice: this must surely apply to the relationship of the accented syllable to its closest context, namely the immediately following syllable.

Storm's view (1892) that there is no definite tonal movement on syllables bearing the short accents ̏ and ̀ is correct for some dialects.

Stojanović's (1892, etc.) designation of ̏ as sharp accent and ̀ as gentle accent has a real basis in the fact that ̏ is abruptly set off by prominence from its context, which is not the case with ̀. The views expressed by Brandt (1895) must be understood in the same way—namely, the statements that the accent ̏ is sharp, whereas the presence of secondary stress on the following syllable makes rising accents less noticeable, so that they give the impression of weak accents.

Šaxmatov (1898) is correct when he states that the pitch level of the syllable immediately following rising accents varies depending on dialect.

Unaccented long syllables are shorter than accented ones, and the vowel under ̀ is usually slightly longer than the vowel under ̏ (Maretić 1899). Maretić's labeling of ̏ as fast and ̀ as slow could be justified insofar as the prominent part of the word comes to an end much faster in words with ̏ than in words with ̀. It would be less appropriate to base such a terminology on the fact that the vowel under ̀ is, on the average (but not always, and not everywhere), slightly (and most often imperceptibly) longer than the vowel under ̏.

The view of Florschütz (1905) that ̏ is a high accent and ̀ a low accent could be acceptable based on the pitch relation between the accented and the postaccentual syllables. Of more limited significance is the circumstance that the average pitch peak of the syllable under ̀ is somewhat lower than the pitch peak of the syllable under ̏.

Ivšić (1911) is correct when he states that "the total impression of the syllable under the accents ́ and ̀ is stronger than the impression of the syllable following ́ and ̀." However, this need not always be due to "both the expiratory force [being] stronger and the pitch [being] higher." There are many dialects in which the latter statement does not hold either with respect to intensity or with respect to pitch; other factors obviously come into play, such as the longer duration of the vowel under the accent and the relaxation that begins during the production of the postaccentual syllable.

Moskovljević's statement (1913) is correct that in Srem the syllable immediately following a syllable with rising accent may even be somewhat higher than the accented syllable. Srem is part of Vojvodina, an area for which this phenomenon has since been well confirmed. Moskovljević likewise senses well that the pitch drop in the syllable under ̑ is much greater than that in the syllable under ̏, and in connection with this he explains correctly the difference between the pitch levels of the vowels immediately following each of these two accents.

Belić (1926–27) observes correctly that the different pitch level of the first postaccentual syllable is the factor that preserves the distinction between the two short accents when the pitch movements within the accented syllables are the same. Belić is likewise correct when he points out that the pronunciation of ̏ in eastern Štokavian areas in "atypical," which in fact means that there is no real pitch fall within the accented syllable.

Jakobson's observation (1931a) that ̀ and ́ are characterized by "Übersilbigkeit" (transsyllabicity) of high tone is excellent. Less accurate is the statement that in other Neoštokavian dialects "Vollsilbigkeit" (the occurrence of high tone only on the accented syllable) has the same function. As for "Unvollsilbigkeit" (occurrence of high tone on part of the accented syllable) as a distinctive feature, this corresponds well to the nature of the ̑ accent, but not at all to the ̏ accent, to which Jakobson attributes the same property.

The accents ̏ and ̑ do indeed "seem to detach the stressed syllable from other syllables" (Belić 1935b).

Miletić's observations (1952) about the influence of sentence intonation on word accents are in principle correct.

The musical transcription of accents given by Peco 1971c is among those that correspond best to instrumental results.

Kašić and Jerković's views (1976), according to which intersyllabic tonal relations are relevant for short accents but not for long accents, appear to be founded on the realization that with long accents the distinction rests primarily on the difference in tonal movements within the accented syllable, which is not so clearly manifested with short accents.

We turn now to views expressed in the literature that have not been confirmed by experimental studies. We will leave aside those claims that by their very nature hardly lend themselves to experimental verification, as well as those that may be considered marginally correct.

The statement that the ̀ accent is "quickly lowered" (Starčević 1812) does not belong in the description of this accent. On the contrary, ̀ is distinguished from ̏ primarily by the fact that the high tone lasts much longer.

Whatever interpretation we may try to apply to Karadžić's (1814) view that "some of the stretching" of the ̑ accent "is transferred to the following vowel," this statement cannot be accepted as accurate.

The views of Miklošič (1852), Karadžić (1858), Bošković (1869, 1878), and Živanović (1874) that reduce the differences between the four accents to differences in duration are far from realistic.

Šunjić (1853) is wrong in assuming that syllables following rising accents are at the same pitch level as syllables following falling accents.

Also wrong is Brlić's view (1854) that the accent ̏ is "low" in contrast with ̀, which is "higher than ̏."

Experimental studies and perceptual tests have failed to support the idea of Mažuranić and others that intensity features are relevant for Serbocroatian accents. In actuality, tone plays a much more important role.

Completely erroneous in Pacel's idea (1860) that the durations of the four accents ̏ : ̀ : ́ : ̑ are in a 1 : 2 : 3 : 4 relationship. Here the difference in duration between the two short accents, as well as the difference between the two long ones, has been excessively magnified, and the whole range represented by 1 : 4 has been at least doubled.

Surprising is the auditory impression of Storm (1892) according to which the syllable immediately following the accent ́ is lower by far than the accented syllable.

No confirmation has been found for the claims of Milas (1898), Kostić (1937), and Tomić (1963) that Neoštokavian distinguishes more than four accents.

Most of Šajković's results (1901) hardly correspond to what is typical for Neoštokavian accents. This applies in particular to the notion that ̀ is a falling accent and that the accent ̑ is characterized by the presence of two pitch peaks, one at the beginning and one at the end of the accented vowel.

Instrumental measurements have generally not confirmed Belić's auditory impression (1926–27) that the intensity of rising accents begins to decrease from the middle of the accented syllable. To be sure, many of the measurements did not include intrasyllabic intensity changes, but only intersyllabic relationships.

Trubetzkoy (1939) was not on the right track in claiming that low register is characteristic for the syllable under ̏. This syllable is, as a rule, set off from its context by higher pitch. Nor has the view been confirmed that pitch is relevant for rising accents, but intensity for ̏.

We can conclude that of the many statements based on auditory impressions, a great number are correct to a certain degree, and that the majority of the significant characteristics of Neoštokavian accents have been perceived by the unaided ear. However, side by side with such valid observations, opinions have been offered that have no basis in objective physical reality. The usefulness of instrumental measurements lies, among other things, in the fact that they make it possible to identify and single out those observations that represent positive and valuable contributions in the scholarly heritage.

Chapter 3
Sentence Prosody

In this chapter we treat the realization of accents in various positions within sentences of several types, as well as some basic intonation patterns manifested over words with different accents. The treatment is much less complete than we would like to offer; we recognize that a great deal of work remains to be done before sentence-level prosody in Serbocroatian has been exhaustively described. Our analysis is based on a corpus of 272 sentences (listed in appendix C), produced by two informants, P.I. and D1. The list of sentences was compiled at the beginning of our reasearch in 1961. It reflects our concerns at that time and does not provide enough material to answer all the questions that have arisen in the course of our work. Likewise, a substantial amount of research in the intonation of tone and accent languages has recently been carried out (e.g., Abramson 1979, Bruce 1977, 1979, Fujisaki, Hirose, and Ohta 1979, Gårding 1977, 1979, Thorsen 1978, 1979, 1980a, 1980b, 1980c); if we were to start our investigation now, it would benefit from the results achieved in these studies. Our analyses were published between 1969 and 1972 (Ivić and Lehiste 1969, 1970, 1972). In this chapter we summarize our results and add some new observations that will round out the picture, fully recognizing the limitations of our presentation.

Chapter 3 falls into two large parts. The first (section 3.2) treats the realization of various accents in different positions within the sentence; basically, this describes the ways in which sentence-level prosody affects word-level prosody. The second part (section 3.3) treats sentence intonation as it may be abstracted from the ways in which the prosodic shape of sentences of the same category is realized when the words of which the sentence consists carry different word accents; thus, it deals with the influence of word-level prosody on sentence-level prosody. Section 3.4 examines experimental research in Serbocroatian sentence intonation performed by other scholars. A summary of our findings concludes the chapter.

3.1 Method, Materials, and Informants

The study of sentence intonation is based primarily on the acoustic analysis of a corpus of 272 sentences produced by informants P.I. and D1. Both speakers have medium-pitched voices (P.I. male, D1 female). The sentences were constructed to contain several instances each of words with the four Štokavian accents. At the time the list was constructed we could not anticipate with certainty what we would find; therefore, we tried to include in the list as many different sentence types as possible, consciously avoiding duplication. In retrospect, this is a drawback: repeated productions of a smaller set of sentences would have yielded more reliable data, which could have been subjected to more rigorous statistical treatment. Our conclusions are therefore primarily based on qualitative rather than quantitative observations.

The 272 sentences contain words with all four accents in the following sentence types:

1. Statement.
2. Statement expanded by a subordinate clause, introduced by the conjunction *da*.
3. Statement expanded by an adversative clause.
4. Statement with emphasis on the sentence-final word.
5. Exclamation.
6. Question with the interrogative adverb *kada*.
7. Question with the interrogative particle *li*.
8. Question with statement wording (morphologically/syntactically unmarked yes-or-no question).
9. Question with statement wording, combined with emphasis on one of the nonfinal words.
10. Question with statement wording, with emphasis on the sentence-final word.

The sentences were read from a randomized list. In sentences containing a word to be produced with emphasis, that word was underlined. The recording of P.I.'s reading of the sentences was made in 1961 at the Haskins Laboratories in New York. D1 read the sentences in 1964 at the recording studio of Radio Novi Sad. The recorded tapes were processed using the same techniques described in chapter 2. Broad-band and narrow-band spectrograms as well as continuous intensity displays were made of all utterances. The materials recorded by P.I. were processed (by I.L.) at the Communication Sciences Laboratory of the University of Michigan; the materials recorded by D1 were analyzed at the Ohio State University. The fundamental frequency of all syllable nuclei was measured at the beginning, peak, and end of each syllable nucleus. Intensity was measured at the peak of the intensity curve within each syllable nucleus.

Since the accentual patterns of Serbocroatian words in sentence-medial position have been described in detail in chapter 2, this section of chapter 3 will concentrate on the realization of accentual patterns in sentence-final and sentence-initial position.

3.2 Accentual Patterns in Words in Various Positions within a Sentence

Details about fundamental frequency and intensity patterns in all ten positions listed above are offered in our earlier publications (Ivić and Lehiste 1969, 1970, 1972). Here we will consider four of the ten positions: final in statements (sentence type 1 in section 3.1), final in nonfinal clauses (sentence types 2 and 3), emphasized final in morphologically/syntactically unmarked yes-or-no questions (sentence type 10), and initial in statements (sentence type 1). Table 3.1 presents average F_0 values and peak intensities in six types of test words occurring in three of these positions in productions by P.I.; table 3.2 presents comparable material for D1. (Initial positions are described in tables 3.5 and 3.6.) Figure 3.1 contains narrow-band spectrograms of four statements produced by P.I. illustrating the manifestation of the four accents in final position in simple statements; figure 3.2 illustrates the manifestation of the accents on the same words occurring in final position at the end of nonfinal clauses.

Sentence intonation will be described in more detail in a later section. By way of anticipatory summary, we can say that simple statements terminate in a fall, the end of nonfinal clauses is characterized by terminal sustain, and yes-or-no questions with emphasis on the final word carry a special low-high intonation contour ("reverse pattern") appearing on the emphasized final word.

3.2.1 Accentual Patterns in Final Position in Statements

A common characteristic of words in final position in declarative sentences is falling fundamental frequency that reaches the lowest limit of the speaker's range and often involves a change in the mode of vibration of the vocal folds: regular phonation gives way to laryngealization—slow and

Table 3.1
Average fundamental frequencies and peak intensities in six types of test words produced by P. I. in three positions: 1–final in statements, 3–final in nonfinal clauses, 10–emphasized final in yes-or-no questions. Frequencies in hertz, intensities in decibels relative to a constant reference level. Laryngealized productions were not included in the averages. N = number of tokens.

			First vowel				Second vowel				Third vowel			
			F_0				F_0				F_0			
Sentence type	Test word	N	Beg.	Peak	End	Intensity peak	Beg.	Peak	End	Intensity peak	Beg.	Peak	End	Intensity peak
1	bȃrku.	5	137	137	115	37.0	(laryngealized			26.0				
					(3 lar.)		throughout)							
3	bȃrku,	4	175	219	215	40.4	204	204	187	38.3				
10	bȃrku?	1	130	108	122	32.0	260	284	220	45.0				
1	čámac.	5	131	131	118	35.7	116	116	114	33.6				
					(1 lar.)		(1 laryngealized)							
3	čámac,	4	161	205	205	35.9	208	210	201	38.3				
10	čámac?	1	135	118	140	32.0	200	235	225	43.0				
1	bȁru.	6	134	134	111	38.8	114	114	122	25.6				
					(1 lar.)		(5 laryngealized)							
3	bȁru,	4	166	220	220	40.8	217	217	180	38.3				
10	bȁru?	1	120	lar.	lar.	37.5	160	250	200	46.0				
1	sèlom.	5	143	143	117	37.5	125	125	125	32.7				
					(2 lar.)		(3 laryngealized)							
3	sèlom,	4	161	200	200	38.4	203	203	183	37.3				
10	sèlom?	1	140	132	140	37.0	200	270	200	47.0				
1	bȁbama.	4	148	148	131	39.7	117	117	113	34.0	(laryngealized)			25.7
			(1 laryngealized)				(1 laryngealized)							
3	bȁbama,	4	168	226	224	42.5	223	225	213	40.3	207	207	189	35.8
10	bȁbama?	1	108	98	110	37.0	160	252	252	48.0	260	260	120	43.0
1	tràvica.	4	144	144	123	41.0	126	127	125	35.4	(laryngealized)			17.0
3	tràvica,	4	168	206	206	37.0	210	216	211	37.7	201	201	181	37.0
10	tràvica?	1	120	106	123	27.0	220	240	223	43.0	256	260	140	41.0

Table 3.2
Average fundamental frequencies and peak intensities in six types of test words produced by D1 in three positions: 1–final in statements, 3–final in nonfinal clauses, 10–emphasized final in yes-or-no questions. Frequencies in hertz, intensities in decibels relative to a constant reference level. Laryngealized productions were not included in the averages. N = number of tokens.

			First vowel				Second vowel				Third vowel			
			F_0				F_0				F_0			
Sentence type	Test word	N	Beg.	Peak	End	Intensity peak	Beg.	Peak	End	Intensity peak	Beg.	Peak	End	Intensity peak
1	bârku.	6	160	160	(6 lar.)	24.0	(laryngealized throughout)			20.0				
3	bârku,	5	182	216	206	28.8	201	201	171	27.1				
10	bârku?	1	149	158	158	22.0	199	199	183	24.0				
1	čámac.	6	151	153	143	24.5	144	159	159	22.2				
					(2 lar.)		(1 laryngealized)							
3	čámac,	5	164	188	188	26.4	227	247	242	28.1				
10	čámac?	1	166	149	158	23.0	166	216	216	27.0				
1	bȁru.	7	149	153	129	21.8	137	137	116	19.1				
			(2 laryngealized)				(4 laryngealized)							
3	bȁru,	4	171	230	230	27.9	249	251	216	26.9				
10	bȁru?	1	(lar.)	208	208	22.0	257	257	199	28.5				
1	sèlom.	6	145	145	125	22.0	133	137	137	19.1				
							(1 laryngealized)							
3	sèlom,	4	175	215	215	26.2	266	232	225	26.5				
10	sèlom?	1	154	149	154	23.0	178	228	228	25.3				
1	bȁbama.	4	228	228	162	24.3	(4 laryngealized)			18.8	(4 laryngealized)			20.3
			(1 laryngealized)											
3	bȁbama,	4	168	196	195	25.9	222	247	243	26.9	249	253	232	24.6
10	bȁbama?	1	158	158	(lar.)	23.0	158	208	208	24.0	208	208	158	26.0
1	tràvica.	5	148	148	141	20.4	145	148	145	22.0	149	149	141	22.3
			(2 lar.)	(3 lar.)	(3 lar.)		(3 laryngealized)				(3 laryngealized)			
3	tràvica,	4	172	193	193	28.3	210	249	236	29.5	255	255	218	27.1
10	tràvica?	1	158	141	166	24.0	166	199	199	28.0	257	257	166	24.0

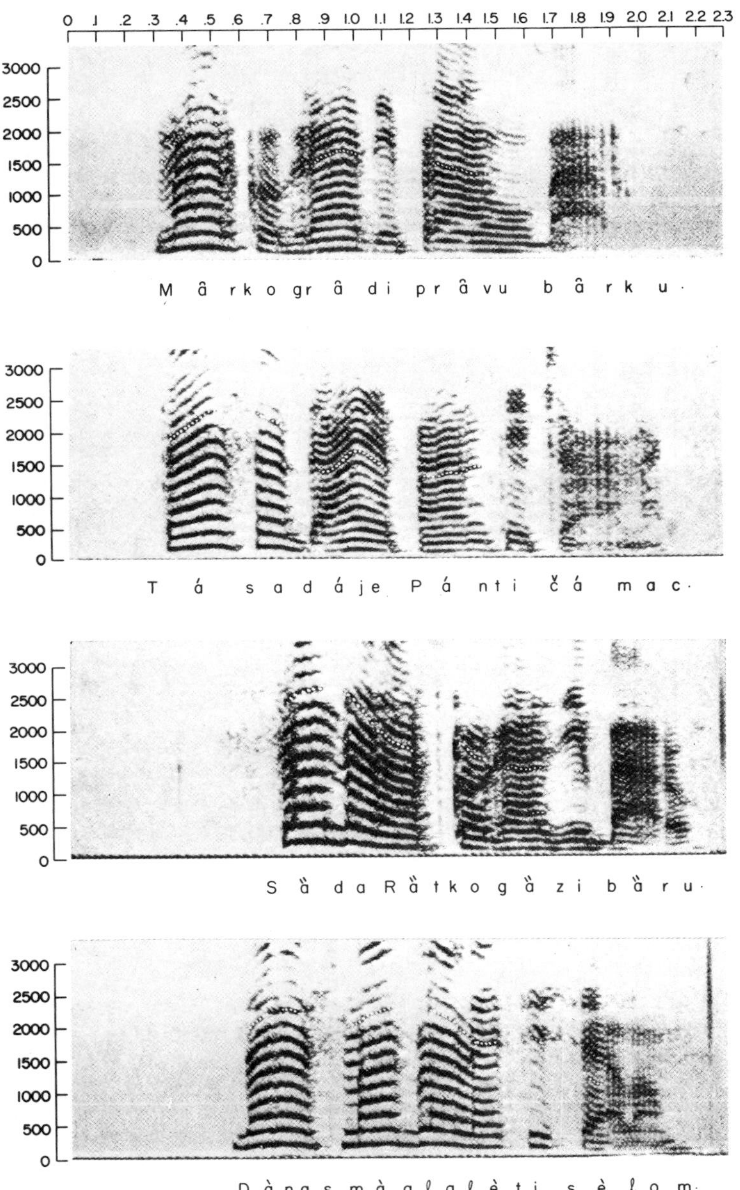

Figure 3.1
Narrow-band spectrograms of four complete statements produced by P. I., illustrating the four Neoštokavian accents in final position

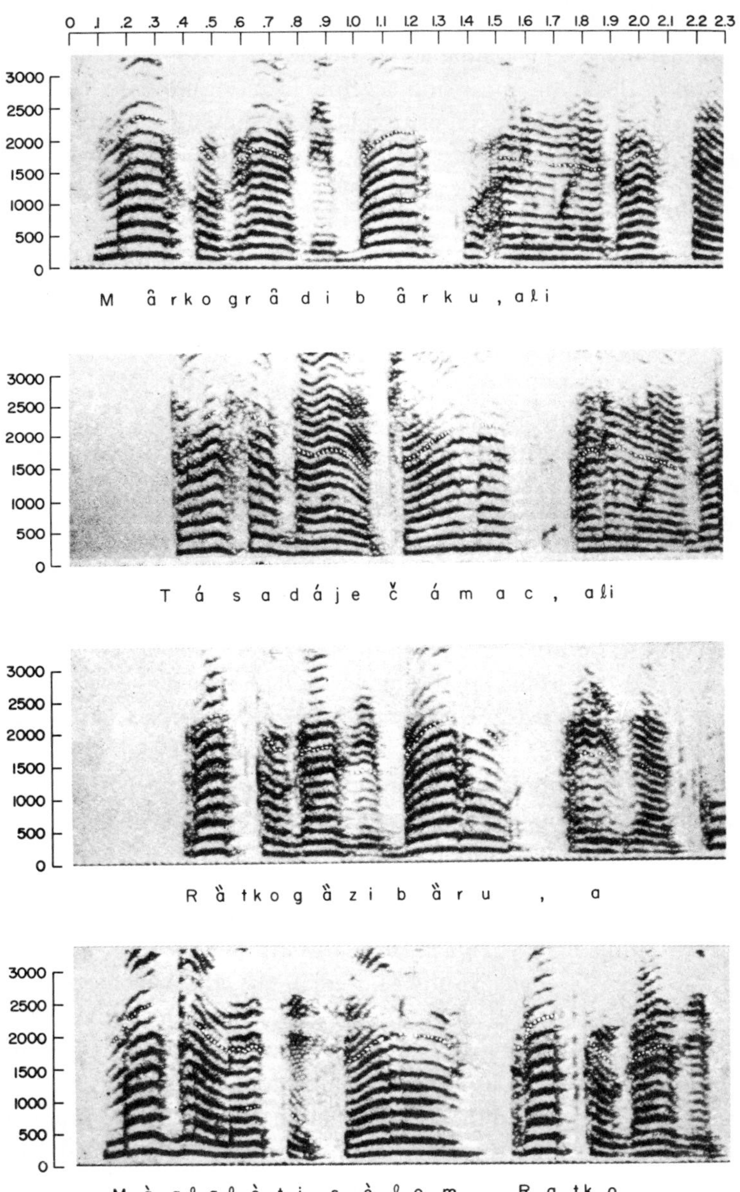

Figure 3.2
Narrow-band spectrograms of four incomplete statements produced by P. I., illustrating the four Neoštokavian accents in final position in nonfinal clauses

irregular vibration of the vocal folds at a pitch that cannot be precisely specified. Generally falling fundamental frequency and laryngealization are present in both falling and rising accents, resulting in many cases in complete neutralization of the opposition between these two accent types.

Thus, in the word *bârku*, produced by P.I., laryngealization started in the first syllable in three instances; the second syllable was either laryngealized or completely voiceless in all productions. Figure 3.1 illustrates a production with laryngealization in both syllables. In the six productions of speaker D1 laryngealization started toward the end of the first syllable and persisted through the second syllable in all instances.

In the five productions of *čámac* by P.I. the end of the first syllable and the whole second syllable were laryngealized in one case; this production is included in figure 3.1. In the six productions by D1 the end of the first syllable was laryngealized in two instances, and the whole second syllable in one instance. As far as the fundamental frequency is concerned, the difference between long falling and long rising accents appears neutralized: in both accentual types fundamental frequency can fall so low that the speaker shifts into a laryngealized mode of phonation. One may notice that laryngealization occurs with much greater frequency in words with the long falling accent; thus, the difference between the two accents may be reduced to the possibility that the final syllable may be still phonated in a word with a long rising accent, whereas it is likely to be laryngealized in a word with a long falling accent.

The same kind of neutralization can be observed in words with short accents in final position in declarative sentences. In P.I.'s production of the word *bȁru* the first syllable nucleus was fully phonated in five out of six occurrences; in the word *sèlom* the first syllable was fully phonated in three out of five instances. In one production of *bȁru* laryngealization started in the second half of the first syllable nucleus; this utterance is reproduced in figure 3.1. In *sèlom* laryngealization started in the first syllable in two instances, one of which is included in figure 3.1. The second syllable was fully phonated in one production of *bȁru* and in two productions of *sèlom*. In productions by D1 two out of seven realizations of *bȁru* were laryngealized in the first syllable; in the second syllable this was true in four out of seven cases. In *sèlom*, on the other hand, all six productions had fully phonated first syllables, and in only one case was the second syllable laryngealized. Thus, in the materials produced by D1 the difference between short falling and short rising accents again appears to lie in the relative susceptibility of the words to terminal laryngealization. This, however, is not so obvious in productions of these words by P.I.

In the word *bàbama* the third syllable was laryngealized in all four productions by P.I.; one of the realizations of *bàbama* was laryngealized throughout. In P.I.'s production of *tràvica* the third syllable was laryngealized in all four productions, whereas the first and second syllables were fully phonated. D1 had more laryngealization than P.I. in both words: in all four productions of *bàbama* the second and third syllables were laryngealized, whereas one of the productions was laryngealized throughout. In *tràvica* D1 had full phonation in two out of five words. In one word laryngealization started at the end of the first syllable and continued to the end of the word; two words were fully laryngealized. Again, there was a certain tendency for words with rising accents to continue regular phonation into postaccentual syllables; but complete neutralization can be observed in those cases in which the whole word was produced with laryngealization.

3.2.2 Accentual Patterns in Final Position in Nonfinal Clauses

Words occurring in final position in nonfinal clauses are characterized by an F_0 rise on the accented syllable and a minimal F_0 fall on the postaccentual syllable. Measured averages are presented in tables 3.1 and 3.2; illustrations are offered in figure 3.2. In most instances the F_0 level reached at the end of the word is higher than the F_0 value at the beginning of the first syllable; the single exception in these materials is the word *bârku* produced by D1, where the average fundamental frequency at the end of the word was lower by one semitone than the beginning F_0 value.

We considered the possibility that the difference between rising and falling accents might be maintained by means of different peak F_0 values on the successive syllables, but this hypothesis turned out to be tenable only as far as the distinction between the long accents is concerned. The two disyllabic words with long accents showed a systematic pattern: for both speakers the F_0 peaks in *bârku* were lower by 15 Hz in the second syllable, and in *čámac* the second peak was higher by an average of 5 Hz for P.I. and 59 Hz for D1. But the average peak F_0 values in the test words with short accents were inconclusive. For P.I. the relationship between the two peaks in *bàru* was -3 Hz and in *sèlom* $+3$ Hz; but for D1 the second syllable of *bàru* was higher by an average of 21 Hz, and the second syllable of *sèlom* by 17 Hz. In productions by P.I., maintenance of the opposition was suggested in the averages for *bàbama* and *tràvica*: in *bàbama* the second syllable was lower by 1 Hz than the first, and the third was lower by 19 Hz; in *tràvica* the second syllable was higher by 10 Hz than the first, and the third was lower by 5 Hz. But for D1 there was no difference between the two word types: the second and third syllables of both *bȁbama* and *tràvica* were higher than the first syllable by comparable amounts (*bȁbama*—51 and 57 Hz, *tràvica*—56 and 62 Hz). We can conclude that the two long accents were basically distinguished in our material, and that traces of the distinction between the two short accents are found only in disyllabic words pronounced by P.I. Notice that in trisyllabic words the accented syllable is farther from the clause end than in disyllabic words.

Next we considered the potential role of the position of the F_0 peak within the accented syllable. Table 3.3 shows average durations of syllable nuclei and distance of F_0 peak from the beginning of the syllable nucleus in the six test words under consideration. As may be seen from the table, a difference exists between long accents and short accents. For P.I. the average durations of the accented long falling and long rising syllable nuclei were 192 and 180 msec, respectively, and the position of the F_0 peak was at 112 and 180 msec; for D1 the corresponding durations were 234 and 208 msec for the accented syllables, and 180 and 208 msec for the positions of the F_0 peak. Thus, the long rising accent always had its peak at the end of the accented syllable nucleus; the long falling accent had its peak at an average of 58% of the duration of the syllable nucleus in productions by P.I. and at 77% of the duration of the syllable nucleus in productions by D1. The position of the peak apparently has no such differentiating function in words with short accents: as may be seen from the table, both short rising and short falling accents had their peak at the end of the syllable nucleus. At least for the short accents, it may be concluded that the opposition is neutralized in positions located at the end of nonfinal clauses.

3.2.3 Accentual Patterns in Emphasized Final Position in Yes-or-No Questions

Yes-or-no questions in which intonation is the only signal of interrogation are characterized by a special prosodic marker that (depending on the sentence) appears on the word in focus or the word bearing emphasis. In our set of sentences (types 9 and 10 in section 3.1) the speakers were requested to emphasize an underlined word, and both speakers applied this prosodic marker to the underlined words in yes-or-no questions. Tables 3.1 and 3.2 contain average F_0 values for occurrences of six such words in final position. In our previous publications we have referred to this prosodic marker as *reverse pattern*, since in most cases the F_0 contour on the accented syllable has a falling-rising shape (containing a "negative peak"), and the postaccentual syllable carries a rising or rising-falling pattern. Figure 3.3 contains examples of reverse patterns appearing on emphasized

Table 3.3
Average durations (in milliseconds) of syllable nuclei and distance of F_0 peak from the beginning of the syllable nucleus in six words produced by P. I. and D1 in final position of nonfinal clauses. Numbers of occurrences as in tables 3.1 and 3.2.

	P. I.						D1					
	First vowel		Second vowel		Third vowel		First vowel		Second vowel		Third vowel	
Test word	Dur.	Peak at	Dur.	Peak at	Dur.	Peak at	Dur.	Peak at	Dur.	Peak at	Dur.	Peak at
bârku,	192	112	94	14			234	180	134	10		
čámac,	180	180	86	16			208	208	90	56		
bȁru,	150	146	122	10			180	180	145	20		
sèlom,	140	140	88	25			125	125	125	38		
bȁbama,	125	120	80	18	125	10	137	120	97	70	130	17
tràvicu,	120	120	63	45	98	10	145	145	95	63	155	10

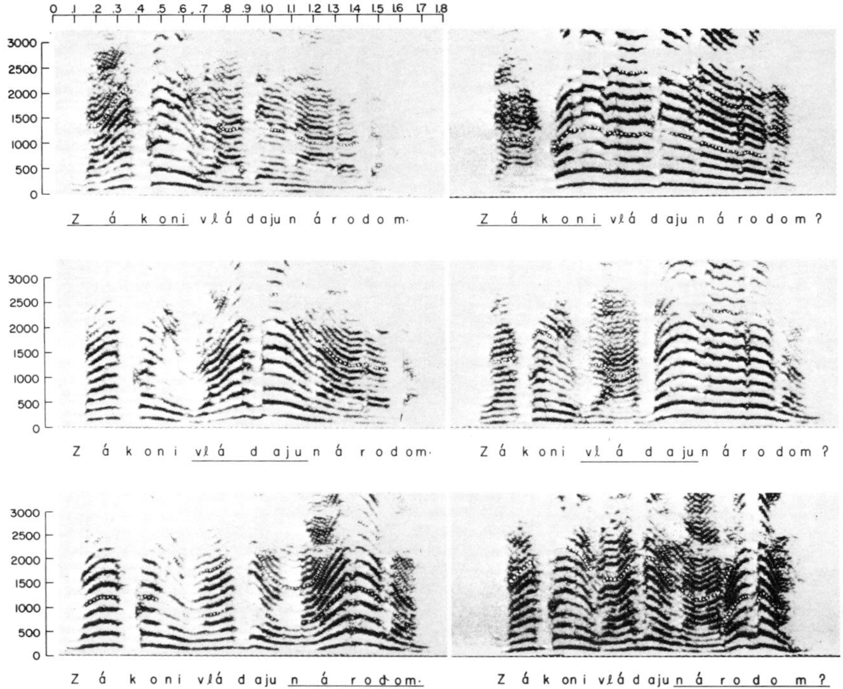

Figure 3.3
Manifestation of emphasis in statements and questions produced by P. I.

words in yes-or-no questions; the figure will be discussed later, since its primary purpose is to illustrate the manifestation of emphasis in various positions. Many other examples are offered in Ivić and Lehiste 1969, 1972, and Lehiste and Ivić 1978.

The opposition between rising and falling accents appears neutralized when the reverse pattern is applied to the word. There are no systematic differences in the F_0 contours. In order to determine whether a difference might be present in F_0 levels, the extent of the difference in semitones was calculated between the "negative peak" in the first syllable and the F_0 peak in the postaccentual syllable in the six test word types under consideration. Table 3.4 contains this information. As may be seen from the table, the two speakers differed considerably in the extent of the F_0 movement: for P.I. the average differences between the extremes were greater than an octave (12 semitones) in almost all cases; for D1 a difference larger than an octave was

Table 3.4
Difference in semitones between the "negative peak" in the first syllable and the F_0 peak of the postaccentual syllable in six test word types produced in emphatic final position in yes-or-no questions by P. I. and D1.

Test word	P. I.	D1
bȃrku?	17	4
čámac?	12	6½
bȁru?	16	12½
sȅlom?	12½	7½
bȁbama?	16	5
trȁvica?	14	6

reached in only one of the test words. No systematic distinction between rising and falling accents can be observed.

3.2.4 Accentual Patterns in Sentence-initial Position

Illustrations of four accentual patterns occurring on first words in complete declarative sentences are contained in figure 3.1. Average F_0 values and intensity peak levels are offered in tables 3.5 (P.I.) and 3.6 (D1). A study of the F_0 values indicates that the accentual patterns are generally kept distinct in sentence-initial position: the degree of neutralization is not comparable to that observed in sentence-final position, although the shape of the F_0 curve in the accented syllable is somewhat affected by the position of the word in the sentence. Table 3.7 provides a comparison of F_0 peak locations within accented syllables in twelve test words with six accentual patterns described here, occurring in four positions within declarative sentences. To make it possible to compare peak F_0 positions in syllable nuclei with different durations and to compare the patterns found in the productions of the two informants, the location of the F_0 peak is expressed in terms of percentage of the average duration of the accented syllable nucleus.

We started our description of word-level accents by observing the manifestation of various prosodic features on test words occurring in medial position in nonemphatic declarative sentences. (See chapter 2 for the description of accents in this "neutral" position.) Column 2 of table 3.7 gives the percentages of accented syllable nucleus duration at which the F_0 peak occurred in test words in medial position, derived from data analyzed in chapter 2. As may be seen from the table, P.I.'s materials show a systematic difference between rising and falling accents in medial position

Table 3.5
Average fundamental frequencies and peak intensities in six types of test words produced by P. I. in three positions: 1–initial in statements, 8–initial in nonemphatic yes-or-no questions, 9–emphasized initial in yes-or-no questions. Frequencies in hertz, intensities in decibels relative to a constant reference level. N = number of tokens.

			First vowel				Second vowel				Third vowel			
			F_0				F_0				F_0			
Sentence type	Test word	N	Beg.	Peak	End	Intensity peak	Beg.	Peak	End	Intensity peak	Beg.	Peak	End	Intensity peak
1	Mârko	8	213	238	219	43.4	204	204	178	42.9				
8	Mârko	4	176	208	200	42.5	192	192	163	42.0				
9	Mârko	1	140	150	150	38.0	235	260	260	45.0				
1	Tása	10	207	239	230	41.2	236	236	211	41.8				
8	Tása	5	165	198	194	40.0	221	225	206	42.7				
9	Tása	1	125	112	138	30.0	220	250	245	43.0				
1	Sȁda	4	202	207	205	40.2	193	193	174	40.5				
8	Sȁda	4	180	192	191	39.9	183	183	175	41.6				
9	Sȁda	1	122	142	142	38.0	220	255	255	48.0				
1	Dànas	7	201	233	233	41.9	236	237	217	41.5				
8	Dànas	4	140	180	180	40.4	185	192	181	40.0				
9	Dànas	1	130	120	130	31.0	140	235	235	41.0				
1	Jàgṇe se	7	210	240	234	43.5	220	220	184	41.7	182	182	163	41.1
8	Jàgṇe se	3	147	187	187	40.3	194	194	168	40.3	160	160	146	38.7
9	Jàgṇe se	1	110	110	110	42.0	220	254	250	45.0	260	260	260	43.0
1	Snȁšice	7	220	241	230	41.0	243	253	240	37.7	217	217	184	42.5
8	Snȁšice	3	160	170	165	39.0	210	215	203	40.3	190	190	148	42.0
9	Snȁšice	1	135	129	132	34.0	220	240	240	37.5	250	252	240	45.0

Table 3.6
Average fundamental frequencies and peak intensities in six types of test words produced by D1 in three positions: 1–initial in statements, 8–initial in nonemphatic yes-or-no questions, 9–emphasized initial in yes-or-no questions (mostly missed by this speaker). Frequencies in hertz, intensities in decibels relative to a constant reference level. N = number of tokens.

			First vowel				Second vowel				Third vowel			
			F_0				F_0				F_0			
Sentence type	Test word	N	Beg.	Peak	End	Intensity peak	Beg.	Peak	End	Intensity peak	Beg.	Peak	End	Intensity peak
1	Mârko	9	227	231	188	32.7	199	199	182	30.4				
8	Mârko	2	205	205	185	32.5	201	201	181	30.0				
1	Tása	12	212	225	225	30.7	237	237	198	29.7				
8	Tása	3	206	214	205	30.3	216	216	192	29.7				
1	Sȁda	5	229	231	212	29.9	210	210	185	29.5				
8	Sȁda	2	224	224	203	28.4	203	203	178	28.3				
1	Dànas	8	221	230	224	32.4	227	228	219	32.1				
8	Dànas	3	202	202	188	28.3	190	190	188	28.3				
1	Jàgņe se	7	224	237	232	32.6	221	221	201	29.9	210	210	181	30.1
8	Jàgņe se	2	199	208	208	31.0	189	189	178	28.5	185	185	166	28.8
9	Jàgņe se	1	228	228	216	33.0	191	191	183	29.0	183	183	166	28.0
1	Snàšice	7	223	252	252	32.7	282	282	258	31.2	235	235	188	31.1
8	Snàšice	4	206	224	221	30.4	261	264	243	29.0	229	229	187	29.6

Table 3.7
Average location of F_0 peak in percent of the duration of the accented syllable nucleus in four positions within declarative sentences, produced by two informants

		P. I.				D1			
Accentual pattern	Test words	Initial	Medial	Final in nonfinal clause	Absolute final	Initial	Medial	Final in nonfinal clause	Absolute final
ˆ ˘	Mârko, bârku	60	25	58	6	19	8	77	4
ˊ ˘	Tása, čámac	82	90	100	6	78	35	100	28
˵ ˘	Sȁda, bȁru	68	48	97	7	27	18	100	33
ˋ ˘	Dànas, sèlom	100	78	100	8	66	8	100	20
˵ ˘ ˘	Jȁgn̯e se, bȁbama	78	45	96	9	66	27	88	8
ˋ ˘ ˘	Snàšice, tràvicu	58	72	100	8	100	20	100	8

in terms of the location of the F_0 peak: in every case the peak is located later in the syllable nucleus in rising accents as compared to falling accents of the same duration in words of the same number of syllables. The picture is less systematic for D1: for the two long accents D1's pattern resembles that of P.I., but F_0 peak position does not distinguish between the two short accents, and the F_0 peak occurs within the first half of the syllable nucleus in every case, regardless of accent type. Initial position (column 1) has the general effect of shifting the F_0 peak closer to the end of the accented syllable nucleus. Interestingly, in the materials produced by P.I. this shift affects falling accents more than rising accents (in two out of the three rising accentual patterns contained in table 3.7, the average location actually shifted slightly forward); on the contrary, in materials produced by D1 initial position affected rising patterns more than falling patterns, although all six patterns show later location of the F_0 peak. Whereas in D1's productions the two short accents were not distinguished on the basis of F_0 peak location in medial position, now there is a clear difference between all three comparable pairs. This does not mean, however, that F_0 peak location in the accented syllable alone could be sufficient for distinguishing between rising and falling accents; consider, for example, the fact that disyllabic words with a short rising accent have the F_0 peak at the same position as trisyllabic words with a short falling accent.

Table 3.7 also provides the background for drawing some generalizations about the realization of the F_0 contour in final position (see the two preceding sections). As becomes obvious from this table, the F_0 peak is effectively located at the end of the accented syllable in final words of nonfinal clauses and at the beginning of the accented syllable in words occurring in absolute final position. The only exception is the long falling accent, which remains distinct from the long rising pattern in comparable position within the sentence. One may draw the conclusion that insofar as the location of the F_0 peak signals rising or falling accents, a neutralization takes place in both positions. This neutralization is directional: at the end of nonfinal clauses falling accents are replaced by rising ones, and in absolute final position rising accents are replaced by falling ones. Clearly the location of the F_0 peak is not sufficient for maintaining the identity of the word-level prosodic patterns within these positions in the sentence.

Another way in which initial position affects the realization of word accents is apparent in the F_0 level. Comparison between tables 3.1 and 3.2 (final position) and 3.5 and 3.6 (initial position) shows that the F_0 level in initial position is considerably higher than the F_0 level in words with the same accentual pattern in final position. In particular, no laryngealization is found in initial position. The difference between initial position and the end of nonfinal clauses is not obvious from F_0 levels; if the distinction is maintained at all, it is probably based on the location of the F_0 peak in the accented syllable (see table 3.7) and in the preboundary lengthening applied to the final syllable (this lengthening will be discussed further in section 3.3.5).

In yes-or-no questions with emphasis on the first word, typical reverse patterns appeared in productions by P.I.; average F_0 values are included in table 3.5. Speaker D1 failed to produce the requested emphasis on the first word of yes-or-no questions. In the one instance in which she produced the sentence in which the first word was underlined (table 3.6, Jàgn̩e se), the phonetic shape of the underlined initial words showed no evidence of emphasis: the F_0 levels are lower than the average for initial position in statements, even though they are slightly higher than in nonemphatic questions, and the utterance was produced without the reverse pattern.

3.3 Characteristics of Sentence Intonation

This section deals with the characteristics that several sentence types have in common independently of the accentual patterns of the words of which the sentences consist. In other words, this section explores sentence-level prosody as it can be abstracted from word-level prosody, as well as the interaction between the two types of prosody. We were particularly concerned with establishing the ways in which prosody is used to distinguish between statements and questions on the one hand and between complete and incomplete statements on the other hand. Measurements made from recorded utterances enabled us to describe the realization of sentences by the speakers; however, before drawing final conclusions from the description of the productions, we wanted to make sure that our speakers had in fact produced the various sentence types in a fashion that was acceptable to listeners within the same speech community. Therefore, we conducted a listening test. The test consisted of three parts. In the first part, sixteen sentences were presented, and the listeners' task was to identify each sentence as a statement or question. The sixteen sentences consisted of eight pairs of statements and yes-or-no questions with identical wording; the only difference between the two members of utterance pairs was sentence intonation. The sentences were selected from P.I.'s production of the list of 272 sentences, rerecorded in random order.

In the second part of the test, eight pairs of utterances were again presented in random order. These utterances were either complete statements or otherwise identical utterances that had been produced as initial clauses of a complex sentence (that is, at the time of the recording, the speaker had continued with another clause). The task of the listeners was to decide whether the sentence was complete or incomplete. The sixteen utterances were rerecorded from the same production of the 272-sentence list by P.I.

The third part of the test was designed to explore the perception of sentence-level stress or emphasis. As noted, readers had been requested to emphasize those words in a sentence that had been underlined in the text given to them. We noticed that in yes-or-no questions, the readers applied the reverse pattern to the word in focus, regardless of whether that word was underlined or not. We perceived these words to carry emphasis, and we wanted to determine whether other listeners would systematically perceive such words as being emphasized, even though the reader had not consciously applied emphasis to them while producing the sentences. This part of the test consisted of 32 sentences, again presented in random order. The test contained statements and yes-or-no questions without emphasis as well as with emphasis on selected words. The listeners' task was to judge whether emphasis was present, and if so, to identify the emphasized words. The test was administered to 32 listeners at the University of Belgrade, using a good quality loudspeaker and a relatively quiet classroom.

The results of the listening tests, together with the stimulus sentences, are given in tables 3.8, 3.9, and 3.10. The results are rearranged so that the presentation follows the basic structure of the test rather than the random order in which the stimuli were actually presented.

Table 3.8 shows the listeners' judgments of whether a sentence was meant to be a statement or a question. It is obvious that listeners had no difficulty in distinguishing between statements and yes-or-no questions. The same is true of listener judgments concerning completeness: table 3.9 shows that the speaker's intention was successfully transmitted to the listeners by prosodic means.

Table 3.10 shows the listeners' judgments concerning presence and location of emphasis. In general, the presence of intended emphasis was easily recognized. There were eight statements containing an emphasized word; with 32 subjects, the total number of potential identifications is 256. In fact, listeners provided 194 identifications, or 75.8%. This percentage would have been higher, if one sentence had not turned out to have been deviant. Sentence 5 yielded 31 judgments of emphasis on the second word, although it had been intended as an example of emphasis on the third word. Upon rechecking the spectrogram, we found that the speaker had indeed

Table 3.8
Judgments of whether the utterance was meant to be a statement or question, made by 32 listeners. The score of ½ indicates that a listener marked both columns in which ½ appears.

Sentence		Statement	Question
1. (7)	Marko gradi pravu barku.	32	0
2. (12)	Marko gradi pravu barku?	0	32
3. (9)	Tasa daje Panti čamac.	32	0
4. (15)	Tasa daje Panti čamac?	2	30
5. (11)	Sada Ratko gazi baru.	32	0
6. (3)	Sada Ratko gazi baru?	1	31
7. (8)	Danas magla leti selom.	32	0
8. (13)	Danas magla leti selom?	½	31½
9. (4)	Majstori štampaju kartice.	32	0
10. (16)	Majstori štampaju kartice?	2	30
11. (5)	Zakoni vladaju narodom.	32	0
12. (14)	Zakoni vladaju narodom?	½	31½
13. (1)	Jagn̦e se daruje babama.	32	0
14. (10)	Jagn̦e se daruje babama?	½	31½
15. (6)	Snašice raznose travicu.	32	0
16. (2)	Snašice raznose travicu?	½	31½

emphasized the third word: this word carried the highest F_0 and intensity peaks in the utterance, and the accented syllable nucleus was longer than any other syllable nucleus in the sentence. We must conclude that a mistake was made in splicing, and that instead of sentence 5, sentence 4 was included twice. If this sentence is left out of the tally, the percentage of correct identifications of emphasis in statements reaches 86.6%.

Emphasis was even more successfully recognized in questions. Out of 256 potential identifications, the listeners provided 242, or 94.5%. All the emphasized words had the reverse pattern. The test also contained eight yes-or-no questions in which the speaker had not been requested to produce one of the words with emphasis; he had, however, produced reverse patterns on these sentences as well. The word with reverse pattern received an average of 23 out of 32, or 72%, identifications as being the bearer of emphasis; the average for intended emphasis in questions was 30.25 out of 32, or 94.5%. One might conclude here that this difference of 22.5% reflects the difference between focus and emphasis; but the material is clearly not extensive enough for drawing any firmer conclusions.

Table 3.9
Judgments of whether the utterance was meant to be complete or incomplete, made by 32 listeners

Sentence			Complete	Incomplete
1.	(7)	Marko gradi pravu barku.	32	0
2.	(11)	Marko gradi pravu barku, . . .	0	32
3.	(1)	Tasa daje Panti čamac.	32	0
4.	(4)	Tasa daje Panti čamac, . . .	2	30
5.	(6)	Sada Ratko gazi baru.	32	0
6.	(10)	Ratko gazi baru, . . .	0	32
7.	(14)	Danas magla leti selom.	32	0
8.	(15)	Danas magla leti selom, . . .	0	32
9.	(5)	Majstori štampaju kartice.	32	0
10.	(16)	Majstori štampaju kartice, . . .	0	32
11.	(12)	Zakoni vladaju narodom.	32	0
12.	(3)	Zakoni vladaju narodom, . . .	3	29
13.	(9)	Jagŋe se daruje babama.	32	0
14.	(13)	Jagŋe se daruje babama, . . .	0	32
15.	(8)	Snašice raznose travicu.	31	1
16.	(2)	Snašice raznose travicu, . . .	0	32

3.3.1 Simple Declarative Sentence

An effective and recently much used way to represent sentence intonation is to plot on a graph the F_0 positions of stressed syllables and unstressed syllables, to connect the peaks and valleys with a line, and to describe the overall intonation pattern of the sentence in terms of the angle of declination of the two lines—topline and bottomline (for a discussion and summary, see, for example, Thorsen 1980b). After considerable experimentation, we decided to adopt a modified version of this procedure for the discussion of Serbocroatian sentence intonation. The reason for the modification is the shifted nature of the Serbocroatian rising accents. A graph representing the peak values of accented syllables and the lowest F_0 values of the postaccentual syllables of two sentences like *Mârko grâdi prâvu bârku* and *Tása dáje Pánti čámac* yielded a deceptively uniform picture and failed to bring out the difference between the word-level accents. We will illustrate the intonation curves with trisyllabic words. For words with falling accents, the graph represents the peak F_0 value of the accented syllable and the terminal F_0 values of the two postaccentual syllables. For words with rising accents, the graph represents the peak F_0 values of the

Table 3.10
Presence and position of emphasis, as judged by 32 listeners. The score of 1/2 indicates that a listener marked both columns in which 1/2 appears.

Sentence	No emphasis	Emphasis on *n*th word 1	2	3	4
1. (13) Marko gradi pravu barku.	31			1	
2. (27) Marko gradi pravu barku?	5		1½		25½
3. (15) <u>Marko</u> gradi pravu barku.		32			
4. (12) Marko <u>gradi</u> pravu barku.			32		
5. (28) Marko gradi <u>pravu</u> barku.		1	31		
6. (8) Marko gradi pravu <u>barku</u>.	8	5			19
7. (24) <u>Marko</u> gradi pravu barku?		32			
8. (3) Marko <u>gradi</u> pravu barku?	1		29	2	
9. (16) Marko gradi <u>pravu</u> barku?				29½	2½
10. (7) Marko gradi pravu <u>barku</u>?	1				31
11. (11) Tasa daje Panti čamac.	32				
12. (23) Tasa daje Panti čamac?	20				12
13. (17) Sada Ratko gazi baru.	31		1		
14. (9) Sada Ratko gazi baru?	6				26
15. (26) Danas magla leti selom.	14		18		
16. (29) Danas magla leti selom?	10				22
17. (10) <u>Danas</u> magla leti selom.	2	29			1
18. (22) Danas <u>magla</u> leti selom.	3		29		
19. (25) Danas magla <u>leti</u> selom.	2			30	
20. (18) Danas magla leti <u>selom</u>.	8			1	23
21. (2) <u>Danas</u> magla leti selom?	1	29½	½		1
22. (20) Danas <u>magla</u> leti selom?	1		30		1
23. (19) Danas magla <u>leti</u> selom?	1		1	30	
24. (21) Danas magla leti <u>selom</u>?	1				31
25. (31) Majstori štampaju kartice.	31			1	
26. (5) Majstori štampaju kartice?	10			22	
27. (14) Zakoni vladaju narodom.	30	2			
28. (4) Zakoni vladaju narodom?				32	
29. (1) Jagņe se daruje babama.	28	½		2½	1
30. (6) Jagņe se daruje babama?	3			29	
31. (32) Snašice raznose travicu.	32				
32. (30) Snašice raznose travicu?	10	1	16	5	

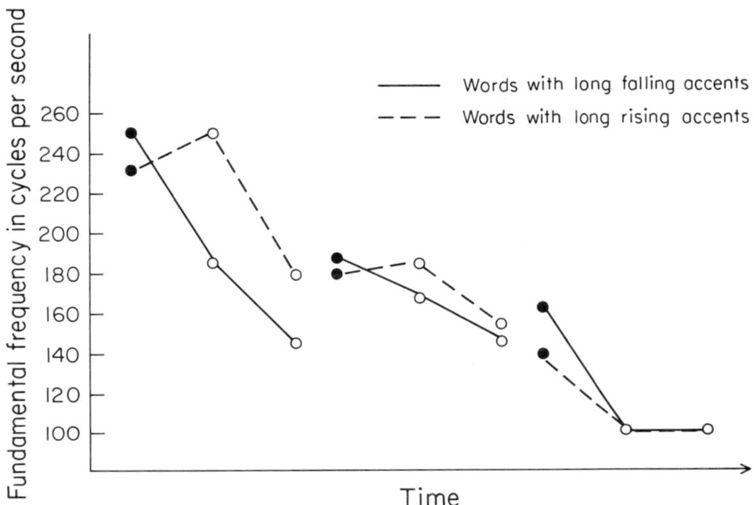

Figure 3.4
Intonation patterns of the complete declarative sentences *Mâjstori štâmpaju kârtice* and *Zákoni vládaju národom*, produced by P. I.

accented and postaccentual syllables and the terminal F_0 value of the third syllable. In this manner, the graph offers both the peak value of the syllable bearing the shifted accent and the peak value observed on the tonal center—the originally stressed syllable. The F_0 movement from the peak of the tonal center to the end of the third syllable is directly comparable to the movement from the peak of the syllable with a falling accent to the end of the postaccentual syllable. Trisyllabic words were selected for the illustrations precisely because they are long enough to reveal the intersyllabic relationships between both shifted and unshifted accented and postaccentual syllables.

Figure 3.4 shows the intonation patterns of the complete declarative sentences *Mâjstori štâmpaju kârtice* and *Zákoni vládaju národom*, produced by P.I. Figure 3.5 presents comparable graphs for the sentences *Jàgn̥e se dàruje bàbama* and *Snàšice ràznose tràvicu*. In each case the point for the third syllable represents the lowest F_0 value that was found at the end of the third syllable nucleus; connecting these points would produce the bottomline. The highest peak in the word occurred in the first syllable in words with falling accents, and either in the accented syllable or the postaccentual syllable in words with rising accents. It is not obvious which of the peaks

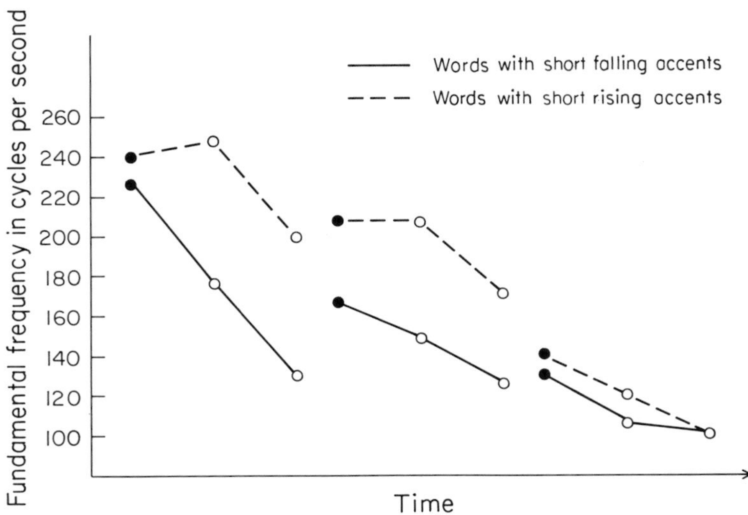

Figure 3.5
Intonation patterns of the complete declarative sentences *Jàgn̦e se dȁruje bȁbama* and *Snàšice ràznose tràvicu*, produced by P. I.

should be used for drawing a topline, and we have refrained from doing it.

For this speaker, laryngealization is represented as a frequency of 100 Hz. Shift into laryngealization took place at approximately this frequency in all but one case: a frequency of 98 Hz, produced with regular phonation, was measured at the end of one utterance (out of 272). It may be noticed that all four productions shown in these figures reached this terminal level, regardless of the accentual pattern occurring on the last word.

Within the three words included in each sentence, all three measurement points are lower in successive words than their counterparts in the preceding word, until the level of laryngealization is reached. The intonation contour of a simple declarative sentence is therefore a falling one. We would like to emphasize here that the graph does truly represent sentence intonation rather than word-level prosody; recall that sentence-initial position affected the realization of the F_0 curve on the accented syllable, moving the location of the F_0 peak closer to the end of the syllable nucleus.

Another observation may be made with regard to differences in the realization of the falling declarative intonation contour with rising and

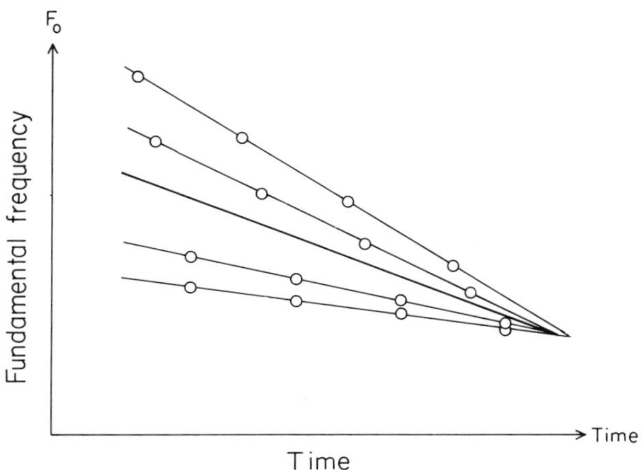

Figure 3.6
Schematic representation of F_0 peaks and valleys occurring in the realization of a declarative intonation contour over sentences consisting of words with falling and rising accents

falling accents: words with falling accents have usually higher peaks and lower terminal values than comparable words with rising accents (for numerical data, see the tables given earlier and those published in Ivić and Lehiste 1969). One might then abstract an intonation contour that represents values intermediate between the peaks and valleys of the words with rising accents. Schematically, the picture might be as in figure 3.6.

In the figure, the top line connects points representing the F_0 peaks of accented syllables with falling accents; the second line from the top connects points representing F_0 peaks on words with rising accents; the bottom line connects points representing terminal F_0 values in words with falling accents, and the second line from the bottom connects points representing terminal F_0 values in words with rising accents. The line between the two representing rising accents shows sentence intonation abstracted from its realizations under the various word accents. It would thus appear that words with rising accents follow the sentence intonation curve more closely than do words with falling accents.

A further schematic figure, 3.7, is based on a comparison of F_0 peaks on the successive syllables of disyllabic words with rising and falling accents. Our data show that in rising accents the peaks have approximately equal values, whereas in falling accents there is a large falling interval. Super-

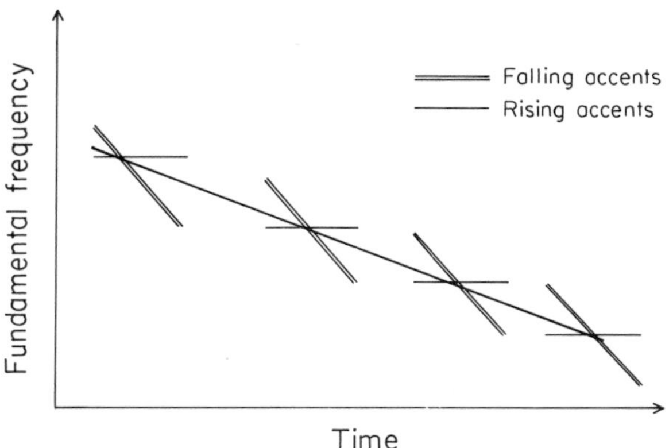

Figure 3.7
Schematic representation of F_0 patterns on words with falling and rising accents superimposed on a falling sentence intonation contour

imposing these patterns on the sentence intonation line results in the picture shown in figure 3.7. Comparing the patterns of rising accents with the sentence intonation curve, one may understand why completely level F_0 curves and equal peaks between the syllables can nevertheless be perceived as rising: they are rising with respect to the declination of the sentence intonation line.

3.3.2 End of Nonfinal Clauses

The continuation of a sentence (as opposed to its termination) is signaled by what we have referred to as "terminal sustain." Figures 3.8 and 3.9 illustrate this phenomenon. Figure 3.8 shows the same two sentences that were represented in figure 3.4, and figure 3.9 the two that were represented in figure 3.5. Terminal sustain affects the level of the test word occurring in preboundary position. (In our materials, test words correspond to phonological words or stress groups; we are not claiming that it is lexical words that constitute the domain of intonation patterns.) Note that it is the level of the whole word that has been raised; the extent of the raising is such that the level of the word is higher than that of the preceding word, although not quite as high as that of the sentence-initial word. Within the word, the relationships of the measuring points to each other are the same as in words in other positions. Thus, there is no terminal rise; the words end at a lower frequency than the F_0 peak in the preceding syllable(s), even though the intervals of fall are smaller than in absolute final position.

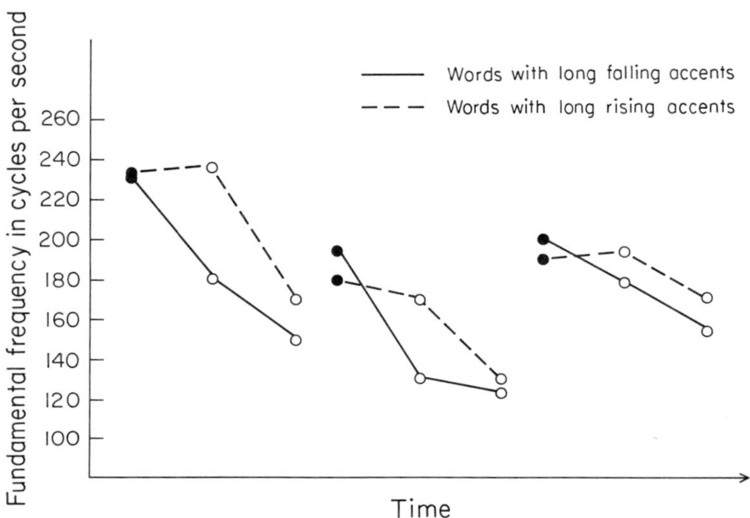

Figure 3.8
Intonation patterns of the declarative sentences *Mâjstori štâmpaju kârtice* and *Zákoni vládaju národom*, produced as first constituent of a compound sentence

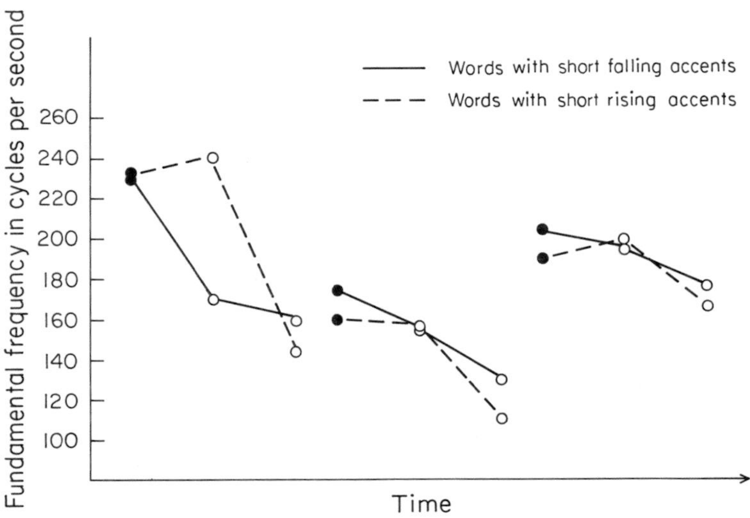

Figure 3.9
Intonation patterns of the declarative sentences *Jàgņe se dàruje bàbama* and *Snàšice ràznose tràvicu*, produced as first constituent of a compound sentence

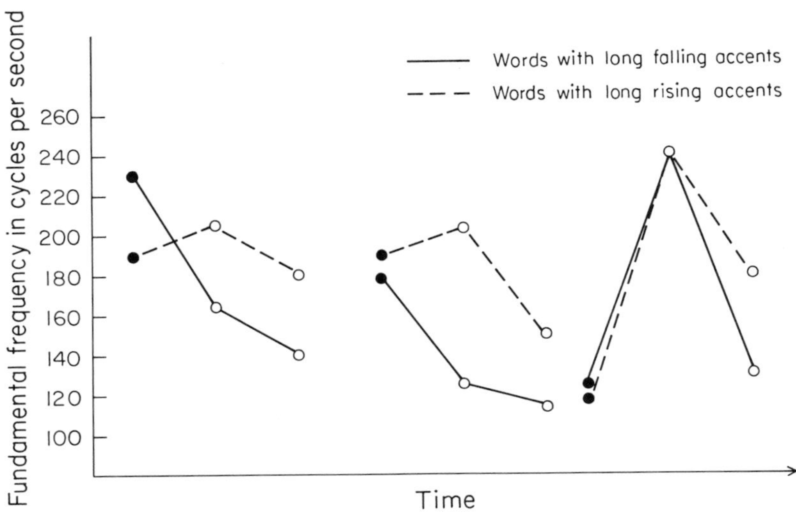

Figure 3.10
Intonation patterns of the sentences *Mâjstori štâmpaju kârtice* and *Zákoni vládaju národom*, produced as nonemphatic questions

3.3.3 Questions

Morphologically unmarked yes-or-no questions contain a word with reverse pattern. Figure 3.10 contains graphs representing utterances 90 and 110 in appendix C—*Mâjstori štâmpaju kârtice* and *Zákoni vládaju národom*—produced as nonemphatic questions. The speaker applied the reverse pattern to the last word in both sentences. Figure 3.11 contains graphs representing utterances 130 and 150—*Jàgņe se dȁruje bȁbama* and *Snàšice ràznose tràvicu*—realized as nonemphatic questions. In uttering these sentences, the speaker produced the reverse pattern on the last word in the sentence with short falling accents, but on the second word in the sentence with short rising accents.

Figure 3.10 shows the neutralization of long falling and long rising accents under the reverse pattern. The realization of the other words is comparable to that of statements. The two sentences represented in figure 3.11 differ in the placement of the reverse pattern and are thus not as easily compared. Note that the postaccentual syllable in words with short falling accents was higher than in statements; this is, however, not a general feature, although it occurred sporadically in other utterances. The F_0 level in the sentence with short rising accents remained high after the reverse

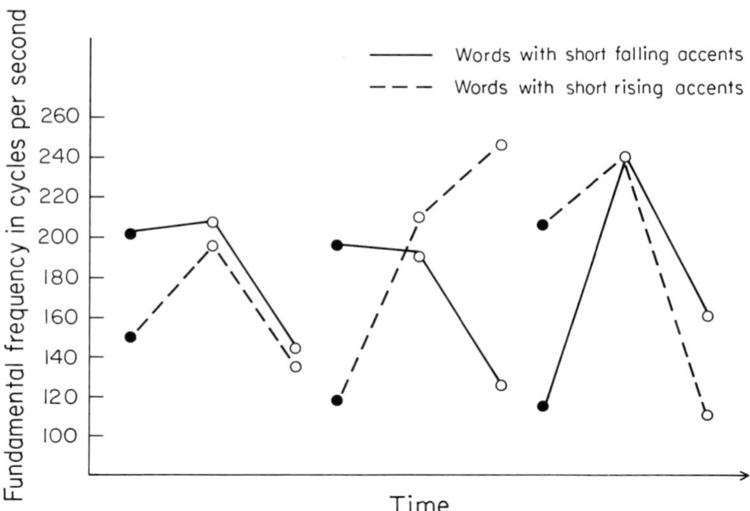

Figure 3.11
Intonation patterns of the sentences *Jàgŋe se dȁruje bȁbama* and *Snàšice ràznose tràvicu*, produced as nonemphatic questions

pattern on the middle word, but the terminal F_0 value nevertheless reached almost the lower limit of the speaker's range. The intonation contour of yes-or-no questions is therefore basically falling, like the intonation contour of statements.

The same basically falling intonation was used in other types of questions. In those questions that began with *kada*, the fundamental frequency applied to the initial interrogative adverb was higher than the average first F_0 peak; this is a characteristic of emphasis (see below). However, after the emphatic interrogative adverb, the sentence was realized with the same intonation that was found in statements. In P.I.'s productions of the ten sentences in which *kada* occurred, the average F_0 peak was 269 Hz; the next word, which is comparable to the first word in a simple statement, had an average F_0 peak of 235 Hz, followed by regular decline. For the sake of comparison, the average F_0 peak on the first word of the ten corresponding statements was 230 Hz.

In sentences with *da li*, the speakers seemed to be free either to use the intonation of declarative sentences or to produce one of the words with the reverse pattern. In sentences with *li* attached enclitically to the predicate, the speakers always used a reverse pattern on one of the words in the

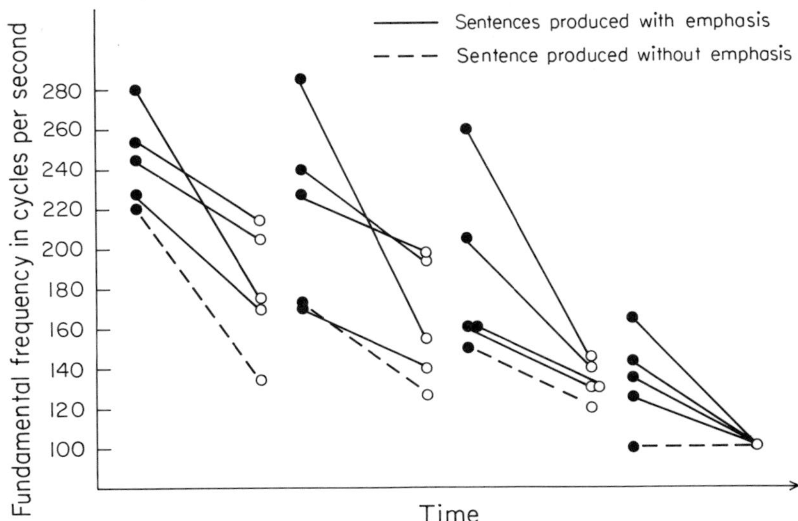

Figure 3.12
Graphs presenting the interval between the F_0 peak of the accented first syllable and the terminal frequency of the postaccentual syllable in five productions of the sentence *Mârko grâdi prâvu bârku* by P. I.

sentence; they differed, however, concerning the selection of the word on which the reverse pattern was manifested. There is evidently some freedom in choosing the focus of an interrogative sentence.

3.3.4 Emphasis

The general characteristics of emphasis include higher fundamental frequency, greater duration, and higher intensity on the emphasized word. For details, see Ivić and Lehiste 1970; here, we illustrate the manifestation of emphasis in different positions within the sentence as well as in different types of sentences.

Figure 3.12 shows graphs presenting the interval between the F_0 peak of the accented first syllable and the terminal frequency of the postaccentual syllable in five productions of the sentence *Mârko grâdi prâvu bârku* by P.I. The sentence with the lowest F_0 values is the sentence produced without emphasis. It may be noted that the first word carried the highest F_0 peak and contained the steepest fall. Initial position is usually in focus in statements, and the shape of the intonation pattern on the first word may be considered a manifestation of focus. The highest F_0 value occurred on the first word when that word carried emphasis. The steep F_0 fall of the emphasized word parallels that of the word in focus; the difference between focus and emphasis is manifested as a difference in F_0 height.

In each of the following words the highest peak and the steepest fall correspond to the production with emphasis on that particular word. (Only one word per sentence was produced with emphasis.) Emphasis on the second or third word in the sentence differed little from emphasis on the first word; in each case the F_0 peak on the emphasized word was the highest in the sentence. This was not true, however, for the production in which the last word carried emphasis: here, the emphasized peak was actually the lowest among the four peaks, which followed the regular declination line. It is instructive to refer back to table 3.10, which gives the results of listeners' identifications of the location of emphasis. Even though the F_0 peak on the emphasized word *bȃrku* was lower than the other three peaks in the sentence, 19 out of 32 listeners identified that word as being emphasized; 8 listeners heard no emphasis, and 5 thought the first word (which carried the highest F_0 peak) had been emphasized.

A comparison of emphasis in statements and yes-or-no questions is offered in figure 3.3. This figure contains narrow-band spectrograms of six sentences produced by P.I. On the left are three productions of the sentence *Zákoni vládaju národom*, produced as statements with the intonation characteristic of declarative sentences, and with emphasis on the first, second, and third word, respectively. On the right are the same sentences produced as emphatic yes-or-no questions, with the reverse pattern on each of the three emphasized words. The effect of the position of the emphasized word within the sentence on the general intonation pattern of the sentence is especially clear in these examples.

3.3.5 Durational Aspects of Sentence-level Prosody

As noted earlier, the position of a word within a sentence affects not only the manifestation of its F_0 pattern, but also its duration. It has been established in several recent studies (for a survey, see Lehiste 1980) that the presence of a syntactic boundary is associated with lengthening of a stretch of speech (syllable, word, or phonological word, depending on the language) preceding the boundary. In the productions of P.I. and D1 we have analyzed the lengthening that occurs at the end of a nonfinal clause (at clause boundary) and in absolute final position in declarative and interrogative sentences. For the sake of comparability with previously presented material we are presenting vowel durations, omitting the analysis of consonants; since it appears, however, that the domain of lengthening is larger than a single segment, some instances where the presence or absence of a consonant adjacent to the vowel may have influenced the results will be pointed out. The results of the analysis are presented in tables 3.11 and 3.12.

Table 3.11 presents data on disyllabic words with four accentual patterns that occurred in the 272 sentences produced by P.I. and D1; table 3.12 presents comparable data for trisyllabic words. Accentual type is indicated in the first column. Then follow four sets of columns. The set entitled "Medial position" contains average durations, in milliseconds, of vowels in words with a given accentual pattern that occurred in nonemphatic second position. The number of analyzed tokens is included (here and in subsequent sets of columns) under N. The second set of columns presents average durations in words with the same accentual patterns that occurred at the end of a nonfinal clause. The third and fourth sets give values for occurrences in absolute final position in declarative and interrogative sentences, respectively. Each set contains a column (headed %) showing the amount of lengthening relative to the duration of vowels found in words with the same accentual type in medial position within the same sentences. Average lengthening has been calculated for all three positions and is given in the last two rows for each speaker in table 3.11 and the last three rows in table 3.12.

It is immediately apparent that preboundary lengthening is indeed present in the sentences produced by these speakers. Because of the limited nature of the material, we do not claim significance for the differences between individual accent types and positions. Nevertheless, some tendencies appear strong enough to be worth mentioning.

For both speakers the amount of lengthening applied to nonfinal syllables (i.e., the first syllable in disyllabic words, and the first and second syllables in trisyllabic words) appears to be comparable for all positions. There are, however, some differences in the lengthening applied to the final syllable. Again for both speakers, the greatest amount of lengthening of the final syllable was found at the end of a nonfinal clause. There is also a tendency for greater lengthening at the end of an interrogative sentence as compared to a declarative sentence. A further tendency appears to be associated with the nature of the accent: lengthening of the final syllable appears to be greater, on the average, after falling accents than after rising accents. For P.I. the average lengthening in the final syllable was 55.7% in words with falling accents and 24.9% in words with rising accents. For D1 the average lengthening was 73.1% after falling accents and 41.9% after

Table 3.11
Durations of syllable nuclei in disyllabic words occurring in different positions within sentences produced by P. I. and D1. Durations in milliseconds. N = number of tokens.

Speaker	Accentual type	Medial position		End of nonfinal clause			End of declarative sentence			End of interrogative sentence		
		N	Dur.	N	Dur.	%	N	Dur.	%	N	Dur.	%
P. I.	˵ ˘	19	113	4	153	35.4	7	166	46.9	10	163	44.2
			89		123	38.2		76	−14.6		97	9.0
	ˋ ˘	20	101	4	140	38.6	4	128	26.7	10	142	40.6
			68		88	29.4		83	22.1		83	22.1
	ˆ ˘	20	143	4	190	32.9	5	176	23.1	10	182	27.3
			65		93	43.1		50	−23.1		96	47.7
	ˊ ˘	17	131	4	180	37.4	5	166	26.7	10	174	32.8
			52		83	59.6		54	3.8		77	48.1
	Average lengthening					36.1			30.9			36.2
						42.6			−3.0			31.7
D1	˵ ˘	12	94	4	180	91.5	7	177	88.3	5	188	100.0
			68		145	113.2		106	55.9		136	100.0
	ˋ ˘	14	81	4	125	54.3	6	130	60.5	7	116	43.2
			62		98	58.1		95	53.2		86	38.7
	ˆ ˘	7	127	5	234	84.3	6	223	75.6	4	193	52.0
			70		134	91.4		102	45.7		93	32.9
	ˊ ˘	13	132	5	208	57.6	6	203	53.8	6	198	50.0
			63		90	42.9		78	23.8		90	42.9
	Average lengthening					71.9			69.6			61.3
						76.4			44.7			53.6

Table 3.12
Durations of syllable nuclei in trisyllabic words occurring in different positions within sentences produced by P. I. and D1. Durations in milliseconds. N = number of tokens.

Speaker	Accentual type	Medial position		End of nonfinal clause			End of declarative sentence			End of interrogative sentence		
		N	Dur.	N	Dur.	%	N	Dur.	%	N	Dur.	%
P. I.	˵ ˘ ˘	13	124	4	125	1.0	4	115	−7.3	9	119	−4.0
			46		80	73.9		75	63.0		78	69.6
			45		125	177.8		70	55.6		77	71.1
	ˋ ˘ ˘	17	107	4	120	12.1	4	133	24.3	9	127	18.7
			72		63	−12.5		50	−30.1		60	−16.7
			64		73	14.1		53	−17.2		66	3.1
	ˆ ˘ ˘	18	118	4	178	50.8	4	180	52.5	9	169	43.2
			48		63	31.3		60	25.0		67	39.6
			46		113	145.7		58	26.1		88	91.3
	ˊ ˘ ˘	17	129	4	178	38.0	4	165	27.9	9	161	24.8
			48		83	72.9		73	52.1		84	75.0
			52		88	90.0		48	−7.7		68	30.8
	Average lengthening					25.5			24.4			20.7
						41.4			27.5			41.9
						106.9			14.2			49.1

D1	˵ ˘ ˘	7	107	4	106	1.0	4	100	−6.5	5	104	−2.8
			66		73	10.6		65	−1.5		69	4.5
			50		141	182.0		70	40.0		77	54.0
	` ˘ ˘	10	100	5	99	−1.0	5	101	1.0	6	99	−1.0
			66		61	−7.6		62	−6.1		62	−6.1
			61		110	80.3		76	24.6		83	36.1
	⌒ ˘ ˘	10	104	3	127	22.1	2	118	13.5	5	113	8.7
			44		70	59.1		85	93.2		72	63.6
			58		88	51.7		93	60.3		87	50.0
	´ ˘ ˘	6	124	4	166	33.9	2	160	29.0	3	156	25.8
			59		75	27.1		73	23.7		79	33.9
			62		101	62.9		88	41.9		60	−3.2
	Average lengthening					14.0			9.3			7.7
						22.3			27.3			24.0
						94.2			41.7			34.2

rising accents. A separate analysis was made of lengthening of final syllables in disyllabic and trisyllabic words with a rising accent on the first syllable. In disyllabic words the final syllable constitutes the tonal center; in trisyllabic words the tonal center is located on the second syllable, and the final syllable is postaccentual in every sense of the word. For P.I. the average lengthening of the final syllable was 30.9% in disyllabic words and 27.2% in trisyllabic words. For D1 the comparable values were 43.3% and 40.5%. The differences are clearly minimal, and the position of the tonal center appears to play no role in determining the amount of preboundary lengthening.

The average durations that appear in the two tables require comment. In several instances the distinction between long and short vowels seems not to have been well maintained by the speakers, especially in medial position. This is at least partly due to the nature of the test words involved. Only vowel durations are included in the averages; but there is some evidence that the duration of a syllable nucleus should be considered to include an adjacent resonant (for a reasoned argument in favor of this proposal, see Lehiste 1972). In these test materials the trisyllabic words with long falling accents were *kârtice* and *štâmpaju*; in both cases a resonant follows the vowel. Words with long rising accents included *vládaju* and *národom*. In *vládaju* a resonant precedes the vowel, and according to the argument presented in Lehiste 1972 the preceding resonant, too, should be considered as part of the duration of the syllable nucleus. The word *národom* introduces a further complication: in final position the lengthening affects both the vowel /o/ and the consonant /m/, but only the vowel lengthening is included in the averages in table 3.12. This may constitute part of the reason that lengthening in words with rising accents was, on the average, smaller than in words with falling accents. Nevertheless, most of the other test words ended in an open final syllable, and the tendency is strong enough to deserve further investigation.

This last observation suggests that sentence-level and word-level prosody influence each other with regard to duration. Different positions within the sentence affect the duration of the word in different ways: compared to words in nonemphatic medial position, clause-final and sentence-final words are lengthened, and lengthened to a different extent depending on whether the utterance is complete or incomplete. But to a certain extent, the nature of the accentual pattern of the word affects the degree of this influence in a particular position: lengthening of the final syllable appears to be greater in most cases, if the word carries a falling accent.

3.3.6 Supplementary Observations

The materials recorded by twelve informants (see section 2.1.3) included a set of four words produced in initial, medial, and final position in the following three frames:

1. . . . se tada potpuno približio.
2. Tada se . . . potpuno približio.
3. Tada se potpuno približio. . . .
   'Then he came completely close to . . .'

The test words were dat.sg.masc. *bràtu* 'brother', dat.sg.neut. *sèlu* 'village', dat.sg.masc. *grâdu* 'city', and dat.sg.fem. *Mári* (feminine name), representing the four accent types. The analysis of these productions showed that the patterns in initial position were basically similar to those in medial position, with usually a somewhat more prominent rise or less prominent fall. In final position there was a considerably lower overall level of fundamental frequency and intensity, and a practically complete absence of rising F_0 movements. The syllable nuclei were considerably lengthened in words in final position. The measurable differences between falling and rising accents, especially the short ones, were greatly reduced. However, in most cases a trace of the distinction remained; in particular, words with falling accents contained a much greater number of laryngealized or devoiced vowels.

Figures 3.13 and 3.14 show broad-band and narrow-band spectrograms of productions of the four test words in initial, medial, and final position by speaker D2. In *bràtu* and *sèlu* the distinction between ̏ and ̀ is maintained in initial and medial position, but neutralized in final position. In fact, this speaker phonated the second syllable of *bràtu* and laryngealized the second syllable of *sèlu* , where one might have expected the opposite. In *grâdu* and *Mári* the falling and rising F_0 movements are distinctive in all positions. Laryngealization started within the first syllable nucleus of *grâdu* in final position; in *Mári* both syllables were fully phonated.

Table 3.13 gives the average values of the F_0 and intensity patterns of the four test words in initial, medial, and final position, produced by the twelve informants.

The characteristics of declarative intonation, described in more detail above for P.I. and D1, were thus fully corroborated by the twelve additional informants.

3.3.7 Direction of F_0 Movement: Conclusions

We can conclude that the general F_0 movement in Serbocroatian sentences

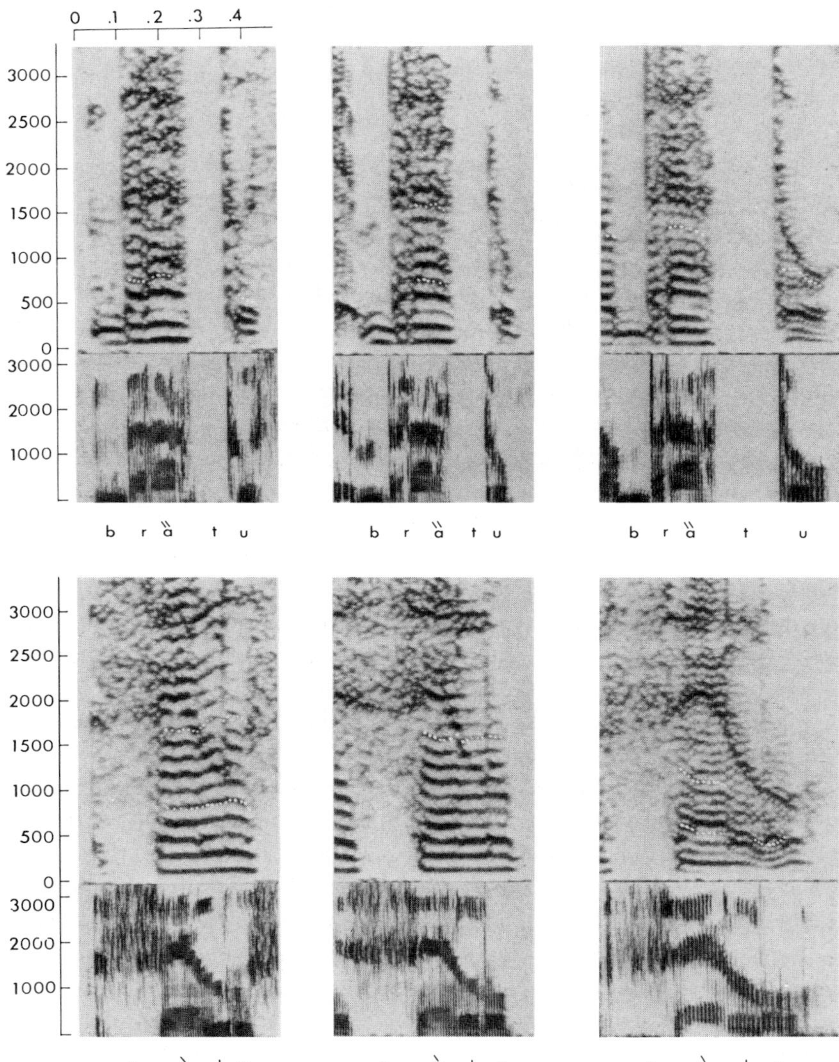

Figure 3.13
Broad-band and narrow-band spectrograms of the test words *brȁtu* and *sèlu*, occurring in initial, medial, and final position in sentences produced by speaker D2

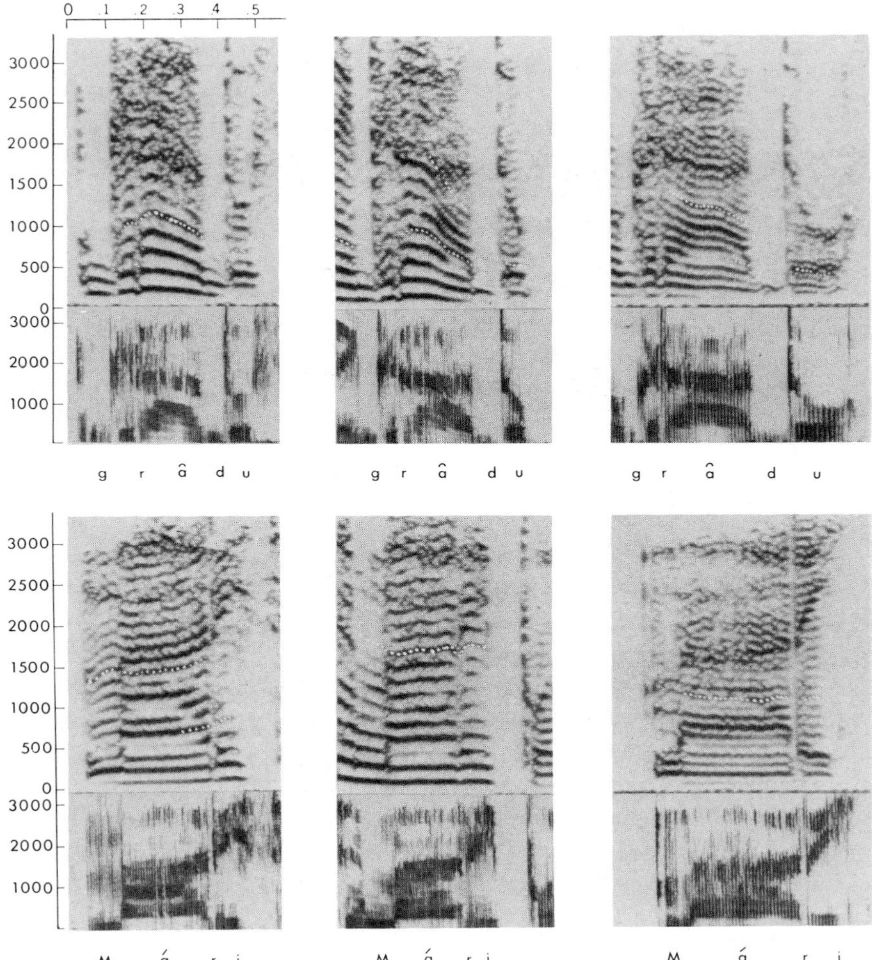

Figure 3.14
Broad-band and narrow-band spectrograms of the test words *grâdu* and *Mári*, occurring in initial, medial, and final position in sentences produced by speaker D2

Table 3.13
Average F_0 and intensity values in four test words in initial, medial, and final position, produced by twelve speakers. Fundamental frequencies in hertz, intensity in decibels.

			F_0 in productions by 6 low-pitched subjects			F_0 in productions by 3 medium-pitched subjects			F_0 in productions by 3 high-pitched subjects			Intensity averaged for all subjects
Word	Position	Vowel	Beg.	Peak	End	Beg.	Peak	End	Beg.	Peak	End	
brătu	initial	a	118	132	131	192	201	180	269	330	324	42.2
		u	122	122	108	222	222	215	229	229	197	34.8
			(2 lar.)			(1 lar.)						
	medial	a	127	141	133	203	220	210	272	300	297	41.5
		u	132	132	108	182	182	157	185	185	174	32.8
			(2 lar.)			(1 lar.)			(1 voiceless)			
	final	a	110	113	98	227	229	203	217	217	192	37.2
		u	70	70	70	93	94	75	158	158	153	26.9
			(4 lar., 1 vl.)			(1 lar., 1 vl.)			(2 lar.)			
sèlu	initial	e	117	117	113	197	200	188	258	276	274	42.9
		u	121	123	115	213	246	237	311	330	292	40.9
	medial	e	115	122	119	184	185	178	260	273	273	41.8
		u	125	128	107	195	212	206	325	331	305	39.1
	final	e	109	109	100	173	173	139	207	207	177	38.1
		u	95	95	84	129	137	131	178	186	186	32.4
									(1 lar.)			

grâdu	initial	a	130	146	122	197	214	159	298	329	262	43.7
		u	111	112	101	143	145	135	245	248	238	39.3
	medial	a	109	113	84	233	250	143	282	315	232	39.3
		u	89 (2 lar.)	92	86	165 (1 lar.)	202	158	192	192	176	35.4
	final	a	89 (1 lar.)	89	71	202	202	127	198	198	163	32.6
		u	102 (5 lar.)	102	96	147 (1 lar.)	152	147	189 (1 lar.)	189	187	29.0
Mári	initial	a	100	120	119	181	196	193	236	278	277	42.3
		i	125	128	121	205	226	226	312	335	313	40.7
	medial	a	99	131	131	197	217	217	251	290	290	41.3
		i	136	138	128	220	236	227	302	324	316	39.4
	final	a	88	90	86	157	157	143	205	205	172	33.2
		i	93 (2 lar.)	95	91	150	153	152	170	173	170	30.8

is falling. Rising movements can occur only in a well-defined set of categories:

1. At the very beginning of the sentence
2. At the end of nonfinal clauses
3. In yes-or-no questions with a "reverse F_0 pattern"
4. In the relation between preaccentual and accented syllables
5. In syllables under a rising accent (in some dialects also in the syllable following a rising accent)
6. (Less systematically) in syllables under a falling accent, especially in the initial part of such syllables

3.4 Experimental Research on Sentence Intonation in Serbocroatian by Other Scholars

Serbocroatian intonation has not been studied very extensively thus far, and many earlier investigations have been based on listening rather than controlled experiments.

3.4.1 Branko Miletić (1937), "Uticaj rečeničke melodije na intonaciju reči"

This article constitutes a report on the first experimental study of Serbocroatian sentence intonation. Miletić discusses the manifestation of word accents in various positions within a sentence, with and without emphasis, in complete and incomplete declarative sentences. The presentation is descriptive rather than quantitative; there is no list of sentences, the number of productions is not specified, and no measurements are reported. Miletić himself served as the speaker. The sentences were analyzed kymographically; the study was carried out in 1935 in the Institute for Experimental Phonetics of the University of Hamburg. Eighteen of the F_0 curves are reproduced in the article to illustrate the various general observations.

Miletić finds that the realization of word tone depends on the position of the word within the sentence. Thus, the word *pût* 'road' had a falling F_0 contour in absolute final position; in medial position the first half of /û/ was level, the second half falling; in initial position the F_0 contour was rising during the first half and falling during the second half. At the end of nonfinal clauses *pût* had a rising-falling F_0 curve on /û/; the fall in the second half terminated at the level of the beginning of the rise. Similar patterns appeared on comparable productions of *djâk* 'student, pupil' and *pàs* 'dog'. The word *déte* 'child' had a level F_0 contour in absolute final position and a rising F_0 contour on the accented syllable at the end of a nonfinal clause. The postaccentual syllable in *dëte* had the same F_0 level as the accented syllable. The relationships were the same for short rising accents.

Miletić also studied the effects of emphasis on word tone. In his pronunciation the two rising accents normally had a level or slightly rising F_0 contour; under emphasis the F_0 contour became rising. The short falling accent was normally slightly falling, and under emphasis either less falling or level. Emphasis affected long falling accents by making the first part more level and increasing the steepness of the fall in the second part. The intervals between the accented and postaccentual syllable remained basically unchanged for all accents, according to Miletić; the duration of all segments, both vowels and consonants, was considerably increased under emphasis.

Since the study involved only one speaker and there appears to have been no attempt to calculate averages, we are essentially dealing with individual productions whose reliability cannot be estimated. The generalizations drawn by Miletić must therefore be regarded with caution. Nevertheless, most of his observations have been substantiated by later research, and his study remains of great historical importance.

3.4.2 R. G. A. De Bray (1960), "The Pitch of Serbo-Croatian Word Accents in Statements and Questions" (see Ivić 1960, Pavlović 1960); (1961), "Some Observations of the Serbo-Croatian Musical Accents in Connected Speech."

De Bray recorded seven statements and six questions containing a slot in which a verb could occur in the third person singular form. Disyllabic 3.sg. forms of four different verbs were alternated in each position, each bearing one of the four accents (*trése* 'shakes', *hvâli* 'thanks', *ìma* 'has', *vȉdi* 'sees'). The number and dialect background of the speaker(s) is not specified; however, De Bray names two persons who read for him fragments from works of Serbian writers. We known from other sources that one of the two persons, Dr. Milka Ivić from Belgrade, also read the test sentences. The recorded tape was then fed to a double-beam cathode ray oscilloscope. One beam produced an oscillogram; the other was passed through a tone analyzer that produced a tracing of the fundamental frequency parallel to the oscillogram. The pitch tracings were used "to confirm aural impressions written down from careful listening to the recordings." De Bray states that "as the investigation concerned the spoken language the point of departure was always the aural impression; and the reaction of the much more sensitive instruments was used to confirm or complete this but never to replace it" (1960:388–389).

De Bray presents his results in the form of a table in which he gives a verbal description of the position of the test word, whether it was stressed, the aural impression, the impression from traces, and the pitch of the subsequent syllable relative to the accented one. He draws the following conclusions. The four different accents preserve their identity over a series of sentences exemplifying some of the main syntactic constructions in Serbian, even though in some instances their phonetic exponents coincide in rise-fall tones, especially for the two short accents. It is striking that the syllable following the ` accent practically always has a low tone in statements. We have reason to believe that the example used for the ` accent, *ìma* 'has', was pronounced *ȉma*, as is normal in Belgrade, where the recording was made, and as it is always pronounced by Prof. Dr. Milka Ivić (see P. Ivić 1960, which was written about a broader and still unpublished version of De Bray's work).

Sentence intonation affects the phonetic realization of the accents in four ways: question intonation demands a high rise; final position demands a fall; initial position is claimed to influence accents, but the specific form of this influence is not indicated; and absence of sentence stress causes a less distinct realization of word accents. According to De Bray, sentence intonations usually have a gradual fall in pitch, even in questions; the voice is maintained at a high or mid pitch at the end of uncompleted sentences or phrases and in the nonfinal clauses of complex sentences. In the fragments from Serbian literature read by his informants De Bray also observed several instances of a "sudden rise" in questions (with statement wording), which obviously corresponds to our "reverse pattern."

3.4.3 Irmgard Mahnken (1964), *Studien zur serbokroatischen Satzmelodie*. (Reviewed by Peukert 1969.)

The studies included in Mahnken 1964 are not really comparable to most of the other studies discussed here, since they are based on subjective listening rather than on objective measurements and systematic listening tests. The materials used by Pollok (1964) also served as the basis of Mahnken's studies. The methodology, described on pp. 42–43, involved repeated careful listening to the recordings and drawing curves by hand that represented the author's auditory impressions. The curves were placed on a five-line grid, whose lines divided a speaker's range into four registers: top, high-mid, low-mid, and low. Each register comprises 4 or 5 semitones. The recordings were also listened to by a (German-speaking) student, who likewise produced schematic pitch curves, and by a native speaker of Serbian. Both made a minimal number of suggestions for changes.

It must be emphasized that the curves are hand-drawn representations of auditory impressions, not instrumental registrations of the F_0 contour. No measurements are presented, and no listening tests are reported. No matter how careful the auditory analysis and how detailed the presentation, the fact remains that the system set up by Mahnken lacks objective confirmation.

These reservations must be kept in mind in considering Mahnken's results and conclusions, which may be summarized as follows.

Mahnken accepts as a premise the findings of Pollok regarding the nature of word-level accents. The rising and falling accents differ, according to this view, with respect to their integration into the "word parabola": ˊ and ˋ fit themselves into the parabola, whereas the accented syllable of ˆ and ̏ constitutes a separate syllable parabola that is set off from the word parabola. According to Mahnken, this is the distinctive characteristic of the Serbocroatian accentual opposition; the F_0 movement within the accented syllables (which can be shown to be significantly different only for the two long accents anyway) is to be considered redundant.

The intonation units within a sentence constitute either rising or falling curves; *thème* is generally rising, *propos* is falling. The smaller curves of syntagmatic units adapt themselves to the direction of the curves representing sentential units. The actual F_0 contour of a syllable that is adapting itself to the syntagmatic curve depends on two factors: its position within the syntagmatic unit (beginning, middle, end) and the direction of the sentential intonation unit into which the syntagmatic unit is integrated. The slope of the sentential intonation curve and the curvature of the syntagmatic parabola exert a (slight) further influence on the actual realization of the F_0 contour on an accented syllable.

The general direction of the intonation of statements is rising-falling, corresponding to the *thème-propos* structure. Differences between declarative sentences are signaled by different terminal cadences. Mahnken classifies them into terminal, semifinal, and progredient (corresponding to our "end of nonfinal clause") cadences, which may be either neutral or marked.

The neutral form of the terminal cadence is characterized by a low-mid to low level of the accented syllable. In syllables with ˆ and ̏ the fall takes place on the accented syllable itself; the postaccentual syllables are level at the extreme low range of the speaker's voice. With ˊ and ˋ the postaccentual syllables participate in the fall. In the marked form of the terminal cadence the accented syllable is in the high register.

The semifinal cadence is a variant of the terminal cadence. There is a fall in the postaccentual syllables, but it does not reach the low register. The semifinal cadence is found in instances in which the sentence is grammatically complete, but the speaker intends to continue his turn.

The progredient cadence is characterized by the nonfalling nature of the syntagma. The register is nonlow, and the syntagmatic curve does not return to the (falling) sentential curve, so that the basic direction of the progredient cadence is rising. This cadence is found when a sentence is grammatically incomplete.

The two basically falling terminal cadences and the basically rising progredient cadence are also distinguished by the specific F_0 contours on the accented syllable. Within the terminal cadence the two rising accents are either very slightly rising, level, or even slightly falling, depending on their position within the word; within the progredient cadence their F_0 movement is very definitely rising. The two falling accents have a prominent fall in the terminal cadence, which continues into the postaccentual syllables. In progredient cadences the syllables with falling accents have a steep rise with a rapid change of direction at the peak. The level of the accented syllable is much higher than that of the preaccentual syllable; the postaccentual syllables are only slightly lower than the accented syllable. The characteristics of a progredient cadence also include lengthening of final syllables.

Questions differ from statements not so much in terms of cadences as in terms of general intonation contour. Statements have a rising-falling intonation; questions starting with an interrogative word have a high peak on the accented syllable of that word, followed by a falling intonation contour. Yes-or-no questions likewise have no specific cadence. Those with interrogative particles (*da li*, *jel*, *zar*, etc.) have a rising-falling intonation contour; those with inversion have a falling contour with a peak on the initial verb form, similar to that of questions with an initial interrogative word. All questions usually end with a marked terminal cadence.

A special kind of intonation contour appeared on short questions introduced with *a* and containing no interrogative elements. In such questions the preaccentual syllables had low register, and the accented syllable had a steep rise, which continued up to the last postaccentual (= final) syllable. This rise, obviously identical with our "reverse pattern," distinguishes such questions from progredient cadences, in which the steep rise is usually restricted to the accented syllable, and the falling movement begins immediately after the syllable carrying the accent.

3.4.4 Per Jacobsen (1964), "Die Bedeutung der Satzintonation für die serbokroatischen Worttöne"

Jacobsen (1964) studied the influence of position within the sentence on the realization of the word tone of the following six words: nom.sg.masc. *ràt* 'war', nom.sg.masc. *sât*, nom.sg.fem. *kàpa* 'cap', nom.sg.masc. *pàtos* 'pathos', past part.nom.sg.masc. *bâčen* 'thrown', nom.sg.masc. *zákon* 'law'. The words were produced in isolation, in initial position of a short sentence, during the first half (but noninitially) in a short sentence, and in sentence-final position. Three informants produced the materials; one was from Zemun, one from Zagreb, and one from Kragujevac. Recording and analysis were carried out at the University of Copenhagen. The analysis was performed using a Frøkjær-Jensen Trans-Pitch Meter and G. Fant's intensity meter; the results were displayed on a four-channel Mingograph that produced a duplex oscillogram, two intensity curves, and a pitch curve. Measurement results are presented in eight tables; all curves are reproduced on pp. 221–231.

The results show that fundamental frequency of the accented syllable is always rising in sentence-initial position, regardless of the shape of the F_0 curve in isolated production. In final position fundamental frequency is falling on the accented syllable. When the word occurred noninitially in the first half of the sentence, all words with rising accents and seven of nine productions of words with falling accents had a rising F_0 movement on the accented syllable; one out of six productions of words with rising accents showed a falling F_0 movement in the accented syllable. Intensity curves did not always parallel the F_0 curves.

Jacobsen devotes one sentence to postaccentual syllables, remarking that in those cases in which word tone and sentence intonation coincide in the beginning of a sentence, the rising movement continues into the following unaccented syllable (or at least into its first half).

Per Jacobsen (1977), "Akcenat i intonacija u srpskohrvatskom jeziku"

The purpose of the study reported in Jacobsen 1977 was to investigate the interaction between word tone and sentence intonation. The materials consisted of six minimally contrastive sets of nonsense words: *pȁpa–pàpa–pâpa–pápa*, *bȁba–bàba–bâba–bába*, and comparable sets for *pipi-bibi* and *pupu-bubu*. These words were placed in three short frames in initial, medial, and final position. The resulting 72 sentences, and 34 meaningful sentences of a comparable structure, were produced three times by a native informant. The recordings were made and analyzed at the Phonetics Institute of the University of Copenhagen.

The results showed that the overall (declarative) sentence intonation falls from the first accented syllable of the sentence, if that syllable bears a falling accent. If the first accented word bears a rising accent, the falling movement starts with the posttonic syllable. In both cases the falling movement continues to the end of the sentence. The unstressed syllables appeared to have a very stable gradually falling F_0 pattern, so that an imaginary straight line could be traced along the F_0 registrations of the unstressed syllables from the first F_0 peak in the sentence to its termination. Jacobsen considers this line to represent the "virtual intonation" of the sentence. Accented short syllables are distinguished not by their F_0 movements, but by F_0 level: syllables with ˵ lie either on or slightly below the imaginary straight line representing sentence intonation, whereas syllables with ` lie considerably below that line. Jacobsen therefore proposes to treat the short rising accent as *low tone* relative to intonation; stating that the short falling accent tends to merge with sentence intonation, he proposes to interpret this accent as *high tone*.

3.4.5 Richard L. Leed (1968), "The Intonation of Yes-No Questions in Serbo-Croatian"

Leed based his analysis of Serbocroatian intonation on two sources. One was a recording accompanying the texbook by Jonke, Leskovar, and Pranjić (1962). The recordings from which Leed's corpus was taken contain the voices of eight different speakers, male and female, using the western variant of the Serbocroatian literary language. The source for the eastern variant was primarily the textbook by Hodge and Janković (1965), in which the sentences through unit 5 are marked for intonation. Leed also mentions an informant speaking the eastern variety, who read the fifty yes-or-no questions from Jonke, Leskovar, and Pranjić's materials. The analysis of the recorded materials was performed aurally. Intonation is described with reference to four numbered levels and with arrows indicating terminal rise or fall.

Leed states that the typical shape of the question intonation contour is fall-rise-fall. If nothing precedes, fall is realized as low pitch. Leed takes issue with De Bray (1960), who had stated that "in no forms of question does the native što-dialect speaker ever raise the pitch of the voice at the end of the utterance" (p. 382); Leed claims that 24% of the yes-or-no questions in his corpus had a fall-rise contour, without a final fall: the pitch remained high to the end of the sentence. Leed says further that the question intonation pattern is much more frequent in the western variety than in the eastern variety, since (according to Leed) the preferred form of the yes-or-no question in the eastern variety is the construction with *da li*, followed by statement intonation. He provides one example with the reverse pattern in a production by his eastern informant (p. 334):

1 3 1 ↓
istina?

3.4.6 T. M. Nikolaeva (1971a), "Sootnošenie slovesnoj i frazovoj melodiki v serbskom jazyke"

Nikolaeva (1971a) investigated the realization of Serbocroatian accents in phrasal units contained in complex sentences. Three speakers produced 60 sentences each. Those sentences that were accepted as well-formed by all three speakers serving as listeners were analyzed oscillographically, and F_0 information was obtained from the oscillograms. Each complex sentence consisted of two interchangeable halves, for example, *Mada je već mrak, ja ipak odlazim–ja ipak odlazim, mada je već mrak* 'Even though it is already dark, I'm nevertheless leaving'. Thus, the same words could occur in several syntactic positions in the same lexical environment.

The clause were divided into two parts: the part containing sentence-level (syntagmatic) stress, and the part preceding the stressed element. In other words, a syntagma was divided into a "cadence" and the part preceding it. Within the cadence, three parts were distinguished: the part preceding the stressed syllable, the stressed syllable, and the syllables following the stressed syllable. In the part preceding the cadence, the beginning and middle part of the syntagma were distinguished.

Nikolaeva studied the F_0 movement in the accented syllable of a word and the relationship of the accented syllable to the neighboring syllables. There were four kinds of F_0 movements within the accented syllable: rising, falling, level, and complex. ("Complex" refers to a F_0 movement that changes its direction more than once, so that it cannot be called either rising or falling.) The F_0 movements in the accented syllable were observed under two kinds of sentence intonation: rising and falling. The results were as follows:

1. Sentence intonation dominates word-level intonation. However, this domination is not absolute. In approximately one-third of the instances a word retained its F_0 movement even when its direction was opposite to that of sentence intonation.
2. It is not true in all cases that words with ̏ have a tendency to acquire level tone in continuous speech, even though they provide the largest number of examples of level tone among the four accents.

3. Words under sentence stress are more strongly influenced by sentence intonation than words not bearing sentence stress. Words with ˆ and ̏ changed less under rising sentence intonation than words with ´ and `; under falling intonation ´ and ` changed less than ˆ and ̏. This was particularly clear with falling sentence intonation superimposed on a word with a long rising accent.

Nikolaeva also compared the fundamental frequency of accented syllables with that of preceding and following syllables under two intonations, with and without sentence stress. There were four possible patterns:

1. The accented syllable has lower fundamental frequency than the preceding and following syllables (H – H).
2. The accented syllable has higher fundamental frequency than the adjacent syllables (L – L).
3. The accented syllable is lower than the preaccentual syllable, but higher than the postaccentual syllable (H – L).
4. The accented syllable is higher than the preaccentual syllable, but lower than the postaccentual syllable (L – H).

These melodic figures can be realized within the sentence under both rising and falling sentence intonation. The analysis of the sentences from this point of view yielded the following results:

1. Only three of the four possible melodic figures appear with each accent. Thus, with rising intonation H – L does not occur; with falling intonation L – H does not appear.
2. The patterns are completely identical for the two falling accents, on the one hand, and the two rising accents, on the other hand.
3. There is no difference between words with and without sentence stress.
4a. The most characteristic movements for the two falling accents are L – L with rising sentence intonation and H – L with falling sentence intonation. This means that under both intonations the postaccentual syllable is lower than the accented syllable.
4b. The most characteristic melodic figures for the two rising accents are L – H with rising intonation and H – H with falling intonation. This means that the postaccentual syllable was higher than the accented syllable under both intonations. According to Nikolaeva, this fact supports Masing's hypothesis about the nature of Serbocroatian accents.
5. The melodic figure L – L was represented in all cases—with all four accents and both intonations, with or without sentence stress. This means that the accented syllable could be set off from its environment by F_0 level.

The short falling accent occupied a special position. This accent stood out from the sentence intonation contour more than the long falling accent, regardless of the F_0 movement within the accented syllable itself.

In the case of rising accents under falling intonation, Nikolaeva observed an almost equal number of instances of the melodic figures H – H (postaccentual syllable is higher than the accented syllable) and L – L (postaccentual syllable is lower than the accented syllable). However, when more than one postaccentual syllable is taken into account, the type L – L becomes L – LH.

Nikolaeva's general conclusions were as follows:

1. Sentence intonation exerts a strong influence on the realization of fundamental frequency in Serbocroatian words.
2. Sentence intonation has the strongest influence on the F_0 movement within the syllable bearing sentence stress; here intonation assimilates the tone on the syllable to itself.
3. The nature of the accent is maintained outside the domain of the accented syllable: accented syllables with rising accents have lower fundamental frequency than postaccentual syllables under both intonations, and syllables bearing falling accents have higher fundamental frequency than postaccentual syllables.
4. It is possible to hypothesize that in Serbocroatian there are not two melodic figures, but one melodic figure that consists of two elements. Accent may be located either on the first part of the figure (in the case of rising accents) or on the second part of the figure (in the case of falling accents). Since the falling accents occur only on the first syllable of a word, the first part of the figure has no opportunity to be realized except in continuous speech.
5. The relationship of the F_0 level of a syllable to that of adjacent syllables and the F_0 movement within the accented syllable itself may be equally valid means of preserving the distinctive nature of an accent under the influence of sentence intonation; both of these means together or either one alone may serve the distinctive function.
6. The instances of heightened F_0 level in postaccentual syllables after rising accents, under falling intonation, when the elevation of F_0 occurs not on the first but on the second postaccentual syllable, suggest that this melodic figure requires a certain time for its realization that does not necessarily coincide with the number of syllables. It might be more appropriate to talk about morae than about syllables in specifying the domain of this figure.

Table 3.14
Number of syllables with two intensity peaks in sentences with rising and falling intonation (Nikolaeva 1973)

Sentence intonation	Number of syllables with two intensity peaks				Long unaccented	Short unaccented
	ˆ	˵	´	`		
Rising	24	15	25	5	6	9
Falling	4	1	5	2	3	2

T. M. Nikolaeva (1971b), "Sootnošenie frazovoj i slovesnoj prosodii (sinxronnoe opisanie). Nekotorye aspekty problemy"
Nikolaeva 1971b offers a preview of materials and results discussed in more detail in Nikolaeva 1973. Two of the three illustrations are not included in Nikolaeva 1973.

T. M. Nikolaeva (1973), "Nekotorye nabljudenija nad sootnošeniem slovesnyx akcentov i frazovoj melodiki v serbskom jazyke"
Nikolaeva 1973 treats the same material as Nikolaeva 1971b. More data are presented; there are 14 examples of oscillographically analyzed sentences and 43 tables containing the results of measurements made from oscillograms. The conclusions concerning F_0 patterns are identical to those presented in Nikolaeva 1971b.

With regard to intensity, Nikolaeva found that F_0 movement and intensity change frequently paralleled each other. There were also numerous instances in which they went in opposite directions. In general, parallel changes in F_0 and intensity were more common with falling sentence intonation than with rising intonation, a fact that Nikolaeva attributes to physiological causes. Relatively more instances of lack of congruence between F_0 and intensity changes were observed with falling accents than with rising accents.

Nikolaeva also studied cases in which a syllable showed two intensity peaks. We reproduce her summary table as table 3.14 (1973 : 188, table 37). On the basis of these data, Nikolaeva concludes that two-peakedness cannot be considered distinctive for any accent type.

Nikolaeva also analyzed the duration of vowels in all syllables and arrived at the following results. Averaged over all productions by her three speakers, the average durations (in milliseconds) of vowels in various positions may be seen from table 3.15 (constructed by us on the basis of Nikolaeva's tables 38–43, pp. 191–193).

Table 3.15
Average durations, in milliseconds, of vowels occurring under various conditions in test materials analyzed by Nikolaeva (1973)

	Accented vowels		Unaccented vowels			
Type of syllable nucleus	Under sentence stress	In continuous speech	In continuous speech	In absolute final position	Before sentence stress	Not before sentence stress
̑	156.8	111.9				
̏	85.3	76.5				
́	143.3	107.0				
̀	84.0	73.4				
Long unstressed vowels			82.9			
Short postaccentual vowels			59.9	86.3		
Short preaccentual vowels					68.8	59.5

In her general conclusions Nikolaeva observes that sentence intonation has a considerable influence on the realization of fundamental frequency and intensity. The only parameter that functioned with absolute regularity was duration: vowels were longer under ̑ and ́ and shorter under ̏ and ̀, and accented vowels were longer than unaccented vowels. This regularity leads Nikolaeva to agree with our formulation of accentedness (Lehiste and Ivić 1963 : 134). Noting the relatively greater duration of preaccentual vowels, which according to her is also present in Russian, Nikolaeva speculates that this greater length may have been phonologized in the Neoštokavian accent shift.

T. M. Nikolaeva (1977), *Frazovaja intonacija slavjanskix jazykov*

Nikolaeva devotes a chapter of Nikolaeva 1977 to Serbocroatian. Her material consisted of eleven sentences produced by one speaker and an unspecified number of sentences produced by three speakers (she refers the reader to Nikolaeva 1973 for more details). The methodology is not described, but it appears that measurements were made of fundamental frequency, intensity, and vowel duration.

Nikolaeva describes six sentence types: declarative sentences, incomplete sentences, general questions (which correspond to our yes-or-no questions), questions with an interrogative word, questions with *a*, and exclamations. The presentation is largely based on existing literature; in particular, Nikolaeva quotes extensively from our work. This is supplemented by results of her own investigations, which generally confirm our previous findings. The one sentence type that we had not described, questions with *a* (e.g., *A vetar*? 'But what about the wind?'), shows the reverse pattern like yes-or-no questions.

3.4.7 Branko Vuletić (1971–72), "Koliko razumijemo intonaciju?"

The author asked an actor to read five sentences in four different emotional modes (fury, irony, happiness, sorrow), and as questions and neutral statements. A listening test was given to three groups of listeners; the first consisted of 145 students at the University of Zagreb, the second of 22 students from the Theatrical Academy in Zagreb, and the third of 70 subjects in France who had no acquaintance with the Serbocroatian language. All three groups succeeded in identifying the questions; their respective scores were 88.27%, 95.45%, and 88.57%. Since no acoustic analyses are reported, it remains unknown what type of intonation the actor had employed in producing the questions.

3.4.8 Edward T. Purcell (1973), *The Realizations of Serbo-Croatian Accents in Sentence Environments: An Acoustic Investigation*

As mentioned in section 2.10.13, this book is a slightly revised version of Purcell's 1970 doctoral dissertation. Excerpts and summaries of the dissertation had been published earlier (Purcell 1971, 1972). We have described the general methodology in chapter 2; here we will summarize the part of Purcell's work that deals with sentence intonation.

Five speakers read a text consisting of 13 sentences, constructed in such a way that 50 test words appeared at the beginning, in the middle, and at the end of statements and questions. Questions in which the test word occurred initially were yes-or-no questions; questions in which the test word occurred medially and finally contained the interrogative particle *li*. Purcell found regular and sizable differences between the average realizations of the four accents in all statement environments. These differences appeared in all acoustic parameters: fundamental frequency, duration, and intensity. There was no neutralization. Statement-initial position was characterized by the highest F_0 peaks, and statement-final position by the lowest ones. Likewise, all relations tended to be more rising in statement-initial position than in any other position, and more falling in statement-final position than in any other position. These findings all correspond to our own. In questions (where a rising question intonation was used, seemingly by only one speaker) "no regular differences could be found between the realizations of any accent that would apply to the realizations of the other three accents in the three question environments" (p. 154). "In other words, it was not possible to establish a concise pattern of relationships differentiating the realizations of any one accent in each of the three question environments" (p. 164). In general, F_0 values were higher for words within a question than for words placed in an equivalent statement environment. None of Purcell's subjects produced the low-high reverse pattern in questions with statement wording. Words occurring in statements showed a higher degree of conformity to what Purcell calls the "normal pattern of accentual differentiation" than the same words in equivalent question environments.

Edward T. Purcell (1974), "A Model of Word Tone, Sentence Intonation, and Segmental Duration in Serbo-Croatian: A Preliminary Report"

This article constitutes a progress report on a synthesis-by-rule analysis of Serbocroatian in which Purcell was engaged at that time; we are not aware of any further publications in connection with this project, although the progress report hints at a continuation. The model presented in the report is based primarily on Purcell's own results, but also incorporates certain findings of others. It generates word tone, sentence intonation, and segmental duration. The model is limited to words of one, two, and three syllables and deals with one type of sentence intonation (a "neutral" declarative statement intonation).

After a string of phonemes has been specified and segmental durations have been assigned, sentence intonation values are calculated. Ten F_0 values are assigned to specific percentage locations within the sentence. The researcher supplies an initial value, which the model uses to calculate the ten values it assigns. The F_0 values representing the sentence intonation are assigned to the sentence as a whole, without regard to words or word boundaries. The initial F_0 value is assigned to the first 10 msec of the sentence. The second value is obtained from the first by multiplying it by 1.15; this value is assigned to the point that represents 15% of the duration of the sentence. The third value is obtained by multiplying the second by 1.07; this value is assigned to a point that represents 35% of the duration of the sentence. The fourth value is obtained by multiplying the third by .94, and so on. A nonlinear interpolation technique is used to supply the intermediate values. The resultant F_0 curve rises in the beginning of the sentence, levels off toward the middle, and then falls until the end.

The next step is calculation of word tone. Using information originally provided in connection with the input string of phonemes, the program identifies accented and unaccented vowels and notes which of the four accents applies to each accented vowel. Word boundaries, which had been likewise included in the segmental input string, are used to mark the endpoints of the domain of a word tone. F_0 values are then calculated for all vowels in the input string. Values for both rising and falling accents are calculated as deviations from the previously defined sentence intonation. Formulas are provided for locating the peak of the F_0 contour closer to the end of the accented vowel if the word appears at the beginning of the sentence, and closer to the start of the accented vowel if the word appears near the end of the sentence. Once all parameters have been specified, they are fed into a synthesizer, the output of which is then available for listening and evaluation.

Purcell provides graphs representing the sentence intonation and the superimposed word tones for four sentences: *Vidim čep tamo* 'I see the cork there', *Vidim pčelu tamo* 'I see the bee there', *Vidim rajčicu tamo* 'I see the tomato there', and *Vidim bebu tamo* 'I see the baby there'. No systematic listening tests or evaluations are reported, but Purcell says that "speech samples synthesized according to the preliminary model may be understandable as Serbo-Croatian to a native speaker, but they do not sound like natural speech" (p. 197). It is quite possible that the unnaturalness is due to the quality of the segmental synthesis; it would be interesting to be able to evaluate the F_0 contours generated by the model, supplied to a better quality segmental string.

3.4.9 Gerhard Neweklowsky (1981a), "Akustisch-phonetische Messungen als Entscheidungshilfe für phonologische Interpretation (am Beispiel der serbokroatischen Akzentuation)"

The study was based on the corpus of 86 sentences used by Ivić and Lehiste 1969. The main purpose of the investigation was to compare the realization of Serbocroatian accents in sentences produced at two different reading speeds, normal and "allegro." Three informants from Bosnia produced the sentences twice, in the two different styles. The recordings were made at the University of Sarajevo in 1979. An acoustic analysis was carried out, but in this publication results are reported for only one of the speakers.

Neweklowsky's results show that sentence intonation influences the realization of F_0 movement within the accented syllable, so that in the beginning of the sentence the F_0 movement is rising in both types of accents, whereas in sentence-final position it is falling. In initial position the distinction between rising and falling accents is maintained on the basis of the relationship between the accented and the postaccentual syllables: in the case of the falling accents the F_0 level (measured in the middle of each syllable) of the two syllables is approximately the same, whereas in the case of rising accents the postaccentual syllable is higher by 2.5 semitones with ` and 4 semitones with ´. In medial position tonal intervals were relatively smaller in allegro speech than in lento speech. In final position of complete statements accent oppositions appeared neutralized under the influence of falling sentence intonation; in incomplete statements, however, the opposition was maintained on the basis of the relationship between the F_0 levels of the two syllables.

The duration of all vowels was compressed in allegro style; the shortening coefficient was 1.49 for ̏, 1.58 for `, 1.68 for ̑, and 1.75 for ´. The average durations of short accented vowels were 62 and 68 msec. Neweklowsky argues that since the integration time of the human ear is approximately 70 msec, tonal movements within short accented vowels would not be discriminable in allegro style. Since the tonal oppositions were not neutralized (except for absolute final position in statements), Neweklowsky concludes that the phonological opposition between rising and falling accents rests solely on the F_0 relationships between the accented and the postaccentual syllables. Thus, accents are indeed disyllabic in Serbocroatian, as Masing had already claimed for the rising accents in 1876.

3.5 The Relationship between Sentence Intonation and Word Accents

After having described the manifestation of word accents in various types of sentences and the manifestation of sentence intonation over words with different accents, we are left with the problem of the interaction between the two systems. It is inevitable that the two systems affect each other, since their manifestation involves the same physiological and physical parameters. In principle, the conflict is resolved in a manner analogous to vector addition: the actual realization of a curve is the combined result of two (or more) forces applied in independent directions. Thus, the types of sentence intonation and the accentual types of words may be viewed as abstract forces that are materialized as components woven into a single, complex realization.

The relative shares of sentence intonation and word accents in the prosodic realization of a sentence vary from situation to situation. In the position that we have called neutral (in the middle of a simple, nonemphatic statement) differences between rising and falling word accents are very clear, whereas in final position these differences are much smaller. Thus, the share of word accent in the ultimate realization of a contour is greater in medial position than in final position. The data presented in chapters 2 and 3 make it possible to establish a partial hierarchy of such positions with respect to the relative degree of significance of sentence intonation in a given situation. On the other hand, there is also a hierarchy of word accents: in identical positions, the difference between the two long accents is always greater than the difference between the two short accents, so that the share of word accent in the realization of a contour is greater when the words carry a long accent. Furthermore, the two short accents in final position are distinguished in trisyllabic words much more clearly than in disyllabic words.

In considering the relative importance of sentence intonation and word accent (from the point of view of establishing a hierarchy among all the components involved in the prosodic realization of a sentence), two kinds of solutions are possible. A quantitative approach would give precedence to sentence intonation for the reason that the differences between realizations of the same word accent in various positions within the sentence are, on the average, greater than the differences between realizations of the same sentence intonation on words with different accents. We believe that it is more meaningful to base the decision on a qualitative approach, taking into consideration the observed phenomena of neutralization. It has been shown that in a series of types of sentence intonation, the opposition between the two short accents was neutralized, and that there were instances in which the contrast between the two long accents likewise disappeared, such as questions where interrogation was signaled by the presence of a reverse pattern; but there were no instances in which sentence-intonational signals would have been neutralized under the influence of word accents.

We conclude, therefore, that sentence intonation is primary, and that word accents cause modification in the realization of sentence intonation. Under some conditions the modifications are very extensive; in other positions they are smaller, and there are certain cases in which the signals of sentence intonation are so prominent that differences in word accents are completely absent.

The decision tree presented as figure 3.15 (Lehiste and Ivić 1978: 127) constitutes an attempt to establish the order in which various decisions must be made in order to arrive at the realization of the prosodic shape of a sentence. Specification of word tone is assumed at this stage (Lehiste and Ivić 1978: 107). We are still very far removed from a formula that would

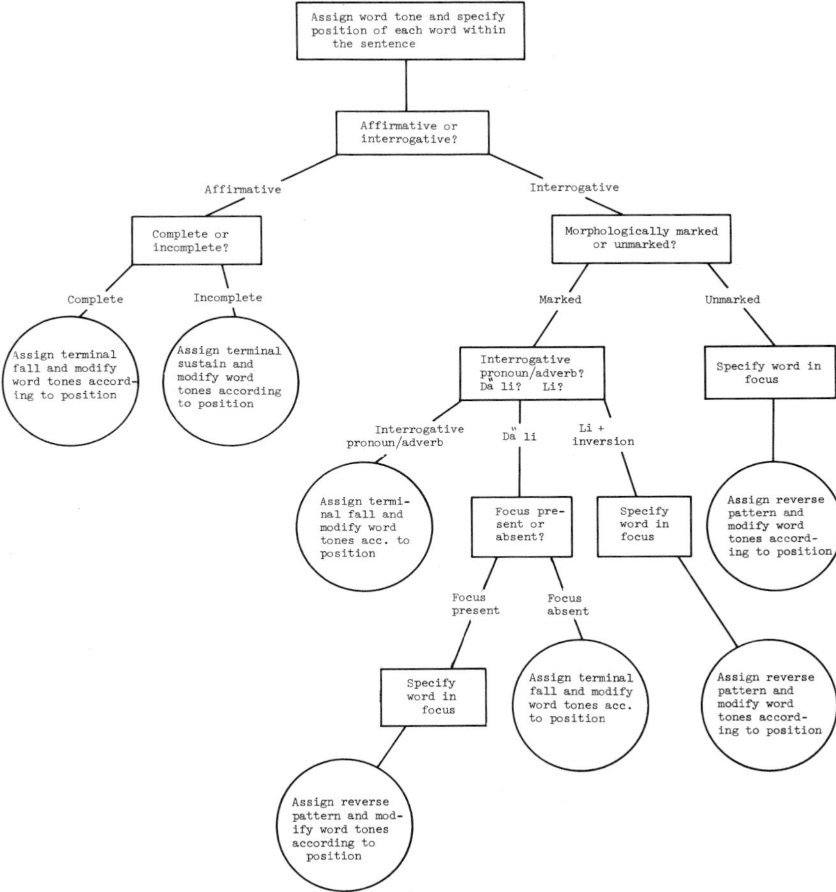

Figure 3.15
Decision tree representing the successive steps involved in the realization of the prosodic shape of a sentence

make it possible to assign numerical values to the various acoustic parameters; but we believe that we have identified the relationships between several of these parameters, and that we have discovered some unity in diversity.

Chapter 4

Phonological Analysis

4.1 History of the Problem

4.1.1 The Views of Jakobson and Trubetzkoy

Neoštokavian accentuation attracted the attention of phonologists at an early date; already in the 1930s the leading scholars of the Prague school occupied themselves with this problem.

Jakobson (1931a) opened the era of the phonological investigation of Serbocroatian accents. According to Jakobson, what is relevant—besides quantity—is tone. Accent falls automatically on the syllable with marked tone (= the accents ` or ´); if marked tone is not present, accent falls on the first syllable (= ̏ or ̑). A relevant characteristic in some dialects is the "vollsilbige Erhöhung der Vokale"—raising of the tonal height of vowels in such a way that the raising encompasses the whole syllable; in other dialects, a relevant characteristic is "übersilbige Erhöhung"—raising that extends beyond one syllable. Both types of raising can occur on any syllable except the last (Jakobson's term "übersilbig" refers to the presence of high fundamental frequency on the postaccentual syllable; relying on Miletić 1926 and Belić 1926–27, Jakobson believed that this phenomenon occurs only in a part of the Neoštokavian dialects). The accent that falls on the first syllable in words without marked tone is "außerphonologisch" (nonphonemic) and "unvollsilbig" (with a domain encompassing less than one whole syllable); otherwise—according to the testimony of Miletić (1926), whom Jakobson quotes—it is more intense than the accent connected with marked tone. The term "unvollsilbig" refers of course to the falling tonal movement, which leaves the final part of the syllable without high tone.

Jakobson's theory about Serbocroatian accents constitutes a breakthrough not only in Serbocroatian, but also in general accentology. Jakobson demonstrated here that certain prosodic systems can be analyzed in a more economical manner than had been the case before. Whereas the traditional view implicitly operated with three distinctive prosodic features (tone, accent, and quantity), Jakobson reduced this number to two, showing that accent placement is predictable on the basis of tone. This theory is particularly attractive in the variant that operates with the concept of "übersilbige Erhöhung," since we know now that high fundamental frequency on two successive syllables is characteristic of so-called rising accents in all Neoštokavian dialects. Thus, when the word does not contain a sequence of two high-pitched syllables, the high pitch falls automatically on the first syllable, which is in complete accord with phonetic reality. Using the term "übersilbig" instead of operating explicitly with tonal height on consecutive syllables may not be logically precise, but it has the advantage that it corresponds well to the native speaker's intuition, according to which the first of the two high-pitched syllables appears as the bearer of the accent. Nevertheless, various authors raised objections to Jakobson's analysis, including the following:[1]

1. From the viewpoint of descriptive economy, this approach has the disadvantage that it retains the distributional restrictions connected with final syllables and monosyllabic words.

2. The syllable bearing the falling accent has all the characteristics of an accented syllable rather than those of an unaccented syllable. This concerns pitch height, intensity, and duration, as well as the phonetic quality of the syllable nucleus. This fact speaks for the necessity of treating falling accents in the same manner as rising accents.

3. The notion that words with falling accents possess no phonological accent conflicts with the fact that words in Serbocroatian are divided into two large categories: accentogenic words and clitics. The difference between them is above all semantic and functional; their unequal prosodic behavior reflects this fundamental difference. If we declare that one subset of accentogenic words, namely those with falling accents, do not possess phonological accent, it becomes necessary to redefine the clitics—that is, to introduce a new feature distinguishing them from words with ̏ or ̑. Whatever feature were introduced, the description would inevitably depart from phonetic reality. At the same time the saving would be lost that had been achieved by qualifying the falling accents as automatic.

4. In the typological set to which European polytonic languages belong, tone is a subcategory of accent rather than a superordinate category.

5. Falling accents also have a distinctive function, since they occur in the same position as the rising accents, contrasting with them.

6. The distributional limitation of falling accents to the first syllable does

not mean that they have no phonological value; this applies also to the changes that they undergo in sandhi.

7. Falling accents may occur beyond the first syllable in combination with proclitics and in compound words of the type *jedinodùšni* 'of the same mind'.

8. The analysis that Jakobson presented was necessary for him in order to remove the obstacle that Neoštokavian accentuation presented for his theory that tonal contrasts are due to accent placement on either the first or the second mora of a long syllable, from which it follows that such contrasts should not be found with short accents.

These objections do not all proceed from the same premises, and they are of unequal character and value, but on the whole they call Jakobson's analysis into serious question. One could, furthermore, raise additional objections: for example, that the morphophonemic description remains at least as complicated under this analysis as under the traditional one. For all these reasons, in spite of its tremendous historical significance, Jakobson's clever and elegant theory failed to provide the definitive answer to the question of the phonological essence of Neoštokavian accentuation.[2] However, in a slightly revised version this theory cannot be easily refuted as a possible solution. It is necessary to start from the notion of accentual word, thus making the appropriate distinction between clitics and accentogenic words (which is indispensable in any realistic analysis), and to leave out the qualification "außerphonologisch" as applied to the falling accents (if place of accent is nondistinctive anyway, then both rising and falling accents are equally "außerphonologisch"). (Compare how this analysis was applied in Ivić (ed.) 1981.) It would be appropriate to add that both rising and falling accents fulfill the culminative function (see section 4.2.2), and of course, the whole analysis may be valid only in its "übersilbig" variety.

The analysis offered by Trubetzkoy (1939) is very close to that of Jakobson and depends upon it. Trubetzkoy nevertheless proceeds from accent rather than from tone, and says that "the truly 'free' accent is musically rising," whereas "the 'falling' accent . . . is . . . only . . . a combinatory variant of the absence of accent which fulfills a demarcative function."[3] This viewpoint has the same virtues and weaknesses as that expressed by Jakobson (1931a).[4] In addition, Trubetzkoy describes the falling accent as "primarily expiratory," in contrast to the rising accent, which is "characterized almost entirely by its musical quality"—an assertion that is by no means confirmed by instrumental research.

The interpretation advanced by Isačenko (1939) agrees with that of

Jakobson (1931a):" . . . im Serbokroatischen wird die den Steigton tragende Silbe als iktisch empfunden. . . . Fehlt eine solche Silbe, dann fällt der 'Iktus' automatisch auf die erste Silbe der expiratorischen Einheit" (. . . in Serbo-croatian the syllable bearing the rising tone is felt to be ictic. . . . When no such syllable is present, the ictus falls automatically on the first syllable of the expiratory unit).

Jakobson returned several times to the problem of the phonological analysis of Neoštokavian accentuation, gradually modifying his theories.[5] His abandonment of the term "übersilbige (or "vollsilbige") Erhöhung" and his replacement of this term by the traditional label "rising" (in 1931b and 1937; also see Jakobson 1971 : 351) constituted a step backward. This applies even more to his analysis of 1949, in which high-toned vowels are opposed to low-toned ones. "High tone" must apparently be understood as so-called rising accents. This view conflicts with the fact that the pitch peak of vowels under a falling accent is, as a rule, higher than the pitch peak in words with rising accents. In later works Jakobson retained the contrast between high and low tone. The innovation of his 1965 paper ("the high pitch, permutative . . . throughout the nonfinal syllables . . . is supplemented by a high/low pitch commutation in the initial syllable") also has other disadvantages. Here the distinction between "Tonstelle" ("position of tone" = permutative high pitch) and "Tonverlauf" ("tonal movement" = commutative high pitch) as independent variables is again introduced into the interpretation of Neoštokavian accentuation, a procedure against which Jakobson himself had justifiedly protested in 1963; at the same time the situation on the initial syllable is obscured by imprecise description.

4.1.2 The views of Trager and Hodge

Trager (1940) followed the Prague school teachings: " . . . falling stress may occur on any syllable of a word. This, when there is no rising stress in the word, is actualized as a loud stress on the first of not more than three syllables" (p. 31). The innovations that Trager introduced into his description have no basis in phonetic reality: he states explicitly that what is relevant is loudness, pitch being concomitant ("automatic"!), and has obtained from somewhere the idea that "every word of more than three syllables must have a rising stress," even though there exist numerous examples like dat.pl. *mâjstorima* 'craftsmen', *vȅrovānje* 'believing (noun)', dat.pl. *kȕkavicama* 'cowards', and gen.sg.masc. *ȉnternacionālnoga* 'international'.

Hodge (1946) refrains from a full description of the prosodic pattern and refers to Trager, but his short, somewhat fragmentary analysis differs considerably from that of Trager. He distinguishes falling pitch with stress (̀ according to his notation) and rising pitch with stress (́), adding that "actual rise and fall is only phonetically discernible on long vowels and *ije*" (p. 112). It follows from this that Hodge did not hear tonal contrasts in short syllables. On the other hand, the contrasts that he found in the sequence *ije* (*ijè* ∼ *ijé*; i.e., *ijȅ* ∼ *ijè* according to traditional transcription) do not in fact exist (most probably, the informants, who were Serbs from Croatia, pronounced something like *ⁱi̯ê* and *ⁱi̯é*, respectively). Hodge transcribes length with two vowel letters (*ràad* 'work', *raáditi* 'to work'), but does not include quantity in the phonemic inventory. Nevertheless, he makes no explicit statement about vowel gemination, which means that no argumentation is offered in favor of the chosen solution.

4.1.3 The views of Kuznecov and Others

After a detailed discussion, Kuznecov (1948) arrives at a conclusion close to the traditional description: primary role belongs to accent, which can be either rising or falling: "Only words and word forms characterized by rising accent may differ with regard to place of accent; only words and word forms that are accented on the first syllable and that are longer than a single syllable may differ with regard to the quality of the accent" (p. 130).

Such an analysis is not economical. It introduces one more feature than is absolutely necessary (place of accent *and* tone in addition to quantity), and it imposes fairly complex distributional rules (separate statement concerning the final syllable and monosyllabic words). It also complicates the morphophonological description of the accentuation to a considerable extent. Finally, this analysis is even not quite exact. It operates with the concepts "falling" and "rising" as if the so-called falling accents were always phonetically falling and the so-called rising accents always phonetically rising. Nowadays it is known (and has been demonstrated in this book) that in syllables under "rising" accents the pitch rise may be absent, and that in syllables under "falling" accents, especially under ̏, pitch is frequently rising or at least predominantly rising. To be sure, it might seem that tradition, which reflects the native speaker's intuition, argues in favor of an analysis based on the opposition between falling and rising accents. However, this analysis is not as traditional as it would seem from the perspective of the terminology in current international use. We showed in chapter 1 that labels such as "short falling accent" appeared only toward the end of the last century and that they became predominant in Yugoslav publications only after a government decree proclaimed in 1932.

Moreover, they never acquired general acceptance among Croatian scholars. It appears that certain older terms might have some advantages over expressions like "short falling" or "long rising." For example, a very interesting terminological solution reserved the labels "falling" and "rising" for the long accents, while the short accents were called "brzi" (̏, fast) and "spori" (̀, slow), which corresponds fairly well to the contrast between the rapid F_0 fall associated with ̏ and the longer maintenance of high F_0 level with ̀, carried over into the following syllable. The same relationships are reflected in terms like "oštri" (̏, sharp) and "blagi" (̀, mild). In both cases the choice of terms seems to reveal an intuitive recognition that the contrast between the two short accents cannot be reduced to the relationship between a fall and a rise.

Kuznecov was the first to point out that the "Serbian stress . . . refers to phonetic features that characterize the whole word [rather than individual phonemic segments—I.L. and P.I.], and that are realized on the basis of opposing whole words to each other" (p. 130). This conclusion, which the author deduced from the fact that the presence of accent on one syllable implies its absence on other syllables, appropriately locates Neoštokavian accents within the sphere of suprasegmental phenomena.

Kuznecov is not the last author whose phonological analysis operates with long and short falling and rising accents. This analysis is supported by Peco (1965b, 1971c) and Brozović (1973), for example, as well as by Lehfeldt and Finka (1969a), Junković (1969–70), and Stankiewicz (1977) (also see Lehfeldt 1970; Hyman (1978) likewise comes close to this view (his footnote 4)). To be sure, Brozović (1973) also presents an alternative phonological analysis, which corresponds to that of Jakobson: if there is a rising tone in the word, accent automatically falls on that tone; in the absence of a rising tone, accent falls automatically on the first syllable and is then falling (in his 1968 publication Brozović presents only the latter analysis, with some reservations concerning special situations). On the other hand, Lehfeldt calls attention to the results attained by members of the generative-transformational school (see section 4.1.5), although he himself operates with the opposition between falling and rising accents. The same analysis forms the basis of a number of articles in language-related journals intended for a broader audience, where the distinctive function of prosodic phenomena is explained and illustrated with minimal pairs (e.g., Sv. Nikolić 1955, Vuković 1972, Sekereš 1973). Finally, the definitions of accents and the accentual symbols used in school grammars continue to imply this analysis (see chapter 1). It is certain that this analysis will remain in use in schools. Of all existing analyses it is closest to the intuition of native speakers, who hear the accent on the syllable that bears the accent sign under this analysis, and as a rule only on that syllable. On the other hand, this analysis systematizes accent types in a logically convincing and elegantly symmetrical manner; native speakers are not in a position to sense its inaccuracies. Supplemented by explanations—already found in some grammars—that the syllable that follows a syllable with rising accent has high tone, and that the short falling accent need not be really falling, this analysis also corresponds to phonetic reality.

In the year 1958 two new conceptions made their appearance, both proceeding from the fact that with falling accents, high tone usually encompasses only one (the initial) mora, but with rising accents, it encompasses two morae separated by a syllable boundary.

In Hodge's 1958 analysis there is only one kind of (primary) stress. The rising accents are treated as stress on two consecutive syllables: nom.sg. *vódá* (= *vòda*) 'water' vs. acc.sg. *vódu* (= *vȍdu*) 'water', nom.sg. *glaává* (= *gláva*) 'head' vs. acc.sg. *gláavu* (= *glâvu*) 'head'. Now we can say that Hodge was wrong in believing that intensity rather than pitch plays the relevant role in the distinction between the two kinds of accents. Moreover, in contrasts such as *vódá* vs. *vódu* the first accent sign is redundant (Browne and McCawley 1965). Hodge and Janković (1965) present generally the same ideas found in Hodge 1958, only with changed transcription (the above-mentioned examples would be written *vóda*, *vòdu*, *glā́va*, *glā̀vu*, with the explanation that the accents ˊ and ˉˊ mean "a carryover of stress into the following syllable") and with acceptance of the role of high F_0 as a physical correlate of accents.

Hodge was followed by Bidwell (1963, 1968), who retains Hodge's original transcription. Bidwell offers the view that alternative phonological solutions (those of Trubetzkoy, Ivić, Browne and McCawley) are all inadequate since they assume that so-called falling accents cannot occur except on the initial syllable, which—according to Bidwell—is not true, since "in the speech of many standard speakers" there exist words like *lavabȍ* 'washstand' and *cirkuzȁnt* 'circus performer', which Hodge's and Bidwell's transcription marks very simply as *lavabó*, *cirkuzánt*.[6] This argument is opposed by Browne and McCawley (1965), who, citing Chomsky, state (p. 147, fn. 1) that minor exceptions (irregularities) no more invalidate a phonemic system than they do a morphological system.[7] Naturally, the real state of affairs is described most adequately and economically when one operates with rules that encompass the vast majority of examples, and when deviations are identified as such and provided with interpretations.[8]

Lüdtke (1959) gives a brief outline of a view that basically coincides with the view expressed in Hodge 1958 (which was unknown to Lüdtke when he wrote his article).

4.1.4 The Views of Ivić (1958, 1961–62, 1965b)

The viewpoint proposed by Ivić (1958) and elaborated in later works (1961–62, 1965b) proceeds from the fact that the number of accentual possibilities in a Neoštokavian word equals the number of syllables: a word of *n* syllables can bear a so-called falling accent on the initial syllable or a so-called rising accent on any syllable except the final one. Thus:

Falling	1
Rising	$n - 1$
Total	n

Since the peak of the falling accents is in the beginning of the word, and the peak of the rising accents, which are disyllabic, near one of the internal syllable boundaries, it suffices to specify the position of the accentual peak in order to obtain complete information about the accentual shape of a word. (Naturally, information about quantity is likewise necessary—a fact that must not be overlooked under any conditions.) Therefore, Ivić introduces an abstract concept of "place of accent" on syllable boundaries on which a syllable begins (transcribed with ': *vo'da* = *vòda*, *'vodu* = *vȍdu*, *glā'va* = *gláva*, *'glāvu* = *glâvu*). The phonetic realization of such an accent is defined as a high pitch on (one or both) adjacent mora(s): voda, vodu, glaava, glaavu (here the word "mora" is used not as a phonemic term, but as a shorthand expression for a short syllable nucleus or one-half of a long syllable nucleus). This kind of interpretation corresponds quite closely to phonetic reality.

The analysis presented in Junković 1968 is essentially identical with that of Ivić, as Junković himself points out.[9] However, in a later article devoted to the popularization of a structural approach to accentuation among the general public (1969–70), Junković does not mention his conclusion of 1968 and returns basically to the analysis implicit in the traditional description.

4.1.5 Generative-Transformational Interpretations

In the early 1960s two representatives of the generative-transformational school, James McCawley and Wayles E. Browne, arrived independently at an even more revolutionary concept: to regard rising accents as a realization of accent on the following syllable (*vodá* = *vòda* vs. *vódu* = *vȍdu*;

McCawley 1963, Browne and McCawley 1965).[10] This analysis became very popular within the generative-transformational school and is typical for it (see, for instance, Halle 1971, 1974). It seems, however, that developments within the science itself during the preceding years had prepared the way for such a view, since at almost the same time authors from quite different circles came out with similar ideas; see Garde (1966a), Stankiewicz (1966), Naylor (1969, 1970), I. Miletić (1974). This solution is closely related to that of Ivić. They share the following advantages:

1. Due attention is drawn to the fact that the following syllable is relevant for the distinction between the two kinds of accents.
2. The number of distinctive prosodic features is limited to two (place of accent and quantity); accordingly, only two signs are necessary.
3. It is clearly indicated that Neoštokavian falls among languages with pitch accent rather than phonemic tone (in this respect Neoštokavian resembles Tokyo Japanese; see, for instance, McCawley 1968 and Ivić 1970b, 1973) and that the number of possible accent placements in a word equals the number of syllables.
4. The distribution of accent is extremely simple (there are no restrictions).
5. The morphophonemic description is substantially simplified (instead of operating with apparently different relations in *kljûč* 'key' vs. gen.sg. *kljúča*, *bȍb* 'broad bean' vs. *bòba*, *jùnāk* 'hero' vs. *junáka*, and *žȉvot* 'life' vs. *živòta*, all these types are unified: *'kljūč–kljū'ča*, *'bob–bo'ba*, *ju'nāk–junā'ka*, *ži'vot–živo'ta*, or *kljú:č–klju:čá*, *bób–bobá*, *juná:k–juna:ká*, *živóı–životá*; the fictitious alternation disappears from examples like 3.sg.pres.imperf. *mȍlī* 'begs' vs. 3.sg.pres.perf. *zàmolī* 'begs', 3.sg.pres.imperf. *brânī* 'defends' vs. 3.sg.pres.perf. *zàbrānī* 'defends'; compare *'molī–za'molī*, *'brānī–za'brānī* or *móli:–zamóli:*, *brá:ni:–zabrá:ni:*).
6. The Neoštokavian accentuation is presented in a form that makes it readily comparable with older Štokavian as well as with Čakavian, Russian, or even Late Common Slavic.

With respect to points 4, 5, and 6, the analysis of the above-mentioned authors possesses certain advantages over that of Ivić: it has a shorter and neater formulation (accent on a syllable, and not on the beginning of a syllable). Besides, in this approach the accent sign is to be put on the syllable carrying the last high tone (in the terminology used in this book).[11] These advantages guarantee a safe future for this analysis. On the other hand, Ivić (1976a) has demonstrated that his own analysis of 1961–62 and 1965 has certain drawbacks that decrease its usefulness. Its underlying forms have an accent between two syllables, which is an abstraction unfamiliar to linguists.[12] The use of the sign ' in this analysis is also unorthodox. In one widespread convention this sign in an example such as *vo'da* would mean an accent on the *preceding* syllable, and in another (the International Phonetic Alphabet) it would denote an accent on the *following* syllable. This is obviously an inconvenience, connected with the fact that the sign stands between the two syllables. It might seem reasonable to use it, when necessary, to denote an abstract accent between syllables, but again, this is not a common practice.

The analysis of Browne, McCawley, Garde, etc., also has some disadvantages. Placing the accent sign on the syllable from which the accent was removed by the Neoštokavian shift eliminates the difference between the older and the Neoštokavian accentuation, which in turn makes this type of accent marking inapplicable in dialectology or for describing the history of the language. It would also be inconvenient for prosodic typology. Moreover, Ivić's solution makes possible a simpler definition of the place of the lengthening and thus of the culminative accent: the first syllable that lies next to the accent sign.

Both analyses have a serious weakness that is somewhat less explicit in the analysis of Ivić: they contradict the native speakers' intuition. Native speakers feel that in words such as *vòda* the accent falls on the first syllable rather than on the syllable boundary (i.e., on both syllables), and they would perceive accent on the second syllable as being definitely alien—for example, as being Russian or Čakavian. However, this does not present any real difficulties in a generative treatment. It suffices to include at the end of the description a few rules specifying the realization of initial and noninitial accents, as for example in Halle 1971. This approach thus does not imply that the accent is in fact pronounced on the place in which the accent mark appears. It is no accident that this type of analysis was introduced by authors belonging to the generative-transformational school and by those working in the field of morphophonemics. What is essential is the fact that this method is very practical for morphophonemic studies,[13] and phonetic reality is an independent problem.[14]

Ivić (1970b, 1973) used the Japanese sign ⌝ to denote the end of the stretch carrying high pitch. Thus, he obtained the transcriptions *voda*⌝ : *vo*⌝*du*, *gla:va*⌝ : *gla*⌝*:vu*, *juna*⌝*:k* (= *vòda*, *vȍdu*, *gláva*, *glâvu*, *jùnāk*). This procedure is close to that applied by Browne and McCawley. The use of the sequence of signs ⌝: after the symbol for the vowel that carries the ˆ accent or stands immediately after the ˋ accent makes it possible to achieve an additional amount of phonetic precision: in such vowels usually only the first half has high fundamental frequency (instances with an F_0 peak on the second half of the vowel under ˆ are rather rare). Of course, the generative approach does not require such phonetic precision: information of this kind is dealt with in low-level rules that derive the phonetic realization from the underlying forms.

4.1.6 The Views of Pollok, Mahnken, and Rehder

In their 1964 publications Pollok and Mahnken introduced completely new ideas concerning the distinction between so-called falling and rising accents. Their formulations differ slightly, but their reasoning proceeds in the same direction. Pollok talks about the tonal parabola of the word and states (p.126) that the pitch curve of rising accents coincides with that parabola ("die steigenden Akzente ˊ und ˋ verlaufen an der Parabel"), whereas the curve of falling accents separates itself from the word parabola ("in einer besonderen Silbenparabel, die zwar an die Wortparabel angelehnt, aber doch auch gegen diese abgehoben ist"). Mahnken, whose presentation is more theoretically oriented and formulated more abstractly, states, "*Distinktive* Relevanz kommt . . . dem *Tonkontinuitäts*-Merkmal in seiner *inter*syllabischen Relation integrierend/abhebend zu; *redundant* ist hier das *Tondimensions*-Merkmal in seiner *intra*-syllabischen Relation steigend/nicht steigend" (*Distinctive* relevance belongs to the sign of *tonal continuity* in its *inter*syllabic integrating/contrastive relationship; *redundant* is here the sign of *tonal dimension* in its *intra*syllabic rising/not rising relationship) (p. 20, emphasis I.M.). Naturally, "integrierend" refers here to ˋ and ˊ, and "abhebend" to ˵ and ˆ.

Critics have not reacted favorably to the ideas of Pollok and Mahnken, particularly because of their insistence upon complicated systems of abstract parabolas of tonal movements, and also because of the scarcity of concrete numerical data concerning measurements, but it must be recognized that their conclusions have a certain basis (cf. our figure 3.7). Still, they are wrong when they explain the rising tonal movement in the syllable bearing ˋ or ˊ as the automatic result of the distribution of these accents, which occur only in nonfinal syllables and thus are located on the rising part of the word parabola. Even if this could be accepted for the initial syllable, such an explanation could not be valid for rising accents occurring on medial syllables. One must not forget that in the majority of instances, or more precisely under unmarked conditions, the tonal movement within a word is predominantly falling, just as it is within a sentence. This means that under ˋ and ˊ we must take into account a rising factor in relation to the general direction of tonal movement, just as under ˵ and ˆ a falling modification of that direction will take place.

The phonological analysis that Rehder presented as the conclusion derived from his listening tests is referred to in our discussion of his book in section 2.10.10.

4.1.7 The Views of Simić (1977)

R. Simić (1977) suggests that with respect to accentuation, Neoštokavian dialects exhibit two phonological systems. One of them—the northern system—is more archaic; in this system, the tonal height of the postaccentual syllable is phonologically relevant. In the more innovative southern system, rising or falling tonal movements within the accented syllable are sufficient to manifest the opposition. This view is not without substance, but the difference between the two regional types has been made overly sharp (e.g., the difference between the behavior of short and long accents has been ignored, as well as the possibility that intrasyllabic and intersyllabic contrasts may work simultaneously and in parallel). In 1978 Simić again posits two systems. In one system, which this time is associated with the northeast, the postaccentual syllable plays the decisive role. In the other, two tonal movements are contrasted within the accented syllable: rising-falling (under ̏ and ̑) and rising (under ̀ and ́). The range of the first movement is from a low level to a middle level, and the range of the second movement is from low to high. Thus, the syllable under the so-called falling accents is attributed a much lower tonal peak than is associated with the syllable under rising accents—a claim that receives no confirmation whatsoever from instrumental measurements. Finally, Simić and Ostojić (1981) briefly outline a theory of three tonal levels. Rising accents are characterized by a rise from a "neutral" level to "high tonality," and falling accents by a movement from "neutral" to "low tonality." This contrast may encompass two successive syllables (primarily in the northeast) or only the accented syllable (primarily in the southwest). Thus, the authors ascribe to falling accents a F_0 peak that is much lower than the F_0 peak of rising accents; such a view contrasts sharply with the results of instrumental measurements.

4.1.8 The Views of Gvozdanović (1980)

Gvozdanović (1980:28) states that "it would suffice to mark the prosodic word boundaries and the distinctively [±rising] syllable in a prosodic word. Within a prosodic word, the [+rising] syllable, if any, has the accent. If there is no [+rising] syllable, then the first, [−rising] syllable is accented." This comes very close to Jakobson's analysis from 1931, with the proviso that [+rising] is defined as "a rising or nonfalling nonrising fundamental frequency that is followed by a high falling fundamental frequency in the next following syllable nucleus," and [−rising] as "a nonfalling nonrising fundamental frequency that is followed by a low falling fundamental frequency in the next following syllable nucleus." Obviously, the characteristics of the two kinds of accented syllable nuclei overlap: [−rising] is always "nonfalling nonrising," and [+rising] can be "nonfalling nonrising." Thus, the only really distinctive element in this analysis is the level of the next syllable (*high* falling vs. *low* falling). This associates Gvozdanović's position with the "übersilbig" variety of Jakobson's view from 1931. However, in section 2.10.14 we have shown that Gvozdanović's descriptions of F_0 movements in syllable nuclei under falling and rising accents are inaccurate. On p. 97 Gvozdanović adds a second rule that is stated to apply to the northeastern variety of the standard language (see section 2.10.14). Here, too, tone is distinctive, the place of accent being regulated automatically. Still, a three-way tonal contrast is implied: ` and ´ are "rising," ̏ and ̑ are "nonfalling nonrising," and postaccentual syllables are "falling." In this way, the saving is lost that had been achieved by qualifying the place of accent as predictable on the basis of tone.

4.1.9 The Views of Hattori (1981)

Hattori 1981 is written in Japanese. We base the following short review on the summary in English and on the lists of examples given in the article.

On the basis of Gvozdanović 1980, Hattori "has come to the conclusion that Standard Serbo-Croatian has the prosodeme" (cf. Hattori 1978). He uses ˆ to denote a marked kernel of a prosodeme and ˇ to denote an unmarked kernel. This gives the transcriptions *păra* (= *pȁra* 'penny'), *pâra* (= *pàra* 'vapor'), *păara* (= gen.sg. *pâra* 'pair'), and *paâru* (= loc.sg. *páru* 'pair'). Later Hattori simplifies this system by leaving out the predictable sign for the unmarked prosodeme: *para* (= *pȁra*), *pára* (= *pàra*), *paara* (= *pâra*), and *paáru* (= *páru*). Obviously, this solution is very close to that of Jakobson 1949, with the proviso that vowel length is regarded as vowel gemination.

4.2 Discussion and Conclusions

In this section we offer our own views on the matters discussed from a historical perspective in section 4.1. Comparing the two sections, the reader will be able to identify the similarities and differences between our views and those of other authors.

4.2.1 Principles on Which a Phonological Analysis of Neoštokavian Accentuation Should Be Based

In our opinion, before embarking upon a phonological analysis of Neoštokavian accentuation, it is necessary to emphasize the unacceptability of all proposals based on two notions that have been shown to be erroneous by instrumental measurements made in the past few decades:

1. that the contrast between the two kinds of accents is due to differences in intensity (or to differences in intensity as much as in fundamental frequency);
2. that the contrast rests exclusively on the falling or rising movement of fundamental frequency within the accented syllable.

The first notion has been refuted most convincingly by Rehder's listening tests, which showed that accents remain recognizable when the intensity differences between recorded accentual minimal pairs have been eliminated by means of "purposeful destruction," whereas they become unrecognizable when their characteristic F_0 patterns are eliminated. Our findings point in the same direction: although the behavior of intensity was completely nonsystematic in the speech of many of our informants, their accents were easily recognizable.[15]

The second notion is disproved by the numerous attested instances of predominantly rising F_0 movement in the vowel under ̏ and ̑ and predominantly falling F_0 movement in the vowel under ̀ or ́. It happens especially frequently that the vowel under ̏ is not (predominantly) falling. The majority of instrumental investigations have shown that ̏ is an accent in the realization of which F_0 rise and fall in the accented vowel are in some kind of balance: either the F_0 levels at the beginning and end of the vowel are equal, or the number of predominantly falling or rising realizations, respectively, is approximately the same, or the typical realization is rising-falling with a peak in the middle of the duration of the vowel.[16] Some researchers have even found predominantly rising F_0 movements in the vowel under ̏.[17] Finally, Ekblom 1917, Miletić 1926, Rehder 1968a and Purcell 1973 found primarily falling F_0 movements, but they all state that their samples included realizations that were primarily rising.

However, there exists a difference that is much more constant than the pronunciation of the vowel under ̏ with falling F_0. This is the contrast between a relatively explicit rise in the vowel under ̀ and a less well defined rise (or lack of it) in the vowel under ̏. Even in cases where the vowel under ̏ is predominantly rising, its F_0 peak usually occurs earlier than in the vowel under ̀, and the F_0 relationship between the beginning and the end of the vowel is less rising. This can be observed in the materials of practically all investigators. Examples of the opposite situation are rare.[18] It happens more frequently that the physical distance between the two realizations of the accented syllable itself is too small to guarantee the maintenance of the distinction in various communicative situations. Furthermore, the numbers presented in most publications are averages, which obscures the fact that there normally exists a large amount of overlap between the ranges of individual realizations.[19]

4.2.2 Distinctive and Culminative Function of Neoštokavian Accents

The single parameter distinguishing between the two kinds of accents that is consistently present in the results of all instrumental investigations, including measurements made of the speech of subjects from different areas of the Neoštokavian territory, is the F_0 relationship between the accented and the postaccentual syllables, found in both the short and the long accents. It would seem to follow from this that only those phonological analyses are correct that operate with the intersyllabic relationship as the distinctive factor and place the accent symbol in a different position for the so-called falling and rising accents (for example, the analyses of Ivić, Browne and McCawley, and Garde). To be sure, it might seem that the native speakers' intuition is contradicted by the claim that the second syllable is relevant for the distinction between the types *vȍdu* and *vòda*, and by placement of the accent mark on that syllable, as in *vodá* = *vòda*; native speakers recognize unequivocally that in both of these examples it is the first syllable that is accented. This counterargument can be turned aside by the statement that it is necessary to distinguish between the distinctive and the culminative functions of prosodic phenomena. As is well kown, the most general function of word accent as a linguistic phenomenon is culminative. To put it briefly, the accent signals the presence of a word in the spoken chain and helps the hearer to divide this chain into words (Jakobson 1971: 118). In Neoštokavian the culminative function is fulfilled by the traditional "accents" on the syllable where the native speakers' intuition and the traditional grammar place them. The distinctive and the culminative functions are dissociated in Neoštokavian (Ivić 1976a: 39). Although the second syllable is relevant for the distinction between the two kinds of accents, the first syllable does indeed fulfill the culminative function.

4.2.3 Nature of the Culminative Accent

In this connection it is necessary to explain what makes the native speaker feel that the culminative accent in disyllabic words with ` or ´ is located on the first syllable, when in most instances that syllable is not more prominent either with regard to pitch or with regard to intensity. Our measurements, corroborated by measurements of other authors, reveal the circumstances that contribute to the perception of the first syllable as being nevertheless more prominent. These include:

1. The vowel of the syllable bearing a rising accent is as a rule considerably longer than that of the next syllable, provided they have the same phonemic quantity (i.e., if they are both phonemically short, or both long). The vowel under ` is usually of the same duration as the vowel under ̏ or even somewhat longer. Thus, the first vowel with high tone shows the characteristic lengthening that marks the presence of an accent.

2. From the point of view of perception it is important that the syllable under ` or ´ is the *first* syllable in the word with prominently high tone.

3. A syllable with rising F_0 movement sets itself off by this fact from the generally falling F_0 curve of a word or sentence, which contributes to its perceptual prominence.

4. Another cue—although one of limited importance—is provided by vowel quality: in words such as *vòda* the first vowel has the timbre of a short accented vowel, and the second vowel has the phonetic quality of an unstressed short vowel (see section 2.5).

5. According to the findings of certain investigators (e.g., Rehder 1968a, Purcell 1973), the intensity of the first syllable is generally higher than that of the second.

6. The F_0 movement in the postaccentual syllable is usually explicitly falling, which contributes to the impression that in that syllable the tension of the speech production mechanism that is normally associated with accentedness is relaxed.[20]

7. The end of the syllable following a rising accent is usually considerably lower than the beginning of the syllable bearing the accent, which compensates for the fact that the F_0 peak of the second syllable is usually somewhat higher than that of the first, or at approximately the same level.

One or the other of the above-mentioned circumstances may not be present in a particular speech sample or a particular corpus of materials. The remaining factors are nevertheless sufficient to guarantee greater prominence for the first syllable—that is, to guarantee the impression that it bears the accent. It is this syllable that behaves like the accented one under emphasis.[21] Very important evidence for the fact that accent is indeed located on this syllable rather than on the following one is contributed by dialectal syncope of the first postaccentual syllable in examples like imper.pl. *nòste* < *nòsite* 'carry' or *kásti* < *kázati* 'to tell'.

4.2.4 Relevance of Listening Tests

Everything said so far is based on the results of instrumental measurements. However, measurements are not sufficient to prove that any particular aspect of the phonetic signal is relevant for the distinction. For this purpose, listening tests are indispensable. Up to now, tests for the distinction of falling and rising accents have been carried out by Rehder (1968a), Lehiste and Ivić (see chapter 2: informal test mentioned in the beginning of section 2.9, as well as Experiment 2, its replication, and Experiment 4), and Purcell (1976, 1981). These tests have revealed a rather complicated picture. As far as short accents are concerned, Rehder 1968a as well as our informal test and Experiment 4 have demonstrated the relevance of the intersyllabic relationship;[22] however, our Experiment 4 also brought out the role of F_0 movement during the accented syllable—a role that is not uniform across listeners from different regions, to the extent that for listeners from Vojvodina, it was practically irrelevant in making a decision about the nature of an accent. Evidence for the relevance of the intersyllabic relationship in the case of long accents is offered by Rehder 1968a, our Experiment 2, its replication, and Purcell 1976, 1981; on the other hand, these same sources also contain evidence about the role of F_0 movement within the accented syllable. A strong argument in favor of the relevance of this movement is likewise the above-mentioned dialectal syncope in word types like *nòste* or *kȁsti*.[23] It is also evident that the intersyllabic relationship plays a relatively greater role with short accents, and the intrasyllabic movement with long accents. In both cases regional differences are of great importance. In the northeast, in Vojvodina, the role of the intersyllabic relationship is most important, in the Neoštokavian areas of Serbia it is somewhat smaller, and in the western territories it is relatively least important (this concerns in particular the southwest; the situation in the northwest is less clear).[24] A correlation appears to exist between this observation and the fact that in the southwest the syllable immediately following a rising accent can be considerably lower than the accented one;[25] we also have reason to believe that the so-called falling and rising accents are more consistently falling and rising in the southwest than in the northeast. Nevertheless, there seems to exist no area in which either of the two relationships would be totally irrelevant for the distinction between the two kinds of accents, just as there are no regions in which either of them would not turn up in the results of instrumental measurements.

At first glance it might seem surprising that listening tests suggest a much greater role for F_0 movement within the syllable under a rising accent than one would assume on the basis of measurement results. This discrepancy can, however, be explained by the consideration that this syllable is the bearer of an accent with culminative function, and hearers have built up an expectation that accented syllables carry the greatest amount of information (segmental as well as prosodic).

The results of listening tests show that the analyses and notations introduced by authors such as Browne and McCawley, Ivić, and Garde, even though they may possess observational and descriptive adequacy at the acoustic level and even though they may be advantageous from a generative or morphophonemic point of view, cannot offer satisfaction when one considers the determination of the phonetic nature of the signals contained in Neoštokavian word accents. These signals can be described more accurately as a contrast between a falling F_0 relationship and a rising F_0 relationship. Falling intervals are usually somewhat greater than rising intervals, so that the falling movements more often that not give the impression of an abrupt fall, whereas the rising movements, especially in the case of intersyllabic relationships, can frequently be reduced to a basically level pitch relation. Nevertheless, one must bear in mind that the general intonational curve in the sentence is falling, so that the considerable fall of accents of one kind and the moderate rise of accents of the other kind modify the general pitch movement within the sentence to approximately the same extent.[26] Both relationships encompass two successive syllables. With a falling relationship, these are, as a rule, the first two syllables of an accented word; with a rising relationship, they can be any sequence of two syllables (with the proviso that the rising movement is typically concluded immediately after the onset of the second syllable of the sequence, so that the F_0 movement within the second syllable is falling). It follows then that the domain of the contrast between falling and rising accents is restricted to the first two syllables. It is understandable that in the case of long accents the share of tonal movement within the accented syllable is greater than in the case of short accents.[27] A long syllable is more prominent than a short syllable, and the longer duration facilitates the perception of tonal movements as well as making possible the achievement of larger intervals. It is equally natural that a prosodic system formulated in this manner is highly redundant. What is redundant under one set of conditions becomes relevant under others. Redundancy guarantees easy communication among people from different districts of the Neoštokavian area, who unerringly identify accents in the pronunciation of speakers of another Neoštokavian dialect with corresponding accents in their own.

It is obvious from these findings that Neoštokavian accents are suprasegmental phenomena and that interpretations are unacceptable according to which they constitute inherent characteristics of vowels—for example, that there exist phonemes like /ȁ à â á/ or even /ȁ à â á ă(unaccented) ā(unaccented)/.

4.2.5 Word Prosody and Sentence Prosody

So far in this section we have talked abstractly about the nature of Neoštokavian accents, as if they existed outside of a sentence or occurred only in intonationally neutral positions. However, within a sentence the falling and/or rising relationships are converted into a falling or rising modification of the sentence intonation curve. In chapter 3 of this book as well as in works of other authors who have described the interrelationship between sentence intonation and word accents in Neoštokavian, there are many examples of instances in which the opposition between falling and rising is converted into an opposition between more vs. less falling or less vs. more rising. This exemplifies the eminently relational character of the opposition between the two kinds of Neoštokavian word accents.[28] This aspect of the phonetic nature of the accents further demonstrates that they belong among prosodic rather than inherent phonetic phenomena.

The contrast between the falling and the rising F_0 relation manifested over the first two syllables of a word implies a peak on the first syllable in the former case and a peak on the second syllable in the latter case. Likewise, a rising relation embracing the second and third syllables implies a peak on the third syllable, etc. Thus, the contrast between fall and rise is reduced to placement of the F_0 peak on different syllables, whereby the number of possible peak locations equals the number of syllables. When the intersyllabic relation in words with rising accent is not really rising but level or even slightly falling, it is appropriate to speak about the last high pitch in the word rather than about the F_0 peak. In any event, it is justified to classify standard Serbocroatian among languages with pitch accent rather than among tone languages. However, the specific feature of this pattern is the fact that here the distinctive "accent" does not coincide with the culminative accent, which also exists in the language and lies on the syllable that precedes the last high pitch whenever the latter is on a noninitial syllable.

The theory of Browne, McCawley, Garde, etc., echoing Masing's final conclusions from 1876, deals with the distinctive accent; it could be made acceptable with the addition of the notion of culminative accent. An alternative would be to give the status of "pitch accent" or "tonal center" to the syllable boundary before the syllable carrying the last high pitch in the word (as in Ivić 1958, 1961–62, 1965a). In any event such analyses would have to be accompanied by rules that, on the basis of the location of the tonal center, will generate the prosodic shape of words with various syllabic and quantity structures. It is equally indispensable to give a rule that will specify the position of the culminative accent. However, if we start from the culminative accent, it is necessary to emphasize that one of the two types of accent is characterized by the carryover of high pitch to the following syllable. That such an analysis, even in its Jakobsonian version, is less economical, especially on the morphophonological level, does not obliterate the fact that it corresponds better to the native speakers' intuition. The peculiar and many-sided character of the acoustic and perceptual realities makes Neoštokavian accentuation a typical case of nonuniqueness of possible phonemic solutions.

4.2.6 Conclusions

We shall summarize our own position, trying to do justice to the complexity of a prosodic pattern in which different factors cooccurring and contributing to the linguistic distinctions are engaged in an interplay of relevancies and redundancies regulated by a number of other factors.

The distinctive mark of Neoštokavian word accents is high pitch. It occurs either on the initial syllable or on any disyllabic sequence in the accented word. In the former case a falling modification is introduced into the pitch contour of the sentence intonation, and in the latter case the modification goes in the rising direction. These modifications embrace two syllables even in the case of the monosyllabic accent, which sets off the initial syllable from the low-pitched second syllable. In both cases both the pitch movement within the first syllable of the disyllabic sequence and the relationship between pitch peaks of the two syllables are involved. Their relative importance depends on several factors, including regional variation. The culminative function is fulfilled by the first high-pitched syllable (the syllable carrying the monosyllabic initial accent or the first syllable of disyllabic accents). In both cases the culminative function is accompanied by a certain lengthening of the pertinent syllable nucleus. The monosyllabic accent also exerts a delimitative function, signaling the beginning of an accentual word.

These are the phonological facts. Naturally, accent symbolization and prosodic morphophonemics require a simplified transcription. In our opinion three proposals are superior to others offered so far. They all use only one accent mark in addition to the length symbol.

1. One may proceed from the fact that the number of accentual possibilities equals the number of syllables in an accentual word, the contrastive

last high pitch being possible on every syllable. This gives the transcription of the type *vodá, vódu, gla:vá, glá:vu* (Browne and McCawley 1965, Garde 1966b, etc.). Here the accent mark indicates the last high pitch.

2. The nature of disyllabic accents can be represented by putting an accent mark between the two syllables. In this case the monosyllabic accent is represented by a sign at the beginning of the word, and the sign indicates high tone on the neighboring syllable(s): *vo'da, 'vodu, glā'va, 'glāvu* (Ivić 1965a).

3. In view of the fact that the monosyllabic accent occurs automatically when there is no disyllabic high-pitched sequence in the word, one can mark the first syllable of the disyllabic sequence, which bears the culminative function, and place no accent mark at all in words with a monosyllabic accent: *vóda, vodu, glá:va, gla:vu* (Jakobson 1931a).

In our opinion solution 2 is in principle the most adequate because it stays in close contact with phonetic reality.

Appendix A
List of Text Words

List of test words used in production experiment (chapter 2), arranged according to accent type and stressed syllable nuclei.

Short Falling Accent

˵ ˘	vȉdi	sees 3.sg.pres.
˘ + ˵ ˘	da vȉdi	that he sees 3.sg.pres.
˵ ˘	ȉgra	plays 3.sg.pres.
˘ + ˵ ˘	da ȉgra	that he plays 3.sg.pres.
˵ ˘	lȉsta	list nom.sg.
˵ ¯	dȉnār	dinar nom.sg.
˵ ¯	pȉsār	clerk nom.sg.
˵ ˘ ˘	ȉzginu	died out 3.sg.aor.
˵ ¯ ˘	ȉz grāda	from the town gen.sg.
˵	svȅ	everything nom.sg.neut.
˘ ˵	za svȅ	for all acc.pl.masc.
˵ ˘	bȅži	run away 2.sg.imper.
˵ ˘	kćȅri	daughter gen.sg.
˵ ˘	lȅti	in summer
˵ ˘	pȅći	stove gen.sg.
˵ ˘	sȅdi	sit down 2.sg.imper.
˵ ˘	sȅli	sat down past part.pl.masc.
˵ ˘	lȅgne	lies down 3.sg.pres.
˘ + ˵ ˘	da lȅgne	that he lies down 3.sg.pres.
˵ ˘	sȅdne	sits down 3.sg.pres.
˘ + ˵ ˘	da sȅdne	that he sits down 3.sg.pres.
˵ ˘	zȅmļe	countries nom.pl.
˵ ˘	rȅbra	ribs nom.pl.
˵ ˘	sȅla	villages nom.pl.

˵ ˘	mȅsto	place nom.sg.
˘ + ˵ ˘	na mȅsto	to the place acc.sg.
˵ ˘	sȅlo	sat down past part.sg.neut.
˵ ˘	zȅmļu	earth acc.sg.
˘ + ˵ ˘	na zȅmļu	to the ground acc.sg.
˵ ¯	mȅsēc	moon, month nom.sg.
˘ + ˵ ¯	na mȅsēc	to the moon acc.sg.
˵ ˘ ˘	zȅleni	vegetables gen.sg.
˵ ˘ ˘	prȅdati	tremble inf.
˵ ¯ ˘	dȅvōjke	girls voc.pl.
˵ ¯ ˘	dȅvōjko	girl voc.sg.
˵ ˘ ˘ ˘	dȅtelina	clover nom.sg.
˵ ˘ ˘ ˘ ¯ ˘	rȅakcionāran	reactionary nom.sg.masc. (indef.decl.)
˵ ˘ ˘ ˘ ˘ ¯ ˘	rȅvolucionāran	revolutionary nom.sg.masc. (indef.decl.)
˵	rȁt	war nom.sg.
˘ + ˵	u rȁt	to the war acc.sg.
˵ ˘	stȁvi	puts 3.sg.pres.
˘ + ˵ ˘	da stȁvi	that he puts 3.sg.pres.
˵ ˘	vȁdi	takes out 3.sg.pres.
˵ ˘	mȁgle	fogs nom.pl.
˵ ˘	pȁdne	falls 3.sg.pres.
˘ + ˵ ˘	da pȁdne	that it falls 3.sg.pres.
˵ ¯	kȁmēn	stone nom.sg.
˵ ¯	mȁzān	smeared pass.part.nom.sg.masc.
˵ + ¯	nȁ brēg	to the hill acc. sg.
˵ ˘ ˘	jȁrica	young female goat nom.sg.
˵ ˘ ˘	zȁigra	began to dance 3.sg.aor.
˵ ˘ ˘	zȁkinu	withdrew one's due 3.sg.aor.
˵ ˘ ˘	prȁvļeno	made pass.part.nom.sg.neut.
˵ ˘ ˘	rȁstera	dispelled 3.sg.aor.
˵ ˘ ˘	sȁstavi	put together 3.sg.aor.
˵ ˘ ˘	stȁjati	stop inf. (imperf.asp.)
˵ ˘ ˘	stȁvite	put 2.pl.pres.
˵ ˘ ˘	rȁzloži	analyzed 3.sg.aor.
˵ ˘ ˘	zȁmoli	requested 3.sg.aor.
˵ + ˘ ˘	nȁ zemļu	to the ground acc.sg.
˵ + ˘ ˘	nȁ vodu	to the water acc.sg.
˵ ¯ ˘	nȁplāti	paid up 3.sg.aor.

˵ ¯ ˘	zȁbrāni	forbade 3.sg.aor.
˵ ¯ ˘	zȁrādi	earned 3.sg.aor.
˵ ¯ ˘	zȁvr̄ši	finished 3.sg.aor.
˵ ¯ ˘	rȁsr̄di	made angry 3.sg.aor.
˵ ¯ ˘	zȁmr̄si	entangled 3.sg.aor.
˵ + ¯ ˘	nȁ rūku	on the hand acc.sg.
˵ + ˘ ¯	nȁ mesēc	monthly acc.sg.
˵ ˘ ¯	Drȁgomīr	(name) nom.sg.masc.
˵ ˘ ˘ ¯ ˘	nȁcionālni	national nom.sg.masc. (def.decl.)
˵ ˘ ˘ ˘ + ˘	nȁrvao se	to wrestle to one's satisfaction past part.sg.masc.
˵ ˘ ˘ ˘	zȁrđao	rusted past part.sg.masc.
˵	zlȍ	evil nom.sg.
˘ + ˵	za zlȍ	for the evil acc.sg.
˵ ˘	gȍri	worse nom.sg.masc. (compar.)
˵ ˘	Kȍļi	(name) dat.sg.masc.
˵ ˘	kȍsi	mows 3.sg.pres.
˘ + ˵ ˘	da kȍsi	that he mows 3.sg.pres.
˵ ˘	mȍli	requests 3.sg.pres.
˘ + ˵ ˘	da mȍli	that he requests 3.sg.pres.
˵ ˘	mȍći	power gen.sg.
˵ ˘	nȍsi	carries 3.sg.pres.
˵ ˘	prȍsi	begs 3.sg.pres.
˵ ˘	sȍli	salt gen.sg.
˵ ˘	gȍre	up
˵ ˘	kȍze	give birth to kids 3.pl.pres.
˵ ˘	pȍļe	field nom.sg.
˘ + ˵ ˘	u pȍļe	to the field acc.sg.
˵ ˘	rȍbe	slave voc.sg.
˵ ˘	tȍpe	cannon voc.sg.
˵ ˘	vȍde	lead 3.pl.pres.
˵ ˘	bȍja	fight gen.sg.
˵ ˘	tȍga	that gen.sg.masc.
˘ + ˵ ˘	za tȍga	for that acc.sg.
˵ ˘	mȍstu	bridge dat.sg.
˵ ˘	sȍbu	room acc.sg.
˘ + ˵ ˘	u sȍbu	into the room acc.sg.
˵ ˘	vȍdu	water acc.sg.
˘ + ˵ ˘	na vȍdu	to the water acc.sg.
˵ ¯	bȍlēst	illness acc.sg.

˵ ¯	dȍnēt	brought pass.part.nom.sg.masc.
˵ ¯	kȍmād	piece nom.sg.
˵ ¯	prȍdāt	sold pass.part.nom.sg.masc.
˵ ¯	gȍlūb	pigeon nom.sg.
˵ ¯	kȍtūr	wheel nom.sg.
˵ ˘ ˘	rȍđeni	born pass.part.nom.pl.masc.
˵ ˘ ˘	pȍgleda	looked 3.sg.aor.
˵ ˘ ˘	ȍstavi	left 3.sg.aor.
˵ ˘ ˘	gȍvori	spoke 3.sg.aor.
˵ ˘ ˘	pȍkosi	mowed 3.sg.aor.
˵ ˘ ˘	pȍlomi	broke 3.sg.aor.
˵ ˘ ˘	pȍsoli	salted 3.sg.aor.
˵ ¯ ˘	dȍnēti	brought pass.part.nom.pl.masc.
˵ ¯ ˘	ȍdlūči	decided 3.sg.aor.
˵ ¯ ˘	prȍsūti	strewn pass.part.nom.pl.masc.
˵ ˘ ¯	dȍgovōr	agreement nom.sg.
˵ ˘ ¯ ˘	kȍlosālni	colossal nom.pl.masc.
˵ ˘ ¯ ˘	kȍlosālan	colossal nom.sg.masc. (indef.decl.)
˵ ˘ ˘ ˘ ˘ ¯ ˘	ȍrganizaciōni	organizational nom.sg.masc.
˵	psȕ	dog dat.sg.
˘ + ˵	na psȕ	on the dog loc.sg.
˵ ˘	kȕka	hook nom.sg.
˵ ˘	s kȕkom	with the hook inst.sg.
˵ ˘	kȕću	house acc.sg.
˘ + ˵ ˘	u kȕću	into the house acc.sg.
˵ ˘/˵ ˘ ˘	ȕmro–ȕmr̥o	dead past part.sg.masc.
˵ ¯	kȕvār	cook nom.sg.
˵ ¯	sȕdār	collision nom.sg.
˵ + ¯	ȕ grād	to the town acc.sg.
˵ ˘ ˘	ȕginu	died 3.sg.aor.
˵ ˘ ˘	ȕpala	inflammation nom.sg.
˵ ˘ ˘	ȕlovi	caught 3.sg.aor.
˵ ˘ ˘	ȕ poļe	to the field acc.sg.
˵ ¯ ˘	ȕzēti	taken pass.part.nom.pl.masc.
˵ ¯ ˘	ȕpāli	set fire to 3.sg.aor.
˵ ˘	tȑči	run 2.sg.imper.
˵ ˘	kȑvi	blood gen.sg.
˵ ˘	Kȑsti	(name) dat.sg.masc.
˵ ˘	Kȑka	(name of a river) nom.sg.

˵ ˘	Kȑsta	(name) nom.sg.masc.
˵ ˘	s Kȑstom	with K. inst.sg.
˵ ˘	pȑstu	finger dat.sg.
˵ ¯	kȑvāv	bloody nom.sg.masc. (def.decl.)
˵ ¯ ˘	kȑvāvi	bloody nom.pl.masc.
˵ ˘ ˘	gȑoce	throat nom.sg. (dim.)

Short Rising Accent

ˋ ˘	lìsta	turns over pages 3.sg.pres.
ˋ ¯	bìrō	office nom.sg.
ˋ ˘ ˘	ìzginu	die out 3.pl.pres.
ˋ ˘ ˘	ìzvadi	takes out 3.sg.pres.
ˋ ˘ ˘	prìselo	stuck in one's throat past part.sg.neut.
ˋ ˘ ¯ ˘	vìnogrādi	vineyards nom.pl.
˘ ˋ ˘	visìna	height nom.sg.
˘ ˋ ˘	planìna	mountain nom.sg.
˘ ˋ ˘	brzìna	speed nom.sg.
˘ ˋ ¯ ˘	prostìtūtka	prostitute nom.sg.
˘ ˘ ˋ ˘	veličìna	magnitude nom.sg.
ˋ ˘	bèži	flees 3.sg.pres.
ˋ ˘	kćèri	daughters gen.pl.
ˋ ˘	lèti	flies 3.sg.pres.
ˋ ˘	pèći	bake inf.
ˋ ˘	sèdi	sits 3.sg.pres.
ˋ ˘	zèmļe	earth gen.sg.
ˋ ˘	sèlo	village nom.sg.
ˋ ˘	rèbra	rib gen.sg.
ˋ ˘	sèla	village gen.sg.
ˋ ¯	pèvāč	singer nom.sg.masc.
ˋ ¯	dèpō	depot nom.sg.
ˋ ¯	nè dām	I don't give 1.sg.pres.
ˋ ˘ ˘	zèleni	green nom.sg.masc. (def.decl.)
ˋ ˘ ˘	prèdati	give up inf.
ˋ + ˘ ˘	nè vidi	does not see 3.sg.pres.
ˋ ¯ ˘	dèvōjke	girls nom.pl.
ˋ +¯ ˘ ˘ ˘	nè nādničiti	not work as a day laborer inf.
˘ ˋ ¯	kolèktīv	collective nom.sg.
˘ ˋ ¯	komèsār	commissary nom.sg.

˘ ˋ ˘ ˘	babètina	old woman nom.sg. (pejor.)
˘ ˋ ˘ ¯	kolèbļivōst	hesitancy nom.sg.
˘ ˘ ˋ ˘	navedèno	quoted pass.part.nom.sg.neut.
ˋ ˘	màgle	fog gen.sg.
ˋ + ˘	nà zlo	to the evil acc.sg.
ˋ + ˘	zà sve	for all acc.sg.neut.
ˋ + ˘	nà psu	on the dog acc.sg.
ˋ ¯	càrīć	wren nom.sg.
ˋ ¯	vàļān	good nom.sg.masc. (indef.decl.)
ˋ ˘ ˘	jàrica	spring wheat nom.sg.
ˋ ˘ ˘	zàigra	begins to dance 3.sg.pres.
ˋ ˘ ˘	zàkinu	withhold one's due 3.pl.pres.
ˋ ˘ ˘	nàseli	colonizes 3.sg.pres. (perf.asp.)
ˋ ˘ ˘	nàlegne	leans on 3.sg.pres. (perf.asp.)
ˋ ˘ ˘	nàsedne	becomes stranded 3.sg.pres. (perf.asp.)
ˋ ˘ ˘	ràstera	dispels 3.sg.pres.
ˋ ˘ ˘	sàstavi	puts together 3.sg.pres.
ˋ ˘ ˘	stàjati	stand inf.
ˋ ˘ ˘	zàpadne	falls into 3.sg.pres.
ˋ ˘ ˘	ràzloži	analyzes 3.sg.pres. (perf.asp.)
ˋ ˘ ˘	zàmoli	requests 3.sg.pres. (perf.asp.)
ˋ + ˘ ˘	nà mesto	to the place acc.sg.
ˋ + ˘ ˘	zà toga	for this acc.sg.masc.
ˋ ¯ ˘	nàplāti	pays up 3.sg.pres.
ˋ ¯ ˘	zàbrāni	forbids 3.sg.pres.
ˋ ¯ ˘	zàrādi	earns 3.sg.pres. (perf.asp.)
ˋ ¯ ˘	ràsr̄di	makes angry 3.sg.pres.
ˋ ¯ ˘	zàmr̄si	entangles 3.sg.pres.
ˋ ¯ ˘	zàvr̄ši	finishes 3.sg.pres. (perf.asp.)
ˋ ˘ ˘ ˘	nàpravļeno	made pass.part.nom.sg.neut.
ˋ ¯ ˘ ˘	zàvīnuti	bent pass.part.nom.pl.masc.
ˋ ¯ ˘ ˘	zàlēpimo	glue up 1.pl.pres. (perf.asp.)
ˋ ¯ ˘ ˘	nàštāmpati	print inf. (perf.asp.)
ˋ ¯ ˘ ˘	zàbrānite	forbid 2.pl.pres.
ˋ ¯ ˘ ˘	zàvr̄nuti	twisted pass.part.nom.pl.masc.
ˋ ˘ ˘ ¯	zàposlenōst	employment nom.sg.
˘ ˋ ¯	barjàktār	ensign nom.sg.
˘ ˋ ˘ ˘ ˘	kolàčićima	cookies dat.pl.
˘ ˋ ¯ ˘	deklàsīran	déclassé pass.part.nom.sg.

˘ ˋ ¯ ˘ ˘	deklàsīrani	déclassé pass.part.nom.pl.
˘ ˘ ˘ ˋ ˘ ˘	nacionàlisti	nationalists nom.pl.
ˋ ˘	gòri	burns 3.sg.pres.
ˋ ˘	kòļi	slaughter 2.sg.imper.
ˋ ˘	kòsi	mow 2.sg.imper.
ˋ ˘	mòli	request 2.sg.imper.
ˋ ˘	mòći	be able inf.
ˋ ˘	nòsi	carry 2.sg.imper.
ˋ ˘	pròsi	beg 2.sg.imper.
ˋ ˘	sòli	salt 2.sg.imper.
ˋ ˘	gòre	burn 3.pl.pres.
ˋ ˘	kòze	goats nom.pl.
ˋ ˘	ròbe	merchandise gen.sg.
ˋ ˘	tòpe	melt 3.pl.pres.
ˋ ˘	vòde	water gen.sg.
ˋ ˘	bòja	color nom.sg.
ˋ ˘	mòstu	bridge loc.sg.
ˋ ¯	vòdīč	guide nom.sg.
ˋ ¯	kòlāč	cake nom.sg.
ˋ ¯	kòpāč	digger nom.sg.
ˋ ¯	kòrāl	coral nom.sg.
ˋ ¯	kòrān	Koran nom.sg.
ˋ ˘ ˘	pògleda	gives a look 3. sg.pres.
ˋ ˘ ˘	ròđeni	born of the same parents nom.sg.masc.
ˋ ˘ ˘	òstavi	leaves 3.sg.pres. (perf.asp.)
ˋ ˘ ˘	gòvori	speaks 3.sg.pres.
ˋ ˘ ˘	pòkosi	mows down 3.sg.pres.
ˋ ˘ ˘	pòlomi	breaks 3.sg.pres.
ˋ ˘ ˘	pòsoli	salts 3.sg.pres. (perf.asp.)
ˋ ¯ ˘	dònēti	bring inf.
ˋ ¯ ˘	òdlūči	decides 3.sg.pres.
ˋ ¯ ˘	pròsūti	strew inf.
ˋ ˘ ˘ ˘	òstavite	leave 2 pl.imper.
ˋ ˘ ¯ ˘	dòlažēņe	coming nom.sg. (subst.)
ˋ ¯ ˘ ˘	òprāvdamo	justify l.pl.pres. (perf.asp.)
ˋ ¯ ˘ ˘	òprāvdati	justify inf. (perf.asp.)
˘ ˋ ˘	biròa	office gen.sg.
˘ ˋ ˘	depòa	depot gen.sg.
˘ ˋ ˘ ˘	okòreli	inveterate nom.sg.masc.

˘ ` ˘ ˘	okòrelim	inveterate dat.pl.
˘ ` ˘ ˘	kostòboļa	gout nom.sg.
˘ ` ˘ ˘	prelòmiše	broke in two 3.pl.aor.
˘ ` ˘ ˘	devòjčica	little girl nom.sg.
˘ ` ˘ ¯	okòrelōst	inveteracy nom.sg.
˘ ˘ ˘ ` ¯	reakciònār	reactionary nom.sg.
˘ ˘ ˘ ˘ ` ¯	revoluciònār	revolutionary nom.sg.
` ˘	kùka	hip gen.sg.
` ˘	s kùkom	with the hip inst.sg.
` + ˘	ù rat	into the war acc.sg.
` ¯	bùnār	well nom.sg.
` ¯	pùdār	vineyard guard nom.sg.
` ¯	rùkāv	sleeve nom.sg.
` ¯	čùvār	guard nom.sg.
` ¯	ćùrān	turkey-cock nom.sg.
` ˘ ˘	ùginu	perish 3.pl.pres.
` ˘ ˘	ùpala	fell in past part.sg.fem.
` ˘ ˘	ùlovi	catches 3.sg.pres.
` + ˘ ˘	ù kuću	into the house acc.sg.
` + ˘ ˘	ù sobu	into the room acc.sg.
` ¯ ˘	ùzēti	take inf.
` ¯ ˘	ùpāli	sets fire 3.sg.pres.
˘ ` ˘ ˘	indùstrija	industry nom.sg.
˘ ` ¯ ˘	golùbārnik	dovecote nom.sg.
` ˘	kr̀vi	blood loc.sg.
` ˘	kr̀sti	baptizes 3.sg.pres.
` ˘	tr̀či	runs 3.sg.pres.
` ˘	Kr̀ka	island of Krk gen.sg.
` ˘	kr̀sta	cross gen.sg.
` ˘	s kr̀stom	with the cross inst.sg.
` ˘	pr̀stu	finger loc.sg.
` ¯	r̀vāč	wrestler nom.sg.
` ˘ ¯	vr̀tirēp	name of a bird nom.sg.
` ¯ ˘	kr̀vāvi	makes bloody 3.sg.pres.
˘ ` ˘ ˘ + ˘	nar̀vati se	wrestle to one's satisfaction inf.
˘ ` ˘ ˘	zar̀đati	rust inf.

Long Falling Accent

⌢ ˘	čȋle	old man nom.sg.

ˆ ˘	rîta	rags gen.pl.
ˆ ˘	s mîrom	in peace inst.sg.
ˆ ˘	lîstu	leaf dat.sg.
ˆ ˘ ˘	krîvite	incriminate 2.pl.pres.
ˆ ˘ ˘	slîstite	wipe out 2.pl.pres.
ˆ	brêg	hill nom.sg.
˘ + ˆ	na brêg	on the hill acc.sg.
ˆ ˘	dête	child voc.sg.
ˆ ˘	svêta	world gen.sg.
ˆ ˘	brêgu	hill dat.sg.
ˆ ˘ ˘	bêlite	whiten 2.pl.pres.
ˆ ˘ ˘	krênuti	set in motion pass.part.nom.pl.masc.
ˆ	dâm	give 1.sg.pres.
ˆ	grâd	town nom.sg.
˘ + ˆ	u grâd	to the town acc.sg.
ˆ ˘	brâni	defends 3.sg.pres.
ˆ ˘	mâri	cares 3.sg.pres.
ˆ ˘	plâti	pays 3.sg.pres.
˘ + ˆ ˘	da plâti	that he pays 3.sg.pres.
ˆ ˘	râdi	works 3.sg.pres.
ˆ ˘	sâdi	plants 3.sg.pres.
ˆ ˘	mâce	kitten 3.pl.pres.
ˆ ˘	râde	work 3.pl.pres.
ˆ ˘	blâga	treasure gen.sg.
ˆ ˘	dâra	gift gen.sg.
ˆ ˘	drâga	dear nom.sg.fem. (def.decl.)
ˆ ˘	grâda	town gen.sg.
˘ + ˆ ˘	iz grâda	from the town gen.sg.
ˆ ˘	lâza	glade gen.sg.
ˆ ˘	mâjka	mother nom.sg.
ˆ ˘	mlâda	bride nom.sg.
ˆ ˘	prâva	genuine nom.sg.fem.
ˆ ˘	râda	work gen.sg.
ˆ ˘	vlâda	governs 3.sg.pres.
ˆ ˘	blâgo	treasure nom.sg.
ˆ ˘	s râdom	with the work inst.sg.
ˆ ˘	Vlâdo	(name) voc.sg.masc.
ˆ ˘	grâdu	town dat.sg.
ˆ ˘ ˘	brânimo	defend 1.pl.pres.

ˆ ˘ ˘	hrâníte	feed 2.pl.pres.
ˆ ˘ ˘	mâzite	pamper 2.pl.pres.
ˆ ˘ ˘	râdite	work 2.pl.pres.
ˆ ˘ ˘	sâdite	plant 2.pl.pres.
ˆ ˘ ˘	štâmpati	print inf.
ˆ ˘ ˘	prâvdati	justify inf.
ˆ ˘ ˘	zâbrani	prohibition dat.sg.
ˆ ˘ ˘	prâvdamo	justify 1.pl.pres.
˘ + ˆ ˘ ˘	da prâvdamo	that we justify 1.pl.pres.
ˆ ˘ ˘	mâjstore	artisans acc.pl.
˘ + ˆ ˘ ˘	za mâjstore	for artisans acc.pl.
ˆ ˘ ˘ ˘	mâjstorima	artisans dat.pl.
˘ + ˆ ˘ ˘ ˘	o mâjstorima	about artisans loc.pl.
ˆ ˘ ˘ ˘	nâdničiti	work as a day laborer inf.
ˆ ˘	bôba	picks berries 3.sg.pres.
ˆ ˘	bôda	stitch gen.sg.
ˆ ˘	bôra	pine gen.sg.
ˆ ˘	kôsa	blackbird gen.sg.
ˆ ˘	lôza	chance in a lottery gen.sg.
ˆ ˘	vôda	leads 3.sg.pres.
ˆ ˘	ļûbi	kisses 3.sg.pres.
ˆ ˘	drûga	comrade gen.sg.
ˆ ˘	kûma	godfather gen.sg.
ˆ ˘	lûda	fools gen.pl.
ˆ ˘	lûka	bow gen.sg.
ˆ ˘	rûža	lipstick gen.sg.
ˆ ˘	sûda	container gen.sg.
ˆ ˘	s drûgom	with the comrade inst.sg.
ˆ ˘	s kûmom	with the godfather inst.sg.
ˆ ˘	rûku	hand acc.sg.
˘ + ˆ ˘	na rûku	on the hand acc.sg.
ˆ ˘ ˘	krûžite	circulate 2.pl.pres.
ˆ ˘ ˘	ļûbite	kiss 2.pl.pres.
ˆ ˘ ˘	ļûtite	make angry 2.pl.pres.
ˆ ˘ ˘	lûdoga	fool gen.sg.masc. (def.decl.)
ˆ ˘	mȓsi	tousles 3.sg.pres.
ˆ ˘	bȓka	moustache gen.sg.
ˆ ˘	kȓpa	rags gen.pl.
ˆ ˘	cȓna	black nom.sg.fem. (def.decl.)
ˆ ˘	Kȓco	(name) voc.sg.masc.

⌢ ˘ ˘	sȑdite	make angry 2.pl.pres.
⌢ ˘ ˘	cȑnite	blacken 2.pl.pres.
⌢ ˘ ˘	cȑnoga	black gen.sg.masc. (def.decl.)

Long Rising Accent

´ ˘	Číle	Chile nom.sg.
´ ˘	ríta	swamp gen.sg.
´ ˘	s Mírom	with Mira inst.sg.
´ ˘	lístu	leaf loc.sg.
´ ˘ ˘	krívite	incriminate 2.pl.imper.
´ ˘ ˘	slístite	wipe out 2.pl.imper.
˘ ´ ˘	brzína	speeds gen.pl.
˘ ´ ˘	planína	mountains gen.pl.
˘ ´ ˘	visína	heights gen.pl.
˘ ´ ˘ ˘	zavínuti	bend inf.
˘ ˘ ´ ˘	veličína	magnitudes gen.pl.
˘ ˘ ´ ˘	kolektívi	collectives nom.pl.
˘ ˘ ´ ˘	kolektíva	collectives gen.pl.
˘ ˘ ˘ ´ ˘ ˘	parafrazírati	paraphrase inf.
´ ˘	déte	child nom.sg.
´ ˘	Svéta	(name) nom.sg.masc.
´ ˘	brégu	hill loc.sg.
´ ˘ ˘	bélite	whiten 2.pl.imper.
´ ˘ ˘	krénuti	set in motion inf.
´ ¯ ˘	pétlōva	roosters gen.pl.
˘ ´ ˘ ˘	zalépimo	stick on 1.pl.imper.
´ ˘	bráni	defend 2.sg.imper.
´ ˘	Mári	(name) dat.sg.fem.
´ ˘	rádi	work 2.sg.imper.
´ ˘	sádi	plant 2.sg.imper.
´ ˘	máce	cats nom.pl.
´ ˘	Ráde	(name) gen.sg.masc.
´ ˘	blága	mild nom.sg.fem. (indef.decl.)
´ ˘	Dára	(name) nom.sg.fem.
´ ˘	drága	dear nom.sg.fem. (indef.decl.)
´ ˘	Láza	(name) nom.sg.masc.
´ ˘	májka	grandmother nom.sg.
´ ˘	mláda	young nom.sg.fem. (indef.decl.)
´ ˘	práva	right gen.sg.

´ ˘	Ráda	(name) nom.sg.masc.
´ ˘	vláda	government nom.sg.
´ ˘	blágo	mild nom.sg.neut. (indef.decl.)
´ ˘	s Rádom	with Rada inst.sg.
´ ˘	Vládo	(name) nom.sg.masc.
´ ˘	grádu	town loc.sg.
´ ˘ ˘	bránimo	defend 1.pl.imper.
´ ˘ ˘	hránite	feed 2.pl.imper.
´ ˘ ˘	mázite	pamper 2.pl.imper.
´ ˘ ˘	rádite	work 2.pl.imper.
´ ˘ ˘	sádite	plant 2.pl.imper.
´ ˘ ˘	závidi	envies 3.sg.pres.
´ ˘ ˘	zábrani	groves nom.pl.
´ ¯ ˘	várnīca	sparks gen.pl.
´ ¯ ˘	spávāņe	sleeping nom.sg.
´ ˘ ˘ ˘	várničavi	sparkling nom.pl.masc.
´ ˘ ˘ ˘	várnicama	sparks dat.pl.
˘ ´ ˘	upáli	set fire to 2.sg.imper.
˘ ´ ˘	zabráni	forbid 2.sg.imper.
˘ ´ ˘	zarádi	earn 2.sg.imper.
˘ ´ ˘ ˘	zabránite	forbid 2.pl.imper.
˘ ´ ˘ ˘	Lazárević	(family name) nom.sg.
˘ ˘ ´ ˘	barjaktári	ensigns nom.pl.
˘ ˘ ´ ˘ ˘	Milovánović	(family name) nom.sg.
´ ˘	Bóba	(name) nom.sg.masc.
´ ˘	Bóda	(name) nom.sg.masc.
´ ˘	Bóra	(name) nom.sg.masc.
´ ˘	Kósa	(name) nom.sg.fem.
´ ˘	lóza	vines gen.pl.
´ ˘	vóda	waters gen.pl.
´ ˘	ļúbi	kiss 2.sg.imper.
´ ˘	drúga	mate nom.sg.fem.
´ ˘	kúma	godmother nom.sg.
´ ˘	lúda	fool nom.sg.fem. (indef.decl.)
´ ˘	lúka	port nom.sg.
´ ˘	Rúža	(name) nom.sg.fem.
´ ˘	súda	court of justice gen.sg.
´ ˘	s drúgom	with the mate inst.sg.fem.
´ ˘	s kúmom	with the godmother inst.sg.
´ ˘ ˘	krúžite	circulate 2.pl.imper.

´ ˘ ˘	ļúbite	kiss 2.pl.imper.
´ ˘ ˘	ļútite	make angry 2.pl.imper.
´ ˘ ˘	lúdoga	fool gen.sg.masc. (indef.decl.)
˘ ´ ˘	odlúči	decide 2.sg.imper.
´ ˘	mŕsi	tousle 2.sg.imper.
´ ˘	bŕka	large-moustached man nom.sg.
´ ˘	kŕpa	cobbler nom.sg.
´ ˘	cŕna	black nom.sg.fem. (indef.decl.)
´ ˘	Kŕco	(name) nom.sg.masc.
´ ˘ ˘	sŕdite	make angry 2.pl.imper.
´ ˘ ˘	cŕnite	blacken 2.pl.imper.
´ ˘ ˘	cŕnoga	black gen.sg.masc. (indef.decl.)
˘ ´ ˘	zamŕsi	complicate 2.sg.imper.
˘ ´ ˘	nasŕni	attack 2.sg.imper.
˘ ´ ˘	rasŕdi	make angry 2.sg.imper.
˘ ´ ˘	zavŕši	finish 2.sg.imper.
˘ ´ ˘ ˘	zavŕnuti	twist inf.

Appendix B
List of Test Words

List of test words recorded by twelve speakers, arranged according to accent type and stressed syllable nuclei.

Short Falling Accent

˵ ˘	da bȉje, ȉgra, lȅti, sȅlo, brȁtu, sȍli, da mȍli, vȍde, bȍja, po ȍku, kȕka, Kȑsta, Kȑstom
˵ ˘ ˘	ȉzginu, nȁbije, rȁstera, stȁjati, rȍđeni, ȕpala
˵ ¯ ˘	prȍsūti, ȕzēti, kȑvāvi
˵ ˘ ˘ ˘	zȁovama
˵ + ¯	ȕ grād
˘ + ˵	u rȁt

Short Rising Accent

ˋ ˘	ìgra, lèti, sèlo, sèlu, sòli, vòde, bòja, kùka, kr̀sta, kr̀stom
ˋ ˘ ˘	ìzginu, zèleni, ràstera, stàjati, zàmoli, ròđeni, dòveo, ùpala
ˋ ¯ ˘	ràsr̄di, òdlūči, pròsūti, ùzēti, kr̀vāvi
˘ ˋ ˘	zelèni, zoòlog
˘ ˋ ¯	barjàktār
ˋ ¯ ˘ ˘	jàūčemo
ˋ + ˘	ù rat
˘ ˋ ˘ ˘	crnòoka

Long Falling Accent

ˆ ˘	čîle, svêta, râda, grâdu, kôsa, rûža, kr̂pa
˘ + ˆ	u grâd

Long Rising Accent

´ ˘ Číle, Mári, Svéta, Ráda, Kósa, rúža, kŕpa
˘ ´ ˘ odlúči, rasŕdi
´ ˘ ˘ plaćao
˘ ˘ ´ ˘ barjaktári

Appendix C

List of Recorded Sentences

List of sentences recorded for the study of sentence intonation and the interaction of word tone with sentence intonation. Speakers were requested to produce the underlined words with emphasis.

Sentences

1. Mârko grâdi prâvu bârku.
2. Mârko grâdi prâvu bârku?
3. Dȁ li Mârko grâdi bârku?
4. Kȁda Mârko grâdi bârku?
5. Grâdi li Mârko prâvu bârku?
6. Grâdi li Mârko bârku?
7. Mârko grâdi bârku, ali mu nedòstaje grâđa.
8. Mârko sad grâdi bârku da otpùtuje ŋóme.
9. Mârko grâdi bârku, Tása mu dáje čámac, a Mârkovica sȅla pa jàūče po sèlu.
10. Mârko grâdi prâvu bârku, a vî níste zȁdovōl̦ni.
11. Mârko grâdi prâvu bârku!
12. Mârko grâdi prâvu bârku.
13. Mârko grâdi prâvu bârku.
14. Mârko grâdi prâvu bârku.
15. Mârko grâdi prâvu bârku.
16. Mârko grâdi prâvu bârku?
17. Mârko grâdi prâvu bârku?
18. Mârko grâdi prâvu bârku?
19. Mârko grâdi prâvu bârku?
20. Mârkovica grâdi bârku.
21. Mârkovica grâdi bârku, pa će plòviti rékom.
22. Mârkovica grâdi bârku?

23. Tása dáje Pánti čámac.
24. Tása dáje Pánti čámac?
25. Dȁ li Tása dáje čámac?
26. Kȁda Tása dáje čámac?
27. Dáje li Tása Pánti čámac?
28. Dáje li Tása čámac?
29. Tása dáje čámac, ali mu nedòstaje vèslo.
30. Tása nam dáje čámac da ga prodámo na tŕgu.
31. Tása dáje čámac, Mârko grâdi bârku, a Ráda nȍsi sȍli i vòde.
32. Tása dáje Pánti čámac, a òvāj se bûni.
33. Tása dáje Pánti čámac!
34. *Tása* dáje Pánti čámac.
35. Tása *dáje* Pánti čámac.
36. Tása dáje *Pánti* čámac.
37. Tása dáje Pánti *čámac.*
38. *Tása* dáje Pánti čámac?
39. Tása *dáje* Pánti čámac?
40. Tása dáje *Pánti* čámac?
41. Tása dáje Pánti *čámac?*
42. Tása mu sad dáje čámac.
43. Tása mu sad dáje čámac, a Kȓsta se kr̀sti.
44. Tása mu sad dáje čámac?
45. Sȁda Rȁtko gȁzi bȁru.
46. Sȁda Rȁtko gȁzi bȁru?
47. Dȁ li Rȁtko gȁzi bȁru?
48. Kȁda Rȁtko gȁzi bȁru?
49. Gȁzi li sȁda Rȁtko bȁru?
50. Gȁzi li Rȁtko bȁru?
51. Rȁtko gȁzi bȁru, a iznad kùka mu se vȉde rȅbra.
52. Rȁtko sad gȁzi bȁru da ìzmakne žèteocima.
53. Rȁtko gȁzi bȁru, Kȓsta tr̀či iz ríta, a Svéta dòšao da glȅda.
54. Rȁtko gȁzi bȁru, a crnòoka Dára sèdi u bârci.
55. Sȁda Rȁtko gȁzi bȁru!
56. *Sȁda* Rȁtko gȁzi bȁru.
57. Sȁda *Rȁtko* gȁzi bȁru.
58. Sȁda Rȁtko *gȁzi* bȁru.
59. Sȁda Rȁtko gȁzi *bȁru*.
60. *Sȁda* Rȁtko gȁzi bȁru?
61. Sȁda *Rȁtko* gȁzi bȁru?
62. Sȁda Rȁtko *gȁzi* bȁru?

63. Sȁda Rȁtko gȁzi bȁru?
64. Rȁtkovica gȁzi bȁru.
65. Rȁtkovica gȁzi bȁru, a kúma se pribli̇̀žāva čámcu.
66. Rȁtkovica gȁzi bȁru?
67. Dànas màgla lèti sèlom.
68. Dànas màgla lèti sèlom?
69. Dȁ li màgla lèti sèlom?
70. Kȁda màgla lèti sèlom?
71. Lèti li dànas màgla sèlom?
72. Lèti li màgla sèlom?
73. Dànas màgla lèti sèlom, ali je bŕka krénuo ȕ poļe.
74. Dànas màgla lèti sèlom da nàjēdi kûma i kúmu.
75. Màgla lèti sèlom, Rȁtko gȁzi po bȁri, a sȅoski psȉ lȁju nȅumōrno.
76. Dànas màgla lèti sèlom, a sȕtra će pȁsti snêg.
77. Dànas màgla lèti sèlom!
78. Dànas màgla lèti sèlom.
79. Dànas màgla lèti sèlom.
80. Dànas màgla lèti sèlom.
81. Dànas màgla lèti sèlom.
82. Dànas màgla lèti sèlom?
83. Dànas màgla lèti sèlom?
84. Dànas màgla lèti sèlom?
85. Dànas màgla lèti sèlom?
86. Ȉzmaglica lèti sèlom.
87. Ȉzmaglica lèti sèlom, a planìna se béli u snégu.
88. Ȉzmaglica lèti sèlom?
89. Mâjstori štâmpaju kârtice.
90. Mâjstori štâmpaju kârtice?
91. Dȁ li mâjstori štâmpaju kârtice?
92. Kȁda mâjstori štâmpaju kârtice?
93. Štâmpaju li mâjstori kârtice?
94. Štâmpaju li kârtice?
95. Mâjstori štâmpaju kârtice, ali môj pȉsār ne pòzīva dèvōjke.
96. Mâjstori štâmpaju kârtice da ih pòšaļu Kósi.
97. Mâjstori štâmpaju kârtice, zoòlozi se sàstaju dvánaestog, a ôn još ȕvēk nȉšta ne pòčiņe.
98. Mâjstori štâmpaju kârtice, a mòji pȉsāri dáju ih Míri.
99. Mâjstori štâmpaju kârtice!
100. Mâjstori štâmpaju kârtice.
101. Mâjstori štâmpaju kârtice.

102. Mâjstori štâmpaju kârtice.
103. Mâjstori štâmpaju kârtice?
104. Mâjstori štâmpaju kârtice?
105. Mâjstori štâmpaju kârtice?
106. Mâjstorice će da štâmpaju.
107. Mâjstorice će da štâmpaju, a mâjstori će da sȅdnu u bìrō.
108. Mâjstorice će da štâmpaju?
109. Zákoni vládaju národom.
110. Zákoni vládaju národom?
111. Dȁ li zákoni vládaju národom?
112. Kȁda zákoni vládaju národom?
113. Vládaju li zákoni národom?
114. Vládaju li národom?
115. Zákoni vládaju národom, ali se tô kàdiji ne dòpada.
116. Zákoni vládaju národom da bi se ìzbegla nèprāvda.
117. Zákoni vládaju národom, sùdije sûde po prâvdi, a vójska se nȉkoga ne bòji.
118. Zákoni vládaju národom, a dvánaest mìnistāra sačiņávaju vládu.
119. Zákoni vládaju národom!
120. Zákoni vládaju národom.
121. Zákoni vládaju národom.
122. Zákoni vládaju národom.
123. Zákoni vládaju národom?
124. Zákoni vládaju národom?
125. Zákoni vládaju národom?
126. Po zákonu će da vládaju.
127. Po zákonu će da vládaju, a po prâvdi će da sûde.
128. Po zákonu će da vládaju?
129. Jȁgņe se dȁruje bȁbama.
130. Jȁgņe se dȁruje bȁbama?
131. Dȁ li se jȁgņe dȁruje bȁbama?
132. Kȁda se dȁruje bȁbama?
133. Dȁruje li se jȁgņe bȁbama?
134. Dȁruje li se bȁbama?
135. Jȁgņe se dȁruje bȁbama, ali se óvca zadȑžāva u planìni.
136. Jȁgņe se dȁruje bȁbama da i òne imaju nȅko zadovóļstvo.
137. Jȁgņe se dȁruje bȁbama, óvca i kòza òstaju u planìni, a snáše ìdu po tràvicu.
138. Jȁgņe se dȁruje bȁbama, a òne ga ispèku na rážņu.
139. Jȁgņe se dȁruje bȁbama!

140. Jȁgŋe se dȁruje bȁbama.
141. Jȁgŋe se dȁruje bȁbama.
142. Jȁgŋe se dȁruje bȁbama.
143. Jȁgŋe se dȁruje bȁbama?
144. Jȁgŋe se dȁruje bȁbama?
145. Jȁgŋe se dȁruje bȁbama?
146. Dȁrujemo ga i bȁbama.
147. Dȁrujemo ga i bȁbama, a nȅ sȁmo devòjčicama.
148. Dȁrujemo ga i bȁbama?
149. Snàšice ràznose tràvicu.
150. Snàšice ràznose tràvicu?
151. Dȁ li snàšice ràznose tràvicu?
152. Kȁda snàšice ràznose tràvicu?
153. Ràznose li snàšice tràvicu?
154. Ràznose li tràvicu?
155. Snàšice ràznose tràvicu, ali im babètine stâlno smétaju.
156. Snàšice ràznose tràvicu da se nàhrāne ôvce i kòze.
157. Snàšice ràznose tràvicu, kòze bȑste u žbûŋu, a ôvce pásu na brégu.
158. Snàšice ràznose tràvicu, a zȁove im dòlaze nà ŋivu.
159. Snàšice ràznose tràvicu!
160. Snàšice ràznose tràvicu.
161. Snàšice ràznose tràvicu.
162. Snàšice ràznose tràvicu.
163. Snàšice ràznose tràvicu?
164. Snàšice ràznose tràvicu?
165. Snàšice ràznose tràvicu?
166. Za snàšice je i tràvica.
167. Za snàšice je i tràvica, a takóđe i rúže.
168. Za snàšice je i tràvica?
169. Kȁmēn su dȍnēle grȁđānke.
170. Kȁmēn su dȍnēle grȁđānke?
171. Dȁ li su kȁmēn dȍnēle grȁđānke?
172. Kȁda su grȁđānke dȍnēle kȁmēn?
173. Kȁmēn su dȍnēle grȁđānke, a grȁđani će ŋíme pòpraviti ȕlicu.
174. Kȁmēn su dȍnēle grȁđānke da se ŋíme pòpravi kȁldrma.
175. Kȁmēn su dȍnēle grȁđānke, ȕlicu su pòpravili muškárci, a ȍpština im je dála kamióne iz depòa.
176. Kȁmēn su dȍnēle grȁđānke, ali ni grȁđani nísu sèdeli u bifèu.
177. Kȁmēn su dȍnēle grȁđānke!
178. Kȁmēn su dȍnēle grȁđānke.

179. Kȁmēn su dȍnēle grȁđānke.
180. Kȁmēn su dȍnēle grȁđānke.
181. Kȁmēn su dȍnēle grȁđānke?
182. Kȁmēn su dȍnēle grȁđānke?
183. Kȁmēn su dȍnēle grȁđānke?
184. Za kȁmēn su sad i grȁđānke.
185. Za kȁmēn su sad i grȁđānke, a àsfalt nȉko ne žèli.
186. Za kȁmēn su sad i grȁđānke?
187. Ràdōjki dònēše kòlāč.
188. Ràdōjki dònēše kòlāč?
189. Dȁ li Ràdōjki dònēše kòlāč?
190. Kȁda Ràdōjki dònēše kòlāč?
191. Dònēše li Ràdōjki kòlāč?
192. Dònēše li kòlāč?
193. Ràdōjki dònēše kòlāč, ali čitaònicu ȉpāk ne osnòvaše.
194. Ràdōjki dònēše kòlāč da ì ŋū mȁlo razvèsele.
195. Ràdōjki dònēše kòlāč, Bòsīļki pečéņe, a Drȁgomīru prázan tàņīr.
196. Ràdōjki dònēše kòlāč, a Beògrađanima ràkije.
197. Ràdōjki dònēše kòlāč!
198. Ràdōjki dònēše kòlāč.
199. Ràdōjki dònēše kòlāč.
200. Ràdōjki dònēše kòlāč.
201. Ràdōjki dònēše kòlāč?
202. Ràdōjki dònēše kòlāč?
203. Ràdōjki dònēše kòlāč?
204. Za Ràdōjku je i kòlāč.
205. Za Ràdōjku je i kòlāč, kao što je rečèno u intervjùu.
206. Za Ràdōjku je i kòlāč?
207. Tȁmo ȉma dȍsta rîta.
208. Tȁmo ȉma dȍsta rîta.
209. Tȁmo ȉma dȍsta rîta.
210. Tȁmo ȉma dȍsta rîta.
211. Tȁmo ȉma dȍsta rîta.
212. Rîta tȁmo ȉma dȍsta.
213. Dȍsta rîta ȉma tȁmo.
214. Ȉma dȍsta rîta tȁmo.
215. Tȁmo ȉma dȍsta rîta?
216. Tȁmo ȉma dȍsta rîta?
217. Tȁmo ȉma dȍsta rîta i svèga drȕgoga.
218. Tȁmo ȉma dȍsta rîta da se zadòvoļe ļûdi.

219. Ȋma li tàmo dȍsta rȋta?
220. Tàmo ȉma dȍsta rȋta!
221. Tàmo ȉma dȍsta ríta.
222. Tàmo ȉma dȍsta ríta.
223. Tàmo ȉma dȍsta ríta.
224. Tàmo ȉma dȍsta ríta.
225. Tàmo ȉma dȍsta ríta.
226. Ríta tàmo ȉma dȍsta.
227. Dȍsta ríta ȉma tàmo.
228. Ȋma dȍsta ríta tàmo.
229. Tàmo ȉma dȍsta ríta?
230. Tàmo ȉma dȍsta ríta?
231. Tàmo ȉma dȍsta ríta i svèga drȕgoga.
232. Tàmo ȉma dȍsta ríta da se zadòvoļe ļûdi.
233. Ȋma li tàmo dȍsta ríta?
234. Tàmo ȉma dȍsta ríta!
235. Tàmo ȉma dȍsta rȋta, ali nȉko nȅ zna zà tō.
236. Tàmo ȉma dȍsta ríta, ali nȉko nȅ zna zà tō.
237. Tàmo ȉma dȍsta rȋta, ali tô nȉkome nìje pȍznāto.
238. Tàmo ȉma dȍsta ríta, ali tô nȉkome nìje pȍznāto.
239. Ako tàmo ȉma dȍsta rȋta, zȁšto ste ȍnda mène zváli?
240. Ako tàmo ȉma dȍsta ríta, zȁšto ste ȍnda mène zváli?
241. Vȑlo je dòbro sȅlo.
242. Vȑlo je dòbro sȅlo.
243. Vȑlo je dòbro sȅlo.
244. Vȑlo je dòbro sȅlo.
245. Sȅlo je vȑlo dòbro.
246. Ono je sȅlo dòbro.
247. Ono je sȅlo vȑlo dòbro.
248. Vȑlo je dòbro sȅlo?
249. Vȑlo je dòbro sȅlo?
250. Vȑlo je dòbro sȅlo i svȉ su ņíme zȁdovōļni.
251. Vȑlo je dòbro sȅlo da bi ugòdilo svíma.
252. Vȑlo je dòbro sȅlo, a nȉko nȅ zna zà tō.
253. Vȑlo je dòbro sȅlo, ali tô nȉkome nije pȍznāto.
254. Ako je vȑlo dòbro sȅlo, zȁšto ste ȍnda mène zváli?
255. Dȁ li je dòbro sȅlo?
256. Vȑlo je dòbro sȅlo!
257. Vȑlo je dòbro sèlo.
258. Vȑlo je dòbro sèlo.

259. Vȑlo je <u>dòbro</u> sèlo.
260. Vȑlo je dòbro <u>sèlo</u>.
261. Sèlo je vȑlo dòbro.
262. Òno je sèlo dòbro.
263. Òno je sèlo vȑlo dòbro.
264. Vȑlo je dòbro <u>sèlo</u>?
265. Vȑlo je <u>dòbro</u> sèlo?
266. Vȑlo je dòbro sèlo i svȉ su ŋíme zȁdovōļni.
267. Sèlo je vȑlo dòbro da bi ugòdilo svíma.
268. Vȑlo je dòbro sèlo, a nȉko nȅ zna zà tō.
269. Sèlo je vȑlo dòbro, ali tô nȉkome nȉje pȍznāto.
270. Ako je sèlo vȑlo dòbro, zȁšto ste ȍnda mène zváli?
271. Dȁ li je dòbro sèlo?
272. Vȑlo je dòbro sèlo!

Glosses

1. Marko builds a real boat.
2. Marko builds a real boat?
3. Does Marko build a boat?
4. When does Marko build the boat?
5. Does Marko build a real boat?
6. Does Marko build a boat?
7. Marko builds a boat, but he is short of material.
8. Now Marko builds a boat in order to depart on it.
9. Marko builds a boat, Tasa offers him a rowboat, and Marko's wife sits screaming in the village.
10. Marko builds a real boat, and you aren't satisfied.
11. Marko builds a real boat!
12. <u>Marko</u> builds a real boat.
13. Marko <u>builds</u> a real boat.
14. Marko builds a <u>real</u> boat.
15. Marko builds a real <u>boat</u>.
16. <u>Marko</u> builds a real boat?
17. Marko <u>builds</u> a real boat?
18. Marko builds a <u>real</u> boat?
19. Marko builds a real <u>boat</u>?
20. Marko's wife builds a boat.
21. Marko's wife builds a boat, and she will sail along the river.
22. Marko's wife builds a boat?

23. Tasa is offering Panta a rowboat.
24. Tasa is offering Panta a rowboat?
25. Does Tasa offer a rowboat?
26. When does Tasa offer a rowboat?
27. Is Tasa offering Panta a rowboat?
28. Is Tasa offering a rowboat?
29. Tasa is offering a rowboat, but it lacks an oar.
30. Tasa is offering us a rowboat so that we can sell it on the market.
31. Tasa offers a rowboat, Marko builds a boat, and Rada brings salt and water.
32. Tasa is offering Panta a rowboat, and the latter is complaining.
33. Tasa is offering Panta a rowboat!
34. *Tasa* is offering Panta a rowboat.
35. Tasa is *offering* Panta a rowboat.
36. Tasa is offering *Panta* a rowboat.
37. Tasa is offering Panta a *rowboat*.
38. *Tasa* is offering Panta a rowboat?
39. Tasa is *offering* Panta a rowboat?
40. Tasa is offering *Panta* a rowboat?
41. Tasa is offering Panta a *rowboat*?
42. Now Tasa is offering him a rowboat.
43. Now Tasa is offering him a rowboat, and Krsta is crossing himself.
44. Now Tasa is offering him a rowboat?
45. Now Ratko is wading through the puddle.
46. Now Ratko is wading through the puddle?
47. Is Ratko wading through the puddle?
48. When does Ratko wade through the puddle?
49. Is Ratko wading through the puddle now?
50. Is Ratko wading through the puddle?
51. Ratko is wading through the puddle, and above his hip one can see his ribs.
52. Now Ratko is wading through the puddle in order to run away from the reapers.
53. Ratko is wading through the puddle, Krsta is running away from the marsh, and Sveta came in order to watch.
54. Ratko is wading through the puddle, and dark-eyed Dara is sitting in the boat.
55. Now Ratko is wading through the puddle!
56. *Now* Ratko is wading through the puddle.
57. Now *Ratko* is wading through the puddle.

58. Now Ratko is *wading* through the puddle.
59. Now Ratko is wading through the *puddle*.
60. *Now* Ratko is wading through the puddle?
61. Now *Ratko* is wading through the puddle?
62. Now Ratko is *wading* through the puddle?
63. Now Ratko is wading through the *puddle*?
64. Ratko's wife is wading through the puddle.
65. Ratko's wife is wading through the puddle, and the godmother is approaching the rowboat.
66. Ratko's wife is wading through the puddle?
67. Today mist is flying over the village.
68. Today mist is flying over the village?
69. Is mist flying over the village?
70. When does mist fly over the village?
71. Is mist flying over the village today?
72. Is mist flying over the village?
73. Today mist is flying over the village, but the man with a long moustache went to the field.
74. Today mist flies over the village to anger the godfather and the godmother.
75. Mist is flying over the village, Ratko is wading through the puddle, and the village dogs are barking tirelessly.
76. Today mist is flying over the village, and tomorrow it will snow.
77. Today mist is flying over the village!
78. *Today* mist is flying over the village.
79. Today *mist* is flying over the village.
80. Today mist is *flying* over the village.
81. Today mist is flying over the *village*.
82. Is it *today* that mist is flying over the village?
83. Today *mist* is flying over the village?
84. Today mist is *flying* over the village?
85. Today mist is flying over the *village*?
86. A haze is flying over the village.
87. A haze is flying over the village, and the mountain is white with snow.
88. A haze is flying over the village?
89. The craftsmen are printing the cards.
90. The craftsmen are printing the cards?
91. Are the craftsmen printing the cards?
92. When do the craftsmen print the cards?
93. Are the craftsmen printing the cards?

94. Do they print cards?
95. The craftsmen are printing the cards, but my clerk still does not invite the girls.
96. The craftsmen are printing the cards in order to send them to Kosa.
97. The craftsmen are printing the cards, the zoologists are going to meet on the twelfth, and he still does not begin anything.
98. The craftsmen print the cards, an my clerks give them to Mira.
99. The craftsmen are printing the cards!
100. The *craftsmen* are printing the cards.
101. The craftsmen are *printing* the cards.
102. The craftsmen are printing the *cards*.
103. The *craftsmen* are printing the cards?
104. The craftsmen are *printing* the cards?
105. The craftsmen are printing the *cards*?
106. The craftsmen's wives will print them.
107. The craftsmen's wives will print, and the craftsmen will sit in the office.
108. The craftsmen's wives will print them?
109. Laws govern the people.
110. Laws govern the people?
111. Do laws govern the people?
112. When do laws govern the people?
113. Do laws govern the people?
114. Do they govern the people?
115. Laws govern the people, but the judge does not like it.
116. Laws govern the people so that injustice can be avoided.
117. Laws govern the people, the judges judge according to justice, and the army does not fear anybody.
118. Laws govern the people, and twelve ministers make up the government.
119. Laws govern the people!
120. *Laws* govern the people.
121. Laws *govern* the people.
122. Laws govern the *people*.
123. *Laws* govern the people?
124. Laws *govern* the people?
125. Laws govern the *people*?
126. They will govern according to the law.
127. They will govern according to law, and they will judge according to justice.

128. Will they govern according to law?
129. The lamb is donated to the old women.
130. The lamb is donated to the old women?
131. Is the lamb donated to the old women?
132. When is it donated to the old women?
133. Is the lamb donated to the old women?
134. Is it donated to the old women?
135. The lamb is donated to the old women, but the sheep is retained on the mountain.
136. The lamb is donated to the old women so that they too can have some pleasure.
137. The lamb is donated to the old women, the sheep and the goat stay on the mountain, and the young married women go to fetch some grass.
138. The lamb is donated to the old women, and they barbecue it.
139. The lamb is donated to the old women!
140. The *lamb* is donated to the old women.
141. The lamb is *donated* to the old women.
142 The lamb is donated to the *old women*.
143. The *lamb* is donated to the old women?
144. The lamb is *donated* to the old women?
145. The lamb is donated to the *old women*?
146. We donate it to the old women, too.
147. We donate it to the old women, too, and not only to the small girls.
148. Do we donate it to the old women, too?
149. The young married women spread the grass.
150. Do the young married women spread the grass?
151. Do the young married women spread the grass?
152. When do the young married women spread the grass?
153. Do the young married women spread the grass?
154. Do they spread the grass?
155. The young married women spread the grass, but the old women constantly disturb them.
156. The young married women spread the grass in order to feed the sheep and the goats.
157. The young married women spread grass, the goats browse in the bushes, and the sheep graze on the hill.
158. The young married women spread the grass, and their sisters-in-law visit them in the field.
159. The young married women spread the grass!
160. The *young married women* spread the grass.

161. The young married women *spread* the grass.
162. The young married women spread the *grass*.
163. The *young married women* spread the grass?
164. The young married women *spread* the grass?
165. The young married women spread the *grass*?
166. Grass, too, is for the young married women.
167. Grass, too, is for the young married women, and likewise the roses.
168. Is the grass, too, for the young married women?
169. Stone was brought by female citizens.
170. Stone was brought by female citizens?
171. Was stone brought by female citizens?
172. When did female citizens bring the stone?
173. Stone was brought by female citizens, and male citizens will repair the street with it.
174. Stone was brought by female citizens so that the pavement can be repaired with it.
175. Stone was brought by the female citizens, the street was repaired by the men, and the community office gave the trucks from the depot.
176. Stone was brought by the female citizens, but the male citizens were not sitting in a bar either.
177. Stone was brought by female citizens!
178. *Stone* was brought by female citizens.
179. Stone was *brought* by female citizens.
180. Stone was brought by *female citizens*.
181. *Stone* was brought by female citizens?
182. Stone was *brought* by female citizens?
183. Stone was brought by *female citizens*?
184. The female citizens, too, now favor stone.
185. The female citizens, too, now favor stone, and nobody wants asphalt.
186. The female citizens, too, now favor stone?
187. They brought a cake for Radojka.
188. They brought a cake for Radojka?
189. Did they bring a cake for Radojka?
190. When did they bring a cake for Radojka?
191. Did they bring a cake for Radojka?
192. Did they bring the cake?
193. They brought a cake for Radojka, but they still did not found a reading room.
194. They brought a cake for Radojka in order to cheer her up too.

195. They brought a cake for Radojka, roast meat for Bosiljka, and for Dragomir an empty plate.
196. They brought Radojka a cake, and brandy for the people from Belgrade.
197. They brought a cake for Radojka!
198. They brought a cake for Radojka.
199. They brought a cake for Radojka.
200. They brought a cake for Radojka.
201. They brought a cake for Radojka?
202. They brought a cake for Radojka?
203. They brought a cake for Radojka?
204. The cake, too, is for Radojka.
205. The cake, too, is for Radojka, as it was said in the interview.
206. The cake, too, is for Radojka?
207. There are enough rags there.
208. There are enough rags there.
209. There are enough rags there.
210. There are enough rags there.
211. There are enough rags there.
212. Rags are there in sufficient quantity.
213. Enough rags are there.
214. There are enough rags there.
215. There are enough rags there?
216. There are enough rags there?
217. There are enough rags there, and enough of everything else.
218. There are enough rags there to satisfy the people.
219. Are there enough rags there?
220. There are enough rags there!
221. There is enough swampland there.
222. There is enough swampland there.
223. There is enough swampland there.
224. There is enough swampland there.
225. There is enough swampland there.
226. Swampland is there in sufficient quantity.
227. Enough swampland is there.
228. Enough swampland is there.
229. There is enough swampland there?
230. There is enough swampland there?
231. There is enough swampland and everything else there.
232. There is enough swampland there to satisfy the people.

233. Is there enough swampland there?
234. There is enough swampland there!
235. There are enough rags there, but nobody knows about it.
236. There is enough swampland there, but nobody knows about it.
237. There are enough rags there, but this isn't known to anyone.
238. There is enough swampland there, but this isn't known to anyone.
239. If there are enough rags there, why did you call me?
240. If there is enough swampland there, why did you call me?
241. It sat down very well.
242. It sat down very well.
243. It sat down very well.
244. It sat down very well.
245. It sat down very well.
246. It sat down well.
247. It sat down very well.
248. It sat down very well?
249. It sat down very well?
250. It sat down very well and everybody is pleased with it.
251. It sat down very well in order to please everybody.
252. It sat down very well, but nobody knows about it.
253. It sat down very well, but this isn't known to anyone.
254. If it sat down very well, why did you call me?
255. Did it sit down well?
256. It sat down very well!
257. The village is very good.
258. The village is very good.
259. The village is very good.
260. The village is very good.
261. The village is very good.
262. That village is good.
263. That village is very good.
264. The village is very good?
265. The village is very good?
266. The village is very good and everybody is very pleased with it.
267. The village is very good in order to please everybody.
268. The village is very good, but nobody knows about it.
269. The village is very good, but this isn't known to anyone.
270. If the village is very good, why did you call me?
271. Is the village good?
272. The village is very good!

Notes

Chapter 1

1. For an insight into the variety of dialectal prosodic patterns, including those of non-Štokavian (i.e., Čakavian and Kajkavian) dialects, see Ivić 1974–75.

2. The quotation is from Daničić 1851, reprinted in Daničić 1925: 1 (all of Daničić's accentological studies are collected in this book). We find practically the same formulation in Daničić 1850: 3—only the examples, which Daničić had not originally provided with accent marks, now carry the following accents: *gláva*, *prâvda*, *màgla*, *slȁma*. (The meaning of these words is 'head', 'justice', 'fog', 'straw'.) Peco 1981 deals with Daničić's accentological works.

3. Partial reviews of older studies of Neoštokavian accentuation are offered by Novaković (1873), Masing (1876), Brandt (1880), Jakšić (1891), Šajković (1901), Kuhač (1908), Pollok (1957), Peco (1971c), Magner and Matejka (1971), Ivić (1974–75, 1976a), and Šojat (1981). Some of these reviews also discuss how other types of Serbocroatian accentuation are described in the works of old grammarians and lexicographers—matters that we will not discuss here. See also the bibliographies of Hraste (1956) (additions in Ivić 1959b), Ivić and Lehiste (1967), and Matešić (1970).

4. Drechsler 1912a, 1912b. Ivšić (1912) also mentions Starčević's accentuation, emphasizing that Drechsler had called it to his attention. Later authors who have written about Starčević's accents are Anić (1967–68, 1968), Vince (1973), and (from a phonemic viewpoint) Jakobson 1931a: 177 and Junković (1978).

5. In each case Milovanov also provided Serbian equivalents for his own Latin terms.

6. However, a footnote on p. 19 (concerning the examples *cȑvēn* 'red color, redness', written *crvên* and *cr̀ven*) gives the impression that Milovanov sensed a difference between the two short accents ("I think that they cannot be separated, although it seems to me that there is some kind of difference between them").

7. Regarding accentuation in Karadžić 1818, see Ivić 1966.

8. If we interpreted Kolarović literally, we might say that his formulation "reč još traje" (the word goes on (after ` and ´)) may be related to the fact that after these accents there must occur at least one additional syllable, whereas ̏ and ̂ may also

appear on examples like *mrȁz* 'frost' and *dâr* 'gift'. However, among Kolarović's examples are words like *jȁbuka* 'apple' and *pûtnik* 'traveler', in which additional syllables occur after ̏ and ̑, respectively, indicating that he was aware that the occurrence of additional syllables was not restricted to those accents after which "reč još traje." Therefore, it is more probable that he wanted to say that the prosodically prominent part of the word continues after the syllable bearing ̀ or ́, whereas that part is completed on the syllable bearing ̏ or ̑.

9. Kolarović's views about accents are discussed by Stojanović (1924:456–7) and by Živanović (1976a). However, these two authors appear not to have grasped how far ahead of his time Kolarović was in this respect.

10. Even in works published as late as 1849 and 1851 Karadžić still used the symbol ̀ for ̏ (see Karadžić 1896:6, 307).

11. In Karadžić's and Daničić's works postaccentual length is transcribed with the symbol ̑ and is treated as identical to the long falling accent (gen.pl. *pûtnîkâ* 'travelers' = *pûtnīkā*). Miklošič 1852 pointed out that different entities are involved and proposed that postaccentual length be indicated by a macron (̄), a practice that was eventually adopted by other scholars, even though Karadžić and Daničić persisted in their previous usage, and even though Daničić fervently defended this usage in polemical writings.

12. Evidence exists, provided by Daničić himself, of his participation in providing accent symbols for the words included in Karadžić's dictionary of 1852 (see Pavić 1885:183). It is interesting that in his 1847 publication Daničić himself had not distinguished between ̀ and ̏.

13. Information about Šunjić's views concerning accents is unsatisfactory in the otherwise very useful study of Pudić (1960).

14. In the 1850 edition of Fröhlich's grammar, published during the writer's lifetime, the so-called Slavonian accentuation is represented, which is basically different from Neoštokavian accentuation.

15. Concerning Masing's life and work, see Bulatova 1975.

16. Nowadays it is known that these are characteristics of the dialect of Žarkovo and neighboring villages, in the development of which new waves of migration played no part (Ivić 1978). It is more relevant that in that region the older Štokavian accentuation is still prevalent (type *kraljȉca*, *sačûvam* rather than *kràljica*, *sàčūvam*), which raises the possibility that Masing may have actually observed an accentuation different from Neoštokavian. In addition, the geographical position of Mrkopalj, which together with two or three neighboring villages constitutes a Neoštokavian oasis in non-Štokavian territory in western Croatia, might give rise to the idea that the local dialect there is not typically Neoštokavian. Nevertheless, neither Kovačević nor other critics expressed such reservations, probably because the state of Serbocroatian dialectology at the time did not make it possible. Anticipating later developments, we can say that it is now clear that such assumptions would be unwarranted. Masing's notations do indeed reflect Neoštokavian accentuation, which means that the Mrkopalj dialect had preserved a "good" Neoštokavian pronunciation, and that the informant who was born in Žarkovo

and educated in Belgrade had generally adopted the norms of the literary pronunciation.

17. Maretić (1879) uses the equations *â* = *ȁa* and *á* = *aà*, but does not take up the question of the correctness of Masing's views.

18. Following Karadžić and Daničić, Maretić writes ˆ instead of ¯, but states that the symbol ˆ beyond the first syllable signifies only length, not accent.

19. Jakšić says that these terms were used by Daničić, but we have not succeeded in finding them in Daničić's writings, either in those quoted by Jakšić or in others. Jakšić further recalls Bošković's terms—̏ "oštar" (sharp), ̀ "blag" (gentle), ́ "otegnut" (stretched), ˆ "snažan" (strong)—and asserts that they correspond better to the actual pronunciation of the accents in question. (These labels are different from the ones found in the already mentioned textbooks published by Bošković in 1869 and 1878, but they correspond to those used by Stojanović in 1892 (except for the term "otegnut" for ́; Stojanović uses "visok").)

20. There is no evidence in Storm's book that he was acquainted with other points of view.

21. Parentheses indicate terms that apply simultaneously to ̏ and ̀. Slanted lines indicate terms that describe, not the accents themselves, but their graphic symbols.

22. It is interesting to note Rešetar's reaction (1902: 252) to Gauthiot's finding that the vowel under ˆ is really falling with regard to pitch and intensity and that vowels under ̀ and ́ are indeed rising, whereas the vowel under ̏ is level in both respects. About ̏, Rešetar says,

...was mich, aufrichtig gesagt, nicht wenig wundert, denn es scheint mir noch immer, dass ich auch in solchen Fällen wie *ȅto*, wo also die erste Silbe aus einem einzigen stimmhaften Laute besteht, ein Sinken des Tones in der Silbe höre; doch ist das der Punkt, wo ich am ehesten geneigt wäre, eine Koncession zu machen. (...frankly, this surprises me not a little, since it still seems to me that I hear falling pitch even in cases like *ȅto* ['look!', interj.], where the first syllable consists of a single voiced sound; but this is the point where I would be relatively most willing to make a concession.)

23. Judging by all available evidence, Belić must have had in mind Bosnia, Hercegovina, neighboring areas of Crna Gora, and possibly also Dubrovnik.

24. In the course of our research we surveyed a substantial number of works by these authors from the period before 1932, but this survey did not encompass their whole output up to that time.

25. These labels were also used in the textbook by Florschütz published during World War II (Florschütz 1943).

Chapter 2

1. The instrument is described in detail in Pulgram 1959 and in Potter, Kopp, and Green 1966.

2. For details, see Ivić and Lehiste 1967: 62–68.

3. For details, see Ivić and Lehiste 1967: 75–84.

4. More details are to be found in Lehiste and Ivić 1973a.

5. More details are to be found in Ivić and Lehiste 1979.

6. We gratefully acknowledge the assistance of Professor Gunnar Fant.

7. For details, see Lehiste and Ivić 1972.

8. We thank Dr. Lloyd Nakatani for his help.

9. The technique is described in detail in Lehiste, Olive, and Streeter 1976.

10. Unfortunately, the test words *vode* and *moli* had to be discarded because of a technical problem with the synthesis.

11. We are grateful to Dr. David Pisoni and Dr. Diane Kewley-Port for their assistance.

12. More details are to be found in Lehiste and Ivić 1973b.

Chapter 4

1. This interpretation has been criticized by a considerable number of authors, among them Kuznecov (1948), Pollok (1957), Ivić (1958, 1959a, 1965b), Lüdtke (1959), Peco (1965b), Garde (1966b), Rehder (1968a), I. Miletić (1974), and Stankiewicz (1977) (in his 1959 publication Stankiewicz supports Jakobson's views). We summarize some of these criticisms, with added comments.

2. This view has continued to receive support; later publications sustaining it include Stankiewicz 1959, Brozović 1968, and Ivić (ed.) 1981. Gvozdanović 1980 likewise comes close to this view.

3. Trubetzkoy had already briefly presented his views about Neoštokavian accentuation in his publications of 1936, 1938a, and 1938b, emphasizing that the so-called falling accents are in fact boundary signals.

4. The authors cited in note 1 usually also deal with the views of Trubetzkoy. Van Wijk 1940 and Gvozdanović 1980 do likewise.

5. Muljačić (1964) and Ivić (1965b) deal with the evolution of Jakobson's ideas.

6. The question whether such examples can be considered acceptable in the standard language has provoked long and bitter discussions. See, for example, Rončević 1950, Belić 1950–51, Moskatelo 1954, Brozović 1955, Moskovljević 1957, Frančić 1963a, Stevanović 1963, Jonke 1964, Anić 1969, 1972, 1975, Marković 1972, Vuković 1972.

7. Bidwell responded to this in 1968, maintaining that every description "at one point must account for the 'irregularity' noted above," so that "I see no gain in economy," whereas with regard to generality he states that his own "analysis also includes no positional restraint on stress." Bidwell is wrong on this point. It is not without importance at which level exceptions are handled. When exceptions have been identified as such, a wide area remains available for generalizations about what is normal in the language, but when the exceptions are placed on the same level as normal phenomena, such generalizations are impossible. Bidwell's own analysis of standard Serbocroatian accentuation cannot be called general; he operates with

disyllabic and monosyllabic noninitial stress, which introduces an additional category and complicates the picture to a great extent.

8. We are talking about several categories of examples:

1. Compound nouns like *poljoprȉvreda* 'agriculture' or *Jugoslâvija* 'Yugoslavia', where a juncture occurs before the syllable with ̏ or ̂
2. Loanwords like *asistȅnt* 'assistant', *interesȁntan* 'interesting', and *televȋzija* 'television'
3. Plural genitives like *Dalmatȋnācā* (... nom.sg. *Dalmatínac*) 'Dalmatian', where the accentual relationship has been analogically carried over from examples like nom.sg. *vrábac* 'sparrow' : gen.pl. *vrâbācā*
4. A few words of an expressive nature, such as *jedvȁ* 'barely', *tamȁn* 'just (adv.)'
5. A very small number of words of other categories, usually words of recent and bookish origin, such as *verovȁtno* 'probably'.

In the vast majority of these cases alternative pronunciations are found, which are sometimes more common than pronunciations with ̏ or ̂ on the noninitial syllable.

9. To be sure, he adds that a difference exists consisting of the fact that "pour Ivić, l'accent est distinctif au même titre que la quantité" (for Ivić, accent is distinctive for the same reason as quantity), whereas for himself, "l'accent ne peut assumer qu'une fonction contrastive" (accent can only assume a contrastive function). However, in his manual on Serbocroatian dialectology (1958), quoted by Junković, Ivić did not go into the question of the nature of accentual contrasts (on this, see for example Ivić 1973) but tried to demonstrate which phenomena are phonologically relevant in Serbocroatian.

10. McCawley states in the first footnote of his 1963 paper that he and Browne "discovered independently" the possibility of describing Serbocroatian accents in this manner.

Our transcription of the examples (*vodá*, etc.) corresponds in principle to that employed by Browne and McCawley (1965). However, in examples such as *vódu* or *glá:vu* they would leave out the accent symbol because in syntagms with proclitics the accent is retracted to the proclitic.

11. Authors belonging to the generative-transformational school did not formulate their rules in this way. McCawley (1963) speaks simply of high-pitched syllables, whose peculiarity is that they "start on a high pitch." Thus, the first syllable in words like *vòda* (*vodà* in McCawley's notation) is considered low-pitched, which does not correspond to phonetic reality. Browne and McCawley (1965), as well as Halle (1971), do not raise the question of the invariant phonetic characteristics of a syllable on which they place the accent mark. Of course, their formulations could be easily adjusted or added to.

12. However, compare Hayata 1973: 143: "We assume that in Japanese the carrier of abstract accent marks is not the syllable but rather the syllable boundary."

13. Such a procedure made it possible for Garde to categorize morphemes successfully as *morphèmes auto-accentués*, *morphèmes post-accentués*, *morphèmes pré-accentués*, and *morphèmes inaccentués*, so that the classification of individual Ser-

bocroatian morphemes coincides in most cases with the classification of corresponding Russian morphemes.

14. Stankiewicz (1977: 515) states that "the difference between a phonological and a morphophonological interpretation of accents is relevant in its entirety," and, as far as the phonological interpretation is concerned, he returns to the traditional analysis that operates with falling and rising accents. Naylor (1969: 80–81) treats the difference between phonological and morphophonemic levels in a similar manner.

15. Further evidence about the redundancy of intensity can be found in the works of other authors, even if they themselves do not draw this conclusion. Thus, Pollok (1964: 20) and Purcell (1973: 260–266) present tables from which it can be seen that the ranges of intensity peak values found in words with falling and rising accents overlap completely. In both kinds of accents the intensity peak may be located either on the accented syllable or on one of the following syllables, its occurrence on the first syllable being the most frequent case. Still, the percentage of examples with the peak on a nonfirst syllable is greater with rising accents. Naturally, neither the presence of the peak on the first syllable nor its occurrence on one of the other syllables serves as a signal of the presence of one or the other accent.

16. Gauthiot 1900, Popovici 1902, Ivković 1912, Appel 1950, Peco and Pravica 1972.

17. Ekblom 1924–25, Pollok 1964, Jacobsen 1967.

18. Our table 2.6, which contains data for three speakers, shows a more falling F_0 movement in the syllable under ` than in the syllable under ̏.

19. This becomes particularly clear from a study of frequency diagrams. Thus, the diagram found in Rehder 1968: 109 shows that there are examples with falling fundamental frequency in the vowel under ` as well as examples with rising fundamental frequency in the vowel under ̏. Figure 2.2 in this book shows a similar picture. Notice that in both cases the average $F_0$ movement is more rising in vowels under ` than in vowels under ̏.

20. The significance of the falling movement in the postaccentual syllable has been emphasized particularly by Gvozdanović (1980, as well as earlier works).

21. The importance of this criterion for accentedness was pointed out by Pešikan (1977: 510).

22. The high perceptibility and the important role of tonal height in the syllable immediately following a rising accent has also been confirmed, in a certain sense, by listening tests reported in Ivić 1970a and Nakađima 1981.

23. To be sure, one might think that the weakening of the first postaccentual syllable in word forms like imper.pl. *nòsite* > *nòste* 'carry' is paralleled by a raising of pitch on the following syllable (-(*t*)*e*), which makes possible the appearance of forms like *nòste*. However, in some—although few and rare—dialects one finds examples like *nód* < *nóde* 'there' or *kònj* < *kònji* 'horses'. The contrast between ´ or ` in such examples and ˆ or ̏ in examples like *rôd* 'relatives' or *kȍnj* 'horse' demonstrates that in these dialects the intrasyllabic F_0 movement is a sufficient signal of the distinction

between the two kinds of accents, even in the case of short accents. This was pointed out, in a somewhat different fashion, by Stankiewicz (1977 : 515).

24. Regional differences in the realization of Neoštokavian accents have been discussed by many authors, including, among others, Masing (1876), Šaxmatov (1898), Belić (1911, 1926–27, 1948, etc.), Moskovljević (1913), Jakobson (1931a), Miletić (1952), Peco (1971c), Simić (1977, 1978), Gvozdanović (1980), Simić and Ostojić (1981). In general, what has been reported does not contradict the results of our listening tests offered in this book. We would like to draw attention in particular to the landmark observations of Moskovljević 1913 and Belić 1926–27.

25. This can be seen most clearly in the results of Purcell's measurements (1973).

26. Even when the F_0 peak in the syllable immediately following a rising accent is somewhat lower than the peak of the accented syllable, the intersyllabic relationship remains rising when measured against the intonation curve of the sentence in what we have called neutral position (within a statement except in absolute initial or absolute final position, or immediately before a new clause within the same sentence).

27. No listening experiments have been carried out to test our hypothesis that the role of the postaccentual syllable may be greater in words of the type ˵ ¯ and ˋ ¯ (i.e., where the accented syllable is short and the postaccentual syllable is long).

28. Relativity as an essential characteristic of prosodic phenomena has been mentioned by such authors as Jakobson and Halle (1956) (cf. Jakobson 1971 : 481) and Lunt (1963).

Bibliography

AfslPh	*Archiv für slavische Philologie*
ARIPUC	*Annual Report of the Institute of Phonetics, University of Copenhagen*
GlSAN(U)	*Glasnik Srpske akademije nauka (i umetnosti)*
JF	*Južnoslovenski filolog*
NJ (n.s.)	*Naš jezik* (nova serija)
NSSVD	*Naučni sastanak slavista u Vukove dane*
Rad JAZU	*Rad Jugoslavenske akademije znanosti i umjetnosti*
RFFZ	*Radovi Filozofskog fakulteta u Zadru*
SEEJ	*Slavic and East European Journal*
TCLP	*Travaux du Cercle linguistique de Prague*
ZFL	*Zbornik za filologiju i lingvistiku*
*	Items marked with an asterisk are referred to in the text but are not specifically concerned with Serbocroatian accentuation.

In the case of textbooks that have appeared in several editions, only certain editions are entered in the bibliography.

*Abramson, Arthur (1979). Lexical tone and sentence prosody in Thai. *Proceedings of the Ninth International Congress of Phonetic Sciences, Copenhagen 6–11 August*, ed. E. Fischer-Jørgensen, J. Rischel, and N. Thorsen, Vol. II, 380–387. Institute of Phonetics, University of Copenhagen.

Ajanović, M., and M. Minović (1971). *Srpskohrvatski/hrvatskosrpski jezik*. Zavod za izdavanje udžbenika, Sarajevo.

Aleksić, Radomir, and Mihailo Stevanović (1946), *Gramatika srpskog jezika*. Belgrade.

Anić, Vladimir (1967–68). Akcentološki članci Šime Starčevića. *Jezik*, 15, 114–121.

Anić, Vladimir (1968). Akcenat u gramatici Šime Starčevića. *RFFZ*, 7.

Anić, Vladimir (1969). O jednom akcenatskom procesu u različitim službama književnog jezika. *Jezik*, 16, 84–89.

Anić, Vladimir (1972). O akcentu složenica u hrvatskosrpskom jeziku. *RFFZ*, 9, 25–29.

Anić, Vladimir (1975). Akcenatska adaptacija internacionalnih riječi u suvremenom književnom jeziku. *Zbornik Zagrebačke slavističke škole*, 3, 93–99.

Appel, Wilhelm (1950). Gestaltstudien. A Untersuchungen über den Akzent in der serbokroatischen Sprache. *Wiener slavistisches Jahrbuch*, 1, 53–70.

Arbuzova, I. V., P. A. Dmitriev, and N. I. Sokal' (1965). *Serboxorvatskij jazyk*. Izd. Leningradskogo universiteta, Leningrad.

Babukić, Věkoslav (1839). *Grundzüge der illirischen Grammatik*. Mit einer sprachvergleichenden Vorrede von Rudolph Fröhlich. Vienna.

Barić, Eugenija, Mijo Lončarić, Dragica Malić, Slavko Pavešić, Mirko Peti, Vesna Zečević, Marija Znika (1979). *Priručna gramatika hrvatskoga književnog jezika*. Školska knjiga, Zagreb.

Barjaktarević, Danilo (1964–65). Srednjoibarska govorna zona. *Zbornik Filozofskog fakulteta u Prištini*, 2, 57–113.

Becker, Lee A. (1979). *The Leftward Movement of High Tone*. Indiana University Linguistics Club, Bloomington, Ind.

Becker, Lee A. (1979). A contribution to an explanation of the Neo-Štokavian accent retraction. *ZFL*, 22/1, 87–94.

Belič (= Belić), Aleksandar (1910). *Zametki po čakavskim govoram*. Otdel'nyj ottisk iz Izvestij Otdlenija russkogo jazyka i slovesnosti Imperatorskoj Akademii Nauk, toma 14, 1909 g., kn. 2. St. Petersburg.

Belić, Aleksandar (1911). Review of Broch 1910. *Rocznik slawistyczny*, 4, 189–199.

Belić, Aleksandar (1926–27). Review of B. Miletić 1926. *JF*, 6, 225–232.

Belić, Aleksandar (1931). L'accent de la phrase et l'accent du mot. *TCLP*, 4, 183–188.

Belić, Aleksandar (1934). *Gramatika srpskohrvatskog jezika za drugi razred srednjih i stručnih škola*. Geca Kon, Belgrade.

Belić, Aleksandar (1935a, 1936). O rečeničnom akcentu u kastavskom govoru. *JF*, 14, 151–158; 15, 165–169.

Belić, Aleksandar (1935b). Jezik i muzika. *NJ*, 3/6, 161–166.

Belić, Aleksandar (1948). *Savremeni srpskohrvatski književni jezik. Prvi deo: Glasovi i akcenat*. Naučna knjiga, Belgrade.

Belić, Aleksandar (1950–51, 1951–52). Iz novije akcentuacije. I. *NJ*, n.s. 227–237. II. *NJ*, n.s. 3, 149–153.

Belić, Aleksandar (1960). *Osnovi istorije srpskohrvatskog jezika. I. Fonetika*. Univerzitet u Beogradu, Belgrade.

Berlić, Andreas Torquat (= Brlić, Andrija Torkvat) (1854). *Grammatik der illyri-*

schen Sprache wie solche im Munde und Schrift der Serben und Kroaten gebräuchlich ist. Vienna.

Bidwell, Charles E. (1963). The phonemics and morphophonemics of Serbo-Croatian stress. *SEEJ*, 7, 160–165.

Bidwell, Charles E. (1968). Accent patterns of the Serbo-Croatian noun. *Folia Linguistica*, 2/1–2, 18–28.

Bogorodickij, V. (1912). *Dialektologičeskie zametki*. IX. Iz nabljudenij nad serbsko-xorvatskim literaturnym proiznošeniem. *Russkij filologičeskij vestnik*, 67/1–2, 201–206.

Bošković, Jovan (1869). *Izvod iz srpske gramatike za učenike srednjih škola. Sveska prva. O glasovima i rečima*. Četvrto izdanje. Belgrade.

Bošković, Jovan (1878). *Izvod iz srpske gramatike. Knjiga prva. Glasovi, reči, oblici*. Sedmo izdanje. Belgrade.

Boyer, Paul (1900). La langue et la littérature en Bosnie-Herzegovine. *Revue générale des Sciences*, 11, 335–343.

Brabec, Ivan, Mate Hraste, and Sreten Živković (1965). *Gramatika hrvatskoga ili srpskog jezika*. Zagreb.

Brandt, Roman (1880). *Načertanie slavjanskoj akcentologii*. St. Petersburg.

Brandt, Roman (1895). *Kratkaja fonetika i morfologija serbskogo jazyka*. Moscow.

Braun, Maximilian (1964). Review of Mahnken 1962a. *International Journal of Slavic Linguistics and Poetics*, 8, 131–133.

Brok, O. (= Olaf Broch) (1910). *Očerk fiziologii slavjanskoj reči*. Enciklopedia slavjanskoj filologii 5/2. St. Petersburg.

Broch, Olaf (1911). *Slavische Phonetik*. Carl Winter, Heidelberg.

Browne, Wayles E. (1971). Review of Matešić 1970. *SEEJ*, 15, 351–355.

Browne, Wayles E. (1972). Review of Magner and Matejka 1971. *SEEJ*, 16, 503–508.

Browne, Wayles E. (1975). Phrase stress in Serbo-Croatian and English. *Kontrastivna analiza engleskog i hrvatskog ili srpskog jezika* 1, 169–171. Institut za lingvistiku, Zagreb.

Browne, Wayles E., and James McCawley (1965). Srpskohrvatski akcenat. *ZFL*, 8, 147–151.

Brozović, Dalibor (1955). Akcentuacija tuđica na *-or* u hrvatskom jeziku. *Jezik*, 3/4, 118–123.

Brozović, Dalibor (1968). O fonološkom sustavu suvremenog standardnog hrvatskosrpskog jezika. *RFFZ*, 7, 20–39.

Brozović, Dalibor (1972). Review of Matešić 1970. *Jezik*, 19/4–5, 123–139.

Brozović, Dalibor (1973). O fonološkim sustavima suvremenih južnoslavenskih jezika. *Makedonski jazik*, 24, 7–31.

*Bruce, Gösta (1977). *Swedish Word Accents in Sentence Perspective*. CWK Gleerup, Lund.

*Bruce, Gösta (1979). Word prosody and sentence prosody in Swedish. *Proceedings of the Ninth International Congress of Phonetic Sciences, Copenhagen 6–11 August*, ed. E. Fischer-Jørgensen, J. Rischel, and N. Thorsen, Vol. II, 388–394. Institute of Phonetics, University of Copenhagen.

Budmani, Pietro (1867). *Grammatica della lingua serbo-croata* (*illirica*). Vienna.

Bulatova, R. V. (1971). Novye issledovanija po serboxorvatskoj akcentologii. *Sovetskoe slavjanovedenie*, (7) 6, 85–91.

Bulatova, R. V. (1972). Review of Matešić 1970. *Sovetskoe slavjanovedenie*, (8) 6, 108–111.

Bulatova, R. V. (1975). Leongard Gotthil'f Mazing (1845–1936). *Tartu ülikooli ajaloo küsimusi*. I., 142–158. (TRÜ ajaloo komisjoni materjalid.) Tartu.

Butler, Th. (1972). Review of Magner and Matejka 1971. *General Linguistics*, 12, 94–96.

Chlumský, Josef (1925–26). La mélodie des voyelles accentuées en tchèque avec mention de l'état en serbe et en allemand. *Slavia*, 4, 1–25.

Daničić, Đuro (1847). *Rat za srpski jezik i pravopis*. Budapest. (Budim).

Daničić, Đuro (1850). *Mala srpska gramatika*. Vienna (Beč).

Daničić, Đuro (1851). Nešto o srpskijem akcentima. *Slavische Bibliothek*, 1, 97–110. (Reprinted in Daničić 1925.)

Daničić, Đuro (1925). *Srpski akcenti*. Srpska kraljevska akademija, Belgrade and Zemun.

De Bray, R. G. A. (1960). The pitch of Serbo-Croatian word accents in statements and questions. *Slavonic and East European Review*, 38, 380–393.

De Bray, R. G. A. (1961). Some observations of the Serbo-Croatian musical accents in connected speech. *Study of Sound* (Tokyo), 9.

Dešić, Milorad (1963). Akcentovanje uzvika. *NJ*, n.s. 13, 239–245.

Divković, Mirko (1879). *Hrvatska gramatika za srednje i nalik im škole. I. Dio: Oblici*. Zagreb.

Divković, Mirko (1895). *Oblici hrvatskoga jezika za srednje škole*. Izdanje peto. Zagreb.

Divković, Mirko (1903). *Oblici i sintaksa hrvatskoga jezika za srednje škole*. Tenth edition. Zagreb.

Divković, Mirko (1917). *Oblici i sintaksa hrvatskoga jezika za srednje škole*. Izdanje dvanaesto prerađeno. Zagreb.

Dmitriev, P. A., and G. I. Safronov (1975). *Serbo-xorvatskij jazyk*. Leningrad.

Drechsler, Branko (1912a). Dr. Ante Starčević. Književna studija iz doba apsolutizma Bachova. *Hrvatsko kolo*, 7, 355–408.

Drechsler, Branko (1912b). Pop Šime Starčević. *Veda*, Gorica, II.

Ekblom, R. (1917). Beiträge zur Phonetik der serbischen Sprache. *Le monde oriental*, 1–77.

Ekblom, R. (1924–25). Zur čechischen und serbischen Akzentuation. *Slavia*, 3, 35–44.

Ekblom, R. (1930). *Zur Entstehung und Entwicklung der slavobaltischen und nordischen Akzentarten*. Uppsala.

Fancev, Frano (1907). Beiträge zur serbokroatischen Dialektologie. Der kaj-Dialekt von Virje mit Berücksichtigung der Dialekte Podravina's (Koprivnica-Pitomača). *AfslPh*, 29, 305–389.

Finka, Božidar (1964–65). Utvrđivanje kvantitativnih odnosa u hrvatskosrpskom jeziku. *Jezik*, 11, 86–89, 111–117.

Finka, Božidar (1965). Jedna usporedba dijalekatskog izgovora s književnim jezikom—akcenatsko-ekspiratorna rečenična linija u jednom čakavskom govoru i u književnom hrvatskosrpskom jeziku. *Naučno društvo Bosne i Hercegovine, Radovi*, 26, 141–147.

Finka, Božidar (1977). Dugootočki čakavski govori. *Hrvatski dijalektološki zbornik* (Zagreb), 4, 7–178.

*Flanagan, J. L. (1957). Estimates of the maximum precision necessary in quantizing certain "dimensions" of vowel sounds. *Journal of the Acoustical Society of America*, 28, 533–534.

Florinskij, T. D. (1895). *Lekcii po slavjanskomu jazykoznaniju*. Kiev.

Florschütz, Josip (1895–96). Prilog za razumijevanje hrvatskoga i njemačkoga akcenta. *Nastavni vjesnik*, 4, 43–47.

Florschütz, Josip (1905). *Gramatika hrvatskoga jezika za ženski licej, preparandije i više pučke škole*. Zagreb.

Florschütz, Josip (1910). Litavci. *Prosvjeta* (Zagreb), 18, 669–673, 706–713, 741–745, 762–778.

Florschütz, Josip (1943). *Hrvatska slovnica za srednje i slične škole*. Prerađeno izdanje. Zagreb.

Frančić, Vilim (1963a). Dublety akcentowe w serbochorwackim języku literackim. *Studia linguistica in honorem Thaddaei Lehr-Spławiński*, 209–212. Warsaw.

Frančić, Vilim (1963b). *Gramatyka opisowa języka serbochorwackiego*. Państwowe wydawnictwo naukowe, Warsaw.

Fröhlich, R. A. (1865). *Theoretisch-praktische Grammatik der ilirischen Sprache, wie solche in Kroatien, Slavonien, Dalmatien und der Militärgrenze üblich ist*. Vierte

Auflage, bearbeitet und mit Übersetzungsstücken versehen von J. Macun. Vienna.

Fry, D., and Đ. Kostić (1939). *A Serbo-Croat Phonetic Reader*. London.

*Fujisaki, H., K. Hirose, and K. Ohta (1979). Acoustic features of the fundamental frequency contours of declarative sentences in Japanese. *Annual Bulletin, Research Institute of Logopedics and Phoniatrics* (University of Tokyo), 13, 163–173.

Garde, Paul (1966a). Fonction des oppositions tonales dans les langues slaves du sud. *Bulletin de la Société de linguistique de Paris*, 61/1, 42–56.

Garde, Paul (1966b). Les propriétés accentuelles des morphèmes serbo-croates. *Scando-Slavica*, 12, 152–172.

Garde, Paul (1967). Principes de description synchronique des faits de l'accent. *Phonologie der Gegenwart*, 32–45. Hermann Böhlaus Nachf., Graz, Vienna, and Cologne.

Garde, Paul (1968). *L'accent*. Presses universitaires de France, Paris.

Garde, Paul (1976). *Histoire de l'accentuation slave* 1–2. Collection de manuels de l'Institut d'études slaves VII, Paris.

Garde, Paul (1981). L'accent du verbe serbo-croate: Essai d'analyse bisynchronique. *Revue des études slaves*, 53/3, 381–402.

*Gårding, Eva (1977). *The Scandinavian Word Accents*. CWK Gleerup, Lund.

*Gårding, Eva (1979). Sentence intonation in Swedish. *Phonetica*, 36, 207–215.

Gauthiot, Robert (1900). Étude sur les intonations serbes. *Mémoires de la Société de linguistique de Paris*, 2, 336–353.

Gopić, Josip (1907). *Prilog poznavanju akcenatske teorije Mažuranićeve s obzirom na komentatorska domišljanja*. Knjižnica "L. K. H. M. S." II, Zagreb.

Gramatička terminologija (1932). Ministrarstvo prosvete Kraljevine Jugoslavije. Srednjoškolska terminologija i nomenklatura knj. I sv. I. Belgrade.

Grubor, Đuro (1909). *Recenzija hrvatske ili srpske gramatike za srednje škole od kr. univerz. prof. dra T. Maretiča*. Zagreb.

Gudkov, V. P. (1969). *Serboxorvatskij jazyk*. Izd. Moskovskogo universiteta, Moscow.

Gvozdanović, Jadranka (1973). Development of the prosodic system in Serbo-Croatian. *Dutch Contributions to the Seventh International Congress of Slavists*, 95–106. Mouton, The Hague.

Gvozdanović, Jadranka (1977). Tonal accents in Scandinavian and Slavic languages. *Phonologica 1976*. (Innsbrucker Beiträge zur Sprachwissenschaft, 19.) Innsbruck.

Gvozdanović, Jadranka (1979a). A perception test of prosodic features in Standard Serbo-Croatian. *Proceedings of the Ninth International Congress of Phonetic Sciences, Copenhagen 6–11 August*, ed. E. Fischer-Jørgensen, J. Rischel, and N. Thorsen, Vol. I, 377. Institute of Phonetics, University of Copenhagen.

Gvozdanović, Jadranka (1979b). Descriptive and explanatory adequacy and co-existing language analyses–Illustrated by examples from Serbo-Croatian phonology. *Sciences of Language* (Tokyo), 7, 181–191.

Gvozdanović, Jadranka (1980). *Tone and Accent in Standard Serbo-Croatian.* (Schriften der Balkankommission, Linguistische Abteilung, 28.) Verlag der Österreichischen Akademie der Wissenschaften, Vienna.

Gvozdanović, Jadranka (1981). On explaining sound change in terms of the system that gives rise to it. *Phonologica 1980.* Akten der Vierten Internationalen Phonologie-Tagung, Wien, 29. Juni–2. Juli 1980, 179–185. (Innsbrucker Beiträge zur Sprachwissenschaft, 36.) Innsbruck.

Gvozdanović, Jadranka (1982). Development of tones in languages with distinctive tonal accents. *Papers from the Third International Conference on Historical Linguistics*, ed. J. Peter Maher, Allan R. Bomhard, and E. F. Konrad Koerner, 39–49. (Current Issues in Linguistic Theory, 13; Amsterdam Studies in the Theory and History of Linguistic Science, 4.) John Benjamins, Amsterdam.

Halle, Morris (1971). Remarks on Slavic accentology. *Linguistic Inquiry*, 2/1, 1–19.

Halle, Morris (1974). Remarks on Slavic accentology. *Slavic Forum, Essays in Linguistics and Literature*, ed. M. S. Flier, 17–41. Mouton, The Hague.

Hamm, Josip (1949). Štokavština Donje Podravine. *Rad JAZU*, 275, 1–70.

Hamm, Josip (1967). *Kratka gramatika hrvatskosrpskog književnog jezika za strance.* Školska knjiga, Zagreb.

Hattori, Shirô (1978). The prosodeme. *Proceedings of the Twelfth International Congress of Linguists, Vienna, August 28–September 2, 1977*, 774–776. Innsbruck.

Hattori, Shirô (1981). On the Serbo-Croatian prosodemes. (In Japanese.) *Sciences of Language* (Tokyo), 8, 157–164.

*Hayata, Teruhiro (1973). Accent in Old Kyoto and some modern Japanese dialects. *Sciences of Language* (Tokyo), 4, 139–180.

Hodge, Carleton T. (1946). Serbo-Croatian phonemes. *Language*, 22, 112–120.

Hodge, Carleton T. (1958). Serbo-Croatian stress and pitch. *General Linguistics*, 3/2, 43–54.

Hodge, Carleton T. (1965). Review of Lehiste and Ivić 1963. *Language*, 41, 534–537.

Hodge, Carleton T., and Janko Janković (1965). *Serbo-Croatian Basic Course.* Vol. 1. Department of State, Foreign Service Institute, Washington, D.C.

Horálek, K. (1961) Zum gegenwärtigen Stand der slavischen Akzentologie. *Zeitschrift für slavische Philologie*, 29, 357–379.

*House, A. S. (1959). A note on optimal vocal frequency. *Journal of Speech and Hearing Research*, 2, 55–60.

Hraste, Mate (1956). Bibliografija radova iz dijalektologije, antroponimije, toponimije i hidronimije na području hrvatskoga ili srpskoga jezika. *Hrvatski dijalektološki zbornik* (Zagreb), 1, 387–479.

Hraste, Mate (1957). O kanovačkom akcentu u Hrvatskoj. *Filologija*, 1, 59–75.

* Hyman, Larry M. (1978). Tone and/or accent. *Elements of Tone, Stress, and Intonation*, ed. Donna Jo Napoli, 1–20. Georgetown University Press, Washington, D.C.

I(lijć) J. (1860). *Srpska pismenica*. Novi Sad.

Isačenko, Alexander V. (1939). Zur phonologischen Deutung der Akzentverschiebung in den slavischen Sprachen. *TCLP*, 8, 173–183.

Isačenko, Alexander V., and Hans-Joachim Schädlich (1963). Erzeugung künstlicher deutscher Satzintonationen mit zwei kontrastierenden Tonstufen. *Monatsberichte der Deutschen Akademie der Wissenschaften zu Berlin*, 5, 365–372.

Ivcovitch, Miloche (= Ivković, Miloš) (1912). Contribution à l'étude des intonations serbes. *Revue de phonétique*, 2, 201–212.

Ivić, Pavle (1949–50). O govorima Banata. *JF*, 18, 141–156.

Ivić, Pavle (1958). *Die serbokroatischen Dialekte* I. Mouton, The Hague.

Ivić, Pavle (1959a). Die Hierarchie der prosodischen Phänomene im serbokroatischen Sprachraum. *Phonetica*, 3, 23–39.

Ivić, Pavle (1959b). Review of Hraste 1956. *ZFL*, 2, 183–198.

Ivić, Pavle (1960). *Studija o srpskohrvatskim akcentima i intonaciji* od dr Redžinalda de Breja. *GlSANU*, 12/1, 42–43.

Ivić, Pavle (1961). The functional yield of prosodic features in the patterns of Serbocroatian dialects. *Word*, 17, 293–308.

Ivić, Pavle (1961–62). Broj prozodijskih mogućnosti u reči kao karakteristika fonoloških sistema slovenskih jezika. *JF*, 25, 75–113.

Ivic, Pavle (1965a). Prozodijski sistem savremenog srpskohrvatskog standardnog jezika. *Symbolae linguisticae in honorem Georgii Kuryłowicz*, 136–144. Wrocław, Warsaw, and Cracow.

Ivić, Pavle (1965b). Roman Jakobson and the growth of phonology. *Linguistics*, 18, 35–78.

Ivić, Pavle (1966). O Vukovom Rječniku iz 1818. Pogovor. In Karadžić (1818) (reprint 1966) 17–188.

Ivić, Pavle (1967a). Diskusioni metodi Đorđa Kostića. *Delo*, 13, 755–761.

Ivić, Pavle (1967b). Srpskohrvatski akcenti i istina. *Delo*, 13, 223–233.

Ivić, Pavle (1970a). Ogled percepcije srpskohrvatskih akcenata pri obratnoj reprodukciji magnetofonskog snimka. *Prace filologiczne*, 20, 95–104.

Ivić, Pavle (1970b). Prosodic possibilities in phonology and morphology. *Studies in General and Oriental Linguistics Presented to Shirô Hattori on the Occasion of His Sixtieth Birthday*, ed. Roman Jakobson and Shigeo Kawamoto, 281–301. TEC, Tokyo.

Ivić, Pavle (1973). The place of prosodic phenomena in language structure. *Sciences of Language* (Tokyo), 4, 103–138.

Ivić, Pavle (1974–75). Die prosodischen Typen in den serbokroatischen Dialekten. *Die Welt der Slaven*, 19–20, 199–209.

Ivić, Pavle (1975). O stanju fonetskog i fonološkog ispitivanja srpskohrvatskog jezika. *Vŭprosi na strukturata na sŭvremennija bŭlgarski ezik*, 305–319. Bŭlgarskata akademija na naukite, Sofia.

Ivić, Pavle (1976a). Serbocroatian accentuation: Facts and interpretation. *Slavic Linguistics and Language Teaching*, ed. Thomas F. Magner, 34–43. Slavica Publishers, Cambridge, Mass.

Ivić, Pavle (1976b). Dicussion of Simić 1976. *NSSVD*, 5, 754–755.

Ivić, Pavle (1976c). Discussion of Đ. Živanović 1976. *NSSVD*, 5, 758–759.

Ivić, Pavle (1977). Discussion of Simić 1977. *NSSVD*, 6, 490–492.

Ivić, Pavle (1978). Beleške o biogračićkom govoru. *Srpski dijalektološki zbornik* (Belgrade), 24, 131–176.

Ivić, Pavle, ed. (1981). *Fonološki opisi srpskohrvatskih/hrvatskosrpskih, slovenačkih i makedonskih govora obuhvaćenih Opšteslovenskim lingvističkim atlasom*. (Odjeljenje društvenih nauka 9.) Akademija nauka i umjetnosti Bosne i Hercegovine, Posebna izdanja LV, Sarajevo.

Ivić, Pavle, and Ilse Lehiste (1963, 1965, 1967, 1969, 1970, 1972). Prilozi ispitivanju fonetske i fonološke prirode akcenata u savremenom srpskohrvatskom [književnom] jeziku. I: *ZFL*, 6, 31–71. II: *ZFL*, 8, 75–117. III: *ZFL*, 10, 55–93. IV: *ZFL*, 12, 115–165. V: *ZFL*, 13/2, 225–246. VI: *ZFL*, 15/1, 95–137.

Ivić, Pavle, and Ilse Lehiste (1979). Akustički opis akcenata u jednom kajkavskom govoru. *ZFL*, 22/1, 179–192.

Ivković, Miloš (1911). *Srpska gramatika za prvi razred srednjih škola*. Geca Kon, Belgrade.

Ivšić, Stjepan (1911). Prilog za slavenski akcenat. *Rad JAZU*, 187, 133–208.

Ivšić, Stjepan (1912). Akcenat u gramatici Igńata Alojzije Brlića. *Rad JAZU*, 194, 61–155.

Ivšić, Stjepan (1913a, 1913b). Današńi posavski govor. *Rad JAZU*, 196, 124–254; 197, 9–138.

Ivšić, Stjepan (1936). Jezik Hrvata kajkavaca. *Ljetopis JAZU*, 48, 47–88.

Ivšić, Stjepan (1970). *Slavenska poredbena gramatika*. Školska knjiga, Zagreb.

Jacobsen, Per (1964). Die Bedeutung der Satzintonation für die serbokroatischen Worttöne. *Scando-Slavica*, 10, 210–231.

Jacobsen, Per (1967). The word tones of Serbo-Croatian: An instrumental study. *ARIPUC*, 2, 90–108.

Jacobsen, Per (1969a). De serbokroatiske ordtoner: En instrumental undersøgelse. *Extracta*, 2, 190–195.

Jacobsen, Per (1969b, 1973a). Falling word tones in Serbo-Croatian. *ARIPUC*, 4, 81–88; 7, 265–268.

Jacobsen, Per (1973b). Review of Magner and Matejka 1971. *Kritikon Literarum*, 2, 348–349.

Jacobsen, Per (1977). Akcenat i intonacija u srpskohrvatskom jeziku. *NSSVD*, 6, 47–52.

Jacobsson, G. (1972). The prosodic pattern in isolated words in a Slavic and a non-Slavic language: Comparison of prosodic possibilities in Serbo-Croatian and Swedish Standard languages. *The Slavic Word*, ed. Dean S. Worth, 388–403. Proceedings of the International Slavistic Colloquium at UCLA, Sept. 11–16, 1970. Mouton, The Hague.

Jagić, Vatroslav (1864a). *Gramatika jezika hèrvatskoga osnovana na starobugarskoj slověnštini. Dio pèrvi: Glasovi.* Zagreb.

(Jagić, Vatroslav) (1864b). Opazka uredničtva. *Književnik*, 1, 197–198.

Jagić, Vatroslav (1870). Paralele k hrvatsko-srpskomu naglasivanju. *Rad JAZU*, 13, 1–16.

Jagić, Vatroslav (1930). *Spomeni mojega života* I. Srpska kraljevska akademija, Belgrade.

Jakobson, Roman (1931a). Die Betonung und ihre Rolle in Wort- und Syntagmaphonologie. *TCLP*, 4, 164–182. (Reprinted in Jakobson 1971.)

Jakobson, Roman (1931b). *K xarakteristike evrazijskogo jazykovogo sojuza.* Paris.

Jakobson, Roman (1937). Über die Beschaffenheit der prosodischen Gegensätze. *Mélanges de linguistique et de philologie offerts à Jacq. van Ginneken*, 25–33. Paris. (Reprinted in Jakobson 1971.)

Jakobson, Roman (1949). On the identification of phonemic entities. *Travaux du Cercle linguistique de Copenhague*, 5, 205–213. (Reprinted in Jakobson 1971.)

Jakobson, Roman (1963). Opyt fonologičeskogo podxoda k istoričeskim voprosam slavjanskoj akcentologii. Pozdnij period slavjanskoj jazykovoj praistorii. *American Contributions to the Fifth International Congress of Slavists*, Sofia 1963, 153–176. Mouton, The Hague. (Reprinted in Jakobson 1971.)

Jakobson, Roman (1965). Information and redundancy in the Common Slavic prosodic pattern. *Symbolae linguisticae in honorem Georgii Kuryłowicz*, 145–151. Wrocław, Warsaw, and Cracow. (Reprinted in Jakobson 1971.)

Jakobson, Roman (1971). *Selected Writings I. Phonological Studies.* Second, expanded edition. Mouton, The Hague.

*Jakobson, Roman, and Morris Halle (1956). *Fundamentals of Language.* Mouton, The Hague.

Jakšić, Grgur (1891). Nešto o srpskim akcentima. *Prosvetni glasnik*, 12, 123–128, 180–185, 247–247, 310–315.

Jerković, Jovan (1966). Glasovna struktura jednosložne reči u srpskohrvatskom književnom jeziku–prozodijske karakteristike. *Prilozi proučavanju jezika*, 2, 55–76.

Jonke, Ljudevit (1964). *Književni jezik u teoriji i praksi*. Znanje, Zagreb.

Jonke, Ljudevit, Ema Leskovar, and Krunoslav Pranjić (1962). *Audiovizuelni tečaj hrvatskosrpskog jezika*. Zagreb.

Junković, Zvonimir (1968). La fonction contrastive et l'accentuation du serbocroate. *La linguistique*, 2, 49–60.

Junković, Zvonimir (1969–70). Napomene o naglasku. *Jezik*, 17, 1–10.

Junković, Zvonimir (1970). Naglasak na proklitici. *Jezik*, 18, 4–14.

Junković, Zvonimir (1978). Šime Starčević i fonološki opis novoštokavskih naglasaka. *Jezik*, 25, 80–85.

Junković, Zvonimir (1982). Dioba kajkavskih govora: Porodice, tipovi i savezi. *Hrvatski dijalektološki zbornik* (Zagreb), 6, 191–216.

Kalogjera, D. (1973). Review of Magner and Matejka 1971. *Studia Romanica et Anglica Zagrabiensia*, 33/36, 888–890.

(Karadžić), Vuk Stefanović (1814). *Pismenica serbskoga jezika*. Vienna. (Reprinted in Karadžić 1894.)

(Karadžić), Vuk Stefanović (1818). *Srpski rječnik istolkovan njemačkim i latinskim riječma*. Vienna (Beč).

(Karadžić, Vuk Stefanović) (1824). *Wuk's Stephanowitsch kleine Serbische Grammatik verdeutscht und mit einer Vorrede von Jacob Grimm*. Leipzig and Berlin.

Karadžić, Vuk Stefanović (1833). Predgovor izdateljev. In Milovanov 1833, pp. B–y. (Reprinted in Karadžić 1895.)

Karadžić, Vuk Stefanović (1836). *Narodne srpske poslovice*. Cetinje. (The relevant *Predgovor* is reprinted in Karadžić 1896.)

Karadžić, Vuk Stefanović (1852). *Srpski rječnik istumačen njemačkijem i latinskijem riječima*. Vienna (Beč).

Karadžić, Vuk Stefanović (1858). Pismo Jovanu Steriji Popoviću o srpskoj prosodiji. *Slavische Bibliothek* (Vienna), 2, 232–236. (Reprinted in Karadžić 1896.)

Karadžić, Vuk Stefanović (1894, 1895, 1896). *Skupljeni gramatički i polemički spisi* I, II, III. Državno izdanje, Belgrade.

Kašić, Jovan, and Jovan Jerković (1976). *Srpskohrvatski/hrvatskosrpski jezik. Udžbenik za I razred srednje škole*. Drugo izdanje. Pokrajinski zavod za izdavanje udžbenika, Novi Sad.

Katić, Frano (1915). *Zašto i kako se mijenjaju akcenti u deklinaciji imenica*. Kralj. zemaljska tiskara, Zagreb.

Knežević, Anton (1970). *Homophone und Homogramme in der Schriftsprache der Kroaten und Serben.* (Veröffenlichungen des Slavisch-Baltischen Seminars der Westfälischen Wilhelms-Universität, Münster, Nr. 11.) Otto Hain, Maisenheim am Glan.

Kolarič, Rudolf (1975). Review of Magner and Matejka 1971. *Zeitschrift für Dialektologie und Linguistik*, 42, 223–226.

Kolarović, Emanuil (1827). Nekoliko predloženija sverh azbuke serbskog jezika. *Serbske lětopisi*, 9, 99–141.

Kostić, Đorđe (1937). Vuk i problemi akcenta. *Naša stvarnost*, fasc. 11–12, 5–17.

Kostić, Đorđe (1938–39). Principi Vukove pravopisne reforme. *Glasnik Jugoslovenskog profesorskog društva*, 18, 350–361.

Kostić, Đorđe (1949–50). O jačini naglaska dvosložnih reči pod (̏) i (̀) akcentom. *JF*, 18, 123–131.

Kostić, Đorđe (1950a). Akcenat i rečenička intonacija. *GlSAN*, 2, 316–317.

Kostić, Đorđe (1950b). Intenzitet izgovorenih glasova. *GlSAN*, 2, 317–318.

Kostić, Đorđe (1950c). O jačini naglaska dvosložnih reči. *GlSAN*, 2, 135–136.

Kostić, Đorđe (1951a). O karakteru intenziteta izgovorenih glasova. *GlSAN*, 3, 114–116.

Kostić, Đorđe (1951b). Varijabilnost intenziteta (̂) i (́) akcenta. *GlSAN*, 3, 278–280.

Kostić, Đorđe (1952a). Dejstvo glasovnog konteksta na intenzitet akcenta. *GlSAN*, 4, 114–115.

Kostić, Đorđe (1952b). Fonološke osobine naših akcenata ispred ploziva. *GlSAN*, 4, 328–330.

Kostić, Đorđe (1952c). Uloga zvučnosti u određivanju akcenatskog intenziteta. *GlSAN*, 4, 326–328.

Kostić, Đorđe (1953). Varijaciono polje intenziteta (̏) i (̀) akcenta. *GlSAN*, 5, 139–140.

Kostić, Đorđe (1966). Savremeni problemi jezika. Proučavanje srpskohrvatskih akcenata. *Delo*, 12, 665–677, 834–849, 932–951, 1035–1052.

Kostić, Đorđe (1967). Srpskohrvatski akcenti i istina. *Delo*, 13, 329–336.

Kostić, Đorđe, and Ljubomir Mihailović (1952). Fiziološki prosek trajanja izgovorenih glasova. *GlSAN*, 4, 334.

Kostić, Đorđe, and Pavle Stefanović (1950). Elementi rečeničke intonacije. *GlSAN*, 2, 318–321.

Kostić, Đorđe, and Pavle Stefanović (1951). Intonacione mogućnosti minimalnog glasovnog konteksta. *GlSAN*, 3, 280–281.

Kovačević, Ljubomir (1878–79). Review of Masing 1876. *AfslPh*, 3, 685–696.

Kravar, Miroslav (1963). O logičkom akcentu riječi u srpskohrvatskom. *Zbornik u čast Stjepana Ivšića*, 209–218. Zagreb.

Kravar, Miroslav (1968a). Jedan drugi slučaj logičkog akcenta riječi. *RFFZ*, 7, 41–45.

Kravar, Miroslav (1968b). Problematika naše gradske akcentuacije. *Zadarska revija*, 17/3, 177–190.

Kravar, Miroslav (1974). O grafici književnog akcenta. *Jezik*, 22, 39–51.

Kravar, Miroslav (1975a). Die logische Wortbetonung im Serbokroatischen. *Festschrift für A. Rammelmeyer*, 397–404. Munich.

Kravar, Miroslav (1975b). Review of Magner and Matejka 1971. *Zeitschrift für slavische Philologie*, 38, 378–384.

Kravar, Miroslav (1982–83). Uz recidiv sumnje u naš četvoroakcenatski sistem. *Jezik*, 30/1, 19–25; 30/2, 40–47.

Kuhač, Fr. Š. (1908). Osobine narodne glazbe, naročito hrvatske. *Rad JAZU*, 174, 117–236.

Kul'bakin, S. M. (1915). *Serbskij jazyk. l. Fonetika i morfologija*. Xar'kov.

Kušar, Marcel (1884). *Povijest razvitka našega jezika hrvackoga ili srpskoga od najdavnijih vremena do danas* (preštampano iz Slovinca). Dubrovnik.

Kuznecov, P. S. (1948). O fonologičeskoj sisteme serbo-xorvatskogo jazyka. *Izvestija Otdelenija literatury i jazyka AN SSSR*, 7/2, 125–140.

Kvačadze, V. V. (1967). Ob udarenijax v serbskoxorvatskom jazyke. *Trudy Tbilis. gosud. pedagog. inst.*, 20, 195–202.

Lalević, M. S. (1938). *Gramatika srpskohrvatskog jezika za I razred srednjih i stručnih škola*. III, nepromenjeno izdanje. Belgrade.

Leed, Richard L. (1968). The intonation of yes-no questions in Serbo-Croatian. *SEEJ*, 12, 330–336.

Lehfeldt, W. (1970). Zur Hierarchie der Akzentalternationen im Serbokroatischen. *Folia linguistica*, 4, 299–315.

Lehfeldt, W., and B. Finka (1969a). Das Akzentverhalten im Serbokroatischen dargestellt an den Substantiven. *Die Welt der Slaven*, 14/1, 26–46.

Lehfeldt, W., and B. Finka (1969b). Das Akzentverhalten im Serbokroatischen dargestellt an den Verben. *Die Welt der Slaven*, 14/2, 174–192.

Lehiste, Ilse (1961). Some acoustic correlates of accent in Serbo-Croatian. *Phonetica*, 7, 114–147.

Lehiste, Ilse (1965). Juncture. *Proceedings of the Fifth International Congress of Phonetic Sciences, Münster 1964*, 172–200. S. Karger, Basel and New York.

Lehiste, Ilse (1969). Review of Rehder 1968a. *SEEJ*, 13, 406–410.

* Lehiste, Ilse (1970) *Suprasegmentals*. MIT Press, Cambridge, Mass.

*Lehiste, Ilse (1972). Manner of articulation, parallel processing, and the perception of duration. *University of Essex Occasional Papers*, 13, 1–24.

Lehiste, Ilse (1976). Review of Purcell 1973. *Phonetica*, 33, 142–145.

*Lehiste, Ilse (1980). Phonetic manifestation of syntactic structure in English. *Annual Bulletin, Research Institute of Logopedics and Phoniatrics* (University of Tokyo), 14, 1–27.

Lehiste, Ilse, and Pavle Ivić (1963). *Accent in Serbocroatian: An Experimental Study*. (Michigan Slavic Materials, 4.) Dept. of Slavic Languages and Literatures, University of Michigan, Ann Arbor.

Lehiste, Ilse, and Pavle Ivić (1967). Some problems concerning the syllable in Serbocroatian. *Glossa*, 1/2, 126–136.

Lehiste, Ilse, and Pavle Ivić (1972). Experiments with synthesized Serbocroatian tones. *Phonetica*, 26, 1–15.

Lehiste, Ilse, and Pavle Ivić (1973a). Akustički opis akcenatskog sistema jednog čakavskog govora. *NSSVD*, 3, 159–170.

Lehiste, Ilse, and Pavle Ivić (1973b). Interaction between tone and quantity in Serbocroatian. *Phonetica*, 28, 182–190.

Lehiste, Ilse, and Pavle Ivić (1977). Fonetska analiza jedne slavonske akcentuacije. *NSSVD*, 6, 67–84.

Lehiste, Ilse, and Pavle Ivić (1978). Interrelationship between word tone and sentence intonation in Serbocroatian. *Elements of Tone, Stress, and Intonation*, ed. Donna Jo Napoli, 100–128. Georgetown University Press, Washington, D.C.

Lehiste, Ilse, and Pavle Ivić (1980). The intonation of yes-and-no questions: A new Balkanism? *Balkanistica*, 6, 45–53.

Lehiste, Ilse, and Pavle Ivić (1982). The phonetic nature of the Neo-Štokavian accent shift in Serbo-Croatian. *Papers from the Third International Conference on Historical Linguistics*, ed. J. Peter Maher, Allan R. Bomhard, and E. F. Konrad Koerner, 197–206. (Current Issues in Linguistic Theory, 13; Amsterdam Studies in the Theory and History of Linguistic Science, 4.) John Benjamins, Amsterdam.

*Lehiste, Ilse, Joseph P. Olive, and Lynn A. Streeter (1976). Role of duration in disambiguating syntactically ambiguous sentences. *Journal of the Acoustical Society of America*, 60, 1199–1202.

*Lehiste, Ilse, and G. E. Peterson (1959). Vowel amplitude and phonemic stress in American English. *Journal of the Acoustical Society of America*, 31, 426–435.

*Lehiste, Ilse, and G. E. Peterson (1961). Some basic considerations in the analysis of intonation. *Journal of the Acoustical Society of America*, 33, 419–425.

Leskien, August (1899). Untersuchungen über die Betonungs- und Quantitätsverhältnisse in den slavischen Sprachen. *AfslPh*, 21, 321–398.

Leskien, August (1914). *Grammatik der serbokroatischen Sprache, I.* Carl Winter, Heidelberg.

Liewehr, Ferdinand (1927). *Zur Chronologie des serbokroatischen Akzentes.* Prague.

Lončarić, Mijo (1977). Jagnjedovački govor (s osvrtom na pitanje kajkavskoga podravskog dijalekta). *Hrvatski dijalektološki zbornik* (Zagreb), 4, 179–262.

Lord, Albert Bates (1958). *Beginning Serbocroatian.* Mouton, The Hague.

Lüdtke, Helmut (1959). Das prosodische System des Urslavischen und seine Weiterentwicklung im Serbokroatischen. *Phonetica*, Supplem. to Vol. 4, 125–156.

Lukić, J. (1923). *Glasovi srpskoga jezika.* Geca Kon, Belgrade.

Lunt, Horace (1963). On the study of Slavic accentuation. *Word*, 19, 82–99.

*Maack, A. (1957). Probleme der prosodischen Strukturanalyse. *Zeitchrift für Slawistik*, 2, 394–405.

McCawley, James. D. (1963). Stress and pitch in the Serbo-Croatian verb. *Quarterly Progress Report*, Research Laboratory of Electronics (Cambridge, Mass.), No. 70, 282–290.

*McCawley, James D. (1968). *The Phonological Component of Japanese.* Mouton, The Hague.

Magner, Thomas F. (1966). *A Zagreb Kajkavian Dialect.* (The Pennsylvania University Studies, 18.) Pennsylvania State University, University Park, Pa.

Magner, Thomas F. (1968). Post-Vukovian accentual norms in modern Serbo-Croatian. *American Contributions to the Sixth International Congress of Slavists*, Vol. I, Linguistic Contributions, 227–246. Mouton, The Hague.

Magner, Thomas F. (1981). The emperor's new clothes; or A modest peek at the Serbo-Croatian accentual system. *General Linguistics*, 21/4, 248–258.

Magner, Thomas F., and Ladislav Matejka (1971). *Word Accent in Modern Serbo-Croatian.* Pennsylvania University Press, University Park, Pa.

Mahnken, Irmgard (1962a). *Die Struktur der Zeitgestalt des Redegebildes.* (Opera Slavica, 2.) Vandenhoeck & Ruprecht, Göttingen.

Mahnken, Irmgard (1962b). *Redegebilde oder Zufallsstreuung?* Otto Sagner, Munich.

Mahnken, Irmgard (1964). *Studien zur serbokroatischen Satzmelodie.* (Opera Slavica, 3/2.) Vandenhoeck & Ruprecht, Göttingen.

Mahnken Irmgard (1965). Discussion of Peco 1965b. *Proceedings of the Fifth International Congress of Phonetic Sciences, Münster 1964*, 456–457. S. Karger, Basel and New York.

Mahnken, Irmgard (1967). Zur Frage der binären Oppositionen im Bereich prosodischer Erscheinungen. *Folia Linguistica*, 1, 59–79.

Mahnken, Irmgard, and Josip Matešić (1970). Akzentoppositionen in den serbokroatischen Dialekten: Zum 5-Akzentsystem der slavonischen Mundarten des

Štokavischen. *Proceedings of the Sixth International Congress of Phonetic Sciences, Prague 1967*, 593–596. Prague.

Maretić, T. (1879). *Iz Eneide P. Vergilija Marona I i II pjev. preveo i prilog o akcentu napisao T. Maretić*, 44–55. Izvješće o kralj. velikoj gimnaziji u Zagrebu koncem školske godine 1878/9. Zagreb.

Maretić, T. (1883). O njekim pojavima kvantitete i akcenta u jeziku hrvatskom ili srpskom. *Rad JAZU*, 67, 1–69.

Maretić, T. (1901). *Gramatika hrvatskoga jezika za niže razrede srednjih škola.* Drugo izdanje. Zagreb.

Maretić, T. (1928). *Hrvatska ili srpska gramatika za srednje škole.* Deseto izdanje. Belgrade.

Maretić, T. (1899, 1931). *Gramatika i stilistika hrvatskoga ili srpskoga književnog jezika.* 1 Knjižara L. Hartmana, Zagreb. 2 Obnova, Zagreb.

Marković, Svetozar (1972). O akcentu nekih kategorija riječi koji je u suprutnosti sa akcenatskim sistemom srpskohrvatskog standardnog jezika. *Zbornik radova posvećenih uspomeni Salke Nazečića*, 381–386. Filozofski fakultet, Sarajevo.

Masing, Leonhard (1876). *Die Hauptformen des serbisch-chorwatischen Accents.* Mémoires de I'Académie Impériale des Sciences de St. -Pétersbourg, VIIe série, Tome XXIII, No. 5. St. Petersburg.

Matejka, Ladislav (1967). Generative and recognitory aspects in phonology. *Phonologie der Gegenwart*, 242–253. Vienna, Graz, and Cologne.

Matejka, Ladislav (1973). O kvantitetu kao sustavu u standardnom srpskohrvatskom jeziku. *Slavica Lundensia*, 1, 25–33.

Matešić, Josip (1970). *Der Wortakzent in der serbokroatischen Schriftsprache.* Carl Winter, Heidelberg.

Mažuranić, Antun (1859). *Slovnica hèrvatska.* Zagreb.

Mažuranić, Antun (1860). O važnosti akcenta za historiju Slavjanah. *Programm des K. K. Gymnasiums zu Agram am Schlusse des Schuljahres 1860*, 3–7. Zagreb.

Meillet, A., and A. Vaillant (1924). *Grammaire de la langue serbo-croate.* Paris.

Micklesen, Lew R. (1981). Review of Gvozdanović 1980. *Word*, 32/3, 235–237.

Mihailović, Ljubomir (1952a). Akcenat i trajanje vokala na početku reči ispred ploziva. *GlSAN*, 4, 116–117.

Mihailović, Ljubomir (1952b). Mesto obrazovanja ploziva i trajanje vokala na početku reči ispred ploziva. *GlSAN*, 4, 331–332.

Mihailović, Ljubomir (1952c). Trajanje reči i trajanje vokala na početku reči ispred ploziva. *GlSAN*, 4, 337–338.

Mihailović, Ljubomir (1953). Uticaj artikulacionog mesta vokala na njihovo trajanje ispred ploziva. *GlSAN*, 5, 142–143.

Mihailović, Ljubomir (1956). Uticaj broja i rasporeda konsonanatu u daljem kontekstu na trajanje inicijalnog vokala. *Godišnjak Filozofskog fakulteta u Novom Sadu*, 1, 131–173.

Mihailović, Ljubomir (1957). Uticaj fonetske strukture reči na trajanje njenih delova. *Godišnjak Filozofskog fakulteta u Novom Sadu*, 2, 185–198.

Mihailović, Ljubomir (1975). The phonetic analysis of the accent-intonation complex. *Abstracts of Papers, Eighth International Congress of Phonetic Sciences*, Leeds 1975, No. 200.

Miklosich, Franz (= Fran Miklošič) (1852). *Vergleichende Grammatik der slavischen Sprachen. Erster Band. Lautlehre*. Vienna.

Miklosich, Franz (= Fran Miklošič) (1879). *Vergleichende Grammatik der slavischen Sprachen. Erster Band. Lautlehre*. 2. Ausgabe. Vienna.

Milaković, Dimitrije (1838). *Srbska gramatika sastavljena za crno-gorsku mladež*. Čast prva. Crna Gora.

Milas, M. (1898). Pravi akcenti i fiziologija njihova u hrvatskom ili srpskom jeziku. *Školski vjesnik* (Sarajevo), 5, 511–534.

Miletić, Branko (1926). *O srbo-chrvatských intonacích v nářečí štokavském*. (Facultas Philosophica Universitatis Carolinae, Prace z vědeckých ústavů, 14.) Prague.

Miletić, Branko (1928–29). Povodom Egblumovih radova iz srpske fonetike i slovenske akcentologije. *JF*, 8, 65–82.

Miletić, Branko (1931a). Über vermeintliche Spuren urslavischer Intonationen im Serbokroatischen und Čechischen. *Časopis pro moderní filologii*, 17, 89–105.

Miletić, Branko (1931b). Review of Ekblom 1930. *JF*, 10, 237–244.

Miletić, Branko (1935). O fiziološkom kvantitetu u srpskohrvatskom. *Spomenica desetogodišnjice rada Više pedagoške škole u Beogradu 1924–1934*, 54–79. Belgrade.

Miletić, Branko (1937). Uticaj rečeničke melodije na intonaciju reči. *Zbornik u čast A. Belića*, 219–223. Belgrade.

Miletić, Branko (1939). Über den Ursprung der sekundären Intonationen im Serbokroatischen. *Proceedings of the Third International Congress of Phonetic Sciences, Ghent 1939*, 402–407.

Miletić, Branko (1952). *Osnovi fonetike srpskog jezika*. Znanje, Belgrade.

Miletić, Igor (1974). Markedness in Serbocroatian word accent. *The First LACUS Forum*, ed. Adam Makkai and Valerie Becker Makkai, 235–245. Hornbeam Press, Columbia, S.C.

Milovanov, Luka (1833). *Opit nastavljenja k srbskoj sličnorečnosti i slogomjerju ili prosodii*. Vienna (Beč). (Reprinted in Karadžić 1895.)

Moskatelo, Kuzma (1954). Akcentuacija tuđica na *-or* u hrvatskom jeziku. *Jezik*, 3/2, 51–56.

Moskovlevič (= Moskovljević), Miloš (1913). Review of Bogorodickij 1912. *Izvestija Otdelenija russkogo jazyka i slovesnosti*, 18/3, 384–391.

Moskovljević, Miloš (1921). Nekoliko reči o beogradskom govoru. *Belićev zbornik*, Belgrade.

Moskovljević, Miloš (1957). Neke nove akcenatske pojave u našem književnom izgovoru. *Pitanja savremenog književnog jezika*, 5, 80–85.

Muljačić, Žarko (1964). Review of Jakobson 1971 (first ed., 1962). *Živi jezici*, 6, 79–90.

Musulin, Stjepan (1929). *Gramatika hrvatskoga ili srpskoga jezika za II. razred srednjih i njima sličnih škola*. Zagreb.

Musulin, Stjepan (1935). *Gramatika srpskohrvatskoga jezika za drugi razred srednjih i njima sličnih škola*. Treće izdanje. Zagreb.

Muškatirović, Jovan (1806). *Prične*. Budapest.

Muža, M. E. (no date, 1888?). *Die Kunst die serbo-kroatische Sprache zu erlernen*. Hartleben, Vienna.

Nahtigal, Rajko (1952). *Slovanski jeziki*. Druga, popravljena i pomnožena izdaja. Ljubljana.

Nakađima, Jumi (1981). O percepciji srpskohrvatskih akcenata na osnovu japanskog jezičkog osećanja. *ZFL*, 24/1, 151–163.

Nakić, Anuška (1982). Kontrastivna analiza nukleuskog segmenta u intonacijskoj jedinici engleskog i hrvatskog ili srpskog jezika. *Godišnjak Saveza Društava za primijenjenu lingvistiku Jugoslavije* VI, 23–42. Zagreb.

Nakić, Anuška, and Wayles E. Browne (1975). The intonation of questions in Serbo-Croatian and English. *Kontrastivna analiza engleskog i hrvatskog ili srpskog jezika*, 172–179. Institut za lingvistiku, Zagreb.

Naylor, K. E., Jr. (1969). Morphophonemics of the Serbocroatian declension. *International Journal of Slavic Linguistics and Poetics*, 12, 79–89.

Naylor, K. E., Jr. (1970). On the morphophonemic hierarchy of Slavic accentual systems. *Actes du Xe Congrès international des linguistes*, IV, 181–184. Bucharest.

Nedović, Obrad (1960). *Dikcija*. Savremena škola, Belgrade.

Neweklowsky, Gerhard (1973). Review of Matešić 1970, Knežević 1970, and Magner and Matejka 1971. *Wiener slavistisches Jahrbuch*, 19, 94–104.

Neweklowsky, Gerhard (1976). Die Toneme in einer čakavischen Mundart des Burgenlandes. *Opuscula slavica et linguistica. Festschrift für Alexander Issatschenko*, 269–280. (Universität für Bildungswissenschaften, Klagenfurt, Schriftenreihe Sprachwissenschaft, I.) Klagenfurt.

Neweklowsky, Gerhard (1977a). Discussion of Lehiste and Ivić 1977. *NSSVD*, 6/1, 506.

Neweklowsky, Gerhard (1977b). Discussion of Simić 1977. *NSSVD* 6/1, 506–507.

Neweklowsky, Gerhard (1981a). Akustisch-phonetische Messungen als Entscheidungshilfe für phonologische Interpretation (am Beispiel der serbokroatischen Akzentuation). *Phonologica 1980*, Akten der Vierten Internationalen Phonologie-Tagung, Wien, 29. Juni–2. Juli 1980, 322–328. (Innsbrucker Beiträge zur Sprachwissenschaft, 36.) Innsbruck.

Neweklowsky, Gerhard (1981b). Review of Gvozdanović 1980. *Wiener slawistischer Almanach*, 8, 337–341.

Nikolaeva, T. M. (1971a). Sootnošenie slovesnoj i frazovoj melodiki v serbskom jazyke. *Pamjati akademika Viktora Vladimiroviča Vinogradova, Sbornik statej*, 148–156. University of Moscow.

Nikolaeva, T. M. (1971b). Sootnošenie frazovoj i slovesnoj prosodii (sinxronnoe opisanie). Nekotorye aspekty problemy. *ZFL*, 14/1, 121–139.

Nikolaeva, T. M. (1973). Nekotorye nabljudenija nad sootnošeniem slovesnyx akcentov i frazovoj melodiki v serbskom jazyke. *Strukturno-tipologičeskie issledovanija v oblasti grammatiki slavjanskix jazykov*, 155–196. Moscow.

Nikolaeva, T. M. (1974). Review of Magner and Matejka 1971. *Voprosy jazykoznanija*, fasc. 5, 137–140.

Nikolaeva, T. M. (1975). O vključenii frazovoj intonacii v kompleks sopostavljaemyx slavjanskix faktov. *Obščeslavjanskij lingvističeskij atlas. Materialy i issledovanija* 1973, 152–176. Izd. Nauka, Moscow.

Nikolaeva, T. M. (1977). *Frazovaja intonacija slavjanskix jazykov*. Izd. Nauka, Moscow.

Nikolaeva, T. M. (1981). Fakty slavjanskoj frazovoj intonacii v svete areal'no-tipologičeskogo podxoda. *International Journal of Slavic Linguistics and Poetics*, 24, 23–47.

Nikolić, Berislav (1962). Akcenatski vid proklize i enklize u srpskohrvatskom jeziku. *NJ*, n.s. 12/3–6, 156–178.

Nikolić, Sv. (1955). Akcenti i dužine kao diferencijalni momenti reči u našem savremenom književnom jeziku. *Književnost i jezik u školi*, 2, 50–59.

Novaković, Stojan (1873). Fiziologija glasa i glasovi srpskog jezika. *Glasnik Srpskog učenog društva*, 37, 1–108.

Novaković, Stojan (1879). *Srpska gramatika za niže gimnazije i realke u kneževini Srbiji*. Prvi deo. Nauka o glasovima. Belgrade.

Novaković, Stojan (1884). *Srpska gramatika za niže gimnazije i realke u kraljevini Srbiji*. Prvi deo. Nauka o glasovima. Treće izdanje. Belgrade.

Novakovič, St. (= Stojan Novaković) (1890). *Grammatika serbskago jazyka*. Perevel s serbskago A. Grigorjev. St. Petersburg.

Novaković, Stojan (1894). *Srpska gramatika*. Prvo celokupno izdanje. Belgrade.

Novaković, Stojan (1902). *Srpska gramatika*. Drugo celokupno izdanje. Belgrade.

Pacel, Vinko (1860). *Slovnica jezika Hrvatskoga ili Srbskoga. I. diel. Nauka o prieslovu.* Zagreb.

Pacel, Vinko (1864). Naglas u rieči hrvatskoga jezika. *Književnik*, 1, 108–119, 187–198.

Pavić, Armin (1881). Studije o hrvatskom akcentu. *Rad JAZU*, 59, 1–102.

Pavić, Armin (1885). Đuro Daničić umro 17. studenoga 1882. *Rad JAZU*, 77, 127–202.

Pavlović, Milivoj (1960). *Studija o srpskohrvatskim akcentima i intonaciji* od dr Redžinalda de Breja. *GlSANU*, 12, 41–42.

Pavlović, Milivoj (1966). Intonation des Satzes und Wortakzent. *Die Welt der Slaven*, 380–386.

Peco, Asim (1965a). Ortoepski normativi standardnog ijekavizma. *Književnost i jezik*, 12/3, 27–42.

Peco, Asim (1965b). Valeur phonologique des accents serbocroates. *Proceedings of the Fifth International Congress of Phonetic Sciences, Münster 1964*, 453–456. S. Karger, Basel and New York.

Peco, Asim (1971a). Akcenat reči i akcenat rečenice. *Književnost i jezik*, 18/1, 1–18.

Peco, Asim (1971b). Les accents serbocroates d'après les recherches de la phonétique expérimentale. *Programme du VIIe Congrès international des sciences phonétiques, Résumés*, 140–141. Montreal.

Peco, Asim (1971c). *Osnovi akcentologije srpskohrvatskog jezika.* Naučna knjiga, Belgrade.

Peco, Asim (1971d). Rad na proučavanju srpskohrvatskih akcenata u posleratnom periodu u SR Srbiji. *NSSVD*, 1, 67–73.

Peco, Asim (1972). Priroda neakcentovanih dužina u srpskohrvatskom jeziku. *Zbornik radova posvećenih uspomeni Salke Nazečića*, 387–394. Filozofski fakultet, Sarajevo.

Peco, Asim (1973). Review of Magner and Matejka 1971. *JF*, 29/3–4, 589–594.

Peco, Asim (1975). L'influence de l'intonation sur la nature phonétique des accents dans la langue serbocroate. *Eighth International Congress of Phonetic Sciences, Leeds, Abstracts of Papers*, No. 16.

Peco, Asim (1976). Zum Wesen der Akzente im Serbokroatischen. *Zeitschrift für Slawistik*, 21, 136–144.

Peco, Asim (1981). Daničić kao akcentolog. *Zbornik o Đuri Daničiću*, 227–243. Belgrade and Zagreb.

Peco, Asim, and P. Pravica (1972). O prirodi akcenata srpskohrvatskog jezika na osnovu eksperimentalnih istraživanja. *JF*, 29/1–2, 195–242.

Pešikan, Mitar (1965). *Starocrnogorski srednjokatunski i lješanski govori.* (Srpski dijalektološki zbornik, 15.) Belgrade.

Pešikan, Mitar (1968–69). Review of Magner 1968. *JF*, 27/3–4, 499–506.

Pešikan, Mitar (1977). Discussion of Simić 1977. *NSSVD*, 6/1, 509–510.

*Peterson, G. E., and Ilse Lehiste (1960). Duration of syllable nuclei in English. *Journal of the Acoustical Society of America*, 32, 693–703.

*Peterson, G. E., and N. P. McKinney (1961). The measurement of speech power. *Phonetica*, 7, 65–84.

Peukert, H. (1969). Neuere Arbeiten zur serbokroatistchen Akzentuation, [Review of Rehder 1968, Lehiste and Ivić 1963, Ivić and Lehiste 1963, 1965, 1967, Pollok 1964, and Mahnken 1964.] *Zeitschrift fur Slawistik*, 14/1, 73–76.

Peukert, H. (1972). Review of Matešić 1970. *Zeitschrift für Slawistik*, 17, 137–139.

Pohl, Heinz Dieter (1971). Review of Matešić 1970. *Sprache*, 17/2, 186–187.

Pollok, Karl-Heinz (1957). Zur Geschichte der Erforschung des serbokroatischen Akzentsystems. *Die Welt der Slaven*, 2, 267–292.

Pollok, Karl-Heinz (1964). *Der neuštokavische Akzent und die Struktur der Melodiegestalt der Rede*. (Opera Slavica, 3/1.) Vandenhoeck & Ruprecht, Göttingen.

Pollok, Karl-Heinz (1965). Akzentoppositionen im Serbokroatischen. *Proceedings of the Fifth International Congress of Phonetic Sciences, Münster 1964*, 474–477. S. Karger, Basel and New York.

Popovici, I. (1902). Sur l'accent ̏ en serbocroate. *La parole*, 299–308.

*Potter, Ralph K., George A. Kopp, and Harriet Green Kopp (1966). *Visible Speech*. Dover Publications, New York.

Pudić, Ivan (1960). Univerzalno fonetsko pismo Marijana Šunjića. *Radovi Naučnog društva NR Bosne i Hercegovine*, 13, 191–217. Odjeljenje istorisko-filoloških nauka, Sarajevo.

*Pulgram, Ernst (1959). *Introduction to the Spectrography of Speech*. Mouton, The Hague.

Purcell, Edward (1971). The acoustic differentiation of Serbo-Croatian accents in statements. *Phonetica*, 24, 1–8.

Purcell, Edward (1972). The acoustic differentiation of Serbo-Croatian word-tones in statement environments. *Proceedings of the Seventh International Congress of Phonetic Sciences*, 997–1003. Mouton, The Hague.

Purcell, Edward (1973). *The Realizations of Serbo-Croatian Accents in Sentence Environments: An Acoustic Investigation*. (Hamburger phonetische Beiträge, 8.) Buske Verlag, Hamburg.

Purcell, Edward (1974). A model of word-tone, sentence intonation, and segmental duration in Serbo-Croatian: A preliminary report. *Topics in Slavic Phonology*, ed. D. Koubourlis, 178–202. Slavica Publishers, Cambridge, Mass.

Purcell, Edward (1976). Pitch peak location and the perception of Serbo-Croatian word tone. *Journal of Phonetics*, 4, 265–270.

Purcell, Edward T. (1981). Two parameters in the perception of Serbo-Croatian tone. *Journal of Phonetics*, 9/2, 189–196.

Raić, Jovan (1793). *Sobranie*. Vienna.

Rehder, Peter (1968a). *Beiträge zur Erforschung der serbokroatischen Prosodie. Die linguistische Struktur der Tonverlaufs-Minimalpaare*. (Slavistische Beiträge, 31.) Otto Sagner, Munich.

Rehder, Peter (1968b). Gezielte Destruktion und gezielte Konstruktion. *Slavistische Studien zum VI. Internationalen Slavistenkongress in Prag 1968*, ed. Erwin Koschmieder and Maximilian Braun, 112–120. Munich.

Rešetar, Milan (1897). Neue Ansichten über das Wesen und die Entwickelung der serbokroatischen Accentuation. *AfslPh*, 19, 564–581.

Rešetar, Milan (1898). Review of Šaxmatov 1898. *AfslPh*, 20, 397–405.

Rešetar, Milan (1899). Review of Milas 1898. *AfslPh*, 21, 233–236.

Rešetar, Milan (1900). *Die serbokroatische Betonung südwestlicher Mundarten*. (Kaiserliche Akademie der Wissenschaften, *Schriften der Balkancommission*, Linguistische Abtheilung, I.) Vienna.

Rešetar, Milan (1901). Review of Šajković 1901. *Kolo*, 2/1, 55–58.

Rešetar, Milan (1902). Review of Šajković 1901. *AfslPh*, 24, 251–254.

Rešetar, Milan (1913). Zur Bezeichnung der serbokroatischen Betonung. *AfslPh*, 35, 60–62.

Rešetar, Milan (1916). *Elementar-Grammatik der serbischen (kroatischen) Sprache*. Zagreb.

Rešetar, Milan (1922). *Elementar-Grammatik der kroatischen (serbischen) Sprache*. Zweite durchgesehene Ausgabe. Nakladna knjižara Mirka Breyera, Zagreb.

Ribarić, Josip (1940). Razmještaj južnoslovenskih dijalekata na poluotoku Istri. *Srpski dijalektološki zbornik* (Belgrade), 9, 1–207.

Rončević, N. (1950). Moja predavanja i A. B. Klaić. *Hrvatsko kolo*, 4, 731–740.

Ružić, Žarko (1978). *Osnovi kulture govora*. Pedagoška akademija za obrazovanje vaspitača pedagoških ustanova, Belgrade.

Sadnik, Linda (1971). Review of Matešić 1970. *Anzeiger für slavische Philologie*, 5, 185–187.

Santen, Jadranka (= Gvozdanović, Jadranka) (1972). O fonetičeskoj i fonologičeskoj prirode udarenija v serbskoxorvatskom jazyke. *Sovetskoe slavjanovedenie*, 8/4, 100–105.

Sawicka, Irena (1982). Kontrastivna fonologija srpskohrvatskog i poljskog jezika (II). *ZFL*, 25/1, 7–66.

*Schmitt, A. (1924). *Untersuchungen zur allgemeinen Akzentlehre*. Carl Winter, Heidelberg.

Schooneveld, C. H. van (1959). Serbocroatian conjugation. *International Journal of Slavic Linguistics and Poetics*, 1–2, 55–69.

Sekereš, Stjepan (1966). Govor našičkog kraja. *Hrvatski dijalektološki zbornik* (Zagreb), 2, 209–301.

Sekereš, Stjepan (1973). Razlikovna funkcija naglasaka u hrvatskom književnom jeziku. *Jezik*, 21, 17–27.

Shevelov, George Y. (1964). *A Prehistory of Slavic*. Carl Winter, Heidelberg.

Silić, Josip, and Dragutin Rosandić (1974). *Osnove fonetike i fonologije hrvatskog književnog jezika. Udžbenik za prvi razred srednjih škola*. Zagreb.

Simić, Radoje (1976). O mogućnim uzrocima novoštokavske akcenatske recesije. *NSSVD*, 5, 605–610.

Simić, R., and B. Simić (1981). *Naš jezik i mi*. Belgrade.

Simić, Radoje (1977). Srpskohrvatska ortotonija i slovenski akcent (Sto godina jedne naučne dileme). *NSSVD*, 6, 35–46.

Simić, Radoje (1978). Prozodijski sistem srpskohrvatskog jezika. *Književonst i jezik*, 25/3–4, 307–321.

Simić, Radoje, and Branislav Ostojić (1981). *Osnovi fonologije srpskohrvatskog književnog jezika*. NIO Pobjeda, Titograd.

Simić, Živojin (1883). *Predavanja iz srpskog jezika*. Belgrade.

Simić, Živojin (1922). *Srpska gramatika*. Belgrade.

Skljarenko, V. G. (1972). Review of Lehiste and Ivić 1963. *Issledovanija po serboxorvatskomu jazyku*. Akademija Nauk SSSR, Institut slavjanovedenija i balkanistiki, Moscow.

Sköld, H. (1922). *Zur Chronologie der štokavischen Akzentverschiebung*. (Lunds Universitets Årsskrift, NF 1, 18, 3.) Lund.

Stankiewicz, Edward (1958). Towards a phonemic typology of the Slavic languages. *American Contributions to the Fourth International Congress of Slavicists*, 301–309. Mouton, The Hague.

Stankiewicz, Edward (1959). Review of Ivić 1958. *Word*, 15, 367–376.

Stankiewicz, Edward (1966). Slavic morphophonemics in its typological and diachronic aspects. *Current Trends in Linguistics*, Vol. III: *Theoretical Foundations*. Mouton, The Hague.

Stankiewicz, Edward (1977). Discussion of Simić 1977 (and Ivić 1977). *NSSVD*, 6/1, 513–516.

Starcsevics, Shime (1812). *Novà Ricsôslovica Iliricskà*. Tarst.

Stefanović, Živ. N. (1927). *Gramatika srpsko-hrvatskog jezika za II razred srednjih škola*. Belgrade.

Stefanović, Živ. N. (1936) *Gramatika srpskohrvatskog jezika za prvi razred srednjih škola*. Sedmo popravljeno izdanje. Knjižara Radomira Ćukovića, Belgrade.

Stevanović, Mihailo (1963). Za čuvanje akcenatskog sistema književnog jezika. *NJ*, n.s. 13, 1–10.

Stevanović, Mihailo (1964). *Savremeni srpskohrvatski jezik*. Naučno delo, Belgrade.

Stevanović, Mihailo (1966). *Gramatika srpskohrvatskog jezika za više razrede gimnazije*. Peto izdanje. Cetinje.

Stojanović, Ljubomir (1892). *Srpska gramatika za I razred gimnazije*. Belgrade.

Stojanović, Ljubomir (1898). *Srpska gramatika za prvi razred gimnazije*. Peto izdanje. Belgrade.

Stojanović, Ljubomir (1901). *Srpska gramatika za I razred gimnazije*. Belgrade.

Stojanović, Ljubomir (1920). *Srpska gramatika za I razred gimnazije*. XII izdanje Državne štamparije, Belgrade.

Stojanović, Ljubomir (1924). *Život i rad Vuka Stef. Karadžića*. Belgrade and Zemun.

Stojanović, Ljubomir (1926). *Srpska gramatika za II razred gimnazije*. Sedamnaesto izdanje. Belgrade.

Stojanović, Ljubomir (1936). *Srpskohrvatska gramatika za II razred gimnazije*. Osamnaesto popravljeno izdanje. Belgrade.

Stojanović, Zdravko (1951). Dejstvo akcenta na artikulaciju vokala. *GISAN*, 141.

Storm, Johan (1892). *Englische Philologie*. Zweite... Auflage. I. *Die lebende Sprache. I. Abteilung: Phonetik und Aussprache*. O. R. Reisland, Leipzig.

Šajković, Ivan (1901). *Die Betonung in der Umgangssprache der Gebildeten im Königreich Serbien*. W. Drugulin, Leipzig.

Šaxmatov, A. A. (1888, 1889, 1890a, 1890b). K istorii serbsko-xorvatskix udarenij. *Russkij filologičeskij vestnik*, 19, 157–227; 20, 321–322; 23, 171–218; 24, 1–27.

Šaxmatov, A. A. (1898). *K istorii udarenij v slavjanskix jazykax*. Izvestija Otdelenija russkogo jazyka i slovesnosti Imperatorskoj Akademii Nauk, 3/1, 1–34.

Šivic-Dular, Alenka (1973). Review of Magner and Matejka 1971. *Slavistična revija*, 21, 482–486.

Škrabec, P. Stanislav (1870). O glasu in naglasu našega knjižnega jezika. *Programm des k. k. Gymnasiums zu Rudolfswerth (Novomesto)*, 3–42. Veröffentlicht am Ende des Schuljahres 1870.

Šojat, Antun (1981). Odraz Daničićevih akcenatskih studija u starijoj hrvatskoj akcentologiji. *Zbornik o Daničiću*, 371–379. Belgrade and Zagreb.

Šojat, Antun (1982). Turopoljski govori. *Hrvatski dijalektološki zbornik* (Zagreb), 6, 191–216.

Šrepel, Milivoj (1886). *Akcenat i metar junačkih narodnih pjesama*. Zagreb.

Šuñić (= Šunjić), Marianus (1853). *De ratione depingendi rite quaslibet voces articulatas, seu de vera Orthographia cum necessariis elementis Alphabeti universalis*. Vienna.

Terras, Victor (1964). Review of Lehiste and Ivić 1963. *SEEJ*, 8, 87–88.

Težak, Stjepko, and Stjepan Babić (1973). *Pregled gramatike hrvatskoga književnog jezika za osnovne i druge škole*. VI, prerađeno izdanje. Školska knjiga, Zagreb.

Thomas, Lawrence L. (1960). Review of Ivić 1958. *Language*, 35, 145–152.

*Thorsen, N. (1978). An acoustical investigation of Danish intonation. *Journal of Phonetics*, 6, 151–175.

*Thorsen, N. (1979). Lexical stress, emphasis for contrast, and sentence intonation in Advanced Standard Copenhagen Danish. *Proceedings of the Ninth International Congress of Phonetic Sciences, Copenhagen 6–11 August*, ed. E. Fischer-Jørgensen, J. Rischel, and N. Thorsen, Vol. II, 417–423. Institute of Phonetics, University of Copenhagen.

*Thorsen, N. (1980a). A study of the perception of intonation contours: Evidence from Danish. *Journal of the Acoustical Society of America*, 67, 1014–1030.

*Thorsen, N. (1980b). Neutral stress, emphatic stress, and sentence intonation in Advanced Standard Copenhagen Danish. *ARIPUC*, 14, 121–205.

*Thorsen, N. (1980c). Intonation contours and stress group patterns in declarative sentences of varying length in ASC Danish. *ARIPUC*, 14, 1–29.

Tomić, Josip (1963). Fiziologija i funkcija uzlaznog i silaznog akcenta u genitivu plurala imenica. *Filologija*, 4, 177–190.

Trager, G. L. (1940). Serbo-Croatian accents and quantities. *Language*, 16, 29–32.

Trnski, Ivan (1874). O našem stihotvorstvu. *Vienac* (Zagreb), 6, 490–493, 504–506, 520–522, 536–538, 551–554.

Trubetzkoy, N. S. (1936). Die phonologischen Grenzsignale. *Proceedings of the Second International Congress of Phonetic Sciences*, 45–49. Cambridge.

Trubetzkoy, N. S. (1938a). Die phonologischen Grundlagen der sogenannten "Quantität" in den verschiedenen Sprachen. *Scritti in onore di Alfredo Trombetti*. Milan.

Trubetzkoy, N. S. (1938b). Die Quantität als phonologisches Problem. *Actes du Quatrième Congrès International de Linguistes, tenu à Copenhague... 1936*. Copenhagen.

Trubetzkoy, N. S. (1939). *Grundzüge der Phonologie*. (*TCLP*, 7.)

Ungeheuer, G. (1965). Review of Mahnken 1962a. *Phonetica*, 12, 33–60.

Veber-Tkalčević, Adolf (1873). *Slovnica hèrvatska*. Zagreb.

Vinaver, Stanislav (1952). *Jezik naš nasušni–prilog proučavanju naše govorne melodije i promena koje su u njoj nastale*. Matica srpska, Novi Sad.

Vince, Zlatko (1973). Zasluge Šime Starčevića za hrvatski književni jezik. *Filologija*, 7, 157–201.

Vondrák, Wenzel (1906). *Vergleichende slavische Grammatik. I. Band. Lautlehre und Stammbildungslehre*. Göttingen.

Vuić, Vladimir (1856). *Srbska gramatika za gimnazijalnu mladež Knjažestva Srbije*. Belgrade.

Vujić, Vladimir (1863). *Srbska gramatika za gimnazije u kneževini Srbiji*. Belgrade.

Vujić, Vladimir (1878). *Srpska gramatika za srednje škole*. Peto, prerađeno izdanje. Pančevo.

Vukomanović, Slavko (1967). O jednoj akcenatskoj osobini beogradskog govora. *Prilozi za književnost, jezik, istoriju i folklor*, 33, 43–48.

Vuković, Jovan (1972). Srpskohrvatska književna akcentuacija i funkcionalnost akcenata i kvantiteta. *Književni jezik*, 1/1–2, 47–63.

Vuletić, Branko (1971–72). Koliko razumijemo intonaciju? *Jezik*, 19, 71–74.

Wijk, N. van (1921). Du déplacement de l'accent en serbocroate. *Revue des études slaves*, 1, 28–37.

Wijk, N. van (1939). Zur Geschichte der serbokroatischen Polytonie. *Zeitschrift für slavische Philologie*, 16, 261–269.

Wijk, N. van (1940). *Quantiteit en Intonatie*. (Mededelingen der Koninklijke Nederlandsche Akademie van Wetenschappen, Afd. Letterkunde, Nieuwe Reeks, Deel 3, No. 1.) Amsterdam.

Živanović, Đorđe (1951). *Problemi pozorišnog jezika*. Stručna pozorišna biblioteka, Rad, Belgrade.

Živanović, Đorđe (1976a). Jedan preteča Đure Daničića. *NSSVD* 5, 631–643.

Živanović, Đorde (1976b). Discussion of Ivić 1976c. *NSSVD*, 5, 761–762.

Živanović, Jovan (1874). *Izvod iz srpske gramatike*. Novi Sad.

Živanović, Jovan (1919). *Izvod iz srpske gramatike za I i II gimnazijski razred*. Sr. Karlovci.

Name Index

Subject Index

Accents, long falling, 1, 35, 44–45, 47, 54, and passim
accentus superelevans (greatly raising accent), 4, 173
descendant (falling), 20
dug (obao) (long (round)), 10
dugački (long), 6, 7, 9
forte lungo (strong long), 11
forte o determinato (strong or determinate), 11
gravis, 10
high long, 15
long and strong, 16
long with the grave accent, 7
malo rastegnut (lengthened a little), 3
obli (round), 10, 16, 19
okrugao akcenat (round accent), 6, 10
oštar (sharp), 9, 12
padajući dugi (falling long), 19
silazni (falling), 23, 31
strong, 18, 291
twisted, 9
two-toned accent, 22, 26
utažen (soothed), 10
visokodugi (high long), 17
Accents, long rising 1, 35, 44–45, 47, 54, and passim
accentus prolongans (lengthening accent), 4
acutus, 10, 16, 19
debole lungo (weak long), 11
debole o indeterminato (weak or indeterminate), 11
gentle rising, 22
high, 18, 291
lang (long), 6, 10, 15, 17
long and weak, 16, 26
long with the acute accent, 7
montant (rising), 20
najduži (longest), 6
otegnut (stretched), 291
posve rastegnut (completely lengthened), 3
protegnut (stretched), 6
rastući dugi (growing long), 19
sharp, 9
single-toned accent, 26
uzlazni (rising), 23
uzlazni dugi (rising long), 26
vrlo dug (very long), 7, 9, 10
zavinuti (twisted), 9, 12
Accents, short falling, 1, 18–19, 23, 25, 28, 31, 35, 42, 44, 47, and passim
accentus elevans (raising accent), 4, 173
brzi (fast), 23, 28, 31, 176
dvostruki (double), 16, 19
dvostruki težki (double heavy), 9, 10
fort (strong), 20
forte breve (strong short), 10
gravis, 10
heavy, 12
high, 23, 176
jaki težki (strong and heavy), 9
kratak (short), 6
kurz und tief (short and low), 8, 20
najoštriji (sharpest), 6
oštar (sharp), 9, 10, 15, 17–18, 23, 26, 31, 291
posve kratak (completely short), 3, 20, 173
rezkoe udarenie (sharp accent), 18
schärfer (sharper), 6, 20, 173
sharp and quick, 8
short and sharp, 15
short and strong, 16, 18–19, 23, 26, 31
short with the grave accent, 7, 20